# Mark's Gospel:
# An Actological Reading

ACTOLOGICAL EXPLORATIONS

A series of books published by Wipf and Stock about actology, which understands reality as action in patterns, and so is an alternative to ontology, which understands reality as beings that change.

Also in this series

*Actology: Action, change and diversity in the western philosophical tradition*

Two streams run through western philosophy: one characterized by Being, beings, the unchanging, the static, and the unitary, and the other by Action, actions, the changing, the dynamic, and the diverse. *Actology: Action, change and diversity in the western philosophical tradition*, explores the 'Action' stream as it has wound its way through history, through Heraclitus, Plato, Aristotle, Hegel, Maurice Blondel, Henri Bergson, Teilhard de Chardin, process philosophy and theology, Geoffrey Studdert Kennedy, Ludwig Wittgenstein, and John Boys Smith. The journey enables us to create the beginnings of an 'actology': a way of seeing ourselves, the universe and God in terms of actions in patterns rather than as beings that change. Such an actology offers a complete alternative narrative far more in tune with the diverse and rapidly changing world in which we live than the ontology that has shaped philosophy, theology and much else for the past two thousand years.

# Mark's Gospel:
# An Actological Reading

MALCOLM TORRY

RESOURCE *Publications* • Eugene, Oregon

MARK'S GOSPEL: AN ACTOLOGICAL READING

Actological Explorations Series

Copyright © 2022 Malcolm Torry. All rights reserved. Except for brief quotations in critical publications or reviews, no part of this book may be reproduced in any manner without prior written permission from the publisher. Write: Permissions, Wipf and Stock Publishers, 199 W. 8th Ave., Suite 3, Eugene, OR 97401.

Resource Publications
An Imprint of Wipf and Stock Publishers
199 W. 8th Ave., Suite 3
Eugene, OR 97401

www.wipfandstock.com

PAPERBACK ISBN: 978-1-6667-3683-0
HARDCOVER ISBN: 978-1-6667-9568-4
EBOOK ISBN: 978-1-6667-9569-1

03/30/22

Scripture quotations are from the New Revised Standard Version Bible: Anglicized Edition, copyright © 1989, 1995 National Council of the Churches of Christ in the United States of America. Used by permission. All rights reserved worldwide.

# Contents

| | |
|---|---|
| Preface and acknowledgments | vii |
| Abbreviations | ix |
| Introduction | xi |
| List of commentaries consulted | xix |
| Front Matter Endnotes | xxi |
| Mark's Gospel: An Actological Reading | 1 |
| Endnotes | 275 |
| Bibliography | 291 |
| Subject Index | 293 |
| Scripture Index | 297 |

# Preface and acknowledgments

Mark's Gospel has been a constant companion since childhood, and innumerable theological teachers, fellow students, preachers and study group participants have contributed to my engagement with it. It would be impossible to name all of them, so I shall not try to do so.

The actological "action in changing patterns" lens through which I have here read Mark's Gospel has evolved during the past forty years, beginning with a paper that the late David Edwards, then Provost of Southwark Cathedral, invited me to present at a meeting of a theological society. The idea then took further shape in a sabbatical essay that Robin Gill, then Michael Ramsey Professor of Modern Theology at the University of Kent, and David Atkinson, then Canon Missioner in the Diocese of Southwark, and subsequently Archdeacon of Lewisham and Bishop of Thetford, both read, and on which they offered valuable comment. I then extracted from the essay five articles that Bill Jacob, then Archdeacon of Charing Cross, published in *Theology*, of which he was the editor.[1] In 2014 I retired early from full-time parochial ministry in order to give to the Basic Income debate the time that it needed, and also to return to philosophical and theological study, in relation to which I wrote a Master of Philosophy thesis on action, change and diversity in the western philosophical tradition, which then became *Actology: Action, change and diversity in the western philosophical tradition*, published by Wipf and Stock in 2020.[2] I am most grateful to all of the above, and particularly to my two M.Phil. supervisors, Professors George Newlands and Simon Oliver.

As well as those named above, numerous individuals have contributed to the development of the ideas to be found in this book by their willingness to discuss them with me. Again there are too many to mention, but particularly significant contributions have been made at various stages by Dr. Martin Cressey, Canon John Byrom, Professor Stephen Sykes, the Rev'd James Bogle, Mr. Renford Bambrough, the Rev'd Jed Davis, chaplains of the South London Industrial Mission, members of the congregations of St. Catherine's, Hatcham, St. George's, Westcombe Park, and Holy Trinity, Greenwich Peninsula, and participants in seminars held in relation to the Archbishop's Examination in Theology. I am more than grateful to those who made possible several periods of study leave of varying lengths: staff members and officers of the parishes that I have served for their willingness to shoulder additional burdens; Bishops of

## Preface and Acknowledgments

Woolwich for permissions to take sabbaticals; and St. John's College, Cambridge, for hospitality for varying lengths of time during the past forty years.

I am of course particularly grateful to my wife Rebecca and children Christopher, Nicholas, and Jay, for putting up with my various study and writing projects.

Scripture quotations are from the New Revised Standard Version Bible: Anglicized Edition, copyright © 1989, 1995 National Council of the Churches of Christ in the United States of America. Used by permission. All rights reserved worldwide.

Numbered references refer to endnotes at the end of the introduction and at end of the book. Lettered references in the biblical text refer to footnotes at the bottom of the page.

# Abbreviations

In the notes the following abbreviations are used, with meanings supplied by the publisher of the New Revised Standard Version Anglicized Edition:

| | |
|---|---|
| Aram | Aramaic |
| Cn | Correction: made where the text has suffered in transmission and the versions provide no satisfactory restoration but where the Standard Bible Committee agrees with the judgement of competent scholars as to the most probable reconstruction of the original text |
| Gk | *In the Hebrew scriptures/Old Testament*: Septuagint, Greek version of the Old Testament; *In the New Testament*: Greek text of the New Testament |
| Heb | Hebrew of the consonantal Masoretic Text of the Old Testament |
| Ms(s) | Manuscript(s) |
| MT | The Hebrew of the pointed Masoretic Text of the Old Testament |
| NRSV-ANG | New Revised Standard Version Anglicized Edition |
| Q Ms(s) | Manuscript(s) found at Qumran by the Dead Sea |
| Syr | Syriac Version of the Old Testament |

# Introduction

In the introduction to his *Readings in St John's Gospel*, William Temple wrote this:

> This book is not a systematic commentary or exposition; nor is it intended for scholars or theologians—though whatever value it has for souls on pilgrimage may be as real for them as for others. Again, it is not a series of devotional meditations, though it contains some of these. It has no distinctive and consistent character. But it is an attempt to share with any who read it what I find to be my own thoughts as I read the profoundest of all writings.[3]

The aim of this book is similar: it is not a systematic commentary or exposition; it is not intended for scholars or theologians (although I hope that some might find something of value here); it is not a series of devotional meditations (although some might experience some of what they find here as religiously helpful); and it is an attempt to share with any who read it what I find in my own thoughts as I read the profoundest of all writings: in this case Mark's Gospel rather than John's Gospel. However, there are two differences between the two books: Temple's book was written by one of the giants of the English Church, and this book is not; and this book does have a distinctive and consistent character in one respect: it regards reality as action in changing patterns rather than as things that change.

A further similarity with Temple's *Readings* is that I shall generally be leaving to one side questions of authorship, date, and so on, and also issues relating to the history of the text and the historicity of the events recorded except where such questions relate to the actological readings. In particular, I shall assume that "Mark" wrote this gospel, that it was the Mark who travelled with Paul, and that this same Mark knew Peter and recorded his reminiscences before writing his gospel: although all of these decisions are contestable.[4] In relation to such issues, and also to inform my reading of Mark's Gospel, I have relied on a number of commentaries, a list of which follows this introduction. Important though the issues discussed in the commentaries might be, I shall attempt not to allow them to distract me from an actological reading of Mark's Gospel that I hope will be of service to Christians, and to any who might value a new perspective on Jesus and on the Christian Faith to which he gave birth: a perspective in which thought and practice cannot be separated, and therefore in which Christian belief and Christian discipleship belong together.[5] Mark's Gospel will be mined for what it has always been mined for: resources for Christian life and faith. What will be distinctive will be the character of the shovel used for the mining.

## REALITY AS ACTION IN PATTERNS

What is distinctive about the standpoint from which the gospel text is viewed is that it regards reality as action rather than being. A thought experiment might be in order. Imagine a vast ocean. Nothing is still. It is all constantly in motion at every level: at the level of subatomic particles (which are not particles, but actions in patterns), at the level of the ocean as a whole, and at every level in between. Now in your imagination try to evacuate the ocean of all substance: that is, of the water understood as a thing. See it instead as like the subatomic particles that make it up: that is, as pure action at every level. That action will be in patterns, so it will exhibit elements of stability: we can experience all of it as water. But those patterns constantly change, so throughout, and at every level, it is action in changing patterns. And now look at yourself and see that you are like that as well: nothing is solid, nothing is still—you are action in changing patterns, as is everyone else, everything else, the planet, and the cosmos. Reality is action in changing patterns.

While most of western philosophy has privileged being over action, Being (being itself, and the source of being) over Action (action itself, and the source of all action), the unitary over diversity, the static over the dynamic, the unchanging over the changing, rest over movement, there has also been a thin stream running through the western philosophical tradition that has regarded reality as action, movement, change, and diversity. I explore that stream in *Actology: Action, change and diversity in the western philosophical tradition*.[6] For most of its two thousand year history, Christian theology has been strongly influenced by the philosophy of Plato and his successors: a philosophy that privileges being over action, Being over Action, the unitary over diversity, the static over the dynamic, the unchanging over the changing, and rest over movement. In *Actology* I explore the philosophical tributary in which theologians such as A.N. Whitehead, Pierre Teilhard de Chardin, Geoffrey Studdert Kennedy, and John Boys Smith, work with a more action-focused basis for reality and therefore for theology. That is the agenda that informs these readings in Mark's Gospel. It is always Mark's Gospel that is the centre of attention, but the lens through which it is understood is an understanding of reality as action in changing patterns.

A problem with language—and one that is discussed in *Actology*—is that our noun-based language forces us to experience reality as things that move and change. English is a noun-based language: sentences usually begin with nouns or pronouns, verbs might explain how the object expressed by the noun is acting or changing, and further nouns and pronouns might then refer to further objects. The situation is somewhat different with Hebrew. Sentences usually begin with verbs, and only then do we hear about the person or object that is doing the action. Nouns will often be adapted verbs. But this book is in English; and ancient western philosophy and theology, which inform so much of our modern thought, are in Greek and Latin, which are as noun-based as English. In this situation all we can do is constantly remind ourselves that reality is action in changing patterns, that being is action, and that what is actually happening is that it is all happening. In practical terms, understanding reality as action in changing patterns requires us to concentrate on the verbs, discovering the action, asking about the patterns in which the action occurs, and discovering the ways in which the patterns are changing. It also requires us to ask how what is being said can be understood in terms of actions in patterns rather than in terms of things that change: that is, with reality understood as Action, action, change, diversity, movement, and the dynamic, rather than as Being, being, the unchanging, the unitary, rest, and the static.

Before we launch into Mark's Gospel, I shall explore briefly a few passages from elsewhere in the New Testament to provide something of a taste of how an action-based understanding of reality might influence how we read the biblical text.

## JOHN'S GOSPEL

To begin with: some statements that represent the relationship between Jesus and God that is at the heart of the Christian Faith:

> The Father and I are one;[7]
>
> I am not alone because the Father is with me;[8]
>
> You, Father, are in me and I am in you.[9]

In what sense are Jesus and the Father "one," "with" each other, and "in" each other? Across the Christian centuries multiple attempts to understand this have employed such terms as "person," "substance," "human nature," "divine nature," "being," and so on. On most Sundays, in most parish churches, we say the Nicene Creed, which in the "traditional" version describes Jesus as "of one substance with the Father," and in the "contemporary" version as "of one Being with the Father," with "substance" and "Being" between them representing something like the meaning of the original Greek word *homoousios*.[10] But how are we to understand that? We no longer function with such concepts, which renders the creed, and the heart of Christian doctrine, irrelevant to our Christian lives and to everything else. But what if we were to understand God as Action: that is, as action itself, and as the source of all action; and what if we were to understand Jesus as action in changing patterns, which is what every human being is? And let us now understand these as descriptions of God and of Jesus that are not somehow subsidiary to more foundational understandings in terms of Being, beings,

## Introduction

substance, and so on, but as expressions of the deepest realities of who they are. If it helps: the Being of God is Action, and the very being of Jesus is actions in patterns. This is who they are.

We might now understand the passages quoted above as follows:

"The Father and I are one": God, the creator, the one whom Jesus called "Father," is both the source of all action, and action in particular changing patterns that are the freely chosen changing patterns that constitute God. Jesus is action in changing patterns: and the patterns of action that he is—his love, his healing, his unconditional giving of himself, his anger, his hope, his faith—these patterns are God's patterns. There will be changing patterns that we call Jesus' physical reality that will not be God's patterns of action in the same way that they are Jesus' patterns of action; and there will be changing patterns of action that are God's changing patterns of action that will not be those of Jesus. Those are not relevant to our discussion here. What is relevant here is that Jesus and his Father are one in relation to changing patterns of action in ways in which others of us are not.

"The Father is with me": Here is where those patterns of action that are God and that are not Jesus are relevant. The God who is the source of all action, and is Action itself, is beyond all imagining, and at the same time is more intimate with us than is possible for anyone or anything else. Among the actions in patterns that are God there is an embracing that embraces our actions in patterns—that is, ourselves—in patterns of action that constantly change so as to relate more deeply than we can ever imagine to the changing patterns of action that we are. This God is with Jesus in the same way that God is with us, but inevitably in a unique way simply because Jesus and God share changing patterns of action in a way that applies only to them. Jesus is not Action itself and the source of all action, and is not the infinity of changing patterns of action that God is, and God is not the action in patterns that constitute Jesus' physical reality: so as well as the "oneness," there is a "withness."

"You, Father, are in me and I am in you": We can now see why Jesus could have said that. Changing patterns of action that constitute Jesus are God's changing patterns of action; and changing patterns of action that constitute God are Jesus' patterns of action. That isn't all that is to be said about either of them, but it provides us with sufficient reason to understand Jesus being in God and God being in Jesus in ways that don't apply to the rest of us.

What we have discovered is that reality understood as Action rather than Being, and as action rather than being, can provide us with a conceptual framework within which to understand the heart of the Christian Faith: that Jesus and the Father are one; that the Father is with Jesus; and that the Father is in Jesus, and Jesus in the Father.

To take a passage from the prologue of John's Gospel:

## Introduction

> 1 In the beginning was the Word, and the Word was with God, and the Word was God. ² He was in the beginning with God. ³ All things came into being through him, . . .

> ¹⁴ And the Word became flesh and lived among us, and we have seen his glory, the glory as of a father's only son,[d] full of grace and truth.[11]

We can now make sense of this passage. Those changing patterns of action that are God, that are God's chosen expression of the very heart of God, and that are creative of changing patterns of action that will be other than God's patterns of action—for that is what is required for relationship with a universe and with every changing pattern of action that will evolve within it: those changing patterns of action are the Word of God, which is therefore itself changing patterns of action. This Word "was" God in the sense that the changing patterns of action that constitute the Word are genuinely God's changing patterns of action; and the Word was "with" God in the sense that God is Action, the source of all action, which the Word was not, and God is particular changing patterns of action that the Word was not. As the Word is God's creative patterns of action, it is through the Word that "all things came into being." It is this Word, these creative changing patterns of action, that "became flesh": that is, it is these changing patterns of action that constituted Jesus—they were the changing patterns of action that he was, that constituted his reality. Those patterns of action that we might call Jesus' physical reality were not those of God in the same way, but they were now inseparable from the changing patterns of action that were the Word, so it is entirely right to say that the Word "became flesh." And now that the Word has become flesh in Jesus, Jesus and the Father are "one," the Father is "with" Jesus, and Jesus and the Father are "in" each other.

When he saw the risen Christ, Thomas exclaimed "My Lord and my God!"[12] He had understood that he could call Jesus "God."[13] In two other passages in the New Testament we find what might have been similar identifications between Jesus and God:

> 13 while we wait for the blessed hope and the manifestation of the glory of our great God and Saviour,[f] Jesus Christ . . .[14]

> To those who have received a faith as precious as ours through the righteousness of our God and Saviour Jesus Christ.[c][15]

The original Greek, though, is ambiguous, and possible translations might be "of the great God and our Saviour Jesus Christ" and "of our God and the Saviour Jesus Christ" respectively. Perhaps the ambiguities were purposeful, in the virtuous sense that both the writer and their readers would have understood the same ambiguity:[16] that Jesus

---

d. Or *the Father's only Son*
f. Or *of the great God and our Saviour*
c. Or *of our God and the Saviour Jesus Christ*

both was and was not God—in our terms, that Jesus was uniquely constituted by changing patterns of action that were God's reality as well as his own, but that that was not all that there was to be said about either God or Jesus.

## GOD WHO...

From Paul's letters:

> ... God who justifies;[17]
>
> ... God who shows mercy;[18]
>
> ... God who gives the growth;[19]
>
> ... God who activates;[20]
>
> ... God who raises the dead;[21]
>
> ... God who establishes us with you in Christ;[22]
>
> ... God who said, "Let light shine out of darkness";[23]
>
> ... God who put in the heart of Titus the same eagerness for you that I myself have;[24]
>
> ... God who created all things;[25]
>
> ... God who is at work in you;[26]
>
> ... God who tests our hearts;[27]
>
> ... God who richly provides us.[28]

We occasionally find Paul describing God by using the verb "to be": "God is one,"[29] "God is faithful";[30] but Paul's normative method is to describe who God is by describing the kinds of patterns of action that he experiences: "God who...." This is who God is, because God is what God does. There is no God who exists apart from God's action. God is action in changing patterns, as well as being the ultimate source of all action.

## WE ARE WHAT WE DO

At the beginning of Jesus' ministry, he read from the book of the prophet Isaiah:

> [18] The Spirit of the Lord is upon me,
> because he has anointed me
> to bring good news to the poor.
> He has sent me to proclaim release to the captives
> and recovery of sight to the blind,
> to let the oppressed go free,
> [19] to proclaim the year of the Lord's favour.[31]

# Introduction

This was who he was, and it is what God is. We are what we do. We are our action in patterns, and Jesus' action in patterns was telling good news to the poor, restoring sight, freeing the oppressed, and proclaiming release and the time of God's favor.

The Acts of the Apostles is precisely that: the *acts* of the apostles. The Church then was what it did, and the Church today is what it does, and the Church is Christian to the extent that its pattern of action is Jesus' pattern of action: a changing pattern of action because his was, but still identifiably his. In the same way it is the Church of God if its changing pattern of action is Jesus's changing pattern of action, because then it will be God's changing pattern of action as well.

And none of this will be somehow subsidiary to the reality of God, Jesus, ourselves, the Church, or the world. This *is* the reality of God, Jesus, ourselves, the Church, and the world.

And so to Mark's Gospel, to discover Jesus, and therefore to discover God, in the changing patterns of action recorded there. Whether these readings in Mark's Gospel are true to the text my readers will have to judge, and in particular whether they are true in the sense of truth as changing patterns of action: as truth-seeking.

# List of commentaries consulted

After the writing of a first draft of these readings, a purposely diverse group of commentaries was read before the text was revised.

- C.E.B. Cranfield, *The Gospel according to Mark*. A commentary on the original Greek text of Mark's Gospel.
- R.T. France, *The Gospel of Mark*. A detailed study of the Greek text of the New Testament from a more conservative theological perspective.
- Elizabeth Stuthers Malbon, *Hearing Mark*. A short exposition that treats the gospel as a drama.
- Ched Myers, *Binding the Strong Man*. An account of Mark's Jesus as a non-violent revolutionary.
- D.E. Nineham, *The Gospel of St. Mark*. A commentary that makes full use of the biblical scholarship of its time.
- Rowan Williams, *Meeting God in Mark*. A commentary from a distinctive theological thinker.
- Tom Wright, *Mark for Everyone*. A popular and accessible commentary from a more conservative tradition.

# Front Matter Endnotes

1. Torry, "Action, Patterns and Religious Pluralism"; "A Neglected Theologian"; "'Logic' and 'Action'"; "On Completing the Apologetic Spectrum"; "Testing Torry's model."
2. Torry, *Actology*.
3. Temple, *Readings in St John's Gospel*, xiii.
4. Malbon, *Hearing Mark*, 3.
5. Myers, *Binding the Strong Man*, xxv, xxix, 11.
6. Torry, *Actology*.
7. John 10:30, NRSV-ANG.
8. John 16:32, NRSV-ANG.
9. John 17:21, NRSV-ANG.
10. Church of England, *Common Worship*, 173, 213.
11. John 1:1–3, 14, NRSV-ANG.
12. John 20:28, NRSV-ANG.
13. A version of this interpretation of these passages from John's Gospel was first explored in Torry, "'Logic' and 'Action.'"
14. Titus 2:13, NRSV-ANG.
15. 2 Pet 1:1, NRSV-ANG.
16. Torry, "Two Kinds of Ambiguity."
17. Rom 8: 33, NRSV-ANG.
18. Rom 9:16, NRSV-ANG.
19. 1 Cor 3:7, NRSV-ANG.
20. 1 Cor 12:6, NRSV-ANG.
21. 2 Cor 1:9, NRSV-ANG.
22. 2 Cor 1:21, NRSV-ANG.
23. 2 Cor 4:6, NRSV-ANG.
24. 2 Cor 8:16, NRSV-ANG.
25. Eph 3:9, NRSV-ANG.
26. Phil 2:13, NRSV-ANG.
27. 1 Thess 2:4, NRSV-ANG.
28. 1 Tim 6:17, NRSV-ANG.
29. Rom 3:30; Gal 3:20, NRSV-ANG.
30. 1 Cor 1:19; 10:13; 2 Cor 1:18, NRSV-ANG.
31. Luke 4:18–19, NRSV-ANG; cf. Isa 61:1–2.

# Mark's Gospel: An Actological Reading

## MARK 1:1

1 The beginning of the good news[a] of Jesus Christ, the Son of God.[b][1]

Mark's Gospel begins with what looks like a highly unactological sentence. It would be consistent with the approach of this reading of Mark's Gospel to suggest that if we wish to ask who Jesus is then we should indicate the patterns of action that the gospel is all about and say that that is who Jesus is: he is precisely those patterns of action, and any titles with which we might try to describe him must remain secondary to the drama of his life, death, and resurrection as the definition of who Jesus is.[2] However, Mark's Gospel uses titles of Jesus, and nowhere more clearly than here at "the beginning of the good news": so it is to those titles that we must address ourselves.

The most ancient manuscripts of the gospel are divided as to whether "the Son of God" belongs here or not. Some omit it, some put it in, and some phrase it differently, putting a definite article in front of "God." This is all very confusing. It makes you wonder. If the gospel originally did not say "the Son of God," then it is possible that an early scribe might have put it in, as it would have seemed the obvious thing to write because that is who the scribe would have thought Jesus was. If it was in the gospel originally then it is unlikely that a scribe would have left it out. The balance of probabilities is that it was not there originally: although not everyone would agree with that conclusion.[3] An interesting but unlikely possibility is that the gospel originally started "The beginning of the good news of Jesus Christ, of God." We shall study all of the possibilities:

"Jesus": The meaning is "Savior." In Matthew's Gospel we hear that Jesus' father Joseph was told in a dream, "You are to name him Jesus, for he will save his people from their sins."[4] Throughout his life, Jesus' pattern of action was one of saving people: by healing them, drawing them back into society, forgiving them, and promising that the Kingdom of God would come and was already present.

  a. Or *gospel*
  b. Other ancient authorities lack *the Son of God*

"Christ": This is the Greek equivalent of the Hebrew "Messiah," meaning rescuer, with connotations of military victory, and therefore in Jesus' context connotations of releasing the people of Israel from Roman occupation. But this was not how Jesus understood his messiahship. His kingdom would be established by different means—different patterns of action; and the kingdom would be characterized by his own patterns of action. And liberating people was and is one of those patterns of action, a constantly changing pattern across time, but continually liberating. If we experience Jesus as liberating, then he is Christ for us still.[5]

"Son of God": This term was employed for the kings of Israel, but as with all analogy, it is not easy to be sure precisely what was meant by such sonship of God. What aspects of the relationship between human children and their parents are we intended to understand in relation to Jesus' relationship to God? Interestingly, in an actological context, the meaning might come down to the same as the meaning of "God" as a potential title for Jesus. The sonship analogy might suggest that we would expect to see in Jesus the actions in changing patterns that we would regard as changing patterns of action that constitute God, thus aligning Jesus understood as Son of God with Jesus understood as God. "Son of God" rather than "God" might express some hesitation about identifying Jesus too closely with God, and if any positive evidence ever turns up that says that the original manuscript of the gospel had included "of Jesus Christ, of God," then it would be no surprise that a scribe would have substituted "Son of God" for "God." An actological conceptual framework subverts the intention to distance Jesus from God, and enables Jesus to be identified as God and not just as Son of God.

But having said that, it is unlikely that a first century Jew such as Mark would have used simply "God" to refer to Jesus. The monotheistic habit would have been almost impossible to break, evidence for which is the difficulty of doing that even now. So the original text would have included or omitted "Son of God," and not "of God."

Whether titled simply "Christ" or "Christ, the Son of God," it is Jesus about whom the gospel-writer is going to tell good news: the Greek *euangelion* reflecting a word in the Hebrew scriptures meaning "good news of victory," and at the same time a word used in the Roman empire in relation to the emperor cult: so "the *euangelion* of Jesus Christ" would have been heard as a challenge to the Emperor's authority, and Jesus' expropriation of the terminology would no doubt have been experienced as subversive.[6] The good news to be told here is of God's kingly rule breaking into human history[7] —good news that Jesus will tell, and the good news that is Jesus himself: and Mark tells this good news by telling us what Jesus did, for that is who Jesus is. And there is plenty of action to come in this gospel. Jesus is constantly on the move, and he is constantly doing things, and, as we near the end of the book, he is constantly having things done to him. The book is full not just of general descriptions of action, but of the detail as well, so that we are drawn into the patterns of action. Just as importantly, the gospel expresses the changing of the patterns of action that constitute

Jesus. Everything is action, change, diversity, movement, and dynamic. The book is truly "the good news of Jesus Christ, [the Son of] God."

A further connotation of *euangelion* is that it usually meant an announcement that would change things:[8] so in the context in which it is used here, the implication is that the patterns of action that constituted the good news would change the patterns of action that constitute who we are, and the patterns of action that constitute who I am. Nothing will be left the same by this good news.

As we read the gospel, see it through a lens that understands reality as action rather than being, and therefore find it possible to speak of Jesus as God, because in him we find patterns of action that are God, we shall find ourselves challenged. We shall find our understanding of God reshaped by the patterns of action that we find in Jesus; and we shall find that the patterns of action that we find in Jesus will judge and change the patterns of action that constitute who we are.

And let us be clear at the beginning of this consideration of Mark's Gospel: to say that the changing patterns of action that are Jesus of Nazareth are uniquely God's patterns of action is a choice that we can make or not make. This actological reading of Mark's Gospel will assume that that choice has been made.

## MARK 1:2-3

> 2 As it is written in the prophet Isaiah,[c]
> 'See, I am sending my messenger ahead of you,[d]
>    who will prepare your way;
> [3] the voice of one crying out in the wilderness:
>    "Prepare the way of the Lord,
>    make his paths straight".[9]

The first part of the quotation is not from the book of the prophet Isaiah, but from the book of the prophet Malachi: "See, I am sending my messenger to prepare the way before me, and the Lord whom you seek will suddenly come to his temple."[10] There are lots of mistakes in the Bible. This is not a problem. It is a collection of human books about events: about action in changing patterns. The text and the meanings that we all find in it are themselves changing patterns through which the actions in patterns that constitute our lives can relate to the events: that is, to the actions in patterns that constitute the reality of God active in the world, and in particular to the actions in patterns that constitute Jesus. But as well as mistakes, there are plenty of purposeful alterations. Mark omits Malachi's reference to the temple, instead suggesting that it is to the wilderness that God will come. Mark's Gospel is to an extent a polemic in

---

c. Other ancient authorities read *in the prophets*

d. Gk *before your face*

favor of the oppressed inhabitants of Galilee and of other regions distant in geography, culture and resources from Jerusalem, and against the ruling authorities of his own times—Rome, and the Jewish authorities to whom Rome had delegated limited powers—and also against the violence of contemporary revolutionary individuals and groups. Mark found no shortage of material in Jesus' ministry for constructing such a polemic. We shall not pursue this line of interpretation consistently in these readings, but we shall find that Mark understands Jesus' patterns of action to be a call to the patterns of action of radical Christian discipleship, and to be a model for the patterns of action of such discipleship.[11]

Mark's omission of Malachi's prophecy that "the Lord whom you seek will suddenly come to his temple" raises a more general question: that of the "symbolic order" that Mark employs in his gospel. Those symbols that represent what Jesus struggled against, because he saw them as opposed to the Kingdom of God—for instance, the temple, the sabbath (as understood by the scribes and Pharisees), Jerusalem, foods permitted and foods not permitted[12]—are all institutions represented by nouns, whereas the symbols that represent the Kingdom of God are patterns of action: forgiveness, healing, eating together, and so on—and these are represented by verbs. Institutions are also patterns of action, of course, but it is not insignificant that the symbolic institutions that Jesus saw as opposed to the Kingdom of God are represented by nouns, and that the symbols that represent the Kingdom of God are represented by verbs.

"I am sending . . . before me." The prophet writes that God will send a messenger "before me": that is, before God arrives in judgement. For anyone with ears to hear, the gospel writer is identifying Jesus, the "you" in Mark's Gospel, with God: the "me" in the book of the prophet Malachi. This Jesus is the God who is coming.

Throughout these readings, we shall be concentrating on the verbs, for those reveal who God is; and here God is a sending God. This is who God is. The following quotation—"Prepare the way of the Lord, make his paths straight"—is adapted from a passage in Isaiah: "In the wilderness prepare the way of the Lord, make straight in the desert a highway for our God."[13] The path must be prepared so that God can travel on it. Mark might not have felt able to identify Jesus with God in writing, which he would have done if he had quoted the passage from Isaiah as it appears in the Hebrew scriptures: but that identification would have been in his mind as he adapted the text, and it would have been in the minds of any of his readers who knew the Hebrew scriptures. We too must ponder that identification.

## MARK 1:4-8

> 4 John the baptizer appeared[e] in the wilderness, proclaiming a baptism of repentance for the forgiveness of sins. ⁵ And people from the whole Judean countryside and all the people of Jerusalem were going out to him, and were baptized by him in the river Jordan, confessing their sins. ⁶ Now John was clothed with camel's hair, with a leather belt around his waist, and he ate locusts and wild honey. ⁷ He proclaimed, 'The one who is more powerful than I is coming after me; I am not worthy to stoop down and untie the thong of his sandals. ⁸ I have baptized you with water; but he will baptize you with[f] the Holy Spirit.'[14]

It is the actions recorded here that are the "beginning" of the good news—the good news being Jesus himself[15] —and the actions are those of John the Baptist. This is drama: action in patterns; and the literary form of Mark's Gospel appears to be specifically designed for reading aloud so as to enable Jesus' ministry, death and resurrection to be experienced by its hearers as a single complex event with sections that we might appropriately denote as "acts."[16]

John was what he did: he baptized. This was who he was. And he accompanied his baptizing with proclaiming, which was also who he was. The baptizing was and still is a pattern of actions: it is the submerging of someone in water. The pattern has changed over the years, so there is now a greater diversity, with infants as well as adults being baptized, and with water being poured as an alternative to submersion; and the meanings have changed, and were already changing only a few years after John baptized in the River Jordan: so here we have changing patterns of action that constitute repentance and confession of faith. It is not that the patterns of action accompany the realities: they are the reality. A further pattern of action was the wearing of clothes that mirrored Elijah's, and the doing of actions that Elijah, the forerunner of the Messiah, might have done. These patterns of action constituted John as Elijah, the forerunner, for they were who John was, and they were who Elijah was.

When John baptized those who came to hear him, the baptism was not merely a statement about a deeper reality of some kind: that is, that a commitment had been made to a turning around of someone's life, to a change of mind, which is what the Greek word here translated as "repentance" means. The baptism *was* that commitment, that turning around, that change of mind, that repentance. The baptism was not just a public statement that a decision had been made, it *was* the decision: and that pattern of action would forever have rippled through the changing patterns of action that

---

e. Other ancient authorities read *John was baptizing*

f. Or *in*

constituted the person baptized. The mind—itself changing patterns of action—was changed by the pattern of action that was baptism.

As well as being "a baptism of repentance," baptism was "for the forgiveness of sins," with either the baptism creating the forgiveness, the repentance doing so, or both. Sin is patterns of action that are not God's patterns of action, so sin changes, and Jesus is sinless by definition. God's forgiveness of us is an *aphesis*, a "letting go," a "dismissing of sin." The baptism brings about God's sending away of our sin; or the baptism creates a repentance that sends away sin. So here there are changing patterns of action cascading: baptism changing our minds, and by that means sending away our sin, perhaps in two different ways. The patterns of action that constitute us are changed, there are fewer patterns of action that are not God's, so sin has been sent away; and baptism and repentance precipitate a pattern of action that is God sending away our sin: placing those patterns of action that are not God's beyond the reach of those patterns of action that constitute the relationship between God and ourselves. As well as God being the source of all action, God's relationship with us is constituted by particular changing patterns of action, and our relationship with God similarly: and for those whom John baptized, those patterns of action were no longer disrupted by patterns of action that were not God's patterns of action, even though the reality was that every one of those baptized individuals would have continued to sin. God was positively deciding that the relationship between God and every baptized individual would not be disrupted by the sin constituted by the actions in patterns that all of us are. God would absorb all of it back into the very creative heart of action, into Action itself, to be cleansed and repatterned as patterns of action that constitute God's relationship with us and with the world around us.

So again we have patterns of action intimately entangled: the baptism, the repentance, and the forgiveness—and just as the baptism was the repentance, so, by God's choice, baptism was the forgiveness. The baptized individual was "letting go" of sin; and God was "letting go" of sin back into the source of action, and creating out of it new patterns of action.

And there is yet another important pattern of action here: for John was baptizing in the river Jordan. It was this river that the people of Israel had crossed to leave their slavery in Egypt and to reach the land that they believed God had promised to them; and now John was putting those who came to him under the water and then out again: a pattern of action that was the pattern of action that constituted the leaving of Egypt and entry into the land of promise, and that was still a leaving of slavery to sin and an entry into a land of promise: a new life going in a new direction, a life waiting for the Messiah to come.[17]

While baptism might happen only once, it is a pattern of action that causes ripples throughout a person's life: that is, the pattern of action that is baptism changes the patterns of action that constitute who I am. Repentance is not just once: it is a continuous process of changing one's mind, of taking new directions; and forgiveness is not just once: it is a continuous process of God leaving our sins behind and repairing the damage to ourselves, to others, and to the whole of the created order. And so baptism, repentance, and forgiveness, are constantly interwoven across our lives in ever-changing patterns of action, just as they are interwoven in every baptized individual.

And the baptism had an accompanying meaning. The submersion was a washing, a statement that the person had been cleansed of their sin and that they were forgiven: and because the primary fact was the pattern of action of being baptized, the repentance and the forgiveness necessarily belonged together, with the baptism both representing and achieving both the new direction and the forgiveness. But this left an open question: Did forgiveness require baptism?

Initially Jesus baptized as John did:[18] but we do not hear of him baptizing during the three years or so of his ministry that are recorded in Mark's Gospel. It might be that the radical welcome into the Kingdom of God that Jesus promised to everyone, and particularly to the outcasts, conflicted with the baptism of the relatively few who came seeking repentance and forgiveness.[19] The process was now reversed: no longer was repentance prior to forgiveness: rather, forgiveness ushered in a changed mind, so that now forgiveness was prior to repentance.

Jesus ceasing to baptize did not stop the first Christians from returning to the practice of baptism. Many of them might have been baptized by John, and possibly by Jesus. On the Day of Pentecost following Jesus' resurrection, at the end of his sermon, Peter said this: "Repent, and be baptized every one of you in the name of Jesus Christ so that your sins may be forgiven; and you will receive the gift of the Holy Spirit."[20] Again we find repentance, baptism, and forgiveness, intimately entangled with each other, and now the gift of the Holy Spirit as well: the Holy Spirit who is the action that is God active among and within us, God's changing patterns of action changing our changing patterns of action. As we have seen in this passage, John the Baptist had predicted that the one greater than him would baptize with the Holy Spirit: and while in the whole of Mark's Gospel after verse 13 of this chapter there are only three mentions of the Holy Spirit, in the first thirteen verses there is an equal number of them.[21] Mark wants his readers to grasp early on that Jesus will pour out the Spirit on his followers, and we shall soon find the Spirit descending on Jesus.[22] The prophet Joel, having described the establishment of God's reign of peace and abundance, has God say "Then afterwards I will pour out my spirit on all flesh . . .":[23] so John saying that Jesus would baptize with the Holy Spirit was a statement that Jesus exhibited a pattern of action that both fulfilled a prophecy of the end times, and was a pattern of action that constituted God; and the subsequent descent of the Spirit on Jesus was a fulfilment of at least two prophecies: a fulfilment that identified him as the promised Messiah who would rule as a servant:

> ¹ A shoot shall come out from the stock of Jesse,
>    and a branch shall grow out of his roots.
> ² The spirit of the LORD shall rest on him,
>    the spirit of wisdom and understanding,
>    the spirit of counsel and might,
>    the spirit of knowledge and the fear of the LORD.[24]

> Here is my servant, whom I uphold,
>    my chosen, in whom my soul delights;
> I have put my spirit upon him;
>    he will bring forth justice to the nations.[25]

This Holy Spirit, constituted by the patterns of action that constitute God, is a third member of God. God, the Father and the Creator, is action in changing patterns and the source of all action; Jesus is action in changing patterns that are among the patterns that constitute God, and is also action in changing patterns that are Jesus' physicality; and the Holy Spirit is actions in changing patterns that are God's patterns of action, and in particular those patterns that the Father shares with Jesus—and the particularity of the Holy Spirit is that the Spirit's patterns of action include patterns that today are entangled with every pattern of action that constitutes the universe, the solar system, the planet, you and me, and the very depths of reality, with the result that the Spirit experiences patterns of action not shared with Jesus or the Father. So here we have the beginnings of God as Trinity: God as the entangled actions in changing patterns that are the Father, Jesus, and the Holy Spirit, with shared patterns of action between them, and with those patterns of action that are not shared entangled with each other: so God is both one and a community of three. And beyond all of the patterns of action is Action, action itself, which God is; and God is also patterns of action specific to the Holy Spirit, to Jesus, and to the Father, who is the Creator. Action, action itself, is constitutive of God the Creator, and by their relationship with the Father, Jesus and the Spirit are constituted by Action as well, so they too give birth to action in changing patterns.

The Holy Spirit, or Spirit of God, is the Spirit of Jesus,[26] because both Jesus and the Spirit share changing patterns of action that constitute God, with Jesus and the Spirit each exhibiting patterns of their own as well as patterns of action common to all three of the Father, the Son, and the Spirit. And the Spirit gives birth to gifts, and we can exhibit fruit of the Spirit—love, joy, peace . . .[27] —all of which are patterns of action that are God's patterns of action. The gifts are our activity, and the fruit of the Spirit is actions that we do, and at the same time it is God's action because the actions in patterns bear a family likeness to patterns of action that constitute God.

The Spirit "swept over the face of the waters"[28] of chaos; the Spirit "blows where it chooses, and you hear the sound of it, but you do not know where it comes from or where it goes";[29] and on the day of Pentecost the Spirit came with a "violent wind" and "tongues, as of fire."[30] The Spirit's particular gift is patterns of action characterized by extreme change.

As the Acts of the Apostles relates the story of the early church, we find baptism regularly employed to mark individuals and households becoming Christians.[31] Baptism was the point at which the Holy Spirit was given, and spiritual gifts, such as speaking in tongues, that is, new God-given languages, accompanied the gift. Still baptism was entangled with the changing patterns of action that constitute repentance and forgiveness, but now the practice had been reshaped—but not entirely so—to both represent and achieve admission to the Christian church as an institution as well as to represent and achieve repentance, forgiveness, and the gift of the Holy Spirit.

The meaning of baptism has continued to change. The baptism of infants implies that baptism is admission to the church, and that the representation and achievement of forgiveness has now been separated from the achievement of repentance; and baptism has also come to mean admission to the human family and the granting of names as well as admission to the church.

There is something highly egalitarian about baptism. However much the context of one baptism might differ from another, what is done remains the same. We immerse in water, or we pour water: and at every baptism forgiveness and repentance happen, and the Spirit is given. All of us need baptism for repentance for forgiveness of sins. So should we seek baptism more often than we do? Christian baptism is rightly just once: an action that is the action of the dying and rising of Christ, and thus ourselves dying to an old life and rising to a new one: but what we also need is constant actions in changing patterns that revive the pattern of action that was and remains our baptism. We are always in need of repentance: of changing our minds. We never arrive; we never achieve perfection: and to be constantly actively reminded of our baptisms can prepare us to be more deeply attuned to the patterns of action that are God's action in the world.

## MARK 1:9-13

> 9 In those days Jesus came from Nazareth of Galilee and was baptized by John in the Jordan. [10] And just as he was coming up out of the water, he saw the heavens torn apart and the Spirit descending like a dove on him. [11] And a voice came from heaven, 'You are my Son, the Beloved;[g] with you I am well pleased.'

---

g. Or *my beloved Son*

> [12] And the Spirit immediately drove him out into the wilderness. [13] He was in the wilderness for forty days, tempted by Satan; and he was with the wild beasts; and the angels waited on him.[32]

If John's baptism was for repentance for the forgiveness of sins, why is Jesus being baptized? We can be certain that nobody made up this incident, as it might have been something of an embarrassment to the church that Jesus had been baptized and that the normal meaning of John's baptism was that sin was being confessed, that repentance was taking place, and that forgiveness was being granted.

But perhaps Jesus was sinless, and he was being baptized for others' sin? Perhaps he was being baptized himself so as to institute the sacrament of baptism, just as he shared the bread and wine with his disciples when he instituted the Eucharist, the Lord's Supper? Or perhaps the baptism was for Jesus an act of dedication to his mission, a kind of ordination, rather than a confession of sin?[33] In Matthew's Gospel, a complex dialogue occurs around Jesus' baptism, clearly driven by the problems that Jesus having been baptized by John were bound to raise in the minds of Christians: but there is no such dialogue in Mark's Gospel, so maybe we should regard Jesus as here completely identified with sinful humanity by being sinful humanity.

Jesus went on a journey from Nazareth to where John was baptizing in the River Jordan: he brought himself to John, and John baptized him. That baptism would have generated similar changes in who Jesus was as it created in the many others whom John baptized: so Jesus' mind was changed, and patterns of action that were not God's patterns of action were no longer constitutive of God's relationship with Jesus. He had confessed his sin, he had repented, and he had been forgiven. If we take this seriously, then we have to conclude that Jesus was no stranger to sin. How could he have been? Each of us is actions in changing patterns, and every one of those patterns of action is constantly changed by other changing patterns of action around us: those that constitute our environments, those that impact our senses, the events that surround us twenty-four hours a day. None of us is a self-enclosed individual. And if each of us is changing patterns of actions, then none of us have boundaries. All of us are constantly impacted by the sin of the individuals we encounter, the sin of our societies, institutions, and economies, and the sin of the natural world, and we cannot avoid participating in all of that sin or contributing to it: so Jesus could not have avoided being immersed in the individual, social, institutional, and natural sin around him, could not have avoided that sin influencing the patterns of action that constituted who he was, and therefore could not have avoided inflicting sin on others. If this were not to be the case, then Jesus would have been a self-enclosed individual whose patterns of action had no effect on individuals and the world around him. That was clearly not the case. Jesus had less of a boundary than the rest of us: he was constantly interacting with individuals and with the world around him.

So what can the writer of the Letter to the Hebrews have meant when they wrote: "For we do not have a high priest who is unable to sympathize with our weaknesses, but we have one who in every respect has been tested[w] as we are, yet without sin"?[34] The writer's motive would have been that in this letter, so heavily influenced by the Jewish sacrificial system, Jesus is described as both priest and victim, the sacrificial victim had to be unblemished, and Jesus' priesthood had to be distinguished from the previous priesthood, so the author had to say that Jewish priests had to offer sacrifices for their own sin as well as for that of the people of Israel, whereas Jesus had offered himself, the perfect victim, for the sins of others.[35] But the writer had no need to think in this way. They could equally well have recognized that because he was perfectly human, Jesus could not be perfectly sinless, and that his sacrifice of himself could be for his own sin as well as for the sins of others. Indeed, in the same passage we find a recognition that Jesus was *not* sinless: "Although he was a Son, he learned obedience through what he suffered; and having been made perfect, he became the source of eternal salvation for all who obey him . . . ."[36]

But let us now take seriously the idea that Jesus was "without sin." What could this mean in the context of boundaryless human individuals who cannot insulate themselves from patterns of action that are not only not God's own patterns of actions, but are positively destructive of them? Each of us is not only constantly affected by the multiple individual, corporate, and natural sin that impacts us all the time: we also generate our own patterns of action that are destructive of the patterns of action by which God reveals God, and of the virtuous and loving patterns of action around us. Out of the patterns of action that influence us, our patterns of action create new destructive patterns in the ubiquitous action: patterns of action that spread sin into the individuals we encounter, into our society, and into the natural world. If we choose to call Jesus sinless, then what we must mean is that this was not true for him. The patterns of action that constituted who Jesus was absorbed the sinful patterns of action that impacted him, so that the patterns of action that constituted who he was, and that influenced the patterns of action that constituted other people, his society, and his world, were God's own patterns of action.

But how do we determine that Jesus did this? Of the infinite number of patterns of action that make up an individual's impact on the individuals and the world around them, how do we determine that they were somehow sinless? We don't. All we can do is define them in that way. We have to begin with Jesus, and decide to call sinless the patterns of action that constituted him. And if we are going to do that, then it might be better to use more positive terminology. We might choose to speak of Jesus' perfection; of the perfection of his patterns of action: a perfection that was God's perfection; a perfection of patterns of action that absorbs the imperfections of the patterns of action that constitute individuals, society, and the world, so that those patterns of action become God's patterns of action. All of it is action, all of it is changing, moving,

w. Or *tempted*

dynamic, and diverse: there is no definition of perfection to be pinned down, so there is no definition of sinlessness that we can grasp, and therefore no definition of sin. What we have is Jesus: the actions in patterns that are this human being who is God: that is, for whom the patterns of action that constitute who he is are the intertwined and constantly changing patterns of action of both his human flesh—and so not those of God—and of his divinity: and so those of God. There is no separating of them; the entire constantly changing pattern of changing patterns of actions are who Jesus is, and are his perfection. But this perfection had to be learned:[37] and we shall find in Mark's Gospel some of the events by which that learning occurred.[38] Was that process ever complete? Perhaps as Jesus approached his crucifixion: for if Jesus' struggle with obedience in the Garden of Gethsemane, and during the crucifixion, were the "testing" referred to in the Letter to the Hebrews, then "tested[w] as we are, yet without sin . . . he learned obedience through what he suffered; and having been made perfect . . ."[39] begins to make sense. And so does Jesus' baptism by John make sense. This too was an act of obedience: a necessary baptism for repentance for the forgiveness of sins, a necessary stage on the way to the perfection that absorbs every destructive pattern of action and transforms it into a pattern of action that is God's.

Jesus needed repentance for the forgiveness of sin: he needed to take all of the action in patterns of his surroundings into himself and therefore into the life of God; he needed his mind and therefore the mind of God to be changed; he needed to be constituted by patterns of action that constitute a human individual in relationship with God if God was to be able to relate to human individuals. Only a God with no boundaries can know boundaryless human beings and all other boundaryless realities. Just like the rest of us, Jesus needed God to choose not to permit the vast turbulent sea of sin to disrupt the relationship between God, the world, and every individual: he needed God to absorb all of it, cleanse it, and reconstitute all of reality through constantly new patterns of action. There could not have been a more appropriate action than for Jesus to be baptized.

> [10] And just as he was coming up out of the water, he saw the heavens torn apart
> and the Spirit descending like a dove on him.[40]

Jesus "was baptized": a simple pattern of action. This is what John did to Jesus. But now we have something very different. The combination of tenses and parts of verbs describe a single complex pattern of action. All of it is happening at the same time: the coming up out of the water, the seeing, the tearing of the heavens, and the Spirit descending. It is impossible to separate this into separate events, and we should not try to do so.

There is no suggestion that anyone else saw anything out of the ordinary: "he saw . . ."; so what Mark is recording here is a vision personal to Jesus rather than something that everyone standing there would have seen and heard.[41] But what of

w. Or *tempted*

the other gospels? Matthew's Gospel closely follows Mark's account;[42] but Luke's Gospel separates out the event: "when Jesus also had been baptized and was praying, the heaven was opened, and the Holy Spirit descended upon him in bodily form like a dove": possibly so that near to the beginning of his gospel Luke could emphasize a constant theme: that Jesus prayed.[43] John's Gospel alludes to Jesus' baptism without directly describing it—perhaps for the same reason that we find a dialogue justifying the baptism in Matthew's Gospel—but we are told that John the Baptist saw "the Spirit descending from heaven like a dove, and it remained on him."[44] But we are studying Mark's Gospel, so we must take seriously the fact that what we have here is a single diverse and complex pattern of activity that is entirely that of Jesus.[45] It belongs to no-one else. Jesus came up out of the water, having experienced a baptism for repentance for the forgiveness of sins, and as he did so he saw "the heavens torn apart and the Spirit descending like a dove on him." While the complex event might be properly describable as having parts, there is no need to regard the heavens being torn apart, the Holy Spirit descending like a dove, and the voice that Jesus heard, as separate events happening at the same time.[46] The Holy Spirit descending was the heavens being torn apart, and the voice was the heavens being torn apart. A similar pattern of action occurred at the end of Jesus' ministry, when the curtain of the temple was torn apart, and Jesus' identity as God's Son was again declared, but on that occasion by a Gentile centurion.[47]

However much all of us are without boundaries, and however much the patterns of action that constitute who we are are constantly affected by the changing patterns of action that constitute individuals, institutions, communities, and the world, and that we encounter and that encounter us, there are patterns of action that are momentarily our own, and then cease to be: and in that respect Luke has entirely changed the story by separating out Jesus' seeing the heavens torn apart from the baptism and instead attaching it to his praying. In Mark's Gospel, the instantaneous complex event is purely Jesus' event, and inaccessible to anyone else. The people there at the time had no access to it, and neither do we. In terms of the practicalities, we can only assume that Jesus told his disciples about what had happened as he came up out of the water, and it is of course possible that John the Baptist experienced something of what was going on, and that others did as well: but that is not what we are told here. All of it is purely a complex pattern of action that constitutes who Jesus is and that will constantly ripple through the patterns of action that will constitute who he will be.

So it is with our relationships with ourselves, with God, and to some extent with other people and with the world around us. The patterns of action that constitute who we are are momentarily entirely our own. The next moment they will influence the changing patterns of action that will make us who we are then, as will the actions in patterns around us, and the patterns of action that we have become will influence those. To that initial momentary event neither we ourselves nor other people will ever again have access. An event had occurred—that is, a complex pattern of actions—and nothing would ever be the same again; but neither would there ever be a way back to it, for Jesus or for us. The text is all that we have: a pure pattern that generates actions in ever new patterns for all of its readers down the centuries. Behind the text we can never go. Jesus lived in the past, and the action in patterns that constitute who he was are still the action in patterns that constitute who he is, so using past, present and future tenses of Jesus, as we have done, is entirely legitimate: but we still can't get behind the text and relate directly to the patterns of action that gave birth to it. All we have is the text: a pure pattern that will catalyze changes in the patterns of action that constitute who we are—changes that reflect but do not replicate the patterns of action that constituted the mind of Mark and the events that impacted that mind and the minds of those who told him about them.

So how shall this reader read this text? And how will you read it? I shall read the Spirit as the bond between Jesus and the one he called "Abba"[z],[48] "Father," and whom he knew as the source of action—as Action itself—and as the one who gives birth to loving and creative patterns of action. The Spirit appearing as a dove represents the bond as patterns of action that represent peace between Jesus and his Father: a communion that through Jesus' obedience and God's action would generate a constantly new unity constituted by patterns of action that are both those of Jesus and those of God. This is the unity between them that we explored briefly in the introduction: a unity of patterns of action. At his baptism Jesus had a vision of this bond of unity; and perhaps John the Baptist experienced something of the same.

Heaven had been opened. In fact, heaven had always been open. There is no boundary between God and the cosmos. God is Action and the source of all action, and so is the source of the action that is the cosmos; and the particular patterns of action that gave birth to the cosmos, and that were and are the cosmos, are God's patterns of action; and God constantly relates to the universe in patterns of action that are God's and those of the universe. But here, in the midst of this event of baptism, the opening of heaven was revealed to Jesus, instilling an intimacy with God that would never leave him.

> [11] And a voice came from heaven, 'You are my Son, the Beloved;[g] with you I am well pleased.'[49]

The kings of Israel were called "sons of God," and in Psalm 2 the writer envisages a king saying "He said to me, 'You are my son; today I have begotten you. . . .'" The voice from heaven echoes this psalm, and also a passage about the servant of God in the book of the prophet Isaiah: "Here is my servant, whom I uphold, my chosen, in whom my soul delights."[50] The conflation transitions from the "servant" of Isaiah to the "son" of the psalm, declaring Jesus to be the servant of God who becomes the king of the Kingdom of God: although he would later identify himself anew with the "servant" as

z. Aramaic for *Father*
g. Or *my beloved Son*

well; and the designation as "son" no doubt also confirmed the relationship that Jesus experienced with God as "Abba[z],"[51] "father."

A voice is the quintessential pattern of action. It is purely movement. The speaker activates the air in patterns of their choosing, and the action in patterns changes the patterns of action that constitute the hearer. The hearer hears the message and is changed: but the voice has disappeared. No analysis is possible. We are not told who heard the message, whether it was only Jesus, only John and Jesus, or everyone who was there. All we can know is that Jesus was told that he would be a son of God, and thus a king of Israel: and that he would be a new kind of king because he would be a servant. Already God was pleased, because Jesus was learning obedience: already the patterns of action that he was were the patterns of action that were God, and they were becoming so: for all is action, everything is changing and dynamic, and nothing is achieved or complete. It was the direction that mattered: a trajectory of change towards the perfection that is God, itself a perfection that is never complete or achieved, because God is Action and the source of all action.

Jesus had received a mandate to be both God's son and the servant of God, to rule in the Kingdom of God, and first of all to proclaim the Kingdom's coming in his actions and in his words. He would therefore have to confront those earthly and heavenly powers that resisted the establishment of that Kingdom:[52]

[12] And the Spirit immediately drove him out into the wilderness.[53]

Could Jesus have resisted?

There is no difference between our choosing and our doing, our willing our actions and the actions themselves. We are our action in changing patterns: all of it is actions in changing patterns. Some of it we label conscious; some of it we label choosing or decisions; some of it we think about afterwards—that is, patterns of action that is us thinking entangle with the changing patterns of action in our brains left behind by our previous actions. And sometimes we are "driven": we can watch ourselves acting in patterns and not be entirely sure where it is all coming from: from the action in patterns in our brains that we call our subconscious? From God? From emotional currents around us, breaking through our always porous boundaries and impacting the patterns of action that we are? We might be able to draw such driven action into our thinking and deciding patterns of actions, but sometimes that might not be possible. Whether Jesus could have resisted being driven into the wilderness we cannot know. What we do know is that he was driven there, into the places where devils were known to dwell.[54] A battle between God's Messiah and the powers of evil was expected during the last days, and it is here in the wilderness that that battle begins: not in Galilee or in Jerusalem—although Jesus would experience conflict with evil in both of those places before long—but in the wilderness: the place of the exodus from Egypt, the place of prophecy, and the place where the battle could only be with the cosmic powers of evil

z. Aramaic for *Father*

and not with the human powers that would soon oppose Jesus. The Messiah had been anointed for the task of doing non-violent battle for the Kingdom of God, and now it had begun.[55]

> [13] He was in the wilderness for forty days, tempted by Satan; and he was with the wild beasts; and the angels waited on him.[56]

Matthew's and Luke's Gospels offer us a dialogue between Jesus and Satan. Mark's account is sparse, leaving us to imagine what happened. What we can say is that Satan, "the adversary,"[57] like every other reality, is action in patterns: in this case patterns utterly destructive and disruptive of the patterns of action that constitute God's relationship with us. God is beyond all patterns of actions in the sense that God is Action: the source of all action; but if God is to relate to a cosmos that is constituted by actions in particular changing patterns, then that relationship can only be constituted by actions in particular patterns: patterns particular to God. God's creation of a universe was and is particular patterns of action: patterns of action that have then gone on to change, and to give birth to an infinite number of constantly changing patterns of action. And the patterns of action that constitute God's relationship with us are patterns of action that we find in Jesus: either because that is who he is, or because we choose to find those patterns of action in him, or both.

There is no reason to suppose that those patterns of action that we call the physical world, and that constantly influence the patterns of action that constitute ourselves, are the only ones: so there is no reason to regard Satan and the angels in this passage from Mark's Gospel as somehow less real than the computer on which I am typing this. They were real enough to Jesus; and they are real in terms of our conceptual framework, because the active verbs in this passage relate to the Holy Spirit, to Satan, and to the angels.[58] The heavenly powers are at least as real as terrestrial ones, and perhaps even more so. Perhaps our rather materialist culture has decided to insulate itself against patterns of action to which previous periods of human history were more receptive.

To reiterate: Satan is action in patterns: patterns of action utterly destructive and disruptive of the patterns of action that constitute God's relationship with us. It is this Satan that tempted Jesus to sin by deviating from the mission that he knew God to have given to him to fulfil. Satan's pattern of action is not dissimilar to that at the beginning of the book of Job, where God permits Satan to test Job.[59] Jesus resisted that temptation, and from then on he constantly resisted Satan's tempting of him.[60] Whether the "wild beasts" were the physical animals of the wilderness, or Satan's associates, they were equally malign influences: and the angels were what they say they are: messengers of God, communicators of the patterns of action that constitute God's relationship with us. There are still angels. Our more materialist mindsets might only be receptive to angels of God who are the people and the world around us, or we might also be able to identify messengers of God who are patterns of action in different ways.

Nothing is impossible, and reality is stranger than we can imagine, simply because reality is all action, and there must be patterns of action beyond our imagining.

Did all of this happen at the same time? The temptation, the wild beasts, and the angels? Or were they a string of events separated by time?[61] Either way, Jesus was tempted, and he resisted; the wild beasts might have been demons; and God's messengers came to him, perhaps exhibiting the same patterns of action as the voice at Jesus' baptism when the heavens were opened and the Holy Spirit descended. If reality is action in changing patterns, then it is the events that matter, and the varying time sequences are generated by the changing patterns of action rather than events fitting into an existing framework of time. There might have been differences in time and space between Jesus' battle with evil powers and the battle with evil that the church for which Mark wrote his gospel was having to wage, but if the patterns of action were the same then it was the same battle, regardless of any distance in time: so this account of a battle with evil, and the various encounters between Jesus and evil powers recounted in the gospel, might have been retained in the tradition and recorded by Mark as an encouragement to a church constantly engaged in a battle with evil powers.[62]

## MARK 1:14-15

> 14 Now after John was arrested, Jesus came to Galilee, proclaiming the good news[a] of God,[b] 15 and saying, 'The time is fulfilled, and the kingdom of God has come near;[c] repent, and believe in the good news.'[d] [63]

There is a pattern of action here: first the forerunner, and then the Messiah, who is "more powerful" than John:[64] sufficiently powerful to defeat the power of evil.[65] The forerunner's work is finished, so John the Baptist is now to fade out of the story until the account of his death in chapter 6; and simultaneously with John's disappearance from view is the beginning of Jesus' ministry.[66] The verb is appropriately passive: "John was arrested." Jesus, however, is described using active verbs: he "came . . . proclaiming." Jesus constantly travelled, and Mark's Gospel is full of his journeys. There is also a sense in which the entire gospel is structured around a journey, with the first eight chapters located at the point of departure in Galilee, chapters 9 and 10 recording the journey from Galilee to Jerusalem, and the final six chapters located at the point of arrival in Jerusalem: a structure clearly more related to Mark's theological purpose than to Jesus' practice, which would probably have consisted of numerous visits to Jerusalem during festivals.[67] Jesus was a preacher who travelled; and this is who Jesus was in this event: someone who arrived and proclaimed. What he proclaimed was

a. Or *gospel*
b. Other ancient authorities read *of the kingdom*
c. Or *is at hand*
d. Or *gospel*

urgent: "The time is fulfilled." It is the *kairos* kind of time that has come,[68] not *chronos* time—a significant point or period of time, not time as in a diary. For this gospel, time is not linear, and there are different kinds of time, all overlapping, and all constituted by changing patterns of action: there is the time of the Kingdom of God, that intensifies towards the final establishment of the Kingdom; there is the time of the incarnation: of Jesus' life, death, and resurrection, that merges with the time of the Kingdom of God at Jesus' resurrection; there is the time of the church between the resurrection and the final establishment of the Kingdom of God, or perhaps between the choosing of the first disciples and the final establishment of the Kingdom. And so the beginning of Jesus' ministry was a particularly significant *Kairos*; and what he proclaimed at this *kairos* was the Kingdom of God: active, with its own pattern of action: "the Kingdom of God has come near." But there is more to be said about time. The complex pattern of action that constituted the proclamation of the Kingdom of God's coming and the repentance of those who responded to the summons to trust the good news is to be found here at the beginning of Jesus' ministry, in the church for which Mark was writing, and in the whole church throughout history. This is the same pattern of action, so it is the same event, regardless of the passage of *chronos* time. Throughout Mark's Gospel we shall find patterns of action that belong both in Jesus' ministry and in the lives of his readers, and everywhere we find such patterns of action we shall know that the same events are occurring.[69]

While the term "Kingdom of God" appears only fourteen times in Mark's Gospel, the concept is central to the gospel's narrative and to Jesus' understanding of himself and his mission.[70] The Kingdom of God was an idea with which Jesus' hearers would have been acquainted: it was the rule of God, both as a current reality and as something hoped for:[71] the rule of God who is the source of all action and is the changing patterns of action that we see in Jesus. It is Jesus who is the Kingdom of God come near; and because he is to come again, he is the Kingdom of God that is still to come.[72] Jesus spoke often about the Kingdom of God, usually in parables, which we shall read later: and we shall find in them a Kingdom of God having come near already and still to be completed.

And then the command is issued: "repent, and believe in the good news": presumably the good news that the Kingdom of God has come near. Again, active verbs. With his "repent" Jesus is asking his hearers to change their minds, to choose a new direction for their lives. This is not a conversion experience that happens to someone: it is a positive decision that is being demanded. We are being told to change our minds. And similarly, the "believe" here is not something that happens to us. It is something that we do. So first of all we might not believe, and now we are told to think differently, to take a new direction, and to believe in the good news that the Kingdom of God has come near. "Commit yourself to," or "trust in,"[73] might be a better translation of *pisteuete*, "believe in": a translation more in tune with the preceding *metanoeite*, "repent." Jesus is asking us to turn ourselves around and to commit ourselves to the good news that the Kingdom of God has come near: presumably not the good news that the Kingdom of God has now stopped, like a train outside a station, but rather the good news that it is still on its way and will arrive. And we are to commit ourselves to the good news that it is the Kingdom of *God* that has come near and will arrive: a kingdom that is of the character of the God who is Action, the source of all action, and the changing patterns of action that we see in Jesus. We are being asked to conform ourselves to those changing patterns of action, which means that we are being asked to live in the Kingdom of God now. We are not to wait for it: we are to be it. The Kingdom of God is not a thing. It is not an object. It is a verb: perhaps better expressed as "the ruling that is God," "the liberating that is God," "the unconditional giving that is God." And in any case, "kingdom" is now a somewhat tainted and anachronistic word to use for patterns of action that are always new. "City of God" might be better, or perhaps "community of God." Or maybe we should bypass that imagery altogether, and speak of "the action of God," for that is what we are discussing here: God's activity among us, inviting us to join in[74]—and it is this pattern of action of God's rule, both fulfilled in Jesus and still awaited in its fulness, that has come near.[75]

Just as God's action has come near in Jesus, and in him we see the changing patterns of action that are God and the coming near of God's action, so we are commanded to live that life, to do that action: for we too are action in patterns. We are to turn around, to strike out in a new direction, in new patterns of action that are the patterns of action that constitute the Kingdom of God, the City of God, the community of God, the action of God. If we obey that command, then not only will Jesus live the life of the Kingdom of God, but we shall live it as well. The Kingdom will be us. The action of God will be us: and to that extent we shall be the Kingdom of God, the City of God, the community of God, the action of God, and, to the extent that the patterns of action that constitute who we are conform to the patterns of action that God is, we shall be God.

## MARK 1:16-20

> 16 As Jesus passed along the Sea of Galilee, he saw Simon and his brother Andrew casting a net into the lake—for they were fishermen. 17 And Jesus said to them, 'Follow me and I will make you fish for people.' 18 And immediately they left their nets and followed him. 19 As he went a little farther, he saw James son of Zebedee and his brother John, who were in their boat mending the nets. 20 Immediately he called them; and they left their father Zebedee in the boat with the hired men, and followed him.[76]

Did he simply see them, or was he looking for them? This was the area in which Jesus grew up and in which he was already active as a prophet of the coming Kingdom of God. But whether or not he was looking for them, or simply encountered them as he walked, he called them to follow him: literally to follow—to walk with him, spread good news with him, heal with him. Being a follower of Jesus, and by extension being a Christian today, is to do these things. It is not a state, something achieved, a state of rest: it is changing patterns of action, in tune with the action in patterns that constitutes who Jesus was and is; and the patterns of action that constituted the calling of Jesus' first disciples and their response was, is, and will be the pattern of action that characterizes Christians throughout space and time. Just as Jesus' first disciples gave up livelihoods and family in order to follow Jesus and make new disciples for him—even if their following was only for occasional periods between periods spent fishing and back with their families—so the Christians of Mark's time were giving up livelihoods and families to be Jesus' followers and to make new disciples in their own time, and so in many places today the same is demanded of Jesus' disciples. Jesus was plundering Satan's kingdom then; Christians of Mark's time were doing that too; and so are Christians today.[77]

The deal was clear. If they chose to follow Jesus, then he would "make" them into people who fished for other people: that is, they would join Jesus in doing the work of the Kingdom of God.[78] The initiative would pass to Jesus. He would fashion them into something new. None of us has boundaries, and all of us are constantly remade by the people around us: but here was something more than influence—Jesus' new followers knew that if they chose to follow Jesus then the patterns of action that constituted who they were would change radically, and not in the usual evolutionary fashion in which the patterns of action that constitute us normally change. A better translation might be "I will make you become people who fish for people." Once we understand reality as action in patterns rather than as beings that might change, everything is becoming, nothing is being, unless we understand being as action and becoming. And so if we hear Jesus' call to follow him, and we choose to follow, then he will remake the changing patterns of action that we are, and we will become something new, and then again we shall be changed, and again. Those fishermen were to be made to become fishers of people. What Jesus would make us become would be for Jesus to decide if we chose to follow him.

Simon and Andrew "left their nets." This was no passive action. They walked away from their nets, from the life that they knew, and headed out after Jesus to be remade. The initial preaching tour might have been quite short: perhaps a tour of a few villages, preaching and healing. We soon find them back in their fishing boats: but they were now changed people, and they would continue to follow, and would continue to be remade so that they would become fishers of people. Who they were would be different because their patterns of action would be different: and eventually they would follow Jesus to Jerusalem to watch him being arrested in the Garden of Gethsemane—and then they would continue to follow him, and they would continue to be remade to become fishers of people. The repentance, the changing of the mind, was permanent; they had heard the good news and committed themselves to it; and although there would never be a new state somehow permanently achieved, there was a permanent change of direction, a rupture in the patterns of action, giving birth to wholly new patterns: and still there would always be action and there would always be change.

And then the same happened again, further down the seashore. Jesus called, they "left" their father and his employees, and they "followed." The same pattern, but always new and different. With every action there is further action; with every pattern of action there will be consequential patterns of action; with every change in patterns of action there will be other changes in patterns of action. James' and John's father would be changed: that is, the action in changing patterns that constituted who he was would be radically changed; and to some extent the same would be true for his employees. The ripples would have gone on to the edges of the cosmos and to eternity, as they do for any change in the patterns of action that constitute who we are. There will always be consequences to any action, and particular consequences if Jesus calls, we follow, and Jesus remakes us. Like those early followers, we shall do new things, and we shall be changed.

## MARK 1:21–28

> 21 They went to Capernaum; and when the sabbath came, he entered the synagogue and taught. 22 They were astounded at his teaching, for he taught them as one having authority, and not as the scribes. 23 Just then there was in their synagogue a man with an unclean spirit, 24 and he cried out, 'What have you to do with us, Jesus of Nazareth? Have you come to destroy us? I know who you are, the Holy One of God.' 25 But Jesus rebuked him, saying, 'Be silent, and come out of him!' 26 And the unclean spirit, throwing him into convulsions and crying with a loud voice, came out of him. 27 They were all amazed, and they kept on asking one another, 'What is this? A new teaching—with authority! He[j] commands even the unclean spirits, and they obey him.' 28 At once his fame began to spread throughout the surrounding region of Galilee.[79]

In this passage, and in the following two passages, Mark describes what we might call a typical day in Jesus' ministry, and while doing so he expresses the patterns of action that constituted the whole of Jesus' diverse ministry. Whilst Jesus' disciples are present, it is Jesus himself who acts: most of the active verbs are singular and have Jesus as their subject.[80] A collection of patterns of action has formed a complex pattern of action that constitutes Jesus during his ministry: a pattern of action to which the patterns of action of Christians are expected to bear family resemblances.[81]

"They went," and "he entered the synagogue and taught." Again we find Jesus going, arriving, doing. This is who he was. And in particular, teaching is who he was:

j. Or *A new teaching! With authority he*

and the teaching was "astounding": it changed the people who listened to him so that "they were astounded." There were no boundaries. We cannot defend ourselves against new things. Even if we resist them and build defenses against them, we have still been changed, the patterns of action that we are will always be of a character and in a direction different from the one in which they would have been if we had not been encountered by the new changing pattern of action. Jesus *was* new changing patterns of action, and so his words were as well: and they broke through the already porous boundaries of his audience, and they were changed. This is what authority is: a changing pattern of action that is the ability to create change, the ability to bring about repentance—changes of mind—and the ability to bring about new commitments. Jesus' words and actions shared in the pattern of action that we call "authority": a pattern of action entwined with changing patterns of action that constitute new ideas, new words, and new patterns of action, drawing people into interacting with the new and into leaving behind the old.[82] Those who came to understand Jesus' authority were drawn into the changing patterns of action that Jesus was, and they found themselves in tune with them: new harmonies will have been established, and they will have continued to change in new ways. And so they were drawn into the changing patterns of action that God is: for Jesus' changing patterns of action were those of God as well as those of his humanity. Those sitting in that synagogue were drawn into God, as we are if we hear Jesus' teaching, as we find that it breaks through our boundaries with authority, and as we find that we too are astounded.

I shall not be asking here about the state of the man in the synagogue. These readings in Mark's Gospel are not interested in states of affairs, which are static understandings, but rather in action and change. So what we are interested in here is the man's pattern of action and Jesus' pattern of action.

The "man with an unclean spirit" did not "enter" the synagogue, as Jesus did: but he did "cry out." The pattern of action that he fears is destruction, of himself, of his demons, or of everyone in the synagogue: it is not clear which—simply that he was afraid of the action of destruction. He knows who Jesus is: "the Holy One of God." This is not a Messianic title.[83] It is not a description of a state, but rather a statement of the pattern of action that constitutes the Holy One of God: that is, the destruction of evil—again, not as a characteristic or a state, but as a continual activity.

A better translation would be "And Jesus rebuked him . . ." The final conflict between God and evil that will usher in the end times and the Kingdom of God, and that will cause great suffering as the battle rages, has begun.[84] The evil-destroying pattern of action that is the Holy One of God entangles with the destructive, demonic pattern of action that constitutes the man in the synagogue. "Be silent" was the command; "come out": another command. Words are as much actions in patterns as is anything else. There is no difference between language and anything else in the world. All of it is action in patterns, and all of it belongs together: and so Jesus' words are his action and they are who he is, just as the words that we speak or write are who we are just as much as is any other action in patterns.

Jesus spoke the words—actions in particular patterns—and those words broke through the man's porous boundary and changed the patterns of action that he was. He was convulsed, and he cried out: and in the midst of the diversity that is the patterns of action of each of us there was a bifurcation, and the patterns of action that we might call demonic were so utterly changed that it would not be inaccurate to say that they were destroyed—that they had come out of him. The Holy One of God had indeed destroyed the patterns of action that had declared who Jesus was. If some of the actions in patterns that constitute who we are are radically changed, then all of them are changed, because there are no boundaries between the many different and changing patterns of action that constantly relate to each other in new ways: and so the man was radically changed. There really were convulsions in the patterns of action that he was.

Again Jesus had astounded them: "they were all amazed." The action was Jesus' action, and the spectators were changed, so that genuine enquiry became a new pattern of action experienced by all of them. They were full of questions, which, like commands, change their hearers. The spectators had seen healing activity, and they called it "a new teaching." Were they referring to Jesus' teaching before he was addressed by the man in the synagogue, or were they referring to the healing of the man? Probably both. Exorcism was not a common event, and Jesus was unusual in the centrality that he gave to the activity—no doubt because exorcism was both compassionate rescue of individuals and victory over Satan; and both the manner and the content of his teaching were clearly of a unique authority. The exorcism and the teaching belonged together as a complex changing pattern of action that represented the Kingdom of God.[85] There is no boundary between language and other kinds of action. Every action is language, and language is changing patterns of action. All of it is action in changing patterns. It is Jesus' commands that are his teaching; and it is the healing that occurred that is his teaching. Jesus' speaking to his hearers in parables, and his healing of people living with disability, illness, or possession, were patterns of action that constituted who he was and that changed everyone who experienced them. There was no boundary between them unless we choose to create one.[86]

Still the actions in changing patterns that are who Jesus was and is change us; and still his teaching and his healing are all teaching, they are his communication, they are his impinging on the world around him and around us. All of it is "with authority": it draws us in and asks us to choose to follow him—and if we do that then we shall be changed and we shall become fishers of people for the Kingdom of God.

But not just for then and now: Jesus' action is the action of the future Kingdom of God. Already he lives the life of the Kingdom. There in the synagogue the Kingdom was happening. It could not have been more present, in the sense that the actions in patterns that constitute the Kingdom of God were happening in that synagogue when

Jesus taught the people and then healed the possessed man. The Kingdom of God remains in the future, in the sense that there is much action in patterns that is clearly not the diverse and changing action in patterns that constitute the Kingdom of God: but the Kingdom is already present to the extent that its life is lived, in Jesus, in people around us, and maybe to some small extent in ourselves.

Perhaps the man in the synagogue did not wish to be healed by Jesus, and so rejected him, because his life was stable even if it was a living hell. Perhaps he could not face the changes that Jesus would bring about at the many levels of action that constituted who he was. He knew that nothing would remain unchanged. It was this destruction that he feared. But he met Jesus, Jesus spoke, Jesus acted; the resistance melted away, and the man was utterly changed. He had repented: he had changed his mind, and was now to move in new directions and do new things. He had been liberated for new changing patterns of action. Because changing patterns of action entangle with those around them so that those patterns of action too change in new and unpredictable ways, everyone in that synagogue would have been changed.

The text of Mark's Gospel is not itself action. It is static marks on a page. It is pure pattern: a crystallization of the patterns of action that happened on that day in that synagogue. Those patterns of action gave birth to new changing patterns of action in the people in the synagogue, in Jesus' new followers, and in Jesus himself, as well as in the man healed of his demons; and those changing patterns of action will have encountered yet more changing patterns of action, and then more again, so that the event will have rippled through generations of Jesus' followers by means of a highly complex oral and maybe also written tradition,[87] and would finally have changed the patterns of action that were Mark's brain, his hand, his pen, and his parchment. The pattern was laid down. Yes, it was static and unchanging, even though in some ways changing as manuscript gave birth to manuscript, manuscript to printed book, Greek to translations: but as it travelled, that static pattern engaged with the action in patterns of the minds of its readers and integrated itself into those patterns of action, changing them, and again rippling outwards into yet more changing patterns of action: and in particular into the changed and changing minds of the text's translators, giving birth to new static patterns that we might call cousins of Mark's original: patterns that have then gone on to change myriads more changing patterns of action. The text is a catalyst, sending changing patterns in ever new directions of change.

And so those of us who read Mark's Gospel will be changed, and those of us who seek to follow Jesus will be changed in unpredictable ways. We too will be amazed; we too will ask questions—"What is this?"; we too will find that Jesus' teaching and healing, which together are teaching about the coming Kingdom of God, will change us; and we too will find that Jesus has exercised his authority, and that we will obey his commands.

But will Jesus' fame spread in our secular age? For two thousand years Jesus' life, healings, teaching, death, and resurrection have changed the actions in changing patterns that constitute individuals, communities, institutions, nations, and the world, and those changed patterns of action have then continued to change, burying the changes brought about by Jesus in the distant past of the evolution of the current changing patterns of action that today constitute individuals, communities, institutions, nations, and the world. It is as if we have been vaccinated against Jesus' call to us, so that the changing patterns of action that we now are resist encounters with the changing patterns of action that constitute Jesus and that encounter us through the pure patterns of the gospels and through those individuals, communities, and institutions that follow Jesus today, and whose patterns of action might therefore be more directly affected by the changing patterns of action that were and are Jesus. Those individuals, communities, and institutions might (but might not) exhibit patterns of action similar to Jesus' patterns of action, and the gospels will communicate those patterns: but they will not generate the same radical change that they catalyzed in Jesus' own time, and during the early years of the Christian church.

So how is Jesus' fame to spread today? The gospels remain the same as they were: they are pure pattern—crystallizations of actions in patterns—so we cannot expect anything new from them. One possibility is that we return to this story near the beginning of Mark's Gospel and notice the disruption that Jesus caused in the patterns of action all around him. He said new things, and he did new things, and the waves continue to ripple towards us today. If we are to be followers of Jesus, then we too will do new things and say new things. We shall allow Jesus' changing patterns of action to make new changes in our minds, in our words, and in our actions, and we shall positively seek to change what we say about him, and the ways in which we follow him. As we have discovered with the coronavirus pandemic that continues to cause suffering as I write this, it is viruses that mutate that succeed. Only if we develop previously unknown variants of the good news of Jesus and the Kingdom of God will Jesus' fame spread today. It will still be good news, and it will still be Jesus who is God whose changing patterns of action gave birth to it, but there will be new patterns of actions, constantly changing patterns of action, in amongst which will be new words: for words, too, are changing patterns of action. And so Jesus' fame will continue to spread: and then yet again new kinds of following and new words will have to be found.

# MARK 1:29-34

> 29 As soon as they[k] left the synagogue, they entered the house of Simon and Andrew, with James and John. ³⁰ Now Simon's mother-in-law was in bed with a fever, and they told him about her at once. ³¹ He came and took her by the hand and lifted her up. Then the fever left her, and she began to serve them.

k. Other ancient authorities read *he*

> 32 That evening, at sunset, they brought to him all who were sick or possessed with demons. ³³ And the whole city was gathered around the door. ³⁴ And he cured many who were sick with various diseases, and cast out many demons; and he would not permit the demons to speak, because they knew him.[88]

Now it is both Jesus and his followers who enter somewhere: no longer Jesus alone. He had drawn them into his pattern of action. Jesus entered, came to Simon's mother-in-law, took her hand, lifted her up, and healed her: and forever after Jesus' followers have been going, taking people by the hand, lifting them, and healing them in all manner of ways. But to what extent are our patterns of action Jesus' patterns of action? To what extent can they be?

Reality is action, and action is reality; and what we experience is action in patterns, and those patterns change, so that what we experience is action in changing patterns, and what we are is action in changing patterns. No pattern of action remains as it is, so it is impossible to identify one pattern of action with another, which means that everything is analogy. And not only that: the words that we might use to try to capture a likeness between one changing pattern of action and another constantly change their meanings, because they are constantly in new contexts, and the connections between the words change all the time. Nothing remains the same: and anything that we say about anything will be insecure analogy, even if it is that.

Just as Jesus' first followers had to choose to follow Jesus, and to choose how to follow Jesus, so we must choose whether or not to follow—which means that we shall either follow or not—and we must choose how to follow—which means that we shall follow in some ways and not in others: and none of those ways will be in the ways in which Jesus' first followers followed him. And we shall be left to decide whether our changing patterns of action are a following of Jesus, and to what extent, or whether they are something else entirely. There is only insecure analogy. So if we go to where we are invited, to where there is need, to where love can be exercised, then that going might be more or less a following of Jesus—we shall have to decide; and if we take someone's hand, and lift them up, and they are healed in some way, then that will be more or less a following of Jesus—again we shall have to decide. Nothing is ever the same.

What is still the same of course is that so much action in patterns does not change very much, and in particular that discrimination, oppression, injustice, and exploitation, are still far too common as patterns of action. Why didn't Simon serve his mother-in-law? Jesus might have washed his disciples' feet at his last meal with them before his crucifixion, but does not seem to have offered to help with preparing the meal on this occasion. Jesus still had to learn obedience: and later in Mark's Gospel we shall find occasions on which some of that learning occurred. Those who have followed Jesus throughout two millennia have had to learn obedience, and nobody has succeeded. Christians remain deeply sinful, and the church remains an intensely sinful institution. We never learn, and we frequently drag ourselves along behind the rest of a society that has learnt more quickly to resist discrimination, oppression, and exploitation. There have been brief periods during which Christians have been out in front, creating the liberating change that Jesus learnt to bring about, and that the earliest Christians sometimes managed to exhibit: but those periods have been rare, and too often we have made of our Christian faith a static tradition, and have thought that following Jesus today means following him in the same way that people and institutions followed him at some chosen point in the past. If Christian Faith is a tradition then it is not of that kind: it is a dynamic and ever-changing tradition, which it must be if we are to be followers of the Jesus who was changing patterns of action that were both the changing patterns of action that are God and the changing patterns of action of his humanity. Jesus' changing patterns of action have constantly stimulated new patterns of action in individuals, communities, societies, nations, and the world, and it is those that must constantly change the patterns of action that constitute who we are, so that we in our turn will create constantly new actions and words in the service of Jesus and the Kingdom of God. Still there will only be analogy: but at least there will be an analogy of some kind between the changing patterns of action that Jesus brought about and the changing patterns of action that we become and that we shall bring about, so that perhaps a little more often Christians will be out ahead of the rest of world, destroying demons, taking by the hand, lifting up, healing, and abolishing the exploitation that on this occasion neither Jesus nor his disciples decided to challenge.

> 32 That evening, at sunset, they brought to him all who were sick or possessed with demons. 33 And the whole city was gathered around the door. 34 And he cured many who were sick with various diseases, and cast out many demons; and he would not permit the demons to speak, because they knew him.[89]

On this occasion Jesus did not go to where the need was: those in need were brought to him. Their friends and relatives took action. They, too, were followers: they followed him to where he was staying. And this was not the first time that a crowd gathered around Jesus to hear him teach, to be healed, and to watch him heal. The houses were small, so there was never enough room: which is why the crowds spilled out into the street. And then again Jesus cured people of both disease and demons.

To what extent were the healing events unusual? Unique even? And does it matter? In a context of unique events—and so in the context of all events and of any, because no event is the same as another—drawing clear conclusions, and constructing causal connections, are difficult if not impossible to achieve. Perhaps all that we can say is that it might be appropriate for genuine healing miracles, castings out of demons, and so on, to have taken place, because Jesus' changing patterns of action were and are those of God, and Jesus is the one to whom it has been given to rule in the Kingdom of God: so it would not have been surprising if some of the character of the fully formed Kingdom of God would have overflowed into life on earth both then and today.[90]

During the previous incident in the synagogue Jesus had not been able to prevent the demon-possessed man from telling everyone who he was, but now Jesus is forbidding the demons to speak. To prevent something is as much an action as to do something. For something not to happen is for something to happen. And to make something not happen is to make something happen. There is no lack of action here.

## MARK 1: 35–39

> 35 In the morning, while it was still very dark, he got up and went out to a deserted place, and there he prayed. 36 And Simon and his companions hunted for him. 37 When they found him, they said to him, 'Everyone is searching for you.' 38 He answered, 'Let us go on to the neighbouring towns, so that I may proclaim the message there also; for that is what I came out to do.' 39 And he went throughout Galilee, proclaiming the message in their synagogues and casting out demons.[91]

Luke frequently mentions Jesus praying. Mark mentions Jesus praying just three times: here, in chapter 6, and near the end of the gospel in the Garden of Gethsemane, and always at night:[92] a different method of representing the importance of prayer both for Jesus and for the Christian.

Prayer is patterns of action in our minds, and sometimes it is spoken words. God is Action, is the source of all action, and is characterized by particular changing patterns of action. Some of the patterns in which action occurs are God's patterns, and some of them are ours: but there is still no action to which God is a stranger. This is as true of the action that we might call evil—changing patterns of action that have emerged from patterns to which God gave birth and that now disrupt or destroy God's patterns of action—as it is of evolving patterns of action that remain in tune with God's patterns of action. And so the angel Lucifer, created by God, ended up fighting against God and God's angels.

Prayer is particular kinds of patterns of action in our minds. When we speak words to another person, we change their minds: that is, the patterns of action that are our words change the patterns of action that they are. We might be asking for a particular change in someone's action, or we might have no particular intention but might simply want to create a bond between us. The same is true of God. When we pray, the patterns of action in our minds change the patterns of action that constitute God, and therefore change God. That is inevitable. By praying, we might wish to elicit some particular pattern of action from God, or we might simply be attempting a deeper bond between us. When we speak to someone, we can never predict the effect that our words might have. We cannot determine how the vibrations that we create in the air when we speak will be experienced: that is, how the vibrations that strike the eardrum will change the patterns of action that are the other person's brain, and what further changes will then ensue. We know that we will create change, but we can never know of what kind. The same will be even more true in relation to prayer. We pray, and God is changed: but how, we cannot predict, and we shall never know. This is why when Jesus' disciples asked him to teach them to pray, he told them to say "Your will be done, on earth as it is in heaven."[93] God will be changed by our prayer in the way in which God chooses to be changed by it.

Was Jesus' prayer any different from ours? In one sense no: he was a human being like the rest of us; his mind was changing patterns of action; his prayer was patterns of action in the mind with the explicit aims of changing the mind of God and of creating a deeper bond with God. There is of course a sense in which a deeper bond was not possible, because the changing patterns of action that Jesus was were the patterns of action that were God: but the patterns of action that were his humanity were and were not the patterns of action that were God, so he prayed to deepen the bond between God and himself; and he was moved by the suffering that he found around him, and so prayed that God would cast out evil, heal the sick, and bring hope and liberation.

But it is not only God who is changed: we too are changed as we pray. God's patterns of actions and ours entangling with each other cannot help changing each other: so God changes us as we pray if that is what God chooses to do, just as we change God if that is what God chooses will happen—and presumably we have some choice in the matter, in the sense that we can resist the influence of God's activity. And it is not only God and ourselves who are changed: the universe is changed as we pray. Any changing pattern of action will influence those around it, and those will go on to influence yet others. There are no boundaries. So our prayer will have an infinite number of unpredictable effects on the world. We understand so little about how connected we all are. We now know something about how electrons that have related to each other can still communicate across the vast distances of space, and if reality is action in changing patterns then we would expect one person's activity, including the activity that we call prayer, to change everyone around them. We might resist the influence of others, and they might resist ours, but change will still occur. Our prayer will change God, and God's action in patterns will change the person or the situation for which we pray; and our prayer itself will change them. Quite how will remain a mystery to us.

Jesus prayed in order to bond with God, to seek to be obedient, to pray that God would satisfy the infinite need around him, and above all to pray that God would bring about the Kingdom of God that Jesus' life, teaching, and healing were all about. So we his followers will pray as well. We too must attend to God so that we can open ourselves to God's changing patterns of action. We might choose to do that by developing some kind of silence, which will not be some kind of absence, because our minds are never still: they are constantly action in patterns. What we might in fact mean if we attempt silence is that we are offering an active invitation to God to reshape our minds, to take the patterns of our action and change them in new ways so that they might more closely conform to God's patterns of action. Waiting is not passive: it is a scanning of the horizon—a pattern of action that reflects God's waiting for us.

Jesus sought a time and a place without distractions so that he could be alone with God, so that God and Jesus could tangle with each other with as little interference as possible from other people: but the isolation did not last for long. Soon his disciples came looking for him, bringing to him the needs of the world. They might not have realized that in his prayer Jesus was already dealing with those: for that is what he was doing; and during his time of prayer, God had moved him on, so now he was going to move himself and his disciples on, to new places, to do new things.

Reality is action in patterns, and action in patterns is reality. Prayer is as real as the ground on which Jesus knelt or stood to pray; the journey is as real as the road, and perhaps even more real, because it is the journey that is more clearly actions in changing patterns, although the road is action in patterns as well. Healing, casting out demons, teaching the crowds, moving from town to town: all aspects of reality, and just as real as the people whom Jesus and his disciples would meet on the road and in the towns. There are no boundaries between different kinds of reality: indeed, there are no different kinds of reality. God, Jesus, the people, the land, the solar system, atomic particles, journeys, God's actions, our actions, everyone's actions—our praying—all of it is action in patterns, all of it is real, and all of it is as real as everything else.

As they travelled around Galilee and entered new towns, it was always "the message" that would be proclaimed: the message of the Kingdom of God that had come near; the message of repentance, and of the invitation to believe the good news. As this passage makes clear, this proclamation of the Kingdom of God was Jesus' primary purpose, and it had to take priority over everything else, including healing miracles. This is what Jesus "came out to do": came from Capernaum to do on this occasion, and came from God to do as his life's mission.[94] Always coming and going, always on the move:[95] this was Jesus' pattern of action.

The message was always the Kingdom of God, but always the message would have been different, because Jesus and his disciples would have been different from the way they were in the last town, and there would have been new people to whom they would relate, and each new place would have been different from the last one. And even if the words spoken were the same, their meanings will have changed. A word's meaning is how it connects with everything else: with other words, with the activity that constitutes our minds, with what's going on in other people's minds, and with everything else that is going on. Nothing is ever at rest, and this is particularly true of words. The marks on a page might be the same, but as soon as a word is spoken, the vibrations in the air are new, the sounds that are heard are new, the way that the vibrations on the eardrum affect the changing patterns that constitute the hearers' minds are new: so the meaning of the word will be both new and diverse, and then immediately new and even more diverse as the meaning continues to change. The marks on the page might be the same, but what's going on in the reader's mind changes from reader to reader, and no reading will ever be the same as another, and no reader will be the same as they were the moment before. This book is my reading of Mark's Gospel: but as soon as a sentence is written, my reading of Mark's Gospel will have changed—partly as a result of writing what I have written. And anyone who reads these readings will be changed, so immediately their reading of these readings will change, and then thy will read their own readings of the readings, and so on, and nothing will ever be the same again.

Jesus went travelling so that he could visit the synagogues of the towns around Galilee, and in them proclaim the message of the coming Kingdom of God, and then cast out demons, as he was now used to doing. Jesus was learning obedience to God; he was himself God; and radical evil could not stand the patterns of action that were radically divine.

If we are followers of Jesus, then we too shall proclaim the message that will always be the same and always changing and diverse; if we are followers of the Jesus who taught his disciples to pray then we too shall pray, so that we might change God and the world, and so that we shall be changed; and we too shall cast out evil, disrupting and destroying those patterns of action inimical to the changing patterns of action that constitute God.

And now we know to whom we pray. Of course, God is still a mystery to us. How could it be otherwise? But in Jesus we now know the God to whom we pray, and in purely practical terms our prayer has to be "through Jesus Christ." The patterns of action that constitute Jesus are the patterns of action that constitute God—at least, as far as we are concerned—so it is by praying with and to Jesus that we know to whom we pray, and it is by doing that that we know that our prayers are heard, that they lodge in the very heart of God, and that they change God, the world, and ourselves. The Jesus to whom, through whom, and with whom we pray made no objection when his own praying was interrupted. He will make no objection when we interrupt his communion with God. He will hear us; he will move on; and he will take us with him.

## MARK 1:40–45

40 A leper[l] came to him begging him, and kneeling[m] he said to him, 'If you choose, you can make me clean.' 41 Moved with pity,[n] Jesus[o] stretched out his hand and touched him, and said to him, 'I do choose. Be made clean!' 42

l. The terms *leper* and *leprosy* can refer to several diseases
m. Other ancient authorities lack *kneeling*
n. Other ancient authorities read *anger*
o. Gk *he*

> Immediately the leprosy[p] left him, and he was made clean. [43] After sternly warning him he sent him away at once, [44] saying to him, 'See that you say nothing to anyone; but go, show yourself to the priest, and offer for your cleansing what Moses commanded, as a testimony to them.' [45] But he went out and began to proclaim it freely, and to spread the word, so that Jesus[q] could no longer go into a town openly, but stayed out in the country; and people came to him from every quarter.[96]

A demon-possessed man was healed; Simon's mother-in-law was healed; at sunset people were healed; more demons were cast out; and now a single leper is healed. There would have been a lot of people in need of healing in Galilee: why these, and not others? Casting out evil and healing people who are ill is a divine pattern of action, and contingency is a human constraint. The human changing patterns of action that we are have infinite effects beyond the boundaries of ourselves, but we cannot determine those effects, and the most significant effects will always be those on the changing patterns of action in the temporal and spatial proximity. All Jesus could do was create signs of a Kingdom of God that was near and not yet arrived. He healed individuals, and those healings, like our own relationships with other people, rippled out into the surrounding communities. There were continuing effects: but still local effects. It could not have been otherwise. Jesus was a human being like the rest of us. But still, the Kingdom of God was genuinely present in his changing patterns of action, because his patterns of action were all God's patterns of action: none were not, not even the most intensely human ones, because within each of us there are no boundaries between the many different changing patterns of action that constitute who we are. So every action of Jesus was God's action in ways that our actions are not: but those actions were still human actions, and thus entirely contingent. Some people were healed, and some were not.

But first of all, the man's actions. He came, he begged, and he knelt. We are what we do: and our bodies, everything that they are, and everything that they do, are who we are. We are not some disembodied soul within a body. We are the changing patterns of action that are our bodies, from the subatomic particles, to molecules and microbes, to the limbs, the senses, and the brain: we are what we do. At that moment, the man with the skin disease was the arriving and the kneeling, and those patterns of action were the beginning of the process of his healing: a process that was a changing pattern of action. The initiative was his. He knew that Jesus could choose to heal him, which meant that he knew that Jesus might choose not to do so. And Jesus was "moved with pity": or was he? Some of the ancient documents have "was angry" instead. This was more likely to have been changed to "moved with pity" than "moved with pity" was to have been changed to "was angry": so "was angry" is probably

---

p. The terms *leper* and *leprosy* can refer to several diseases

q. Gk *he*

original. Jesus was angry that Satan was making people suffer, so he was determined to defeat Satan.[97] Either way, Jesus was deeply affected by the suffering around him: so the changing patterns of action that constitute God are always and everywhere moved by human suffering, because there are no boundaries. In this case Jesus' deep compassion resulted in him touching the man, thus making himself unclean, and banishing himself from society for a period, and so enabling him to stand alongside the man suffering from the skin disease. Jesus was not here criticizing the law that someone who touched someone with a skin disease became unclean themselves: he was waging a war with Satan, breaking down barriers, and beginning the establishment of the Kingdom of God. This man's healing, and ultimately the healing of reality by God's infinitely deep compassion, will result in the healing of everyone and everything, in the making whole, complete, just, and beautiful of the universe and whatever else there is. That is not the mystery: the mystery is why that is not already the case; and perhaps our only clue to that mystery is Jesus, and the inevitable contingency resulting from the contingency of any created order that is changing patterns of action that are not God. In this passage in Mark's Gospel we find Jesus bridging the gulf between the contingency of there being particular changing patterns of action that are not God, and a God who is Action, the source of all action, and the particular changing patterns of action that constitute God in God's relationship with every other changing pattern of action. In this one person Jesus, compassion is both human compassion and God's compassion; the healing is human healing and God's healing; the touching is human touching and God's touching.

And then Jesus spoke: "Be made clean!" Our words are patterns of action in the air. They have an effect: they change the patterns of action that they encounter, and new patterns emerge, and they affect other patterns of action, and all of it constantly changes. In this case an effect was an immediate healing: but was it complete? The man with the skin disease (whether leprosy or something else[98]) would have been expelled from society and from human contact. The skin disease had been healed, and Jesus had already touched him: a pattern of action with significant effects on the man himself, on everyone else who was there, on everyone the man knew, and on everyone any of them knew. That touch, that particular pattern of action, was Jesus, and it was God.

The healing was not complete. Jesus "sent him away at once": the word that Jesus used could mean "threw him out," but probably not in the sense that force was used. It was a vigorous sending away. This passage is full of such vigorous action, emphasizing that it is the action that matters: and this was particularly true of what was required of the man who had been healed. The throwing out might have been to enable Jesus to avoid too much publicity, and too much attention being drawn to miracles rather than to proclamation of the Kingdom of God: but the throwing out was also to emphasize the importance of the command to visit the priest.[99] The visit to the priest was prescribed in the Jewish law, and Jesus wanted the man to do what the law prescribed, so that the priest could declare him cleansed of the disease and thus an acceptable person in society. But there might have been two reasons for Jesus insisting that the man should show himself to the priest, and not just one. Firstly, it might have appeared to some that by healing the man by telling him to "be made clean" Jesus was pretending to be a priest. He therefore sent the man to the priest to make it clear that he did not think that he was himself substituting for the prescribed method of declaring someone to have been healed.[100] The second reason related to the healed man himself. The ritual needed to be completed if the man was to find a place in society. Rituals are important: they are patterns of action that do things—they change patterns of action, and they create new ones. Rituals change all the time, but there will always be a certain character to them, a certain consistency, and their effects will be predictable to some extent, although never entirely. A ritual is not a thing: it is an institution; and every institution is a bundle of patterns of action, all interrelating, all relating to patterns of action around them and changing them. The rituals of the Jewish law are institutions with relatively predictable effects; and the effect of the offering that Jesus told the man to take to the priest would have been an examination of his skin by the priest and a reintegration into society. The examination and the ritual would have been a "testimony" to the priests and the people that the man was cured and could re-enter society, but "testimony" might also have a broader meaning here: the healing was testimony to the identity of the healer, and to the nearness of the Kingdom of God that the healing represented.[101] Words are patterns of action that can have multiple different connections with other words and meanings.

We have no idea whether the man went to see the priest. What we do know is that he did what Jesus had told him not to do. Jesus had wanted to maintain a little privacy, but that was now going to be denied to him. Other people were going to determine his movements and how he behaved. Already the man with the skin disease had done this by coming to Jesus, kneeling in front of him, and begging to be healed. That man had caused Jesus' human compassion, and God's compassion. And now a lot of people were going to prevent Jesus from going into towns incognito. Any created order that is not God inevitably does this to God if God determines to relate to what is created. However it came about, there is a cosmos, and God has chosen to relate to it: and in particular to relate to it by being part of it. So now every pattern of action that is God relates to every changing pattern that is not God. Separation is no longer possible. God can no longer avoid compassion: so at the heart of God there is compassion.

One thing that the man's disobedience tells us clearly is that something new was now happening. Whether or not he did eventually go to visit the priest, he clearly felt no need of doing so. He had been healed, and Jesus had touched him, so he was already a member of society, with a new relationship with everyone around him. He had every right to mix in society and tell people what Jesus had done. Jesus was now his authority, and not the priests. This would have been one more reason for the people to seek out Jesus. He offered not only healing but liberation; and he offered the promise of a Kingdom of God in which they would all be released forever from often suffocating and exploitative authority structures. For Jesus, the law of Moses still mattered: he was a faithful Jew, and his God had given to Israel a law that it was their obligation to obey, and that was therefore his obligation to obey. But his patterns of action were telling a new story: he had touched a man whom he ought not to have touched, and by doing that he had already brought the man back into society. No longer was an offering required.

Everyone and everything was now changed: the man who was healed, Jesus, the people who were there, everyone they all knew, and the social and religious structures of that time and place. A single particular pattern of action—a single touch—had achieved all of that. And we too are changed as we read this. God reaches out and touches us, drawing us into relationship with Jesus and with the God whom he was and is: and we also know that God reaches out and touches everyone and everything, drawing everyone and everything into relationship with God. It is the same God, and so the same pattern of action. The patterns change, but just as the patterns of action that constitute us change and are still identifiable as the patterns of action that we are, so Jesus' patterns change and are still identifiable as the patterns of action that he is. He reached out and touched then, and he reaches out and touches now.

## MARK 2:1-12

2 When he returned to Capernaum after some days, it was reported that he was at home. ² So many gathered around that there was no longer room for them, not even in front of the door; and he was speaking the word to them. ³ Then some people[p] came, bringing to him a paralysed man, carried by four of them. ⁴And when they could not bring him to Jesus because of the crowd, they removed the roof above him; and after having dug through it, they let down the mat on which the paralytic lay. ⁵ When Jesus saw their faith, he said to the paralytic, 'Son, your sins are forgiven.' ⁶ Now some of the scribes were sitting there, questioning in their hearts, ⁷ 'Why does this fellow speak in this way? It is blasphemy! Who can forgive sins but God alone?' ⁸ At once Jesus perceived in his spirit that they were discussing these questions among themselves; and he said to them, 'Why do you raise such questions in your hearts? ⁹ Which is easier, to say to the paralytic, "Your sins are forgiven," or to say, "Stand up and take your mat and walk"? ¹⁰ But so that you may know that the Son of Man has authority on earth to forgive sins'—he said to the paralytic— ¹¹ 'I say to you, stand up, take your mat and go to your home.' ¹² And he stood up, and immediately took the mat and went out before all of them; so that they were all amazed and glorified God, saying, 'We have never seen anything like this!'[102]

p. Gk *they*

Conflict with Satan first occurred immediately after Jesus' baptism, and would continue by means of exorcisms: a process that had already begun. In this section, patterns of action that we might describe as conflict become more diverse as powerful groups within Judaism begin their attacks on Jesus.[103] In the first such incident that Mark records, Jesus returns to Capernaum, again people gather, and now it is a paralyzed man's friends who take action. They exercise "faith": and here "faith" must be what they have done, so their faith is the taking apart of the roof and letting their friend down in the middle of the crowd. This is what faith always is. It is not some kind of unchanging state: it is always action in particular patterns. "Now faith is the assurance of things hoped for, the conviction of things not seen."[104] It means to act in the light of the way that things will be, not in the light of how they are now: so for the Christian, faith is to live as if the Kingdom of God has fully come; as if it is no longer "near" but is here. This is what the man's friends have done. Their actions assumed that healing was inevitably available for their friend, as it would be in the Kingdom of God, and they acted accordingly: and in the context of their faith-based relationship with Jesus, a healing occurred.[105] So we shall have faith—or rather, we shall do faith—if we live our lives as if the Kingdom of God were already here in its completion: as if God ruled, and the promised justice, peace, and perfect relationship with God, were already a reality.

On the basis of the faith that he has witnessed, Jesus announces the forgiveness of the man's sins. But why? And what is forgiveness? "I forgive" is a verb, so the one who says "I forgive" is doing something. They are saying to the person they are forgiving that as far as they are concerned there will be no further consequences of whatever is being forgiven. It does not mean that the sin has not happened. Actions cannot be undone. And neither does it mean that there will be no further consequences, because any pattern of action will affect an infinite number of patterns of action forever: the ripples will never subside completely. But the one who forgives is still saying: as far as I am concerned, there will be no further consequences of your sin, at least to the extent that I can achieve that.

But Jesus might not have regarded himself as forgiving the man's sins. Perhaps he saw himself as a messenger of the forgiveness that God was bringing about. However, some words later in the passage suggest that more is meant than that: ". . . so that you may know that the Son of Man has authority on earth to forgive sins." If Jesus is identifying himself as the Son of Man, which he does appear to be doing, then he really is saying that he, the Son of Man, is able to forgive the man's sins. He is standing in the place of God, doing something that God does. He is exercising God's forgiveness.

Jesus is not here forgiving the man for anything that he has done to Jesus: at least, we assume that that is the case. What Jesus is doing is saying that as far as God is concerned, there will be no further consequences of the man's sins: and as it is God who is offering the forgiveness, God can ensure that that will be the case. Sin is patterns of action that disrupt or destroy the patterns of action that are God's patterns of action:

so although the sin that the man has committed will continue to disrupt and destroy God's patterns of action wherever the sin is still causing ripples, those sinful patterns of action will no longer interfere with the relationship between God and the paralyzed man. Sin is never forgotten, but its effects can be transfigured when the patterns of action that are God meet it and transform it.

Jesus is here doing God's work. It is God's prerogative to forgive sins done against God, and the pattern of action that we call forgiveness is what God does and so is what God is. Jesus, by forgiving this man, is doing God's work, is doing a pattern of action that is God's pattern of action, and so he is God. We are what we do. And all of this was true for Mark, for the church of his time, and for Christians from then until now: Jesus has the authority to forgive sins—which is presumably why this story was transmitted through the early Christians' oral tradition, and why Mark recorded it in his gospel.[106] It is the same pattern of action then and now: Jesus exercises God's prerogative to forgive sin. And perhaps a further pattern of action was experienced both in this event and in the experience of early Christians: Jesus had employed a healing miracle to validate his authority to forgive sins—he was offering the kind of "sign" that he was usually reluctant to give—and maybe early Christians used healing miracles to validate their ability to forgive sin in Jesus' name:[107] again a repeated complex pattern of action that binds together into a single reality the life of Jesus and the lives of Christians.

Again Jesus' words have been the pattern of action that has created something new—and then yet another group of words creates an effect. Jesus hears the thoughts of some experts in the Jewish law, and he offers the man's healing as proof that he is indeed able to exercise God's forgiveness. So what is going on here? Is the healing simply a statement of Jesus' authority to forgive sins? If so, there is a sense in which the man has become a means rather than an end: an instrument that Jesus can use, rather than someone with infinite worth

On another occasion Jesus was clear that sin is not a cause of disability.[108] So what is the connection between the healing of the man's paralysis and Jesus' declaration of his forgiveness? The connection must be a third factor: the man himself—the person loved by God: not a means, but someone of infinite worth, an Other to whom Jesus must relate and for whom he bears responsibility. We can only speculate, but perhaps Jesus knew that sin and disability were connected in the man's mind, and maybe in the minds of his friends, so for the man to be healed his sins needed to be forgiven.[109] Whether or not that is the case, this man needed his sins to be forgiven, and he needed to be healed of his paralysis, and Jesus was going to do both for him. Both were the work of God, both were of the character of the Kingdom of God, and so, by doing both of them, Jesus was doing the work of God, and therefore was and is God. There was nothing visible to show the scribes when Jesus forgave the man's sins. It was the healing that would be visible, and that would stand as evidence both for Jesus' ability to forgive sins and for his ability to heal: again God's prerogative.

The man did as Jesus told him to do: he stood up, picked up his mat, and went. He was a changed man. His life would now be utterly different. He would have to earn his own living; his relationships with his family and friends would be different; and he would have been faced with the question as to whether he should become an active follower of Jesus—we don't know that he did. Jesus' patterns of action had impacted on the patterns of action that were this paralyzed man, and no doubt on those that constituted his friends as well, and nothing would ever be the same again. And their patterns of action would have affected those that constituted the people they knew; and the scribes and everyone else who was there that day would have talked to other people about what they had witnessed: and the ripples would have carried on going, changing patterns of action and then yet more patterns of action. The forgiveness and the healing would have kept on giving, over and over again, and they still give today.

An interesting possibility is that the words "But so that you may know that the Son of Man has authority on earth to forgive sins" were not those of Jesus, but were words inserted by Mark to make a connection between the healing miracle and Jesus' forgiveness of the man's sins.[110] The difference that this would make is that it would show that the "Son of Man" was a title for Jesus used by the church for which Mark was writing his gospel, rather than a title that Jesus gave to himself: but perhaps it is not such a significant difference after all, because Jesus uses the title on other occasions, and Mark's church would only have used the title if Jesus had used it. In terms of the pattern of action that constitutes the heart of the narrative—the lowering through the roof, and the man taking up his bed and leaving the room—there is no difference at all.

It is the "Son of Man" who has authority to forgive sins. This is a highly ambiguous title that Jesus gives to himself,[111] if that is in fact what he is doing. "Son of Man" could mean either "I, myself" or the heavenly figure who approaches God's throne in the vision recorded in the Book of Daniel:

> 9 As I watched,
>> thrones were set in place,
>> and an Ancient One[a] took his throne;
> his clothing was white as snow,
>> and the hair of his head like pure wool; . . .
> ¹⁰ . . . The court sat in judgement,
>> and the books were opened. . . .
>
> ¹³ As I watched in the night visions,
> I saw one like a human being[b]
>> coming with the clouds of heaven.

> a. Aram *an Ancient of Days*
> b. Aram *one like a son of man*

> And he came to the Ancient One[c]
>> and was presented before him.
> [14] To him was given dominion
>> and glory and kingship,
> that all peoples, nations, and languages
>> should serve him.
> His dominion is an everlasting dominion
>> that shall not pass away,
> and his kingship is one
>> that shall never be destroyed.[112]

And if this "human being, " this "Son of Man," was the figure that Jesus was referring to, was he referring to himself or to someone else? Was he the one who was going to come to the Ancient of Days, or was he expecting someone else to be that person? Jesus had just said "so that you know that the Son of Man has authority to forgive sins," and he has just forgiven the man's sins: so the only conclusion that we can draw is that either Jesus was simply calling himself a human being to whom had been given authority to forgive sins, or that he saw himself as the one who was to come to the Ancient of Days and that he already had the authority to forgive sins that would be his when that happened. Or perhaps Jesus called himself "Son of Man" because the passage in Daniel gave it messianic overtones but not the kinds of nationalistic meanings that "Son of God" or "Son of David" might have implied.[113] Perhaps Jesus had a mixture of reasons for calling himself "Son of Man." What is fairly certain is that he was not referring to someone else, simply because he was the one who had just forgiven someone's sins.[114]

Who was the "one like a son of man" in the vision? The Book of Daniel is full of imagery. The beasts are often other nations, which rather suggests that the human figure is Israel, the nation now to be given authority over the others. If this is an identification that Jesus would have made, then he was identifying himself with the nation of Israel. Or perhaps he simply envisaged the figure as a heavenly person and wondered whether it was him. If so, then he was not explicitly identifying himself as God, but rather as a separate heavenly person who would be with God. Perhaps that is all that would have been possible for Jesus' completely Jewish mind. He would not have been able to conceive of himself as somehow God: that would have been a blasphemy too far; but he might well be identifying himself here with a heavenly figure who is already living the life of the Kingdom of God. This does not mean, of course, that we cannot identify Jesus as God as well as as a human being, and also as the Son of Man who would come to the Ancient of Days. Jesus was and is his action in changing patterns, and there is no reason why these could not be the action in patterns that constituted

---

c. Aram *the Ancient of Days*

God, the action in patterns that constituted Jesus as a human being, and the action in patterns of a heavenly figure who comes to God. This is the same person and different persons: which is no longer a logical or any other sort of impossibility once we set God, human beings, and heavenly beings, free from being beings and define them as changing patterns of action.

And the man who was forgiven and healed: he was now different patterns of action—patterns probably changing very fast: and the changing would never cease. And we, by entering into the patterns of action that we find in this story, will find ourselves in the story, being forgiven and healed by Jesus.

This is a particularly significant story because in a sense it sums up the whole of Mark's Gospel.[115] It includes Jesus teaching, healing, announcing forgiveness, being condemned for assuming authority that is God's alone, and being vindicated. The event is a pattern of action that will be constantly reflected in patterns of action throughout Mark's Gospel that culminate in Jesus' death and resurrection, resulting in a thread of changing patterns of action that bear family resemblances to each other: the family resemblance being a changing pattern of action that constitutes Jesus and that constitutes God.

## MARK 2:13-17

> 13 Jesus[q] went out again beside the lake; the whole crowd gathered around him, and he taught them. 14 As he was walking along, he saw Levi son of Alphaeus sitting at the tax booth, and he said to him, 'Follow me.' And he got up and followed him.
>
> 15 And as he sat at dinner[r] in Levi's[s] house, many tax-collectors and sinners were also sitting[t] with Jesus and his disciples—for there were many who followed him. 16 When the scribes of[u] the Pharisees saw that he was eating with sinners and tax-collectors, they said to his disciples, 'Why does he eat[v] with tax-collectors and sinners?' 17 When Jesus heard this, he said to them, 'Those who are well have no need of a physician, but those who are sick; I have come to call not the righteous but sinners.'[116]

Levi was a Jew who collected taxes, maybe for the Romans, or maybe for one or both of the two Herodian kings who ruled on either side of the Jordan.[117] His name was that

q. Gk *he*
r. Gk *reclined*
s. Gk *his*
t. Gk *reclining*
u. Other ancient authorities read *and*
v. Other ancient authorities add *and drink*

of the tribe that provided the Jewish religion with its priests, symbolizing someone at the heart of Judaism: and yet this man was collecting taxes from his own people to provide the Roman occupying army, and the Roman empire, with resources, or to provide funds for kings whom many Jews regarded as illegitimate, not least because they were Rome's puppets. And his own people were often poor, fleeced by their own landlords and rulers as well as by the Romans. We are not told whether Levi ceased to collect taxes for the Romans or for the local kings. The ways in which the patterns of action that he was were changing would have been changed by Jesus, the changes would have taken off in new directions, and we might guess as to the new directions that Levi would have experienced, but we don't know what they would have been.

Jesus seemed to be intent on creating the most diverse group of followers that he could gather. It would now include one who collected taxes for oppressive rulers, and Simon the Zealot, a terrorist, or something close to that, whose aim in life was to drive out the occupying army and possibly to murder people like Levi. And there were probably women central to Jesus' band of followers as well: although the list of twelve male apostles, mirroring the twelve tribes of Israel and therefore representing a new Israel, suggests that it might have taken Jesus a while to understand the equal status of women.

Just as Jesus had called Simon, Andrew, James, and John, so he now called Levi: and Levi followed; and not only followed, but also invited Jesus to a meal with his friends. Levi would have been regarded as a social outcast, so it is no surprise that his friends were social outcasts as well: tax collectors and sinners—and not only sinners, but unrepentant sinners. Whether Jesus' other disciples were enjoying the experience we are not told: but as there were now many sinners following Jesus, this was presumably a situation that they were getting used to.

Here we discover an aspect of reality alongside reality as action, change, movement, and the dynamic: the aspect of diversity. Just as we are understanding reality less as being, beings, rest, the unchanging, and the static, and seeing it instead as action, actions, movement, change, and the dynamic, so we are now understanding reality more as diversity than as unitary. The more diverse, the more real: and so the Kingdom of God, that reality that God is bringing about, and that we see already in Jesus' patterns of action, will be intensely diverse. A further consequence is that we should understand God as perfect diversity rather than as a unitary being. The real is complex rather than simple: and the ultimate complexity is God. It is therefore entirely appropriate that the ultimate complexity and diversity of the Kingdom of God should be represented by Jesus' complex and diverse group of followers.

The "scribes of the Pharisees" were now quite concerned. These were rabbis who belonged to the Pharisees, a group of Jews for whom both the written and oral laws were the law: a group whose rigorous keeping of the law was a service to Judaism, and whose rigor was an important reason for its survival following the destruction of the temple in 70 CE.[118] It is the other side of that rigor, its inflexibility in the face of immediate human need, that came in for Jesus' criticism, and it was probably inevitable that early Christians, both Jewish Christians who were experiencing freedom from the law, and Gentile Christians, for whom the law had never been an issue, should find much to continue to criticize.

It is clear from a later dispute about the resurrection of the dead[119] that Jesus was theologically on the side of the Pharisees rather than on that of the Sadducees, for whom the written law was just as important, but for whom later theological and legal developments were not. The Pharisees whom we encounter in this event clearly regarded Jesus as a teacher of the law. They would have supposed both him and themselves to be on one side of a line, and unrepentant sinners on the other. The teacher was supposed to keep the law that he taught—as they expected to do—and those who kept the law were in a different category from those who did not (or at least, those who did not keep the law as the scribes of the Pharisees understood it). That was not how Jesus saw it. For him there was a single category. And not only was he saying this: he was enacting it by eating with tax-collectors and sinners. In every culture, and especially in the Jewish, sharing meals together was an important means of social and religious bonding. The changing patterns of action that constitute everyone around the table engage with each other in particularly complex and intense ways, creating a unique community. Here was no theoretical bond between Jesus and unrepentant sinners: here was a close community containing both Jesus and unrepentant sinners.

And this was not simply a single event with no meaning beyond itself: there is a whole new way of life in evidence. All of the significant distinctions have been left behind, and in particular the division between those who obey the biblical commandments and those who do not.[120] Jesus, his disciples, and everyone gathered around Jesus, were already living the life of the Kingdom of God, and already Jesus was king: that is, the patterns of action that constituted who he was and is were the patterns of action that constitute this new community.

What we don't know, of course, is how Jesus' theology evolved over time. At the beginning of his ministry, he was calling on his hearers to "repent": but now he is happy to mix with unrepentant sinners. As he is recorded as saying to the "priests and elders," "Truly I tell you, the tax-collectors and the prostitutes are going into the kingdom of God ahead of you."[121] Jesus learned obedience: and one of the things that he learnt was that the Kingdom of God was not an exclusive club. First of all he had to learn that repentance was not required, which meant that he also had to learn that keeping the law was not required; and we shall soon find that he had to learn that Gentiles, non-Jews, were as much members of the Kingdom of God as Jews were. Jesus changed constantly, so across his ministry his theology was diverse: not just in relation to peripheral things, but in relation to significant theological principles as well. There was little as important to Jews as the privileges of Israel, even if some recognized that Israel's privilege was to be the servant of other nations. There was little as important to Jews as the requirement to keep the law of Moses: and here was Jesus clearly minimizing its importance. Jesus had learnt to accept and to welcome unconditionally: a pattern of action that constituted God and that now constituted him.[122] But precisely how and when various changes to Jesus' theology took place is now hidden from us. The gospels are made up of scattered memories, written or spoken, passed between Christians of the first few decades of the Christian church: memories then brought together by the gospel writers in different orders, with those orders more determined by the writers' own theological priorities than by those of Jesus. But although precisely how Jesus' theology evolved is hidden from us, the existence of the diversity in the gospels makes it clear that evolution certainly took place. Attempts at synthesis are therefore misplaced.

What is not clear is what is meant by Jesus' words in verse 17, and whether this saying originally belonged to this event.[123] The first sentence is clear on its own: yes, it is people who are ill who need a doctor, and not those who are not. And it is clear from Jesus' calling of Levi, and the gathering of the tax-collectors and sinners, that Jesus was calling sinners rather than the righteous. Those whom he called "sinners" probably were unrepentant sinners; and those whom he called "righteous" probably did do their best to keep the law, and probably repented when they failed to do so. But what is the connection between the two sentences? Who are the "sick": the "sinners" or the "righteous"? Perhaps this was a classic piece of ambiguity on Jesus' part. Might he be asking the scribes to ask themselves: Am I perhaps sick and in need of the physician called Jesus? Do I need to be changed by this teacher of the law who welcomes unrepentant sinners into the Kingdom of God ahead of me? Is everyone sick and in need of healing? Jesus' parables had multiple potential meanings, and much else that he said was similarly ambiguous and required attention and decisions from his hearers. Perhaps the same is going on here.

This event would have been remembered by the church and then included by Mark in his gospel because it would have continued to resonate with the early Christians as they handled the inevitable difficulties of increasing diversity in the church: adding Gentiles to Jews, including slaves and masters in the same congregation, women perhaps understanding that Jesus' attitude to women questioned their society's patriarchal attitudes, and so on. At the Eucharist, the central act of fellowship of the church, there would have been people eating and drinking together in remembrance of Jesus who would never have done so in any other context. Jesus' crossing of the boundaries in his own society would have been an inspiration, a challenge, and an encouragement, as church leaders handled the tensions that are bound to have arisen, and of which we can find evidence in Paul's letters and in the Acts of the Apostles.[124] The event recorded here by Mark might also have been an encouragement to understand the Eucharist as a "feast for sinners":[125] that is, an understanding that no moral requirements should be imposed before permitting participation, and perhaps no other requirements either. Today's churches still have much to learn from this event.

Jesus said "I have come..." Come to eat with Levi and his friends? Come to this town? Come from God to you? Perhaps all of those.

## MARK 2:18-20

> 18 Now John's disciples and the Pharisees were fasting; and people[w] came and said to him, 'Why do John's disciples and the disciples of the Pharisees fast, but your disciples do not fast?' 19 Jesus said to them, 'The wedding-guests cannot fast while the bridegroom is with them, can they? As long as they have the bridegroom with them, they cannot fast. 20 The days will come when the bridegroom is taken away from them, and then they will fast on that day.'[126]

Fasting was only a legal requirement on the Day of Atonement, but the Pharisees regarded it as an important accompaniment to prayer.[127] It is a common practice in a number of religious traditions: a practice, a pattern of action, because a change in the patterns of action that are our eating, drinking, and praying. Fasting could be a sign of repentance for sin, or an accompaniment for intercession. It was a symbol of the seriousness of someone's intention: to express sorrow for sin; to respond to God's call; to turn their life around; or to demand something from God. Fasting was good, Jesus did it himself, and he sometimes recommended it. So what is Jesus saying here? This passage follows the meal with the tax-gatherers and sinners. Meals together were for Jesus a promise of the coming Kingdom of God: and in that context fasting was entirely inappropriate. This was an occasion for celebration: that the Kingdom of God was near; that it was coming; that it was, according to one of Jesus' parables, an abundant harvest;[128] and that it was like a wedding banquet to which everyone was invited.[129] We shall soon encounter Jesus' feeding of thousands in the open air as a promise of the Kingdom of God to both Jews and Gentiles alike. On any such celebratory occasion, fasting was an impossibility: and this was particularly true of any celebration of the coming Kingdom of God.

Separately significant is Jesus' identification of himself with the bridegroom at the wedding banquet. *He* is the cause of celebration: so for anyone with ears to hear, he is the coming Kingdom of God that is being celebrated. We might put it like this: the changing patterns of action that constitute Jesus are those of God and of the Kingdom of God. It is the presence of those changing patterns of action that is being celebrated, and that is why fasting is impossible.

There would be time enough for fasting later. Either this last sentence was added by Christians on the basis of their experience of Jesus' absence and of their subsequent practice of fasting,[130] or Jesus foresaw his likely fate and so predicted a period of absence from his disciples. Already John the Baptist was in prison—hence it being appropriate for John's disciples to fast—so Jesus would have been aware that the

w. Gk *they*

disruption that he was causing was likely to end him up there as well, and that an early death might have awaited him as it had awaited John. He was to be "taken away": the same word as appeared in the Greek translation of the Hebrew scriptures in this passage in Isaiah:

> 8 By a perversion of justice he was taken away.
>> Who could have imagined his future?
> For he was cut off from the land of the living,
>> stricken for the transgression of my people.[131]

Perhaps early on in his ministry, if this passage is from that period, Jesus saw himself as the suffering servant of God; or perhaps this passage comes from later on as he became convinced that because he was the servant of God he would have to suffer and die.

Patterns of action belong together: feasting and the Kingdom of God; fasting and the absence of the Kingdom. That is still true. The Kingdom of God has not yet come, so perhaps we should fast; and the Kingdom of God has come in Jesus, and so is already here: so we should not fast. Given that in this contingent life of ours it is impossible to do both at once, the most appropriate approach would be sometimes to fast and sometimes not to do so: which is of course what happens.

## MARK 2:21-22

> 21 'No one sews a piece of unshrunk cloth on an old cloak; otherwise, the patch pulls away from it, the new from the old, and a worse tear is made. 22 And no one puts new wine into old wineskins; otherwise, the wine will burst the skins, and the wine is lost, and so are the skins; but one puts new wine into fresh wineskins.'[x] [132]

This passage looks as if it is about things. That is one way of looking at it. Another way of looking at it is to see it as being about particular kinds of action: particular patterns of action. Cloth shrinks. A tailor sews. Patches pull away. Cloth tears. We put wine. Wine bursts skins. Wine loses itself.

If someone has torn a garment, or it has simply torn through long use, then someone might sew a patch on it. Until a few decades ago, it was common practice to cut worn bedsheets down the middle, join the hemmed edges together ('sides together'), and rehem the new edges, so that the less worn parts ended up in the middle. Socks would be darned; jackets would have patches sewn on the elbows. In our more polluting society, we are more likely to discard worn bedsheets, socks, and jackets, and to purchase new ones: so sewing a patch on torn cloth is now a less understood process. This raises a more general question: to what extent does imagery constructed

x. Other ancient authorities lack *but one puts new wine into fresh wineskins* from less well understood practices still communicate? Does the shepherd who goes looking for an individual sheep still communicate a God who seeks out every errant individual? Does "Kingdom of God" still communicate with people who live in modern democracies? Might "City of God" work rather better?

To return to the sewing of the patch: If the old cloak on which unshrunk cloth has been sewn is washed, then the patch will shrink and pull away from the cloth surrounding it. If we are thinking of the objects involved, then we might interpret this saying as meaning that a new idea such as the equality of Jews and Gentiles, or God's welcome of unrepentant sinners, if tacked onto existing laws and traditions, could cause more damage than was already evident. The saying suggests that this is a bad idea. This particular saying does not suggest that new cloth should only be sewn onto new garments: we have to understand that that is implied, in parallel with the following saying. The implication is that Jesus' teaching, his patterns of action, and his healings, belong in a wholly new context: that of the Kingdom of God. The second saying has the same meaning. New wine has to be put into new wineskins. If it is put into old ones then it is more likely to break the skins and be lost. Jesus' welcome of unrepentant sinners, his healing on the sabbath, the equality of Gentile and Jew that he will soon learn, and so on, belong in the new context of the Kingdom of God, and in the context of contemporary understandings of the law and accompanying legal traditions they cannot have the effect that they should have, and they can cause damage.

But if we are thinking about the actions, then we might understand the sayings differently. We might understand the sewing as Jesus' teaching and healing, and the pulling away and the tearing as the ways in which the teachings, healings, and miracles were pulling apart the fabric of laws and traditions. Interestingly, this verb-based interpretation does not require us to understand the idea that new cloth should only be sewn onto new garments, which is not in the text anyway: so it is this interpretation that makes more sense of the text that Mark's Gospel presents to us. Similarly with the pouring of new wine that causes old skins to burst. Jesus healed on the sabbath, he welcomed unrepentant sinners, he would drive traders out of the temple precincts, and he would teach that the first would be last and the last would be first. Existing laws and traditions would be unable to hold such new patterns of action, so both would be destroyed. And might the pouring out of the wine be a reference to the pouring of wine at Jesus' last meal with his disciples before his crucifixion: a pouring that represented the pouring out of his blood? Jesus' patterns of action would result in his death.

In the context of a verb-based interpretation, the first saying does not need a balancing "new cloth needs to be sewn onto new garments" line in order to make sense, so it is at least possible that the second does not need the phrase "but one puts new wine into fresh wineskins." Some ancient manuscripts don't include it, so it looks as if it might have been added later by a scribe who thought that they knew what Jesus was saying when in fact they might not have done. If the last phrase of the saying is original, then it is saying that new wine should be poured into new wineskins: Jesus' teachings and healings belong in the new context of the Kingdom of God—but then we are back into an object-based interpretation and we have lost the action-filled interpretation that a verb-based interpretation offers to us.

In this case replacing a noun-based interpretation with a verb-based interpretation explains the textual history, suggesting that it might be the actions rather than the objects in which Mark was interested, because that is what Jesus was interested in. The sayings are about the effects that Jesus' patterns of actions were having, and the effects that they would continue to have: entirely appropriate meanings for this position in the gospel.

This reading of the passage stays closely with the text and with Jesus' proclamation and representation of the Kingdom of God that his ministry was all about: but the passage might also invite us to reflect on the whole of the exercise attempted by these readings in Mark's Gospel. We are employing a particular interpretative method, in the sense that we are understanding reality to be action in changing patterns, and we are imposing that understanding on the text. Is this to sew new cloth onto an old garment, and to put new wine into old wineskins? Might we be causing an even larger tear in the old garment than was there already? And splitting the old wineskin so that the wine is lost? The Christian Faith is already in trouble in a secularizing world: might our attempt at a new reading of the text end up misrepresenting the gospel-writer's intentions, and thus result in a misreading of the text rather than a reading of it? Might we find ourselves with even less access to the Jesus behind the text than we might have had before? Might we be displacing other possible readings that might be somehow more true to the original meaning of the text?

In response: We always bring to a text some understanding of reality; if we do not bring to it an understanding that reality is action in changing patterns, then we shall bring to it an understanding that reality is things that change; and as far as we can tell, the former understanding is at least as ancient as the latter. The philosophers that we now see as somehow originating the two different understandings are Heraclitus and Parmenides, and they both lived about two thousand five hundred years ago. So it is no new understanding of reality that we are bringing to the text: it is at least as ancient as the understanding that we generally bring to it without even noticing that we're bringing a particular understanding of reality to it.

Secondly, Mark's Gospel is full of action, so an understanding of reality as action in changing patterns might be more appropriate to an understanding of it than one of things that change; thirdly, an "action in changing patterns" conceptual framework might be more attuned to our fast-changing world than a "beings that change" framework, so the former might be more likely to enable the text to communicate with us than the latter; fourthly, a beings that change framework has had a good run—it has shaped Christian doctrine since early Christian theologians read Plato—so it's probably time to try something new; and fifthly, what we are attempting is a particular "reading," not "the only way to read." The more different ways of reading the biblical text that we can muster, the deeper will be our reading of it, and the more we shall learn. The more conceptual frameworks that we can bring with us to the text, the deeper will be our understanding of it, and the deeper will be our knowledge of the realities that gave birth to the text.

## MARK 2:23–28

> 23 One sabbath he was going through the cornfields; and as they made their way his disciples began to pluck heads of grain. 24 The Pharisees said to him, 'Look, why are they doing what is not lawful on the sabbath?' 25 And he said to them, 'Have you never read what David did when he and his companions were hungry and in need of food? 26 He entered the house of God, when Abiathar was high priest, and ate the bread of the Presence, which it is not lawful for any but the priests to eat, and he gave some to his companions.' 27 Then he said to them, 'The sabbath was made for humankind, and not humankind for the sabbath; 28 so the Son of Man is lord even of the sabbath.'[133]

What is Jesus saying when he compares his disciples' behavior with that of David and his companions when they ate the bread that only the priests were allowed to eat? Is he simply saying that David was flexible with the law, so his own disciples could be flexible with it as well?[134] Or is he comparing two patterns of action, and in particular the pattern of action that constitutes who David was in that situation with the pattern of action that constituted who he was as he and disciples walked through the cornfield? David was a future king, already anointed by Samuel, but not yet enthroned because Saul was still king. Jesus might have been saying by his actions and words that he too was a king waiting to be enthroned.[135] The Kingdom of God was near, and when it came he would receive authority to rule the nations. Is this to press too far a similarity between two patterns of action? Without knowing what was in Jesus' mind, that question is impossible to answer: but it does rather look as if Jesus was claiming an authority at least as great as David's, and that because David broke the law, and could have his action approved by the scriptures, and therefore by God, so he could break the law and have his action approved.[136]

Whether verse 28 is part of what Jesus said, or is a comment by Mark to draw out the meaning of the event for the church for which he was writing, could be argued either way. Would Jesus have used a designation for himself that would have been understood by the Pharisees as blasphemous, as it was at his trial? If not, then verse 28 is a comment by Mark. But if the phrase could have been understood to mean "anyone is lord of the sabbath" then this might be something that Jesus would have said.[137] Or even if it was ambiguous, meaning both "anyone is lord of the sabbath" and "I am lord of the sabbath," then it might still be something that Jesus would have said during an event that was already characterized by conflict. Christians kept Sunday, the day of resurrection, as their significant day of the week, and so relegated the Jewish sabbath to a secondary position, or abandoned it completely. This event, and other incidents during which Jesus showed himself to have authority over what could and could not be done on the sabbath, would have been retained in the tradition to provide authority for substituting Sunday for the Jewish sabbath, and Christian worship for sabbath laws, and the saying in verse 28 might have emerged within the tradition to make explicit the meaning of the remembered incidents. Mark might have written the event and this verse into his gospel for the same reason.[138]

So what does "the Son of Man is lord of the sabbath" mean for us? Does Jesus mean that any human being is lord of the sabbath? This is what the first part of the sentence implies. Or does he mean here the heavenly figure who comes to the Ancient of Days? This figure is given authority and so could well be regarded as lord of the sabbath. Or does he mean "I am lord of the sabbath"? Perhaps Jesus was ambiguous in relation to the first two of those possibilities, his disciples came to understand the third, and we are invited to understand all three possible meanings.

There was nothing illegal about plucking corn grains while walking through a field.[139] What was against the law was working on the sabbath. The sabbath was a day for doing different things, although it was not intended entirely as a day of rest. Patterns of action proper to the sabbath were the worship of God; reading the scriptures; the sharing of meals together (preferably prepared the day before); and a limited amount of travel. The law relating to the sabbath had experienced a certain amount of elaboration. This was inevitable: any law leaves a lot of decisions still to be made, and if a government wants to reduce people's ability to exercise discretion then regulations will be formulated. This is what had happened in relation to the definition of "work" as it applied to the sabbath. Work was not permitted, so what was work had to be defined.

Laws and regulations constrain the patterns in which action can occur, and they constrain the ability of patterns of action to change. Laws and regulations are certainly required, because one person's pattern of action can restrict another person's pattern of action, and can compromise its ability to change: but laws and regulations can also enable an individual or group of individuals to dismantle the ability of boundaries to change.

Jesus clearly thought the Pharisees' implied definition of work to be ridiculous. The question of whether plucking grain was theft does not arise: the Pharisees thought that it was work, whereas Jesus and his disciples could not see how it could be included in any definition of work intended by the Jewish law, which stated that "the seventh day is a sabbath to the Lord your God; you shall not do any work."[140] Jesus had already healed a man on the sabbath—he simply could not see how that could be against the law of God; and now he meets what he clearly regards as a ridiculous understanding of the meaning of "work" as it related to the sabbath with what is in fact an equally ridiculous response.

We still have difficulty with the definition of "work." Just two of the different meanings available are "any purposive activity" and "activity for which someone is paid." These are very different. I am not being paid for writing this, so is it "work"? A related question is this: Why should work be required before we receive the resources that we need to live on? The planet is generous with its gifts, and the wealth of a society is as much a product of previous generations as it is of today's population, so should not those resources be simply shared out equally between everyone currently alive? Of course, tasks need to be done, and there is no reason why a monetary incentive should not be used to ensure that they are, particularly if they are not particularly pleasant: but that is no reason for regarding work of particular kinds as a normative requirement before resources can be received. In many societies we do in fact distribute resources in a variety of different ways—in the UK, healthcare is freely distributed on the basis of need; and Child Benefit is distributed unconditionally—so we have already recognized that work is not necessarily required before resources can be allocated. There is no reason why we should not separate work and resources even further as long as the work required for the functioning of society still gets done.

"The sabbath was made for humankind." The sabbath was *made*: Just as God made the first six days, so God made the seventh. This might have been the day on which God rested from his labor, but the day had to be made before he could do that. Every pattern of action is a result of work, and there is a sense in which every pattern of action is work, and every changing of a pattern of action is work.

What are we to make of the idea of the sabbath? There is no Christian sabbath. Sunday has sometimes been treated as one, but it is not the sabbath: it is a weekly celebration of Jesus' resurrection. It is therefore appropriate to undertake particular kinds of work on it: worship of the God who raised Jesus from the dead; study of the Christian scriptures; and generally celebratory activity, such as the sharing of meals. But it is not a sabbath in the sense of the Jewish sabbath. There is no requirement to rest or not to work. However, if we are followers of Jesus, then we shall also want to give effect to the idea that "the sabbath was made for humankind." Christians who are also Jews might still want to keep the Jewish sabbath, but Gentiles too might want to keep a sabbath of some kind so that we can give effect to Jesus' saying that the sabbath was made for humankind. As a society we ought to insist that everyone can experience at least one day a week in which an employment contract cannot require work from them. This will not be because there is anything wrong with work, or that there is something wrong with paid work or with employment contracts: it is simply that diversity is good for us, and, conversely, that doing the same things all the time is bad for us. Action is always in patterns, and those patterns need to be diverse: so for at least one day a week to be for different kinds of work, and in particular for work that we want to do rather than work that is required of us, is something that we should all require of each other. Any regulations relating to that one day a week should understand that the day is a gift to us: it is made for us, and not us for it: so any social or individual expectations should be purely about nothing particular being required.

This author attempts to spend approximately one day a week with the computer turned off. This might not be a Saturday, and it might not be a Sunday. It can be any day. The purpose of the chosen prohibition is to create an important diversity in the patterns of action that constitute who I am, and to free time for work that I might not find time for on other days. Other people might make different choices as to what is to be different on their own chosen Christian sabbath. It is the diversity that matters: the change in the changing patterns of action. Just as Sunday, the celebration of Jesus' resurrection, should be defined by particular patterns of action, and is not some kind of pause in the action, so any chosen Christian sabbath will be for particular chosen patterns of action rather than for an absence of action. We and everything else are action in changing patterns; all of it is work; and diversity of work does us good. God worked to make this gift available to us, so we must work to make it good for us and for others.

## MARK 3:1-6

> 3 Again he entered the synagogue, and a man was there who had a withered hand. ² They watched him to see whether he would cure him on the sabbath, so that they might accuse him. ³ And he said to the man who had the withered hand, 'Come forward.' ⁴ Then he said to them, 'Is it lawful to do good or to do harm on the sabbath, to save life or to kill?' But they were silent. ⁵ He looked around at them with anger; he was grieved at their hardness of heart and said to the man, 'Stretch out your hand.' He stretched it out, and his hand was restored. ⁶ The Pharisees went out and immediately conspired with the Herodians against him, how to destroy him.[141]

This is a variation on a theme. We have already read how Jesus cast out an evil spirit on the sabbath, permitted work on the sabbath, and healed a man whose sins he had pronounced forgiven. This is a new combination of familiar elements: a physical healing on the sabbath.

Unlike the paralyzed man lowered through the roof, in this case the man whom Jesus intended to heal was told to "come forward." He heard the command and obeyed it. Forever after he would be the person who chose to hear Jesus' command and to do as he was asked. Presumably he could have refused. This withered hand might have been a ticket to a life of begging and of not having to earn his own living, and it might have elicited sympathy among his family and friends. There might have been all kinds of secondary gains to keeping his withered hand. Because Jesus did not ask whether he wished to be healed, he was left with a choice: to go forwards, or to stay where he was. The pattern of action that he chose would affect every future changing pattern of action that would constitute who he was. He went forwards, and in that action became a follower of Jesus, as the four fishermen, Levi, and the others had done.

As for the Pharisees, there were some patterns of action that they would have permitted on the sabbath, such as limited travel, the eating of meals, and the reading of the scriptures, but some that were not explicitly permitted and so were not permitted, such as healing a withered hand. The problem for them was that if Jesus was permitted one of these not explicitly permitted patterns of action, then there would be no end to the kinds of work that would be regarded as permitted. The prohibition of "work" on the sabbath had given rise to a raft of regulations—a "fence"—so that activity essential to daily life could continue at the same time as every other kind of work being prohibited. Jesus was now breaking down the fence in a highly provocative manner:[142] and if he could breach this fence, then how many others might he destroy? How many people might follow him into such disobedience to the regulations? How would the social fabric survive the rapid expansion of the number of patterns of action that people might allow themselves? As far as the Pharisees were concerned, Jesus' destruction of the fence required Jesus' destruction: a pattern of action that would put an end to the patterns of action that constituted Jesus. But of course it would not put an end to them. First of all, the changing patterns of action that constitute who we are constantly entangle with the changing patterns of action that constitute the individuals, communities, and institutions around us, so Jesus' actions would continue to ripple out forever even if their source were to be destroyed; and secondly, in Jesus' case, there would be a resurrection: the changing patterns of action that constitute Jesus would be transfigured and would continue to change the changing patterns of action that would constitute myriads of individuals, communities, societies, institutions, and nations, both through the experiences of his disciples immediately following his death, and from then until now through Jesus still at work in the world through his Spirit—that is, through his changing patterns of action still changing the changing patterns of action that constitute the universe and every pattern of action within it, and particularly through the church when its changing patterns of action are those of Jesus.

As far as Jesus was concerned, there was a simple distinction relating to the kinds of work that were appropriate to the sabbath: patterns of action that did good were to happen, and patterns of action that would do harm were not. This understanding clearly permitted the healing of the man's hand. The Pharisees' understanding did not permit that. And perhaps also in Jesus' mind was the closeness of a Kingdom of God in which all would be healed, a closeness that demanded new patterns of action in the present, and not just in the future. The Pharisees had hardened their hearts against such a possibility.[143] Jesus therefore "looked . . . with anger," and he was "grieved." Emotions are particular changing patterns of action that constitute who we are, and they deeply affect all of our other changing patterns of action. Jesus' humanity was our humanity, and he felt with our feelings. His anger was human anger, and his grief human grief. But Jesus is also patterns of action that constitute God, and we cannot divide him: so it is the whole Jesus who was angry and who grieved.[144] In Jesus, uniquely, patterns of action that are God were and are entwined with the patterns of action that were and are his humanity, and the anger and the grief were and are the anger and grief of God, for no pattern of action is immune to any other. And so anger and grief are eternally emotions that God experiences, and there are no changing patterns of action that are God's patterns of action that remain untouched by Jesus' anger and grief. God is angry, and God grieves.

This raises the difficult question of the often petulant and vicious God of the Hebrew scriptures, the Christian Old Testament. Here we meet a God who orders genocide, and who behaves like an abusive parent as he punishes, banishes, destroys, and then rescues his chosen people.[145] It is all very well rationalizing these texts by suggesting that for the prophets it was psychologically easier to cope with a God understood as himself punishing Israel than with one so weak that he could not stop surrounding nations from killing Israelites, looting them, and then carrying them off into exile: but we are still left with a God very different from the one that we find in Jesus. Perhaps there really is this diversity of patterns of action in God. In the end, this is a problem that we do not have to resolve. We are here studying Mark's Gospel, and not the Hebrew scriptures: and in this gospel we find a Jesus, and therefore a God, angry with a righteous anger in the face of a regulatory framework and its defenders in which there is no understanding of the law as a gift designed to enhance the life of a community; and we find a God grieving that so many people are unable to repent: to change their minds. They have "hard hearts," and cannot see that healing would be an entirely appropriate kind of work to add to the rather restricted list of tasks permitted on the sabbath.

For the Pharisees, the sabbath law had become a boundary marker, marking out a category of faithful Jews.[146] In one sense that was not a problem. Communities need boundaries. But this was not the positive meaning that the sabbath held for Jesus. For him it was a gift, and a promise of a Kingdom of God in which all would be healed: so healing a man on the sabbath was the most appropriate action possible. If we are followers of Jesus, then we too will regard the sabbath as a promise of the Kingdom of God. This will be rather complicated for Christians as there is no Christian sabbath. However, Sunday, as the day of resurrection, is for Christians a promise of the coming Kingdom of God, and so on that day in particular we shall seek opportunities to enact the Kingdom of God in the midst of the daily lives of ourselves, our families, communities, and institutions; and we might also choose our own sabbaths—days for different kinds of work, both for ourselves as individuals and for our communities and societies—and on those days we shall attempt to embody in our patterns of action the Kingdom of God for which we hope. The patterns of action that constitute the world change constantly, so Sundays and sabbaths from the past will not necessarily be a useful guide to what they should look like today. In every new context we shall have to ask which particular patterns of action might best constitute a promise of the Kingdom of God that we have seen lived in Jesus, and particularly in the kind of event that took place in that synagogue when Jesus called forward the man with the withered hand.

## MARK 3:7-12

> 7 Jesus departed with his disciples to the lake, and a great multitude from Galilee followed him; 8 hearing all that he was doing, they came to him in great numbers from Judea, Jerusalem, Idumea, beyond the Jordan, and the region around Tyre and Sidon. 9 He told his disciples to have a boat ready for him because of the crowd, so that they would not crush him; 10 for he had cured many, so that all who had diseases pressed upon him to touch him. 11 Whenever the unclean spirits saw him, they fell down before him and shouted, 'You are the Son of God!' 12 But he sternly ordered them not to make him known.[147]

Again there is travelling: Jesus with his disciples; the crowds coming to hear him. And there is plenty of other action as well: the readying of a boat, the crushing of Jesus by the crowd, the curing of diseases, and members of the crowd jostling to touch Jesus. The unclean spirits fell in front of him (not the people possessed by them); they shouted out who Jesus was; and he ordered them not to do so. Jesus' relationships with his close followers, with the crowd, and with realities beyond the material, are all described in terms of his patterns of action and of theirs. This *is* their relationships with each other. It is not that there are various relationships, and these actions are expressing them: the actions in diverse and changing patterns *are* those relationships.

They came to hear Jesus and to be healed by him because they had heard "all that he was doing." This was who Jesus was. It was not that he was the Son of God who happened to do these things: these patterns of action constituted the Son of God; and these patterns of action tangled with the patterns of action that constituted the people around him, and with the active realities to which they related, and they changed all of those myriad patterns of action.

We really are what we do. It is not that there is some "I" that does things: the patterns of action simply are who we are. The actions in patterns that constitute what we call atomic particles; the constantly changing actions in patterns that constitute molecules, cells, organs, hormones, bacteria: this is what we are and who we are. The body is a vast network of action in changing patterns, and some of those patterns of action constitute what we call the brain, in which there are some particularly complex patterns of action: but all of it belongs together, there are no separate bits, there is no

"I" that we can separate from the changing patterns of action that constitute our bodies. This is who we are.

And because the changing patterns of action that constitute us constantly relate to the changing patterns of action that constitute other people, we have no boundaries: the patterns of action that constitute other people constantly change ours, so there is a sense in which they are us and we are them. Jesus was constantly remade by the crowd and by his disciples, and they by him. Jesus, teaching and healing on the seashore, wondering whether he would have to climb into the boat if he wasn't to be pushed into the sea by the crowd, was called the Son of God, an analogy that expressed the fact that changing patterns of action that were uniquely his were patterns of action that were God: so he was God, and those changing patterns of action affected those that constituted his disciples and the members of the crowd, and so all of them shared in the changing patterns of action that were God.

These words that we are reading in Mark's Gospel are a crystallization of that event on that day on that seashore. They are pure pattern. There is no action in the text. But the text is born of action: the event and the people themselves; the telling of the event from person to person during the early years of the Christian church; and Mark's pondering of what he has heard, and his writing of the text: and if we are reading a translation of the New Testament, then the action in patterns that constitutes the translators are changed by Mark's text, which determines the words that they write: and it is those words that we read. And if Mark's Greek text was altered or added to during its transition from manuscript to manuscript, then the patterns of action that constituted the scribes were changed by the texts that they received, and in turn determined the words that were written in the new manuscripts. As we read the text, our changing patterns of action are changed by all of those patterns of action. Genuine communication of the event on the seashore takes place, because at the root of all of those texts, and of all of the actions in patterns that have given rise to them, are the actions in changing patterns of the event on the seashore. Relationships happen. We really are there with Jesus, his disciples, and the crowd, because those changing patterns of action are changing the patterns of action that constitute who we are.

Precisely which words are in the text really matters, because different words will have different effects on the text's readers. Here Jesus does not disown "Son of God," and the text implies that he agreed with its use in relation to who he was. He was no warrior king, which is how "Son of God" was sometimes used in the Psalms: but the unclean spirits were right to use the term—and Jesus recognized that they were right to use it—because Jesus' changing patterns of action were uniquely those of God as well as those of his humanity. By "Son of God" Christians now mean Jesus: he is now the definition of that term; which means that the changing patterns of action that constitute who Jesus is constitute the meaning of that term: but not only those, for the myriad of changing patterns of action that have related to those words have constantly changed the connections between that terminology and other words and their meanings in an evolving and turbulent sea of connections between words in the minds of billions of readers. The meanings that we ascribe to "Son of God" will be influenced by the term's meanings in the minds of our teachers, the writers of commentaries, and so on: and the meaning that each of us ascribe to the words "Son of God" will constantly be changed by our new experiences of those words, and of any words and ideas to which they might become connected in our highly active minds. We never simply receive an idea, a concept, a bundle of words: the word is a pattern of action in our brains, and that pattern of action is constantly changed by other changing patterns of action. Nothing is ever fixed. There is a sense in which we shall never understand by "Son of God" what was meant by it by Jesus and by others during that event in Galilee: although from the fact that Jesus asked the unclean spirits not to use that name for him we can conclude that it carried political implications that might have brought an early end to his ministry had the idea spread that he was a warrior king: but whatever the term's meaning, there is a sense in which the patterns of action that were those words, and the many meanings that were connected with them then, continue to influence us via the text. No one meaning of "Son of God" will be the same as any other, and the words will mean different things to each of us, and each of our meanings will be different at different times: but still there will be connections, because the meanings of "Son of God" intended by the unclean spirits, and understood by Jesus, his disciples, the crowd, and countless people since then, continue to influence the connections that we make to it as we read the text and our brains connect to the changing patterns of action that constitute the words in our brains that are constituted by multiple other changing patterns of action.

What does it mean to touch someone? It means to reach out to them; to engage with them; and to be changed by them. In relation to physical touch—which is what is in view in this passage from Mark's Gospel—touch is the engaging of one body with another, and therefore of one person with another.

Paul called the church the body of Christ: and he meant what he wrote. He meant that the church really is the body that is the risen Christ, and so is the risen Christ. My body is the changing patterns of action that constitute the person that I am—I am my patterns of action: so by the church being the body of Christ we mean that its changing patterns of action are those of the risen Christ, and therefore of Jesus: for the identity between Jesus and the risen Christ is the identity between their changing patterns of action. If I touch the church, or the church touches me, then I touch Jesus, and Jesus touches me. If reality is action, and action is reality, and the reality that we experience is action in changing patterns, then the most real touching possible is when the action in patterns that constitutes me touches the action in patterns that constitute the church: if, that is, the church really is the body of Christ—that is, if its patterns of action are those of Jesus. If the church is patterns of action that heal and liberate, then we, like members of the crowd on that seashore, will want to touch the church, the risen Christ, Jesus. Jesus was already living the life of the Kingdom of God—that is, the patterns of action that constitute the Kingdom of God—and so by touching such a church we shall be touching the risen Christ, and therefore Jesus, and therefore the Kingdom of God. We shall be engaging with Jesus past, present, and future, with an engaging that is as real as any other, and more real still because it will be an engagement with God who is not only changing patterns of action but is the very source of action itself.

## MARK 3:13-19a

> 13 He went up the mountain and called to him those whom he wanted, and they came to him. 14 And he appointed twelve, whom he also named apostles, to be with him, and to be sent out to proclaim the message, 15 and to have authority to cast out demons. 16 So he appointed the twelve:[z] Simon (to whom he gave the name Peter); 17 James son of Zebedee and John the brother of James (to whom he gave the name Boanerges, that is, Sons of Thunder); 18 and Andrew, and Philip, and Bartholomew, and Matthew, and Thomas, and James son of Alphaeus, and Thaddaeus, and Simon the Cananaean, 19 and Judas Iscariot, who betrayed him.[148]

To climb a mountain was a recognized preliminary to a divine act.[149] This pattern of action had a meaning—indeed, it was a meaning; and this passage goes on to be full of patterns of action of which the verbs constitute the meanings: he went, he called, they came, he appointed, he named; with the intention of action: to be with, to be sent, to proclaim, to have authority, to cast out. It is this complex pattern of action that constitutes a group of people as disciples of Jesus. Twice the text says that Jesus "made the twelve."[150] This is what the calling, appointing, and giving of authority did then and does now: it makes disciples, with "disciple" being not a state, but action in patterns. And Judas, too, is defined by the pattern of action that constitutes who he was: he is his "handing over" of Jesus.[151]

What Jesus appointed was a diverse community to do these things. The Kingdom of God was and would be the changing patterns of action of a community of liberated individuals, so the proclamation of it would have to represent those changing patterns of action, and so would need to be done by a community. The calling of twelve men was a clear reference to the twelve tribes of Israel (Ephraim and Manasseh often being called half-tribes in order to preserve the list of twelve). Ten of those tribes had been lost when the population of the northern kingdom of Israel was taken into exile by Assyria. Only the tribes of Judah and Benjamin survived. There was a further exile, but it does not appear to have erased the identities of those two remaining tribes, so their identities survived into the time of Jesus. What Jesus was explicitly doing was

z. Other ancient authorities lack *So he appointed the twelve*

constituting a new Israel to fulfil the task originally intended:[152] that it should be a light to the world, and a servant to the nations. Following the resurrection it was only Peter among this group of twelve who exercised any significant leadership in the church, as Jesus' brother James and then Paul became the leaders of the church in Jerusalem and around the Mediterranean respectively:[153] but the twelve men chosen by Jesus would have fulfilled the missionary task given to them by Jesus during his ministry, and would have continued to represent the new Israel that would extend its boundaries to take in the Gentiles.

Why was it all men? How did the women who followed Jesus fit into this picture? Was the choosing of men a purely practical matter?—it was safer to send men out to travel the country than it was to send women to do so? But what is significant for us here, as always, is the verbs: Jesus went, he called, they came, he appointed, and he named the twelve, so that they would be a community that would be sent, would proclaim, would have authority, and would cast out evil: not just during his ministry, but following his resurrection—a task that they fulfilled, and that they were able to fulfil because they had been with Jesus.[154]

This calling, appointing, and sending, was Jesus' pattern of action then, so it is his pattern of action now: yes, always changing in relation to new and changing contexts, but still recognizably one of the myriad patterns of action that is who Jesus was and still is. So this is his pattern of action today: he still finds a context in which he can gather us and we can hear him; he still calls us to that place; we can still choose to join him; he still appoints us; and he still names us—and the verbs apply to any and all of us, whatever our gender, ethnic origin, sexual orientation, or whatever. We might not be members of the original group of twelve apostles, but we are still called to be apostles in relation to the meaning of the word: people who are gathered and then sent.[155] For the intention is still the same, although constantly changing in new contexts. Jesus still calls us to be with him; to be sent; to proclaim the coming Kingdom of God, and Jesus as its new kind of king; to have authority; and to cast out evil. How we do all of this will be largely up to us, but only if these verbs represent who we are can we call ourselves followers of Jesus.

All of these verbs matter, and not just some of them: so it is as important that we should "be with" Jesus as it is that we should proclaim Jesus and his Kingdom; and it is as important that we should proclaim as that we should be with him. But this raises the question as to whether every individual follower should be expected to exercise all of these patterns of action, or whether the whole of the church should ensure that it is exercising all of them, and that individuals should be exercising those to which they are most fitted: that is, those patterns of action that mesh more easily with the changing patterns of action that constitute who we are. Jesus appointed "the twelve" to do these things, which means that today he appoints the church to do them, and not necessarily each individual. As Paul emphasizes, God gives different gifts to different members of the church so that the entire body of Christ, the whole church, might fulfil God's purpose for it.[156] And so in the church today we should expect to find evangelists, healers, those who cast out evil, and those who are with Jesus, which suggests that the church needs enclosed monastic orders just as much as it needs full-time evangelists. Jesus appointment of "the twelve," and Paul's passages about the members of the body of Christ receiving different gifts, suggests that each of us should seek out the particular verb or verbs among the verbs in the text that most clearly relate to the changing patterns of action that constitute who we are, and that we should put energy into developing the patterns of action that those verbs represent. It might still be true, though, that all of the verbs apply to all of us to some extent. As Jesus charged the twelve with the tasks for which he had chosen them, each of those twelve individuals was addressed by each of the verbs. This is a clear invitation to all of us to ask how we might best exercise those patterns of action that might not so easily fit with the patterns of action that we are. The natural evangelist might ask themselves how they could more often "be with" Jesus; and the natural recluse who has given their life to prayer might ask themselves how they could more often evangelize. By taking on all of the patterns of action to which Jesus was inviting the twelve, we shall more completely fulfil the vocation of a follower of Jesus, we shall more completely embody the church understood as multiple and complex changing patterns of action, and we shall more completely embody the Kingdom of God that the apostles were called to represent.

As we have read Mark's Gospel, we have frequently found ourselves encountering and using the words "choice" and "choose." Jesus chose to do things, and those around him chose to do things. But what does it mean to choose? Does it mean anything more than that we simply do what we say we have chosen to do? Is choosing to do something in any sense different from simply doing it? Perhaps the minimal requirement for using the words "choice" or "choose" is that what we find ourselves doing is not in fact something that is done to us. When we say that we have chosen to do something, we are saying that the pattern of action that we have done emerges from the patterns of action that constitute who we are as well as from those that constitute people and situations around us. But do we mean any more than that? Do we mean that a pattern of action in our brain preceded the patterns of actions that involved our limbs, for instance? We might mean that: although now we might be aware that that might not have been what happened, because evidence suggests that physical movement can occur before the brain's activity, which means that what is in fact happening is that the brain is rationalizing instinctive activity after the event. What is happening is still emerging from the patterns of action that constitute who we are, but the order in which things are happening might not be what we think it is.

And does any of this actually make any difference? Patterns of action in our brains, and patterns of action in the other parts of our bodies, such as in our spinal cords, in distributed neural networks, and in the muscles themselves, are all patterns of action that are ours: they emerge from our existing changing patterns of action as well as from those patterns of action that impact us: such as Jesus' calling of us, and other people's responses to his calls to them. Jesus finds a context in which he can call us, he calls us, we might respond, he might appoint us to tasks, and he might name us as apostles, as people who are sent. The call will be to be with him, to be sent, to proclaim, to have authority, and to cast out evil. These are patterns of action that might entangle with the patterns of action that constitute who we are, and they might become our changing patterns of action: integral parts of the networks of changing patterns of action that constitute who each of us is. So we shall be changed, and the patterns of action that constitute Jesus and his Kingdom will continue to engage with our world and with the people around us.

## MARK 3:19b–30

> Then he went home; [20] and the crowd came together again, so that they could not even eat. [21] When his family heard it, they went out to restrain him, for people were saying, 'He has gone out of his mind.' [22] And the scribes who came down from Jerusalem said, 'He has Beelzebul, and by the ruler of the demons he casts out demons.' [23] And he called them to him, and spoke to them in parables, 'How can Satan cast out Satan? [24] If a kingdom is divided against itself, that kingdom cannot stand. [25] And if a house is divided against itself, that house will not be able to stand. [26] And if Satan has risen up against himself and is divided, he cannot stand, but his end has come. [27] But no one can enter a strong man's house and plunder his property without first tying up the strong man; then indeed the house can be plundered.
>
> 28 'Truly I tell you, people will be forgiven for their sins and whatever blasphemies they utter; [29] but whoever blasphemes against the Holy Spirit can never have forgiveness, but is guilty of an eternal sin'— [30] for they had said, 'He has an unclean spirit.'[157]

If reality is action, then God is Action, the source of all action. There are then theoretically two options for God's relationship with the reality that is ourselves and everything that we know and experience. One option is that a pattern of some kind spontaneously appeared in the chaotic sea of action. This is rather like Lucretius's suggestion that turbulence and then new stabilities had emerged from a laminar flow of atoms because just one atom happened to deviate from its path. In this scenario, no relationship between God and the evolving universe is either required or possible. A second option is that God is the source of all action and that God is also constituted by changing patterns of action that are particular to God. This is what the book of Genesis envisages when it says that a wind from God, or the Spirit of God, moved over the face of the waters.[158] What followed was an ordered creation that we might understand as action in changing patterns, and, in particular, changing patterns of action to which God could relate. If this second option is what occurred then the changing patterns of action that constitute God constantly change, and are changed by the evolving universe.

This is the context for the evolution of evil. A universe that is changing patterns of action, however influenced by God's patterns of action, will generate myriads of new patterns of action, and those will instantaneously generate others, and so on: so it is inevitable that at any one time there will be patterns of action that oppose and contradict contemporary patterns of action that constitute God. We might term such patterns of action "evil." Some of them will be done by human beings, but others will occur across the cosmos—for instance, the consequences of an expanding star or a black hole swallowing a planet on which conscious life has evolved don't bear thinking about—and of course across our own planet. A visit to Herculaneum and Pompeii, Roman towns buried by an eruption of Vesuvius, is a sobering experience. There is no reason why the patterns of action that we might call evil should be less diverse than those that we might call good: by which we might mean changing patterns of action that mesh well with God's changing patterns of action.

Those who had met Jesus were telling his family that he had become irrational: which in their terms he clearly was. He was describing a Kingdom of God, and therefore a way of life that in many ways was opposed to the realities that everyone knew. Jesus was calling for liberation from traditional constraints, and he was promising something for which there was little evidence, and we can understand how such calls and such promises might destabilize individuals and communities. His family were presumably concerned for his safety, so they were on their way to find him and presumably to try to persuade him to desist. We shall soon find them trying to talk to Jesus.

We then find the scribes, the interpreters of the law, who no doubt credited themselves with the ability to decide what was evil and what was not, accusing Jesus of "having Beelzebul," or Satan: that is, of being possessed by the prince of the devils. They were putting Jesus into a category:[159] a too common pattern of action throughout history. Instead of getting to know Jesus as the individual changing patterns of action that he was, their minds were identifying him with a changing pattern of action that he was not, which of course would permit changing patterns of action on their part that would have been a lot less possible if they had not put him into the "devil" category.

This was a culture in which evil patterns of action were personalized as Beelzebul, as still happens in many cultures today. This is not irrational. When we see evil patterns of action exhibited by someone, then we either attribute those patterns of action to them, or we attribute them to some pattern or patterns of action that are influencing those that constitute who they are. If in a court of law someone is convicted of murder, then we are assuming that the evil pattern of action that is the killing of someone has been generated wholly or mainly by the patterns of action that constitute who the murderer is, and in particular by those patterns that we think of as decision-making. If, however, we find that the murder was the result of mental illness—that is, of changes in the brain that bypass rational decision-making patterns of action—then we might lock the perpetrator in a secure unit, and attempt to bring the brain's evil activity under control. We might also recognize that changing patterns of action throughout someone's life—for instance, constant abuse of various kinds—has so influenced someone's patterns of action that we cannot hold them entirely responsible for a murder, particularly if the murder was of one of their serial abusers. And if we were to live in a society that personalizes evil patterns of action as invisible evil conscious beings, then we might attempt to dislodge those beings.

Jesus cast out demons: his presence, his actions, and his words—that is, the changing patterns of action that constituted who he was—actively opposed the evil patterns of action that were entangled with afflicted individuals' other changing patterns of action, and as this passage makes clear, by casting out minor demons Jesus was casting out Satan himself.[160] The demons had to leave, and the person was changed. In this context it was not irrational for the scribes to accuse Jesus of being Beelzebul or Satan, evil personified, and therefore able to ask the demons to leave, for such minor demons were regarded as Satan's servants. Jesus' response was equally rational. Evil patterns of action tend to generate more of the same: they do not themselves neutralize evil patterns of action. Only good patterns of action, and particularly those that are God, can do that. And more than that: if we understand Beelzebul to be the source of evil patterns of action, then simply casting out one of his servants will achieve little, because more of them will arrive. Only tackling the source of evil itself will make a true casting out of evil possible. Hence the saying about the strong man's house: only if the patterns of action that function as the source of evil patterns of action can be dissolved can people trapped by evil be rescued from it. A war between two kingdoms is envisaged: ultimately the Kingdom of God will be victorious, because it will destroy the source of evil patterns of action and not just the evil patterns themselves. One of the patterns of action that constituted Jesus was his battle with evil powers: a battle that would result in his suffering and death. Passages such as the one that we are studying here might have been retained in the tradition and recorded by Mark as an encouragement to early Christians who were suffering persecution to see themselves as engaged in Jesus' battle with evil powers and to know that this would result both in their suffering and in the coming of the Kingdom of God;[161] and this particular passage might have been retained in Christian memory because it is a clear declaration that Jesus is the one who will bind "the strong man"—which could be interpreted as the ruling authorities, heavenly evil powers, or both: an identification that might well have confirmed the ruling authorities in their desire to have Jesus killed.[162]

To understand reality as action in patterns reduces considerably the distance between ourselves, who might or might not understand evil as in some sense separate from the natural and human patterns of action of which we have some understanding, and those who live in cultures that personalize evil and believe that there are evil beings that we cannot see and that constantly influence us; and it also reduces the distance between us and people who believe that our good actions are the result of angels or good spirits taking care of us and guiding our behavior. The good as changing patterns of action that reflect the character of the changing patterns of action that constitute God, and evil as changing patterns of action that oppose or destroy God's changing patterns of action, can make sense of both personalized good and evil and an understanding of good and evil as terminology for different kinds of natural and human patterns of action. Either way, Jesus can cast out evil, back then in Galilee, and today in whatever culture his patterns of action, which are God's patterns of action, relate to the patterns of action that constitute ourselves, the world, and the cosmos. The passage describes two kingdoms in conflict: kingdoms that remain in conflict today.

An alternative translation for "the strong man" would be "the power": that is, evil patterns of action. The patterns of action that constitute Jesus are already being shown to be stronger than "the power"—they are already "binding" "the power"—so eventually all such evil patterns of action will be overwhelmed by patterns of action that constitute God and the Kingdom of God.[163]

If by forgiveness we mean that someone can determine that evil patterns of action that have affected them will be absorbed by their own patterns of action, and will no longer influence their own future changing patterns of action, then each of us can forgive, and God can forgive. God, as the source of all action, clearly has absolute freedom to develop whatever patterns of action God wishes to evolve. God cannot help being affected by the evil patterns of action that human beings and the natural world generate, but can ensure that they will never affect the quality of the relationship that God has with the natural world and human beings. Such a relationship will be constantly good patterns of action. This is the judgement on those evil acts: that as far as God is concerned, they will go no further. Our evil actions will of course continue to affect everyone around us, and it will be up to them to forgive us; and it will be up to us to forgive evil acts done to us: and all of that forgiveness will only ever be partial. God's forgiveness will be different: it can be absolute, because whatever evil pattern of action we throw at God, God can ensure its absorption by God's own changing patterns of action, enabling God to exercise a renewed relationship with us in every new moment.

So what should we make of Jesus' words about "blasphemies against the Holy Spirit" not being forgiven? As the passage makes clear, the context is important. Jesus has been irked by the scribes' accusation. He is a human being, like the rest of us. He might be God, in the sense that his action in changing patterns is uniquely God's patterns of action in ways in which ours are not: but human emotions were just as much a part of who Jesus was as they are of who we are. He wants to warn the scribes from Jerusalem that their accusations, which confuse evil with good, and good with evil,[164] and that confuse the Holy Spirit—God's activity—with the devil's activity,[165] might not be forgiven. The Holy Spirit is the pattern of action that we see in Jesus' exorcisms, whereas the scribes are suggesting that the pattern of action that they see in the exorcisms is that of "the power," or Satan.[166] Perhaps if the scribes are not able to recognize a pattern of action as God's, when that is what it is, then they will not be able to recognize God's offer of forgiveness for what it is. So Jesus sets them a question: Are their accusations a sin against the Holy Spirit?[167] This does not mean that God was not going to forgive them, or that Jesus would not relent and forgive them: but it does recognize the seriousness of the conflict between "the power" and the Kingdom of God.

Jesus is also here emphasizing that he has the authority to make these decisions. He had authority to announce the forgiveness of the sins of the man lowered through the roof, and he was now saying that he could also decide that certain sins were not going to be forgiven, including the false accusations of the scribes.

## MARK 3:31–35

> 31 Then his mother and his brothers came; and standing outside, they sent to him and called him. 32 A crowd was sitting around him; and they said to him, 'Your mother and your brothers and sisters[a] are outside, asking for you.' 33 And he replied, 'Who are my mother and my brothers?' 34 And looking at those who sat around him, he said, 'Here are my mother and my brothers! 35 Whoever does the will of God is my brother and sister and mother.'[168]

Throughout this chapter of Mark's Gospel we find a distinction between those "inside" and those "outside." The Twelve are insiders; the scribes are outsiders; and now Jesus' family, whom we have already encountered setting out to try to interrupt Jesus' ministry, are revealed as outsiders in contrast to Jesus' disciples, those gathered "around him": the distinction being graphically represented by the "outsiders" being outside the house, and the "insiders" inside it. The distinction continues into chapter 4, with the outsiders receiving only parables, and the insiders being offered an interpretation.[169] Whilst "inside" and "outside" might not be verbs, they still represent alternative patterns of action that we might describe as "following Jesus" and "distancing from Jesus."

"Who is my mother?" The obvious answer is: the woman who gave birth to me, whose egg was fertilized, whose womb housed me for nine months, whose muscles pushed me out into the world. That complex pattern of action ripples through the changing patterns of action that constitute who I have been across my lifespan, and it still influences the changing patterns of action that I am. But there have been other patterns of action as well: breastfeeding, clothing, hugging, conversation, feeding, potty training, reading—the myriad patterns of action that constitute the care of a child, and that forever influence the patterns of action that the child becomes. These patterns of action might involve the mother who gave me birth, but they might not. There might have been two

a. Other ancient authorities lack *and sisters*

or more mothers in each of our childhoods. And at various times in our lives there might have been even more mothers: If a mother disappeared from our life for whatever reason, then our father might have been our mother, or an aunt or an uncle might have fulfilled the role, or a grandmother or grandfather, or a neighbor. During our teenage years an elderly lady who helped to run the youth club might have fulfilled a motherly function: for that is what we are discussing here. The person who is my mother, or the people who were and are my mothers, are constituted by changing patterns of action that will forever ripple through the changing patterns of action that at every point in our lives determine and constitute who we are. For some children, whole new families become their mothers, or occasionally an institution will fulfil the role. Each of us will be able to look back and decide who our mothers have been: and in some cases the woman who gave birth might not be in the list, because they died, the child was removed from them, they abandoned the child, or they did not care for the child: their patterns of action were not those of a mother, so they were not a mother to the child. Whether they can later become a mother to the adult will depend on whether the patterns of action that we call reconciliation and forgiveness can reignite the patterns of action that constitute mothering. What we are discussing here might be better described by using the verb "to mother" than by using the noun "mother."

And as we grow older, and if our parents live on, then our parents might be those to whom we relate adult to adult; and as we continue to age, our parents might become those for whom we care. The direction and character of the relationship constantly changes: new patterns of action evolve that constitute the relationship between us afresh in every moment. None of what has constituted the relationship, and none of what each of us is, will ever be left behind. Every changing pattern of action constantly affects the vast networks of patterns of action that constitute who each of us is in the world: and it is these networks that are eventually broken apart by death and that can therefore cause the emotional traumas that we might experience.

Other relationships are of course similar. A brother or sister will normally be the person given birth by my mother, or sometimes by my father's former or subsequent wife, and whose childhood is spent in the same family as mine. But there will be many variations on this theme. Perhaps "brothering" and "sistering" might be a better way of defining the relationship. And similarly, of course, with fathering.

Jesus did not say that Mary, James, and the rest, were not his mother, brothers and sisters. What he did say was that those listening to him were his mother, brothers, and sisters; and he explains why—there was a bond between them formed by a common pattern of action: the kind of common pattern of action that might evolve within a natural family. In any family that is anything like normal, the changing patterns of action that constitute who each of us is will relate to those that constitute every other member of the family. There will be no boundaries, so we shall constantly find our patterns of action adapting to those around us. Commonalities will emerge. The same was true of Jesus' disciples: doing the will of God—seeking to know it, committing to it, and doing it—bound them together in a single network of patterns of action that was as integrated as that of the best of families. As always, it is the verbs that matter. It is those who do the will of God that are Jesus' mother, brothers, and sisters. Family is something that we do, so if we are disciples of Jesus, then the patterns of action that constitute who we are will also constitute us as members of his family.[170]

Ludwig Wittgenstein wrote about "forms of life" in which we can discover "family resemblances." It is not that there is a single identifiable pattern of action that we find identically in every separate instance: it is rather that a wide diversity of patterns of action can be identified as belonging to the same family. We can find similarities between them, not some kind of identifiable common pattern: and if we do propose some common pattern, then all we have done is add yet one more form of life to the collection, and the family resemblance has become even more complex. This is what is happening here. No two of the individuals in that room would have shared the same changing pattern of action. All of them will have been different: but there would have been "family likenesses" between their "forms of life": and they would all have borne similarities to the changing patterns of action that constituted Jesus, and therefore to the changing patterns of action that constituted God. It is in this sense that Jesus was doing the will of God, and that his disciples were doing the will of God as well: their changing patterns of action bore family resemblances to the changing patterns of action that were God's changing patterns of action.

We find Paul using a similar image of the church, the members of which were bound together in a single network of patterns of action constituted by a common baptism, a common faith, a common sharing of the bread and wine at the Lord's Supper, and a common Holy Spirit who gives gifts to the church: all changing patterns of action that constitute who the members of the church are, and that held them together in a single network then, and hold us together in a single network today. The forms of life of members of the church bear family resemblances to each other, just as did those of Jesus' disciples.

Within the network of Jesus' disciples were evident the kinds of commonalities and mutual caring found in the best of families, so he was able to say that those gathered around him were his mother, brothers, and sisters. They mothered, brothered, and sistered him. Paul would have said something similar of the church. Elsewhere Jesus calls his disciples "children,"[171] completing the circle of relationships: they were parents and children to each other: that is, their patterns of action were those of both parents and children—they parented and childed each other, for just as "to mother," "to brother" and "to sister" are appropriate verbs to describe how Jesus saw his disciples, so "to child" and "to parent" are equally appropriate verbs to describe the mutual relationships of caring and common purpose between Jesus and his followers.

While it is true that Jesus did not disown his mother, brothers, and sisters during this episode, it is also true that he did not grant them any special status. His disciples were just as much his mother, brothers, and sisters as were Mary, James, and his other brothers and sisters. In the Kingdom of God all human institutions are relativized. Nothing is any longer fixed in any kind of pattern, structure, or hierarchy. Everything changes, because reality is action, and the Kingdom of God is action in changing patterns. In John's Gospel we find not only Jesus telling his mother Mary and his disciple John that they are now mother and son, but we also find Jesus as servant of the disciples at the last supper.[172] The old structures are dissolved: the Kingdom of God is entirely new changing patterns of action that sometimes dissolve, and always relativize, the old ones. This lesson Jesus' disciples and then the church had to learn, and we are still learning it, over and over again. Reality is no longer Being, beings, the unchanging, rest, and the static, if it ever really was: reality is Action, action, change, movement, and the dynamic.

"Mother, brothers and sisters." Why not "father . . ." We do not hear about Jesus' father in Mark's Gospel. The most likely reason is that he had died. Later in the gospel, Jesus is described as "the carpenter," and his mother and four of his brothers are named, and his sisters are again mentioned.[173] Perhaps Jesus had taken over the family firm on his father's death, and his mother, brothers, and sisters had come to find him on this occasion to persuade him to get back to work rather than go preaching and healing with his band of disciples. We can only speculate. If Mark knew any of the stories in circulation about Jesus' birth and childhood, then they clearly held no interest for him. What mattered was Jesus' proclamation of the Kingdom of God, and his living out of the life of that Kingdom along with the band of disciples gathering around him. It was these who were as much his mother, brothers, and sisters, as were the group of blood relatives gathered at the door. These were the ones who, like Jesus, were seeking the will of God and doing it, which presumably meant believing the good news of the Kingdom of God:[174] and Mary and the rest would belong to that family if they did so as well. We find out later that Mary and at least some of the others did. During Jesus' ministry, during the years immediately after it, and still today, family relationships as understood by Jesus are constituted by the changing pattern of action that is doing the will of God.[175] And it remains the case that being a family is patterns of action and not simply genetic coding.

"He looked at them." Jesus looks at us, and if he finds us seeking to do God's will and then doing it, then we too are his mother, brothers, and sisters.

# MARK 4:1-9

> 4 Again he began to teach beside the lake. Such a very large crowd gathered around him that he got into a boat on the lake and sat there, while the whole

> crowd was beside the lake on the land. ² He began to teach them many things in parables, and in his teaching he said to them: ³ 'Listen! A sower went out to sow. ⁴ And as he sowed, some seed fell on the path, and the birds came and ate it up. ⁵ Other seed fell on rocky ground, where it did not have much soil, and it sprang up quickly, since it had no depth of soil. ⁶ And when the sun rose, it was scorched; and since it had no root, it withered away. ⁷ Other seed fell among thorns, and the thorns grew up and choked it, and it yielded no grain. ⁸ Other seed fell into good soil and brought forth grain, growing up and increasing and yielding thirty and sixty and a hundredfold.' ⁹ And he said, 'Let anyone with ears to hear listen!'[176]

For the time being we shall leave to one side the interpretation of this parable in verses 13 to 20 and interpret the parable for ourselves by concentrating on the verbs: a process encouraged by the Greek word *parabolei*, which comes from the verb *paraballō*, "to throw alongside," that is, to throw a story alongside reality in order to illuminate it.[177]

Again the crowds have gathered, and now the boat is not just prepared in case Jesus needs it: he has to climb into it so that he can gain the distance from the crowd required for effective delivery. And the first thing he tells his hearers to do is to "listen!" To listen is not simply to hear. It is a different pattern of action that actively engages the ears, the eyes, and the brain. Hearing allows the patterns of action communicated to the brain by the vibrating ear drums to be ignored, stored for later access, or passively allowed to make whatever connections they can in the midst of the noise of other internal activity. Listening, on the other hand, positively creates connections between the patterns of action communicated to the brain and as many as possible of the other changing patterns of action that make up our lives. Jesus is asking his hearers to do that—to listen: because if they do that then they will be changed, and will not only grasp the character of the Kingdom of God, but will begin to live it as well.

They are to listen to parables. When originally spoken, these would have been patterns of action that did not simply result in patterns of action in the hearer's brain that we might describe as knowledge:[178] rather, they were designed to result in complex changing patterns of action related to the whole of who the hearer was: that is, to the changing totality of the patterns of action that constituted who they were. The written text will not have quite the same impact as hearing Jesus tell his parables for the first time would have had, but the text can still act as a broad catalyst that stimulates change in the patterns of action that constitute who we are: not just creating new patterns of action in the brain that we might call knowledge, but inspiring change in all of the changing patterns of action that constitute who we are. To "listen" to a parable is to be changed.[179]

There has been understandable discussion as to the weight to put on verse 8, and the weight to be given to the parable as a whole with all of its detail. Is the detail there to emphasize the significance of the final harvest, or does each element of the detail contribute to the meaning of the parable? Is the parable about the different soils, and therefore different people's different relationships with the good news of the Kingdom of God, making the parable a call for action? Or is it about the opposition facing the Kingdom of God, and its final arrival? Or is it about the fact that the Kingdom of God really had come, and that all that was required was recognition of that?[180] Should it be called "the parable of the sower," "the parable of the soils," "the parable of the seeds," or "the parable of the harvest"?[181] Whatever Jesus intended—and it is possible, and perhaps likely, that he would not have wished to choose between a variety of options—verse 8 is the conclusion, the punchline, so that is where we shall begin.

The final verse of the parable is all verbs: "brought forth," "growing up," "increasing," "yielding": and then again the command to listen. The central message is clearly that the Kingdom of God will "bring forth," "grow up," "increase," and "yield," or rather better, "carry," which is the literal meaning of the Greek text. And so the Kingdom of God will bring forth, will grow up, will increase, and will carry a harvest: indeed, it will *be* the bringing forth, the increasing, the growing up, and the carrying. What will constitute the harvest? What does the "fruit" or "grain" mean? It will be the Kingdom of God: but that Kingdom will be constituted by patterns of action, so, as always, it is the verbs that matter.

The pattern of action represented by the parable, both in relation to the outcome expressed in verse 8, and by the detail, reflects that to be found in a prophecy in Isaiah:

> [10] For as the rain and the snow come down from heaven,
>> and do not return there until they have watered the earth,
> making it bring forth and sprout,
>> giving seed to the sower and bread to the eater,
> [11] so shall my word be that goes out from my mouth;
>> it shall not return to me empty,
> but it shall accomplish that which I purpose,
>> and succeed in the thing for which I sent it.
> [12] For you shall go out in joy,
>> and be led back in peace;
> the mountains and the hills before you
>> shall burst into song,
>> and all the trees of the field shall clap their hands.
> [13] Instead of the thorn shall come up the cypress;
>> instead of the brier shall come up the myrtle;
> and it shall be to the Lord for a memorial,
>> for an everlasting sign that shall not be cut off.[182]

Jesus might have had this passage in mind as he told his parable, not only in relation to the abundant harvest that represented the Kingdom of God, but also in relation to the detail of the parable: so we shall study that detail, and first of all as a contrast to the bringing forth of the harvest.

Everything goes wrong: it looks as if the crop will fail. The Kingdom of God would not come: the sowing of the seed might look like a promise of something to come, but the seed is eaten, or the young plants wither or are strangled. So it must have felt sometimes to Jesus and his followers. They proclaimed and they healed, but the world was not changed, the Kingdom of God had not come. One aspect of the message of the parable is that the Kingdom of God would come with difficulty, and it would not come straight away. This was not a promise of a military victory over the Romans. This was a promise of an emerging reign of God that would meet setbacks but would in the end come to fruition.[183] The Kingdom of God would come. There would be a harvest: and not just a harvest, but a massive harvest. This is the message to the crowd: it might not look as if a Kingdom of God would be brought to birth, but it will be.

Or perhaps the different parts of the detail of the parable do matter: and if they do then it will be the verbs that tell the story. Birds came and ate the seed, so it did not even have time to germinate. If the sowing of the seed was Jesus' proclaiming, healing, and casting out, then for some people and in some places—presumably among the scribes, and in the towns that would reject Jesus' disciples when they arrived—the Kingdom of God would not even begin to grow. And in places where the proclamation was initially heard as a promise of the Kingdom's coming, and the Kingdom of God began to be lived, then resistance to it from the forces of evil might kill it, or it might get submerged by the demands of social norms, the law, or any of the other institutions that controlled people's lives. There was little hope that the Kingdom of God would take root and grow. But that was not the end of the story. There would after all be a harvest: the Kingdom of God was near, and it would come.

Whether we regard the detail as significant, or the first part of the story as a more general statement that it really did not look as if the Kingdom of God had any chance of growing, it is still verse 8 that matters. The Kingdom of God was a bringing forth, a growing up, an increasing, and a yielding, or a carrying. God would bring about the Kingdom of God. Indeed, God *was* the bringing about of the Kingdom, for the bringing forth, the growing up, the increasing, and the carrying, are action in patterns that constitute God. The Kingdom of God is not some static object: it is God's changing patterns of action breaking into the changing patterns of action that constitute our world: ourselves, our families, our communities, our nations, our institutions . . . ; and Jesus' parable tells us that however bleak the prospects of that happening might appear, it will happen. In spite of the setbacks recorded in chapters 2 and 3 of Mark's Gospel, the Kingdom of God would come.[184] The patterns of action that constituted the Kingdom of God would defeat those that opposed them. The seed was already being sown in Jesus' own life and ministry, so already the seed was germinating, and the plants were beginning to grow. The harvest might not be just yet, but already the shoots would be visible, and although some of the proclaiming, healing and casting out would have no effect, some of it would bear fruit to an astonishing degree.

I have here offered readings of Jesus' parable: particular readings, at this particular moment, in this particular place. As we shall discover in the next section of Mark's Gospel, the point of a parable is to leave interpretation open, and certainly not to close it. My interpretation ought to be different the moment I've written it, and no two individuals will interpret the parable in precisely the same way. That is entirely as it should be.

Again at the end of the parable Jesus asks his hearers not just to hear, but to listen: having heard the parable, they must engage with it, and they must seek the connections with their own lives and with their own worlds. Jesus is asking his hearers to ensure that what they have experienced in his ministry should at least begin to have an effect; that they should prevent the forces of evil from destroying the first signs of the Kingdom's coming; and that they should not permit the law, social customs, or any of the institutions of their society, to submerge the growth of the Kingdom of God. And they should look to see where the proclaiming and the healing was already bearing fruit, and then nurture the growth, in their own lives and in the world around them. This was and is to be no passive watching of things happening: it was and is to be an active engagement in the growing of the Kingdom of God in their midst and in ours.

This is how Jesus intends all of the parables to be listened to rather than just heard. They are designed to reveal a new reality to every individual in the crowd.[185] The words are action in patterns, and they have an effect: they engage with the changing patterns of action that constitute ourselves and the worlds in which we live. And just as the words were addressed to the crowd on the lakeside, so they are addressed to us through the medium of the text: a crystallization of Jesus' action in changing patterns that changes the action in patterns that constitute ourselves and our worlds. The effects will not be the same as those brought about by Jesus' spoken words, because scribes' and translators' patterns of action have contributed to the text and thus to its effects: but still Jesus' words will change our changing patterns of action, and will therefore change who we are—particularly if we listen.

## MARK 4:10-20

10 When he was alone, those who were around him along with the twelve asked him about the parables. [11]And he said to them, 'To you has been given the secret[b] of the kingdom of God, but for those outside, everything comes in parables; [12] in order that

"they may indeed look, but not perceive,

b. Or *mystery*

> and may indeed listen, but not understand;
> so that they may not turn again and be forgiven.'"
>
> 13 And he said to them, 'Do you not understand this parable? Then how will you understand all the parables? [14] The sower sows the word. [15] These are the ones on the path where the word is sown: when they hear, Satan immediately comes and takes away the word that is sown in them. [16] And these are the ones sown on rocky ground: when they hear the word, they immediately receive it with joy. [17] But they have no root, and endure only for a while; then, when trouble or persecution arises on account of the word, immediately they fall away.[c] [18] And others are those sown among the thorns: these are the ones who hear the word, [19] but the cares of the world, and the lure of wealth, and the desire for other things come in and choke the word, and it yields nothing. [20] And these are the ones sown on the good soil: they hear the word and accept it and bear fruit, thirty and sixty and a hundredfold.'[186]

Throughout these readings in Mark's Gospel my normal practice has been to take the text at face value, and to assume that it records what Jesus actually said. This passage requires us positively to decide whether or not Jesus said the words at the beginning of this passage. If he did not say them, then they might have evolved from Christian experience that the meanings of the parables were not clear, perhaps because their contexts had been lost, and perhaps also from Christians believing that the parables must have been designed to obscure rather than to reveal: an understanding encouraged by the Isaiah prophecy.[187] The interpretation given in the text might then have been a Christian attempt to understand the meaning of the parable, with the detail being a result of Christian experience.

If Jesus did say what Mark says that he said, then he was granting privileges to the twelve and to "those around him," whereas in relation to most of his actions it was to unrepentant sinners to whom privileges were granted. As reality is action, it is to Jesus' patterns of action that we must look if we want to know the truth about him, which suggests that while he might have spent time teaching his closest followers, he might not have privileged them with an interpretation of a parable that he did not give to the crowd. On the other hand, it is not impossible that Jesus decided to provide his disciples with a particular interpretation that might have been useful to them in their own ministries. And perhaps after Jesus told the parable, the Twelve and a few others gathered around him to ask for an interpretation whereas other people did not, rather than Jesus taking the initiative: so perhaps the origin of this passage is in the experience of an interpretation given to some and not to others. This would suggest that it was not Jesus who was making a distinction between insiders and outsiders, but people themselves deciding to which group they would belong.[188]

What was being granted to the group gathered around Jesus on that day was the revelation of the *mustērion* of the Kingdom of God: a secret that was now

c. Or *stumble*

revealed—that is, a secret of which the revelation was *given*. The *mustērion* of the Kingdom of God is not an object that we can receive and possess: it is a constant giving, a constant revealing, and the character of the pattern of action that is the revealing is a pattern of action of the Kingdom of God itself. But an act of giving can be received or rejected, or perhaps not even recognized for what it is: so there are some who receive the *mustērion*, and some who do not. So again, it might not be Jesus who is choosing who is "around him" and who is not, but the hearers of the parable who choose whether or not to be "around him." This interpretative possibility is in fact consistent with the context in which these verses are placed. The parable that Jesus has just offered makes it clear that it is the quality of the soil that determines whether the seed results in a harvest.[189]

The three lines beginning "they may indeed look . . ." are a quotation from the prophet Isaiah,[190] so maybe a further possibility is that Jesus was simply reflecting on the fact that his experience was similar to that of the other prophets who were heard but not understood. So was Jesus simply encouraging himself that he was not alone with this experience, and that it had in fact been prophesied and so was bound to occur?[191] Or was he saying something particular to his own activity? Perhaps that the Kingdom of God had come in his own person, that for the time being that was God's secret, that that is what the parable was about, and that his closest disciples had now been let into the secret?[192] Or that the parables would be heard but not understood, and so were not in practice communication of the Kingdom of God's coming, except for those gathered around him: so that the result of hearing the parables was that many of the hearers neither perceived nor understood?[193] Or perhaps that the parables would not function as invitations to live the life of the Kingdom of God because people hearing them would not turn and be forgiven, although those closest to Jesus might? The parables were often not understood, and quite often they did not result in their hearers changing the directions of their lives: so perhaps these elements of the text are the result of Christians employing a passage from the prophets to enable them to understand why so many people had not been changed when they heard Jesus tell his parables. So perhaps either Jesus or the early Christians, or perhaps both, understood that it was somehow God's intention that the parables should not be understood, just as it was God's intention that the words of the prophets should not be understood. Is this simply saying that the fact that Jesus is uniquely God has to be hidden if Jesus' life and death are to be a human life and a human death? God's revelation is a "veiled revelation": genuinely revelation, and genuinely veiled: hence Jesus' use of parables, which are revelation with hidden meanings, and his healing miracles, which are revelation frequently accompanied by a demand for secrecy.[194]

And perhaps this is one of those occasions when we wish that we could hear Jesus' tone of voice. If we could, then we might know whether the words were intended to be irony, and perhaps deeper irony than we might have thought: and we might also begin to wonder whether Isaiah was being equally ironic.[195] Perhaps in response to his disciples' question, Jesus is saying that they know the secret, when in fact they do not; and he says that he tells parables so that people cannot understand, whereas they were actually told because they were the best way to provide understanding.[196] Perhaps that is all there is to it: particularly as later in this chapter we find Jesus saying that whatever is secret will be revealed.[197] Speaking is a complex changing pattern of action, and all of it communicates: the words, the intonation, the facial expression—all of it is a single complex pattern of action, and the written text always crystallizes only a tiny part of it, and it is that minuscule crystallized pattern that we then receive and interpret through the complex changing patterns of action that constitute our brains, and so we are changed. We can choose to label what we receive as "straight statement," "irony," or something else, and how we label it, and therefore interpret it, will determine how the patterns of action that constitute us will be changed by what we read in Mark's Gospel.

As for why Jesus did use parables to communicate the Kingdom of God: He simply believed that they were the most appropriate type of discourse for doing that. The Kingdom might have come near, and it might have been slowly coming to birth, but it was not yet fully in evidence. The patterns of action that constitute the Kingdom of God really were difficult to perceive in the midst of the daily life of the time, and there was a great deal happening that was clearly not the Kingdom of God. It was because the Kingdom is patterns of action that are slowly emerging that the parable was the most appropriate vehicle for communication. A parable sets the mind to work and forces it to make connections; and at the same time it is not purely descriptive, and so does not restrict the understanding: for to restrict what we might be able to understand would reduce our ability to find the Kingdom of God at work in ways that might surprise us. The Kingdom of God, like all reality, is changing patterns of action. To attempt to describe it in some kind of literal way would be to treat the Kingdom of God as some kind of fixed reality, whereas that is precisely what it is not. It is the changing patterns of action of God: a dynamic reality in relation to which any grasp of it that we might experience can only be momentary. Any set of words that attempted to describe the Kingdom of God as if it was an object would fail to understand the Kingdom of God, whereas a parable is open to multiple and changing interpretations, and is thus entirely suited to the communication of a multiple and changing reality.

"To you has been given the secret of the kingdom of God." Those of us happier than first century Jews to use the name of God might translate this as "God has given to you the secret of the Kingdom of God." Here is what revelation is: God gives. It is not an object, it is a pattern of action: God gives; God reveals. And because God is Action and the source of all action, and God is changing patterns of action, the giving is always a new giving: new in every different time, and new in every different place. What God gives is the secret of the Kingdom of God: that it has already been lived in Jesus, that it is still lived in Jesus, that it is near, that it is coming, and that it will come.

The interpretation of the parable of the sower that we find in verses 13 to 20 is equally problematic in relation to the question as to whether Jesus spoke these words. If Jesus said these words then he was fixing the meaning of the parable and stopping the words of the parable from enabling his disciples to understand the Kingdom of God as a dynamic reality that has to be perceived anew in every moment. A possible explanation for the existence of this interpretation in Mark's Gospel is that it might have emerged from early Christian experience[198] and been in circulation in the churches that Mark knew, in either oral or written form, and so was travelling with the parable itself, so that both the parable and the interpretation arrived together as Mark was writing his account of Jesus' parables. But this is speculation, and it is perfectly possible, as we have suggested, that after Jesus had told the parable, those around him might have asked for its meaning and been given this particular interpretation or something like it.[199] What we do know is that this interpretation was made, so we must discuss it.

The interpretation of the parable that I have offered understands it as a promise of the Kingdom of God's coming: in spite of everything, it will come. If the detail of the sower and the seed means anything in particular, rather than being simply required by a narrative that leads to an abundant harvest, then it means Jesus' life of preaching and healing, and it means Jesus' living of the Kingdom of God, which is the same thing. It is the good news of the Kingdom of God that is sown, and so it is either God or Jesus that sows it—and Jesus might have been perfectly happy for the hearer to decide who was doing the sowing. The interpretation that we find in the gospel is very different from this. It is entirely individualized: it is about the effect of Jesus' words on the lives of individuals: or is it? There really is some genuine confusion here. The pattern of the text suggests that the seed represents Jesus' words: but then it is the hearers whom we find sown on the path, on rocky ground, among thorns, or "sown on the good soil."[200] Something strange has happened to this interpretation as different narrators or scribes have passed it on from person to person. We probably have two interpretations mixed up here: one that regards Jesus' hearers as the seed that gives birth to the Kingdom of God, and the other that understands the seed to represent Jesus' words. Either way, the parable is about individuals. It is individuals who hear the word. Satan might then "take away" the word; persecution might result in the individual "falling away"; and wealth, and the problems of daily life, might prevent Jesus' words from bearing fruit. And then there are some who "hear the word and accept it and bear fruit": presumably in terms of faith in Jesus and of a redirected life.

Even if Jesus did not intend such an allegorical interpretation, there is no reason to dismiss it as in some sense untrue to the parable.[201] The whole point of the parable form is to allow the hearer to make decisions about the parable's meaning so that they can integrate the meaning that they have discovered into their lives. But perhaps we should at least attempt to reconcile this interpretation with the one given in the previous section: and we can do that if we understand the interpretation in the text as an understanding of how the emerging Kingdom of God can affect the individual: and it may be that Jesus himself gave to his own parable such an interpretation in order to encourage individual faithfulness.[202] Just as the Kingdom of God as a whole can be compared to an abundant harvest, so the emergence in an individual of the changing patterns of action that constitute the Kingdom of God can be regarded as an abundant harvest. There need be no conflict between different interpretations: they will bear family resemblances to each other—and unusually in this instance we are able to define that likeness: it is constituted by the parable itself, and ultimately by Jesus telling the parable on a lakeside in Galilee about two thousand years ago.

If we are to "listen" to Jesus' parable of the sower then we shall need as many interpretations as we can get. We never access a text without interpreting it. The text on its own is changing patterns of action crystallized into pure pattern, and as we read the text the pattern engages with the changing patterns of action that constitute us, and it changes them, and therefore changes us. Interpretation is both essential and inevitable. To fix on just one interpretation will be to impoverish our understanding of the parable: conversely, to seek out the widest possible variety of interpretations will enrich our understanding of Jesus' words. And we might find ourselves particularly prizing those interpretations that relate to the ways in which the Kingdom of God relates to our own lives. Perhaps that is why some early Christian preacher or scribe attached to the parable the interpretation that we find in Mark's Gospel.

## MARK 4:21-25

> 21 He said to them, 'Is a lamp brought in to be put under the bushel basket, or under the bed, and not on the lampstand? 22 For there is nothing hidden, except to be disclosed; nor is anything secret, except to come to light. 23 Let anyone with ears to hear listen!' 24 And he said to them, 'Pay attention to what you hear; the measure you give will be the measure you get, and still more will be given you. 25 For to those who have, more will be given; and from those who have nothing, even what they have will be taken away.'[203]

Precisely how collections of Jesus' sayings came about is forever hidden from us; and so whether the sentences that make up this collection ever belonged to the same event we shall never know. Texts have effects: they impact the changing patterns of action that determine what we do, how we think, and who we are; so to take this collection of sentences as a single text will have different effects from treating it as separate sentences, each with its own effects. We shall treat the sentences separately.

What is light? It behaves as if it is particles, and it behaves as if it is wave motions: and not wave motions in some substance, but simply wave motions. This combination of behaviors means that if we understand reality as action in changing patterns, then light is action in changing patterns with a certain amount of stability about them.

Light passing through a narrow slit will split into a particular pattern that we interpret as the pattern that particles would generate, but there is no reason to think that solid particles—solid and unchanging beings—exist here. This is simply one of the patterns of action that we call light. And to take another pattern of action: in relation to other action in changing patterns, we interpret light as having a particular speed, and we understand other speeds in relation to the speed of light. Again we are discussing the patterns of action that we call light. There are wave motions that pass through solid objects (although no solid object is in fact solid in the normal meaning of that word. Objects that appear to us to be the most solid of objects—for instance, mountains—are in fact seething networks of changing patterns of action at every level). And there are wave motions that cannot penetrate the patterns of action that we call objects. Light is one of those wave motions: it is a pattern of action that cannot merge with and pass through solid-object patterns of action. A light source—a combination of changing patterns of action that emit the wave motions that we call light—will not light a room if the light is stopped by a well-made basket or a bed. Only if the light is unhindered will it light the room: that is, this action in patterns will impact other changing patterns of actions that will absorb some of the wave frequencies and emit others, sending colored light to the retinas in our eyes. A chain reaction emerges: changing patterns of action emitting the pattern of action that we call light; that pattern of action tangles with the changing patterns of action of objects in the room, and a new pattern of action results from the entanglement, which strikes the retina, and the changing pattern of action that constitutes its cells and the nerve cells behind them will then transmit patterns of action to parts of the brain—itself a vast network of action in changing patterns—which understands the changing patterns of action as color, and that color then contributes to a picture of objects in a room: a picture that is constructed across the networks of action in patterns from which our brains are constructed.

What does Jesus mean by this short parable about light? Perhaps that the Kingdom of God, and therefore Jesus himself, is "a lamp" that might at the moment appear to be "under the bushel basket," but that would one day be "on the lampstand," enabling everything "hidden" to be "disclosed" and "anything secret" to "come to light": hence the command to listen.[204] Earlier in this chapter we find an understanding that the good news of the Kingdom of God might be a secret shared only with a few, but we can now see that that could only be a temporary phase, and that any secrecy will be brought dramatically to an end. Not only is the hiddenness prior to the revelation, but it is for the very purpose of the revelation.[205] Jesus' ministry, and the Kingdom of God's hidden growth, are essential prerequisites for the Kingdom of God's final arrival. This is a changing pattern of action that is God's, Jesus's, and the Kingdom of God's changing pattern of action, which is why it must be the disciples' changing pattern of action as well.[206]

Parables can have multiple meanings, so perhaps Jesus is also asking his followers not to stop the action in changing patterns that constitute the Kingdom of God from emerging into the wider world, but rather to allow those changing patterns of action to tangle with the world around them so that recipients of the effects of those entanglements might understand the world anew as it is enlightened by the Kingdom of God. But how does the idea at the heart of the parable that hiddenness is for the purpose of revelation fit with the two interpretations that we now have of it?

Normally the whole point of hiding something is to keep it hidden, and the point of keeping something secret is to stop it from coming to light. The patterns of action that constitute hiding and keeping secret have these predictable effects on surrounding patterns of action unless new patterns of action impact them and release whatever is hidden or reveal whatever is secret. Jesus frequently inverted norms, and here he is inverting the norms of hiding and secrecy. Here the point of hiding something is to disclose it, and the point of keeping something secret is to reveal it. An analogy might be the wrapping of a gift. We wrap gifts with the intention of their recipients revealing them. The Kingdom of God is like such a gift: God has hidden it with the intention that it should be revealed in Jesus' teaching and healing ministry and in that of his disciples; and God has kept it a secret so that Jesus and his disciples can tell the world about it. And the same was true of Jesus' status as Messiah: initially kept secret—and the disciples were told to keep it secret—throughout the first half of the gospel, and subsequently revealed during the second half: and what was revealed was a Messiah whose task was to suffer.[207] These are God's changing patterns of action: the pattern of hiding—that is, enclosing—changing to the pattern of disclosing—that is, releasing; the pattern of keeping secret—enclosing—changing to the pattern of revealing—releasing; and above all the changing patterns of the Kingdom of God and of the giving of gifts. These are God's changing patterns of action, and they are those of Jesus, constituting him as God as well as as a human being like the rest of us.

The two sayings at the beginning of this passage end with a command to "listen": to pay attention and to be changed by what we hear; and the next two sayings begin with the same command: "Pay attention." The overall effect of the passage as a whole is intensified: these are sayings designed to change us by influencing the changing patterns of action that constitute who we are so that we become different people: because that is what we become when our patterns of action radically change.

"The measure you give will be the measure you get." Is this simply a statement of fact? That what we give to our families, to our communities, to our customers, to our vocations, and to whatever networks of changing patterns of action with which we engage, will determine to a large extent what they give to us? Yes, this might well be such a sensible and obvious statement. What Jesus is doing here is setting the stage for yet another transformation of a normative pattern of action. It is the second part of the sentence that matters: "and still more will be given you." God and the Kingdom of God do not operate in the way in which things normally work. They do not constitute a market economy. God and God's Kingdom give abundantly and take no notice of the extent to which we give. This somewhat contradicts other statements and parables that we find in the gospels, particularly in relation to forgiveness, where God's forgiveness of us appears to depend on our willingness to forgive others:[208] but still, this is what Jesus is saying here: that God's pattern of action is to keep on giving, so that is the character of the coming and already near Kingdom of God, and that is his character as well. The pattern of action at the heart of the Christian Faith is grace: a continual generous and unconditional giving. If we are to be followers of Jesus, then it is clear that this must be our pattern of action as well—a continual generous and unconditional giving of ourselves. Our giving will never match the unconditionality and generosity of Jesus's patterns of action, and the fact of God's generous and unconditional giving means that God's giving to us does not depend on our ability to emulate Jesus' generous and unconditional giving: but still, it is to such unconditional generous giving that we are invited. And not just ourselves as individuals. The Kingdom of God as well is constituted by changing patterns of action characterized by continual generous and unconditional giving, so the networks of changing patterns of action that constitute our societies, economies, and institutions must also be constantly entangled with patterns of action characterized by continual generous and unconditional giving. Some of them are: the UK's National Health Service is an obvious case, and so is the UK's unconditional Child Benefit. We could do with more of the same: the next obvious candidate is an unconditional income for every individual. By such means the Kingdom of God comes nearer to us as the patterns of action that constitute it become the patterns of action of our own societies and communities.

The final saying in this short collection really does seem to be a piece of observational economics. In the world as it is today, those who have much end up getting more, and those who have little find themselves losing what little they have. Inequality increases. This is the same message as that of the parable of the talents in Matthew's Gospel: the anxiety induced by having very little results in risk aversion and in failing to gain what those who have more are able to gain more easily.[209] There is no redeeming second part to this saying: no promise that something different is on the way. The patterns of action of this world will be with us for a while to come, and this final short saying draws our attention to them and presents us with a challenge: how will we change them so that the world becomes a signpost towards the Kingdom of God rather than a signpost away from it? Presumably Mark has included this saying at this point in his gospel because he understood it to have a spiritual meaning; or perhaps it had collected a spiritual meaning as it made its way through early Christian tradition.[210] We are of course at liberty to understand a similarly spiritual meaning: but if so then we ought also to recognize that when Jesus spoke these words he was probably referring to economic realities, and that that original meaning was a statement that the Kingdom of God requires a transformation of economics just as much as it requires a transformation of our spiritual lives.

## MARK 4:26–29

> 26 He also said, 'The kingdom of God is as if someone would scatter seed on the ground, ²⁷ and would sleep and rise night and day, and the seed would sprout and grow, he does not know how. ²⁸ The earth produces of itself, first the stalk, then the head, then the full grain in the head. ²⁹ But when the grain is ripe, at once he goes in with his sickle, because the harvest has come.'[211]

Fewer parables are recorded in Mark's Gospel than in the other gospels, and this is the only one that begins with the words "The kingdom of God is . . . ," although it is fairly clear that the other parables are at least potentially about the Kingdom of God. So what we have here is analogy: A story about scattering, sleeping, rising, sprouting, growing, not knowing, producing, ripening, and going to reap the harvest. The parable is all action, which suggests that, by analogy, the Kingdom of God is also all action: and because the Kingdom of God is the rule of God, the patterns of action that constitute the Kingdom of God are those that constitute God—and so God's patterns of action are scattering, sleeping, rising, sprouting, growing, not knowing, producing, ripening, and going to reap the harvest. And by starting with "The kingdom of God is as if . . . ," Jesus is relating the Kingdom of God to the whole of the story: so to the seed that sprouts, grows, and ripens, as well as to the farmer who scatters the seed, sleeps, rises, and goes to gather the harvest.

By the scattering, Jesus could mean either his own ministry, or God's constant relating to the people of Israel and to the world as a whole, through the act of creation, the giving of the law, the prophecy of the prophets, and, according to Psalm 19, through the created order itself. The Kingdom of God is here envisaged as a widely scattered reality. God's changing patterns of action are to be found all over time and space, and wherever those patterns of action are to be found, the Kingdom of God will come into existence. So now the Kingdom of God is both the farmer and the scattered seed: both the changing patterns of action that constitute God, and the same changing patterns of action in among the changing patterns of action that constitute the life of the world.

By the sleeping and rising, day by day, is Jesus simply drawing our attention to the passing of time, or is he indicating that the farmer remains busy with the farm even though he has no direct relationship with the way in which the crop is growing? The addition that the farmer "does not know how" the seed turns into the crop does not decide the matter. Perhaps Jesus meant both of the possible meanings of the sleeping and rising to be understood. What matters is that the crop continues to grow.

And the seed does sprout and grow. The Kingdom of God has come near, and there are signs of its coming, in Jesus' proclamation and healing, and across time and space. Just as Jesus' words about the secret are followed by a parable about revelation, so here hiddenness is followed by visibility.[212] Wherever we catch glimpses of the changing patterns of action that constitute God—those changing patterns of action that we find in Jesus—there we can see the Kingdom of God coming into existence. This is no one-way process. Signs of the Kingdom of God's coming can as easily disappear as they can emerge: but still we can find ever new signs of God's rule coming about.

It is the earth that produces "of itself," and the farmer "does not know" how the growth happens. We might have more understanding than they had in Jesus' time, but there is still a mystery about the germination of seed, the growth, the production of seed, the germination of seed, and so on, over and over again. If we take this detail seriously then God does not know how the Kingdom of God comes into existence. It is the earth—the planet, and everything that happens on it—that is where it all happens; and it happens in accordance with how the earth functions. The farmer plays no part in it. Is this true of God? Does God abandon the Kingdom's growth to us to manage? —to the planet, its people, its flora and fauna, it's tectonic plates, its oceans, and so on? Does God take no further hand in it? But perhaps we are not meant to find detailed meaning in every detail of the story. Perhaps the same question must be raised in relation to the parable of the sower:[213] Is the meaning of the parable located in its punchline, or is the detail meant to furnish the reader with the parable's meaning? Perhaps both: and if so, then we must take seriously the idea that God leaves us with the responsibility of ensuring the growth of the Kingdom of God, but that in the end it is God who will ensure that growth occurs.[214]

The grain ripens, and the sickle goes in to reap the crop. This is how the prophet Joel described a coming judgement on the nations around Israel:

> 12 Let the nations rouse themselves,
>> and come up to the valley of Jehoshaphat;
> for there I will sit to judge
>> all the neighbouring nations.
> [13] Put in the sickle,
>> for the harvest is ripe.
> Go in, tread,
>> for the wine press is full.
> The vats overflow,
>> for their wickedness is great.[215]

However, there is no sense in Jesus' parable of a judgment on some and not on others, or even of judgment. The prophet's imagery has been repurposed. The sickle reaping the crop is now the gathering of all of the nations into the Kingdom of God.

But which is the harvest? The ripened crop, or the harvested crop? The perfect tense of "The harvest has come" could mean either of these. Perhaps the meanings are in fact the same meaning. When the Kingdom of God is fully come, God's will will be done, God's rule will have arrived, the changing patterns of action that constitute God and that constitute Jesus will be the changing patterns of action that all of us somehow inhabit and exercise. Not only will we live in that completion, characterized by God's patterns of action, but because we shall be constituted by God's changing patterns of action, we shall be God in that sense: not the source of action, and not experiencing and exercising all of the changing patterns of action that constitute God, but still experiencing and exercising patterns of action that constitute God. We shall be "in God": so the ripening of the harvest and the gathering of the harvest are the same thing: or rather, are the same changing patterns of action. This is the punchline, and so even if the rest of the detail is meant to be only preliminary to the sentence at the end, the message of the parable is that the Kingdom of God will come, we shall belong to that Kingdom of God, and the Kingdom of God and therefore we ourselves will find ourselves experiencing and exercising the changing patterns of action that constitute God.

We don't need to decide whether the details of the story are meant to be detailed analogies of the Kingdom of God, or that it is the punchline that matters and everything else is designed to draw our attention to it. Diverse interpretation is entirely in order. No word or string of words has a fixed meaning, so what meanings any of us draw from parables such as this one really will be up to us, and all of our interpretations will be different. Each sentence, each phrase, and each word of this parable can be interpreted in widely different ways. But whatever meanings we develop, we cannot escape the beginning of the passage: "The kingdom of God is as if . . . ." One thing that we cannot escape is that Jesus intended the parable to be about the Kingdom of God. This is non-negotiable: so however we interpret the text, we must draw attention to the Kingdom of God, and must treat the parable as if it is about the Kingdom of God. We might treat the farmer as the Kingdom of God, but we might not. What we cannot avoid is the fact that in this parable the harvest is the Kingdom of God, and that the parable is an invitation to us to conform our lives to that Kingdom of God, and to see them transformed so that they more nearly experience and exercise the changing patterns of action that constitute God. In that sense we become God: except that we don't, because God is Action and the source of action, as well as being particular changing patterns of action. In this life all we can ask for and aim at is to reflect in the activity of our own lives the changing patterns of action that we see in Jesus. We shall never be Action and the source of action, but what we can legitimately hope for is to see the changing patterns of action that constitute God being experienced and exercised by us, partially in this life, and finally in the next. We hope for the continuation of the patterns of action that constitute who we are, and that these will be conformed to those changing patterns of action that we find in Jesus Christ. If that were to become so for every aspect of the created order, then the Kingdom of God will have come.

## MARK 4:30-34

> 30 He also said, 'With what can we compare the kingdom of God, or what parable will we use for it? [31] It is like a mustard seed, which, when sown upon the ground, is the smallest of all the seeds on earth; [32] yet when it is sown it grows up and becomes the greatest of all shrubs, and puts forth large branches, so that the birds of the air can make nests in its shade.'
>
> 33 With many such parables he spoke the word to them, as they were able to hear it; [34] he did not speak to them except in parables, but he explained everything in private to his disciples.[216]

Jesus here makes an explicit connection between parables and comparisons. The parables are designed to tell his hearers what the Kingdom of God is like. And yet again he offers a parable of growth. A tiny seed is sown, and it grows, and it puts forth branches. But what is the meaning here? The huge growth—"the greatest of all shrubs . . . large branches"—or the fact that birds make nests in the bush? Multiple meanings are surely a possibility: The Kingdom of God just keeps on growing; Jesus' ministry in Galilee and its initial success might look less than impressive, but God would still bring in the Kingdom of God;[217] and there is room in the Kingdom for everyone.

The parable echoes a passage from the prophet Ezekiel:

> 22 Thus says the Lord God:
> I myself will take a sprig
> > from the lofty top of a cedar;
> > I will set it out.
> I will break off a tender one
> > from the topmost of its young twigs;
> I myself will plant it
> > on a high and lofty mountain.
> [23] On the mountain height of Israel
> > I will plant it,
> in order that it may produce boughs and bear fruit,
> > and become a noble cedar.
> Under it every kind of bird will live;
> > in the shade of its branches will nest
> > winged creatures of every kind.[218]

This follows a passage about God's judgement on unfaithful Israel, and in that context it represents God doing something new. The new thing will not look much to start with, but it will grow huge, and a wide variety of wildlife will find a home there, presumably meaning that many nations will dwell together in the new community that God will found.

But why did Jesus not tell a parable about a cedar tree? Maybe there were no longer many cedars for Jesus to refer to. They had all been culled, so Jesus chose a plant with which his hearers might have been better acquainted: but the message was the same. Or perhaps there was another reason for choosing a shrub rather than a tree. Might the choice of a shrub have been an indication that the Kingdom of God would be human-sized: for individual children of God, from whichever nations they might come? A human-sized shrub to represent a human-shaped Kingdom of God, perhaps? And perhaps there was another reason for choosing a mustard plant: If the seed pods ripen and crack, then tiny seeds can be scattered over a wide area, resulting in rather more mustard plants than the landowner might have intended. Perhaps this pattern of action represents a pattern of action that constitutes the Kingdom of God: once it has taken root it not only grows into a human-shaped community, but its patterns of action continue to spread and are difficult to control.[219]

Using language is always a matter of comparing: it is an active process, a changing pattern of action. Our brains connect with spoken and written words, and with spoken and written sentences, and connect them with other words and sentences. And those will always have been connected with other words and sentences, so a vast network of connections takes shape: a changing network, because every new word added to the network, and every new combination of words, will change all of the others in the network: and then the next moment all of the words and sentences will be in new contexts, and so will experience different connections, constantly creating new networks. Language is never fixed: meanings constantly evolve. So Jesus' parable of the mustard seed would have meant one thing to a wealthy man who owned a field, and another to someone desperate to plunder the field for firewood. And the meaning of the parable will be entirely different today from what it was when Jesus told it to the crowd. Many city-dwellers today have neither fields nor gardens, and might not regularly see trees at all. For them the image will be either meaningless, or its meaning will be positively alien, declaring the Kingdom of God to be not for them. We must therefore be at liberty to tell new parables: perhaps "The Kingdom of God is like a tiny hamlet with just three cottages, and it grows into a vast city, and millions of people from all over the world come to live in it." Changing the words might convey a meaning more similar to that of Jesus' parable in its original context than would a telling of Jesus' parable today. And perhaps this exercise reveals another possibility: that in this parable "Kingdom of God" should become "City of God": again because the different words might carry a meaning more similar to the original meaning of "Kingdom of God" than the words "Kingdom of God" might carry today.

Language constantly evolves, as does everything else: which suggests another relationship—that there are no boundaries between language and everything else. All of it is changing patterns of action, and all of it relates to all of it. To see an object is to experience pulses in the brain relating to other pulses, and all of it is the result of light striking the retina, which in turn results from light striking the object. Everywhere there is action in changing patterns. And language is pulses in the brain connecting with networks of pulses, and all of it is the result of sound waves reacting with the eardrum, which in turn result from the speaker omitting sound waves by vibrating their vocal cords and moving their mouth, which in turn is the result of pulses in their brain. All of it is physical reality: not in the sense of some fixed solid entity, but in the sense that all of it is action in changing patterns. Such connections are easier to express within a conceptual structure based on reality as action in changing patterns. A conceptual structure based on beings that might change makes it difficult to draw comparisons between language and objects in the world, whereas a conceptual structure based on action that might occasionally and temporarily fall into patterns which then continue to change makes it easier to compare language with objects. Spoken language is action in changing patterns, and written language is relatively static patterns that have resulted from changing patterns of action in its authors and translators and that result in changing patterns of action in its readers.

The second paragraph of this passage reveals a social hierarchy. Jesus appears to have chosen particular people to assist with the proclamation of the Kingdom of God and with healing people as a sign of the Kingdom's coming: but it is also clear that no status was being ascribed. They were being chosen for a task. And of course, it may well be that Jesus spoke differently to the "disciples," his more dedicated followers. He needed to educate them sufficiently to enable them to prepare towns and villages for his arrival, and to ensure that they could speak truthfully about the Kingdom of God. He might also have wanted to see a particular lifestyle lived out among them, so education in a pattern of life that cohered with the life of the Kingdom of God would have been important. However, this passage in Mark's Gospel hints at more than that. By suggesting a contrast between what was taught to the crowd and what was taught to the disciples, a social hierarchy is conveyed. This might be what Jesus intended, but it might also be what emerged among the apostles and other close disciples, both during Jesus' ministry and after it, as the church evolved as an institution.

Institutions evolve. An institution is not an object: it is not a fixed entity of some kind. It is not best described as a being. The community of Jesus' disciples was a shifting network of individual people, each of whom was a vast network of changing patterns of action, and between whom complex networks of relationships evolved and constantly changed. After Jesus' resurrection, the network of disciples evolved into a loose association of followers of Jesus who experienced themselves as empowered by the Holy Spirit: by the Spirit of Jesus; and as all institutions do, this one then started to formalize and to develop networks of relationships that had more of a stable pattern to them. Those now vast networks of changing relationships continued to spread and change, and sometimes to settle into what might have looked like a fixed pattern: but then the context would have changed, the institution would have adapted to it, and so the pattern of action would have changed over and over again. The church has never experienced a period during which change has not happened, and it never will. Reality is action in changing patterns, so although change might sometimes be fast and sometimes slow, there will be nothing that is not action in changing patterns. Social and economic institutions change all the time, and individuals change all the time, so the church—an institution among other institutions—must change all the time, and all of the church's members must change all the time.

Is there *anything* that doesn't change? Does the gospel—the good news of Jesus Christ—change? Yes, it does. Its changing patterns of action are permanently connected to the changing patterns of action that constituted Jesus and his disciples in Galilee through the changing networks of patterns of action that have constituted the world and the church through the past two thousand years, and they are permanently connected with God, who is always the source of all action and so in that sense is a permanent and unchanging reality: but although being the source of all action can only be a mystery to us—although perhaps one that will one day be revealed—God is towards us particular changing patterns of action, and God's reality as Action itself could not be further from beings, Being, the unchanging, the unitary, rest, and the static. God is the absolutely dynamic reality; the world as a whole and everything in it are entirely dynamic realities; the meanings of words change all the time; our actions change their meanings all the time . . . . There is nothing that is not action, movement, diversity, change, and dynamic. There is nothing at all that does not change: not Christian doctrine; not Christian living; not Christian proclamation; not healing . . . . Above all, the church changes all the time. Every member changes all the time, and the institution of the church as a whole is a vast seething network of action in changing patterns. The church and all of its members have their roots in events back in history: do those events not remain unchanged, so giving a solid and unchanging basis to the church? No, they do not. There might be a sense in which the events do not change: but because reality is action in changing patterns, anything about historic events that is not action in changing patterns has no reality. Any reality that historic events now have is the changing patterns of action that constitute them today: that is, the events conveyed and interpreted across two thousand years. Events never stop: they never cease to influence future patterns of action. It is not simply that our interpretations of the events change: the events themselves—or rather, anything about them that is action in changing patterns—constantly change across history and today. It is not that there are fixed events and changing interpretations: anything about the events that relates to us simply has to be dynamic, and there is no element of that relationship that does not change. History is constantly rewritten because the events change.

The church changes, with nothing left unchanged: so although it is possible that Jesus implemented a social hierarchy among his disciples, it is equally possible that Mark recorded in his Gospel the situation that he found in the church of his own day—presumably with different kinds of education being given to different groups of Christians, and in general an evolving social structure in which statuses were ascribed—and that he wrote that situation back into Jesus' context. We still find the church selecting different groups for different treatment, and we still find the ascription of status.

Just like Jesus' hearers back then, we hear his teaching "as we are able to hear it." Because his words have to connect with the existing changing patterns of action that constitute our brains, there might be some words and sentences that we are simply not able to process, and particularly words and sentences that we cannot process at the point at which they are heard or read. The disciples were becoming used to hearing Jesus teach, so they would have slowly developed a capacity for hearing it and for explaining it to others they met. But someone who might have heard of Jesus for the first time, and had gone to hear him preach, would not have developed the capacity to hear the teachings that Jesus gave to his disciples, but were able to hear the parables and at least begin to receive something from them. A natural hierarchy of understanding would then have developed: but still no statuses were being ascribed, except those based on Jesus' statements that the first would be last and the first last, and that tax-collectors and sinners would enter the Kingdom of God before the chief priests and elders.[220]

## MARK 4:35-41

> 35 On that day, when evening had come, he said to them, 'Let us go across to the other side.' 36 And leaving the crowd behind, they took him with them in the boat, just as he was. Other boats were with him. 37 A great gale arose, and the waves beat into the boat, so that the boat was already being swamped. 38 But he was in the stern, asleep on the cushion; and they woke him up and said to him, 'Teacher, do you not care that we are perishing?' 39 He woke up and rebuked the wind, and said to the sea, 'Peace! Be still!' Then the wind ceased, and there was a dead calm. 40 He said to them, 'Why are you afraid? Have you still no faith?' 41 And they were filled with great awe and said to one another, 'Who then is this, that even the wind and the sea obey him?'[221]

This passage begins a section of Mark's Gospel full of action, of an increasing sense of excitement, and of Jesus' authority;[222] and this account in particular is full of movement and change. The verb tenses heighten the sense of action: the verbs that structure the first part of the event are in the present tense, which contrasts them with the imperfect tense used to describe continuing aspects of the situation; and the aorist (point-in-time past) tense is used for Jesus' decisive action that delivers an immediate calming of the sea.[223] Reality is action, change, movement, diversity, and generally dynamic. The sea is quintessentially real. So is everything else, because everything is action, change, movement, diverse, and dynamic: but the sea so obviously has this character that it might be the best image that we can offer for the nature of reality. Of course, there are patterns in the action. Water molecules remain water molecules: but those too are better understood as action in patterns rather than as objects of any kind. At that level, the sea is relatively stable patterns of action; and gravity—itself changing patterns of action—ensures that the body of an ocean and its surface remain fairly stable patterns of action: but throughout, and at every level, the patterns change. The sea is changing patterns of action. It is superbly real.

Because we cannot see the air for most of the time, it is not such an obvious image for reality, but it is just as quintessentially real as is the sea. At every level, the planet's atmosphere is action in changing patterns; and when the air above the sea is particularly turbulent, the water closest to the ocean's surface can also become particularly turbulent. There are no boundaries here. The air and the sea become a single vast sea of action in changing patterns. A certain amount of separation continues to be maintained by the pull of gravity on the water, but there is no separation of the patterns of action that are the sea and the air above it. The whole is turbulent action in changing patterns.

And neither are there any boundaries between the changing patterns of action of the sea and the atmosphere, and the changing patterns of the boat and its occupants. Nothing is insulated from anything else. The combination of the moving air and the moving sea, and the force of gravity, cause the boat to tip from the horizontal, to be pushed upwards by the rising water, and to be pulled down again by gravity as the water falls, so that water sloshes into the boat. And the combination of all of those changing patterns of action impact the bodies of the disciples, and of the sailors in the other boats, and the connections between the movements of their bodies, and the brain's processing of the light waves reaching their eyes and the sound waves reaching their ears, cause the patterns of action that constitute their brains to change into a pattern of action that we might call "terrified." But not Jesus. He was asleep: changing patterns of action of the brain that repair the patterns of action of the body, and particularly of the brain, that have suffered particular turbulence during the day. In sleep, light waves no longer impact the retina, and sound waves might have to be particularly insistent if they are to break through the brain's existing activity, and similarly in relation to someone shaking the rest of the body: but eventually the sleep patterns of action are invaded—so Jesus woke up to the cries of his frightened disciples.

Jesus uttered words of rebuke to the air and the sea—changing patterns of action in the air—and the patterns of action that constituted his brain changed: and the changing patterns of action were his, and they were God's, and the patterns of action that constituted the sea and the atmosphere were changed. The words "Peace! Be still!" were creative, just as God's words at the creation gave birth to new changing patterns of action.[224] As the formless chaos was given new patterns then, and as God's controlling of the sea and its contents was God's creative and sustaining activity,[225] so now the sea and the air experienced new changing patterns of action.

There are echoes here of a prophecy in Daniel. Four beasts emerge from the sea, God's court sits in judgement, one beast is killed, the others have their dominion removed from them, and then comes the "one like a human being[b] coming with the clouds of heaven" to be presented to the Ancient One.[226] Jesus might have expected the disciples to hear echoes of this passage, and of the creation story at the beginning of the book of Genesis, in his defeat of the sea's turbulence, and particularly the passages in the psalms in which God is asleep, is called on to awake and save Israel, and stills the waves;[227] and it appears that the disciples did make such connections. Many early Jewish Christians suffering persecution would certainly have heard these echoes.[228] Jesus was God, creating order out of formless chaos, and rescuing those being submerged by deadly turbulence; and he was the Son of Man who would rule once evil had been defeated. And again we have a changing pattern of action that we find throughout Mark's Gospel, and particularly at the end: evil appears to be in control, but Jesus defeats it.[229]

The rebuke to the disciples hardly seems fair. Fishermen were well aware of the possible consequences of storms. Their reactions were perfectly natural under the circumstances. So what did Jesus mean by the suggestion that if they had had faith then they would not have been afraid? "Faith is the assurance of things hoped for, the conviction of things not seen."[230] Faith is patterns of action in the brain that relate to a situation that is not the one represented by the sense data that our brains are collecting and processing. When the images and sound waves were so insistently terrifying, it's surely a bit much to expect the disciples to exercise patterns of action that we might call faith that God would preserve Jesus and themselves for the tasks ahead, and that therefore they did not need to fear the storm. It would have been difficult to submerge the changing patterns of action driven along by the sights and sounds of the storm around them. And it was not entirely true that the disciples had no faith. After all, they did wake Jesus and expect him to be able to do something about the storm. Their faith that the Kingdom of God would come, and that they were seeing signs of its coming, would have been growing: but it was also no doubt true that their faith was not strong, and that immediate sensations could easily compromise it.

Awe was clearly an appropriate new pattern of action for them, as was the question that they could not resist asking themselves: "Who then is this?" This was Jesus,

b. Aram *one like a son of man*

constituted by changing patterns of action that were the changing patterns of action that constituted God as well as changing patterns of action that constituted him as the human being that he was. It was God's creative action that they had witnessed. There never had been a boundary between God's changing patterns of action and the changing patterns of action that constitute the cosmos and everything in it: but now that absence of a boundary has become clear to them, and they are appropriately awe-struck. Understandably the disciples ask: "Who then is this, that even the wind and the sea obey him?" No answer is given, which suggests that Mark is directing the question to us, his readers.[231] The written question is a crystallized pattern of action, which means that it is pure pattern, which in turn means that the patterns of action that constitute who we are will engage with this pure pattern and will be changed by it. Underlying the text is a question spoken by the disciples, perhaps with significant force and emotion behind it, and the pure pattern of the text communicates that spoken question to us, so that it is the disciples who address us here, asking us to decide who Jesus is. We might offer this response: This individual sitting in the boat was unlike any other in the sense that the changing patterns of action that constituted who he was were by God's action uniquely those that constituted God. In everyone else, the changing patterns of action that constitute God relate to the changing patterns of action that constitute human beings, but there are inevitable incompatibilities, which imply boundaries between the changing patterns of action that constitute God and some of those that constitute the people to whom God has related. But in Jesus there are no such incompatibilities, and no such boundaries. Here, in this person in their boat who was catching up on his sleep, there was someone utterly unique in whom they had witnessed the creative action of God.

The stories and teachings that we find in the gospels represent a very small proportion of the things that Jesus did and said during his journeys around Galilee, around the surrounding areas, and to Jerusalem. Vast amounts have been lost. What we have in the gospels is accounts passed from individual to individual, from Christian community to Christian community, first in verbal form and then in writing: and those accounts will have been passed from generation to generation because the patterns of action that they represented somehow meshed with the patterns of action that constituted the church at the time. This particular story, in which Jesus' words still the turbulence and rescue his followers, must have been particularly meaningful for churches suffering persecution of one kind or another, or simply suffering internal or external turbulence of some kind. The telling or the reading of the story in the congregation would have enabled the members of the church to relive the event, to experience afresh the changing patterns of action of the storm, of Jesus' disciples' reaction to it, and of Jesus' stilling of the waves, and they would have married those patterns of action to the changing patterns of action in their minds in relation to the experiences of the church in their own time. A certain coherence will have been experienced between those patterns of action: and then new faith and confidence would have been brought about by Jesus' "Peace! Be still!" now addressed to their own circumstances. The disciples had been saved through the storm, so they would be.

We are living many years after those early communicators of the story, but still the patterns of action in our minds that relate to the turbulence of our own world find themselves in relation to the patterns of action of the storm, of the boat, of the disciples, and of Jesus. We experience coherence between them, and we still hear "Peace! Be still!" addressed to the world in which we live. And the call for greater faith is addressed to us as it was to the disciples; and we too experience awe, and we ask "Who then is this?". We might not put the answer in the same way that the early Christians would have answered that question, but the verdict will be the same: This Jesus is changing patterns of action that are God.

## MARK 5:1-20

5 They came to the other side of the lake, to the country of the Gerasenes.[d] ² And when he had stepped out of the boat, immediately a man out of the tombs with an unclean spirit met him. ³ He lived among the tombs; and no one could restrain him any more, even with a chain; ⁴ for he had often been restrained with shackles and chains, but the chains he wrenched apart, and the shackles he broke in pieces; and no one had the strength to subdue him. ⁵ Night and day among the tombs and on the mountains he was always howling and bruising himself with stones. ⁶ When he saw Jesus from a distance, he ran and bowed down before him; ⁷ and he shouted at the top of his voice, 'What have you to do with me, Jesus, Son of the Most High God? I adjure you by God, do not torment me.' ⁸ For he had said to him, 'Come out of the man, you unclean spirit!' ⁹ Then Jesus[e] asked him, 'What is your name?' He replied, 'My name is Legion; for we are many.' ¹⁰ He begged him earnestly not to send them out of the country. ¹¹ Now there on the hillside a great herd of swine was feeding; ¹² and the unclean spirits[f] begged him, 'Send us into the swine; let us enter them.' ¹³ So he gave them permission. And the unclean spirits came out and entered the swine; and the herd, numbering about two thousand, rushed down the steep bank into the lake, and were drowned in the lake.

14 The swineherds ran off and told it in the city and in the country. Then people came to see what it was that had happened. ¹⁵ They came to Jesus and saw the demoniac sitting there, clothed and in his right mind, the very man who had had the legion; and they were afraid. ¹⁶ Those who had seen what had happened to the demoniac and to the swine reported it. ¹⁷ Then they began to

d. Other ancient authorities read *Gergesenes*; others, *Gadarenes*
e. Gk *he*
f. Gk *they*

beg Jesus[g] to leave their neighbourhood. [18] As he was getting into the boat, the man who had been possessed by demons begged him that he might be with him. [19] But Jesus[h] refused, and said to him, 'Go home to your friends, and tell them how much the Lord has done for you, and what mercy he has shown you.' [20] And he went away and began to proclaim in the Decapolis how much Jesus had done for him; and everyone was amazed.[232]

Jesus is now extending his ministry beyond mainly Jewish territory into the much more diverse population on the other side of Lake Galilee. The very fact that pigs were being kept implies Gentile farmers, because as far as Jews are concerned pigs are unclean animals and are not to be eaten.

As soon as Jesus arrives, another casting out event unfolds. Again the evil spirits—for this time there is more than one—know who Jesus is, and they use his name in an attempt to control him. They fail, and are forced to provide their own name.[233] The encounter results in the possessed man being healed, the evil spirits' request to enter the pigs—perhaps motivated by a desire to avoid the suffering that would result from Jesus' final victory over evil[234]—and the pigs being drowned in the lake. Quite why Jesus consented to the evil spirits' request to enter the pigs we simply cannot know. It would appear to be a bizarre and cruel thing to do, and perhaps it was.[235] But that was not the end of the story. The people of the town asked Jesus to leave. It would appear that they did not ask him to leave because the pigs had been drowned—perhaps it was Jews who had come to see what had happened, and if so they might not have been too worried about a herd of pigs. What seems to have perturbed the people of the town was finding the man in his right mind. Perhaps they had become accustomed to the mad person among the tombs; perhaps they were unsure what kinds of evil Jesus might cast out next—perhaps evil practices that benefited them; and perhaps it was simply that they could not cope with new things happening.

Is there a political meaning to this story? Does the man living among the tombs represent the conquered peoples of the Roman empire? He has been possessed by a "legion," which was the Roman method of domination.[236] Is Jesus, and now Mark, offering an acted parable which is a statement that Jesus will defeat the kingdoms of this world and bring in his own Kingdom of God? Is the death of the pigs, which were regarded by Jews as unclean, a statement that Jesus was cleansing the territory to prepare it for the Kingdom of God's coming?[237] Is this story a statement that Jesus is the "one like a son of man" who will receive authority to rule the nations? Quite probably: and if so, then the way in which the occupying forces might have been able to interpret Jesus' words and actions might have been another reason for the local population's desire to see the back of Jesus. Their lives were difficult enough, and the thought of Rome sensing rebellion and crushing it might have been rather unwelcome.

g. Gk *him*
h. Gk *he*

Jesus' disciples would by now have been used to him doing new things: healing on the sabbath; announcing the forgiveness of sins; declaring them to be his family; and casting out demons: and now he had done another new thing, this time with a legion of evil spirits involved, and possibly with a political edge to the action. Jesus did not stay in towns in which he was not wanted, and he taught his disciples not to stay where they were not welcome.[238] Jesus' presence either attracted or repelled. Where he and his disciples were welcomed they would proclaim the coming Kingdom of God; and where they were not, they would regard the people who rejected them as already judged by their actions. That would certainly have been true in at least one sense: to reject the bringer of the good news of the Kingdom of God was to reject the Kingdom of God—both the Kingdom of God as it was already lived in Jesus' ministry, and the repentance and belief that would have drawn them into the Kingdom of God already in evidence among them.

Jesus was scary. This is important. The actions in changing patterns that constituted Jesus were those of God, shining a bright light into evil corners with an intensity and an integrity that must have been hard to bear. The many weaknesses of Peter's character were frequently brought to light, as were the sins of the people Jesus encountered. Jesus was certainly experienced as scary by the people of the town in the country of the Gerasenes, which is why they asked him to leave.

The man from whom Jesus had cast out the demons did not ask Jesus to leave. He wanted to travel with Jesus: but Jesus told him to go home to his friends, which means that he must have had some, at least at some point. He was to tell them what had happened to him. He did not just tell his friends: he told the entire region.

Words are important. The word translated as showing mercy is *ēleēsen*, which is the past tense of "to have mercy." The Greek translation of the Hebrew scriptures that the gospel writers would have known had used this verb to translate the Hebrew *chesed*, loving-kindness. This did not mean "mercy," which implies that a punishment had been remitted, but rather an overflowing generous love. This means that here Jesus might have used the word *chesed*, or possibly an Aramaic variant of it. So Jesus was telling the man to "tell them how much the Lord has done for you, and what loving-kindness he has shown to you." There is no sense that he had committed a sin for which he had been forgiven. It was simply God's generous love that had cast the evil out of him.

The use of the words "Lord" and "Jesus" is equally important. Jesus told the man to tell what "the Lord" had done for him. For a Jew "the Lord" would have meant God. Whether the man was a Jew we are not told, but the disciples were Jews, and they would have heard "God" when Jesus used "the Lord": a name frequently used of God whose name *Yahweh* was not normally pronounced by Jews. But when the man went into the towns of the Decapolis, the "ten towns," he told them what *Jesus* had done for him. He had made the connection. The one who had done this was Jesus and it was

God. The releasing of someone from evil was God's work, and Jesus had done God's work and so was God. For this man, reality was patterns of action. "Demoniac" in the translation might be better translated "the one who had been possessed by a demon"; and this man was now "clothed and right-minded": he had put on clothes, and his mind had been put right.[239] And for Jesus to exhibit the patterns of action that were God's patterns of action was to identify Jesus as God.

This passage asks of us in a particularly clear way: What has the Lord done for us? What has God done for us? What has Jesus done for us? What change has happened to us? And how will that relate to the people among whom we live? —for that is the question that now faced the man who had been freed from evil spirits, and one that has faced Christians ever since.[240]

The broader question that must be the context for asking that one is this: How do people relate to each other? If we are constituted by changing patterns of action, then relationships between people must be relationships between changing patterns of action: so it is our actions towards each other that relate us to each other. It is what I do for my wife, my children, my friends, and so on, that constitute my relationships with them. There is no such thing as a non-active relationship. Relationship, like everything else, is a matter of action in changing patterns, and is not some unchanging static reality. It is across vast networks of actions in changing patterns that families, friendships, communities, nations, and so on form relationships within them and between them. Our words are action in changing patterns; what we do for other people is action in changing patterns; if we sent an email then it might be pure pattern, but it is our changing patterns of action that have given it birth, and the changing patterns of action of the recipient will be changed by the pattern and thus by our changing patterns of action. Our feelings are changing patterns of action, and they affect what we say and do, so they are integral to our relationships: and perhaps more directly than we might think, because there are clearly subtle changes across the vast and complex network of action in changing patterns that constitute the universe that form elements of our relationships. If two electrons in different parts of the universe can continue to affect each other if they have ever related to each other, then it would be surprising if relationships between people were to consist entirely of relationships that we could track across the changing patterns of action that we knew to constitute the people involved. The ways in which two people who know each other well can transfer their moods to each other is a clear sign that relationships are highly complex and little understood.

The relationship between Jesus and God will forever be a mystery to us, but because we can say that the changing patterns of action that are Jesus are uniquely those of God, as well as being the changing patterns of action of his humanity, we can begin to understand how in this passage Jesus' "what the Lord has done for you" could be interpreted by the liberated man as "how much Jesus has done for me."[241] We can say the same. Whatever it is that Jesus has done for us is what God has done for us. Here is the beginning of Christology: the understanding of the relationship between Jesus and God. Christology is about action in changing patterns. And here is the beginning of what it is to be a Christian, a follower of Jesus: it is to be changed by Jesus—by the changing patterns of action that he is; and it is do with Jesus the patterns of action that are his: to proclaim with him, to heal with him, to cast out evil with him, to believe and hope with him, and with him to long for the Kingdom of God's coming.

## MARK 5:21-43

21 When Jesus had crossed again in the boat[h] to the other side, a great crowd gathered round him; and he was by the lake. 22 Then one of the leaders of the synagogue named Jairus came and, when he saw him, fell at his feet 23 and begged him repeatedly, 'My little daughter is at the point of death. Come and lay your hands on her, so that she may be made well, and live.' 24 So he went with him.

And a large crowd followed him and pressed in on him. 25 Now there was a woman who had been suffering from haemorrhages for twelve years. 26 She had endured much under many physicians, and had spent all that she had; and she was no better, but rather grew worse. 27 She had heard about Jesus, and came up behind him in the crowd and touched his cloak, 28 for she said, 'If I but touch his clothes, I will be made well.' 29 Immediately her haemorrhage stopped; and she felt in her body that she was healed of her disease. 30 Immediately aware that power had gone forth from him, Jesus turned about in the crowd and said, 'Who touched my clothes?' 31 And his disciples said to him, "You see the crowd pressing in on you; how can you say, "Who touched me?' 32 He looked all round to see who had done it. 33 But the woman, knowing what had happened to her, came in fear and trembling, fell down before him, and told him the whole truth. 34 He said to her, 'Daughter, your faith has made you well; go in peace, and be healed of your disease.'

35 While he was still speaking, some people came from the leader's house to say, 'Your daughter is dead. Why trouble the teacher any further?' 36 But overhearing[i] what they said, Jesus said to the leader of the synagogue, 'Do not fear, only believe.' 37 He allowed no one to follow him except Peter, James, and John, the brother of James. 38 When they came to the house of the leader of the synagogue, he saw a commotion, people weeping and wailing loudly. 39 When he had entered, he said to them, 'Why do you make a commotion and weep? The child is not dead but sleeping.' 40 And they laughed at him. Then he put them all outside, and took the child's father and mother and those who were with him, and went in where the child was. 41 He took her by the hand and

h. Other ancient authorities lack *in the boat*
i. Or *ignoring*; other ancient authorities read *hearing*

> said to her, 'Talitha cum,' which means, 'Little girl, get up!' ⁴² And immediately the girl got up and began to walk about (she was twelve years of age). At this they were overcome with amazement. ⁴³ He strictly ordered them that no one should know this, and told them to give her something to eat.[242]

Everything in this complex narrative is action, movement, and change. Again Jesus arrives, a crowd gathers, and something different happens: it is a leader of the synagogue who comes to ask for help. There was clearly diversity of views about Jesus among the religious institutions of his time. It would appear that some of the Pharisees could see that Jesus might have been a prophet of God. His ideas made them feel uncomfortable, but the ancient prophets were clearly discomfiting to the national and religious leaders of their times, so they ought not to have been surprised that Jesus was having a similar effect: something that some of them clearly understood. We find some of the scribes, the lawyers, against Jesus, and some of them apparently genuinely interested in what he had to say. The synagogues, the local places of prayer and of the reading of the scriptures, were probably quite autonomous, so it would be no surprise to find diversity of view about religiously important matters, just as we find diversity of view about important matters among the religious institutions of any of today's religious traditions. Jesus clearly had no problem responding to this man's request. Whether it was a man living in the cemetery, a blind man begging by the roadside, or a respected citizen in an important official position, Jesus' heart went out to them, and he healed, in order to serve the immediate need and to provide a sign of the Kingdom of God's impending arrival.

During the journey a woman approached Jesus. Menstruation turned women into temporary outcasts, so more frequent losses of blood could cause extreme social isolation. The social stigma attached to this woman's condition caused her to try to conceal her approach. But power had gone out of Jesus as soon as the woman simply touched his clothes. All of us are action in changing patterns, and there are no solid boundaries around us. What we might call our own changing patterns of action are constantly influenced, indeed changed, by the changing patterns of action of the world around us, and particularly by the changing patterns of action of the people around us. In that sense our changing patterns of action are never purely ours. They belong to the world and to the people around us as well, just as their patterns of action belong to us. All of this is true of all of us: but there does appear to have been something unique about the changing patterns of action that constituted Jesus. He was able to create signs of the Kingdom of God's coming in ways in which other people could not, and he was deeply in touch with the thoughts and actions of the people around him. Some of us occasionally glimpse how this might have been, because we can all be deeply affected by the feelings of people we are with, and we can sometimes be aware of what someone might be doing or thinking when they haven't told us. We can be aware of someone emotionally close to us still being alive even when they are not present with us; and we can be aware of the death of someone miles away. There is a normal ubiquitous connectedness of which Carl Jung captured something when he wrote about a collective subconscious. And so here Jesus knew that someone had touched his clothes. Did he know who it was? Was he asking simply to encourage the woman to reveal her faith? Or did he not know? If he did not initially know who it was, then the patterns of action that constituted Jesus that were also patterns of action that constituted God had effected the woman's healing, and because it was God who knew that it was that particular woman who had touched Jesus' clothes in the hope that she would be healed, God met her faith with healing action.[243] Energy had flowed from Jesus to her, and had achieved her healing and therefore her reintegration into society. It was now essential to bring her back into society, and so Jesus turned and either discovered or revealed the identity of the woman who had touched him.

How was it the woman's faith that had made her well when it was Jesus who had done it? It was both of them, working together, as it generally will be when healing occurs: both the healer and the one seeking healing coming together in a single complex changing pattern of action to achieve something new. It was the woman's recognition that Jesus' pattern of action was God's pattern of action,[244] and her touching of Jesus' clothes, that had made the healing possible, so Jesus was correct: it was her faith that had healed her: and so it always was with Jesus' miracles. They were never isolated works of wonder: they were always in the context of relationships of trust within which Jesus' compassion met the person's need, and the result was a foretaste of the new creation of the Kingdom of God.[245]

We know about the woman's health problems, but we do not know what happened to the synagogue leader's daughter. Jesus clearly knew, and he intended to heal her, and if necessary to raise her from the dead. Again he would work with the girl. He would hold her hand—itself a significant pattern of action, as if she was dead then Jesus was risking ritual defilement;[246] and he would tell her to get up, which she did. Always there was action and an invitation to action. And again faith was part of the mix: this time the faith of the synagogue leader: "only believe."

The faith that Jesus was talking about here was not a request for a mental affirmation of any kind. There were certainly mental elements to the woman's approach through the crowd. She had said to herself—for this is what thought is: speaking to ourselves—that if she touched Jesus' clothes then she would be healed. But if she had just thought that and done nothing then there would have been no healing. The faith that Jesus commended was the pushing through the crowd and the touching of his clothes. Faith is a pattern of action: a complex network of purposive activity, aimed at an outcome, specific on each occasion. The woman approached Jesus and touched his clothes. This was her faith. The synagogue leader came to Jesus, made a request, and accompanied Jesus to where his daughter was lying. It was not the synagogue leader who voiced the skepticism. His taking Jesus to his daughter was the faith that Jesus had asked him to exercise, so that is what he did.

And so for us, the faith that Jesus asks of us is not some affirmation of a set of beliefs: it is changing patterns of action that bring ourselves, the people around us, and the world around us, to Jesus to be healed. This is not "acts of faith": this is faith. It is what Jesus discovered in the woman, and what he asked of the synagogue leader.

A consistent command accompanied the requirement of faith: a command to "Go in peace" in the case of the woman, and a command "Do not fear" to the synagogue leader. This was not a wish: it was a command. Jesus was saying that not fearing is something that we do, and that going in peace is something that we do. These are patterns of action that we can choose: that is, we can do them. This was not the only time that Jesus gave the commands "Do not fear" and "Go in peace." They are commands still relevant to all of his followers. There will be healing, the Kingdom of God will come, all are welcome, so we are not to be afraid, and we are to go in peace.

A woman was healed, and a girl was raised from the dead: first the shamed and outcast woman, and then the daughter of the privileged authority-figure, both of whom are equally "daughters." We have here patterns of action that belong to the Kingdom of God: incongruous in relation to a world that had not yet seen the Kingdom of God come in its fulness, but not incongruous in relation to Jesus, who would rule in God's kingdom.[247] The girl would die again, just as Lazarus would die again,[248] so Jesus' resurrection to the eternal life of the Kingdom of God was of an entirely different order:[249] but still the girl being raised to life was a sign of the Kingdom that was near and would come—and the woman would die too, but until then would know herself to be accepted and welcomed. These are all significant patterns of action that constitute the Kingdom of God: and a further and particularly significant pattern of action that we find in this account is the order in which Jesus healed these two "daughters": first the underprivileged, and then the privileged[250]—a pattern of action that constitutes the Kingdom of God.

## MARK 6:1–6a

> **6** He left that place and came to his home town, and his disciples followed him. ² On the sabbath he began to teach in the synagogue, and many who heard him were astounded. They said, 'Where did this man get all this? What is this wisdom that has been given to him? What deeds of power are being done by his hands! ³ Is not this the carpenter, the son of Mary[j] and brother of James and Joses and Judas and Simon, and are not his sisters here with us?' And they took offence[k] at him. ⁴ Then Jesus said to them, 'Prophets are not without honour, except in their home town, and among their own kin, and in their own house.' ⁵ And he could do no deed of power there, except that he

j. Other ancient authorities read *son of the carpenter and of Mary*
k. Or *stumbled*

laid his hands on a few sick people and cured them. ⁶ And he was amazed at their unbelief.²⁵¹

Some patterns of action mesh more easily with others, and some do not. We see examples of this here. Jesus was a network of changing patterns of action, like the rest of us. They had been shaped by his relationships with family members over thirty-something years; and they would have been shaped by his carpenter father, who no doubt taught him the trade; and he would then have become a carpenter: another shaping of his changing patterns of action (although it is odd that there is little sign of carpentering in the parables that the church remembered and passed on). Jesus had now encountered the changing patterns of action of the healings, the crowds, the disciples, and so on, and these had changed the earlier changing patterns of action. Who Jesus was was a vast network of changing patterns of action that had experienced many diverse influences. The extent to which he knew the changing patterns of action that constituted him to be the changing patterns of action that constituted God we cannot know, but he was clearly beginning to understand that he had a particular role to fulfil: the proclamation of the Kingdom of God in his words and in his healing miracles. Jesus' changing patterns of action, now much changed from when he was a younger man, were now meeting again some of the patterns of action that had shaped him as he was growing up, and both he and those among whom he found himself in the synagogue were experiencing a certain amount of dissonance. They understood those aspects of who Jesus was that related to his family and his carpentering, but the teaching and the "deeds of power" were strange to them: these were changing patterns of action that the changing patterns of action that constituted who they were were finding it difficult to relate to, so they were "astounded." The changes had been too wholesale.

Jesus too was experiencing the dissonance. He was coming to understand himself as a prophet: as someone who announces what God is doing and what God will do; and he could sense that his proclamation of the Kingdom of God that God would bring about was not meeting with much of a welcome. The fact that Mary was at the foot of the cross, and that she and at least some of Jesus' brothers and sisters were members of the earliest Christian church following the resurrection, suggests that they were still able to identify with Jesus:²⁵² their patterns of action were able to connect with each other as they continued to change. But some of Jesus' other hearers in that synagogue could not adapt to the new Jesus sufficiently quickly, so rejection was the result.

Mark has placed this story here to emphasize the contrast between the faith of the woman who touched Jesus' clothes and of the synagogue leader, and the lack of faith of the congregation in the synagogue in Nazareth, and to show that Jews had rejected Jesus in much the same way as many Jews continued to reject the Christian gospel in Mark's own time: a rejection that Christians believed to have been prophesied.²⁵³

The generally adulatory pattern of action that Jesus had experienced up to the end of chapter 5 was now being supplanted by a more complex one within a pattern of action that we might term rejectionist.[254] This pattern of action of Jesus' time was being repeated in Mark's own context, so his church's experience of rejection of the gospel was the same reality as Nazareth's rejection of Jesus.

Jesus was "amazed at their unbelief," which we might also translate: he "was amazed at their lack of trust." Again we are not here discussing belief in the sense of affirming a set of propositional beliefs. Their unbelief was active and practical: the immediate activity being chattering among themselves as he was teaching them about the coming Kingdom of God. Maybe there was a parable about a carpenter and they were so busy complaining about Jesus that nobody remembered Jesus' words. Unbelief, like belief, is a pattern of action. It is a resistance to the kinds of activity that belief, or trust, would generate. If belief, or faith—the same word in Greek—is activity to bring people to Jesus to be healed and to hear the Kingdom of God proclaimed, then unbelief is driving people away from the healing and proclamation that Jesus was offering: and the unbelief that Jesus encountered was a pattern of action that rejected the healing that he might have been able to offer to them.

And what precisely is the wisdom that Jesus was offering to them? That the Kingdom of God was coming: and perhaps they did not want their lives disrupted by that eventuality. For the Kingdom of God is that: an eventuality, an event. If Mary sang the Magnificat that we find near to the beginning of Luke's Gospel,[255] and if she continued to sing it and Jesus heard it, then that was where he learnt the revolutionary attitudes that percolated his teaching and his healing miracles. He took no notice of existing hierarchies, except to privilege the outcasts and the stigmatized. In Mary's song the powerful lose their power, the hungry are fed, and those with plenty are sent away with nothing. The Kingdom of God represented a reversal of the world and its economics: a reversal of the situation that Jesus described as those having little having what they had taken from them, and those with more ending up with even more, and in particular with what the poor used to have.[256] The new wisdom that Jesus was teaching might not have been music to the ears of Nazareth's citizens, who would have preferred Jesus to have continued to live quietly as a carpenter, making their chairs, tables, and roofbeams.

But Jesus did heal some people who were sick. He could not resist doing that. The Kingdom of God was characterized by compassion—by a "feeling with": a distinctive pattern of action that simply had to reach out to those in need. But that was all that he could do. Normally Jesus healed when there was at least some kind of responsive faith, as otherwise the miracles would have been purely that and would not have been understood as promises of the Kingdom of God's coming.[257] Maybe some of his hearers had begun to trust him, and to hear his message, making their healing possible: or maybe in this instance he could simply not resist healing those who were in need.

The wisdom that he had to offer was not received; they were not looking forward to the Kingdom of God coming, nor were the good people of Nazareth about to turn around their lives in order to live in their own time and place the life of the Kingdom of God that Jesus so much wanted to be able to tell them about. They were missing something very special: they were missing having the changing patterns of action that constituted who they were reshaped by the changing patterns of action that constituted the coming Kingdom of God: the very same changing patterns of action that they saw in Jesus and rejected. They refused the opportunity to live in their own day the future that God would bring about: a refusal that was a changing pattern of action that would be repeated in changing ways throughout Jesus' ministry, and finally at his death; and that the disciples would experience as well, as we shall discover in the next passage.

Adventures can be difficult to welcome if they might disturb the lives that we are living, particularly if the invitation comes from an aspect of our existing lives, which is what they had thought that Jesus was. For two thousand years Jesus has invited us to go on adventures of ideas, adventures of activity, adventures of discovery, adventures of self-discovery. Jesus still invites us to join him on those adventures: for the Kingdom of God is no static reality—it is constantly changing patterns of action because that is what God is, and the Kingdom of God is the rule of God: a changing rule that invites us to constant repentance, *metanoia*, changing of mind. Jesus is not inviting us into unchanging doctrine, an unchanging tradition, or an unchanging church: he is inviting us into a constantly changing Kingdom of God: so if we do decide to express that in terms of doctrines, traditions, and institutions, then those doctrines, traditions and institutions must share the characteristics of the Kingdom of God to which they must bear witness: so they too will be constantly changing patterns of action, driven along by the God who is changing patterns of action, and in awe of Jesus who is the changing patterns of action that constitute God, who is Action and the source of action.

There will be times when the doctrine solidifies, when tradition ceases to change, and when the church becomes defensive in the face of what looks like the new and the disruptive, just as those hearers in the synagogue defended themselves against Jesus, his wisdom, and his healing miracles. If we are ever tempted to defend ourselves against the constant *metanoia* to which Jesus invites us, then we should turn again to Mark's Gospel, and to this passage about the residents of his home town who defended themselves against the Kingdom of God's coming—and to the many passages about people whose lives were transformed by seeking and welcoming Jesus' wisdom and his healing.

## MARK 6:6b-13

> Then he went about among the villages teaching. ⁷ He called the twelve and began to send them out two by two, and gave them authority over the unclean spirits. ⁸ He ordered them to take nothing for their journey except a staff; no bread, no bag, no money in their belts; ⁹ but to wear sandals and not to put on two tunics. ¹⁰ He said to them, 'Wherever you enter a house, stay there until you leave the place. ¹¹ If any place will not welcome you and they refuse to hear you, as you leave, shake off the dust that is on your feet as a testimony against them.' ¹² So they went out and proclaimed that all should repent. ¹³ They cast out many demons, and anointed with oil many who were sick and cured them.[258]

Everything is action in changing patterns. Now it was not just Jesus travelling and teaching, although he was: now his twelve apostles were being sent to proclaim the Kingdom of God's coming by their words, by healing, and by casting out evil. The sending of the apostles was no longer an intention, it was an actuality: a pattern of action that was words that promised the future pattern of action of sending had now become the pattern of action of sending.[259] And Jesus sent them two by two because it was safer like that: and the staves were for protection as well. But they were to take nothing else, because wherever they arrived everything was to be the exchange of gifts. They were bringing to the villages the gifts of good news, healing, and the casting out of evil—the last of which is the only one mentioned in Jesus' charge to them, although it is clear from verse 12 that they taught and healed as well[260]—and they were to receive the gift of hospitality: itself an affirmation on the part of the village's residents that they had heard the good news and would now be followers of Jesus in the cause of the Kingdom of God's coming.

There were to be no distractions: no moving from house to house (which would in any case have dishonored the original hospitality);[261] and there was to be no negotiation. Everything was to serve the apostles' ability to move from place to place and in each place to exercise the patterns of action that constituted Jesus' mission.[262] The pair of apostles would arrive, a household would welcome them and care for them, and they would preach, heal, and cast out evil. This was Jesus' pattern of action, so it was to be theirs as well. In doing these things they were not only followers of Jesus: they *were* Jesus to the people they were with, they *were* the Kingdom of God come near, and because these were the patterns of action that were God's patterns of action, the apostles would be God in among the village communities. And one further pattern of action was then added: to shake off the dust of any place that did not welcome them. Patterns of action have meanings, and that one certainly did.

This was in many ways the beginning of the church, which is why the story will have been remembered and passed on through the oral tradition, and why Mark would have recorded it in his gospel;[263] and if Jesus envisaged a continuing fellowship of believers after his death and resurrection, then the mission of the twelve might have been intended as an apprenticeship to teach them how to conduct the church's mission.[264] In Paul's words, the church is the Body of Christ. Our bodies are the changing patterns of action that constitute who we are, so Jesus' body was and is the changing patterns of action of who he was and is, and any body of people that exhibits the same changing patterns of action will also be the body of Christ. Later on we shall discuss the church as the Body of Christ in the context of the actions that constituted Jesus' last meal with his disciples before his death. Here we discuss it in relation to the proclaiming, healing and casting out of evil that was Jesus' pattern of action, and the way in which he was now calling on a group of his followers to perform the same pattern of action, which meant that he was calling them to be his body wherever they travelled and proclaimed, healed, and cast out evil. The disciples' pattern of action was the same as Jesus' pattern of action, so they simply were Jesus' body as they did the things that he had authorized them to do, which meant that they were Jesus as they did these things: and the same will be true of every Christian since then who has done those things, and of the whole church as it does them.

One particular action required of the apostles was not one that we have so far heard of Jesus performing: anointing with oil in order to heal the sick. This was clearly a common practice, as we find it in Jesus' parable of the good Samaritan recorded in Luke's Gospel.[265] Although we do not find the practice elsewhere in Mark's Gospel, we do find it discussed in the Letter of James as a practice of the early church:[266] someone who is sick is told to call the elders, who will anoint them with oil; and partly because of this instruction, anointing with oil has remained a practice of the church ever since. It is such patterns of action that bind the church together: the same pattern of action across time for two thousand years, and the same pattern of action across the planet. And it is particularly those patterns of action that constituted Jesus' ministry that bind the church together across time and space: proclamation of the Kingdom of God, healing the sick (mainly by the laying on of hands and prayer, as Jesus did), and the casting out of evil. Whether we are thinking of anointing with oil, proclaiming the Kingdom of God's coming, or the sharing of bread and wine, if reality is action in patterns, then where we find the same patterns of action there is no boundary: it is the same reality, undivided by time.[267]

This raises the important question as to whether the church should today be conducting exorcisms. We are aware from accounts in the gospels that what was sometimes interpreted then as possession by evil spirits was what we would now interpret as illness, particularly if the illness was either mental illness or epilepsy. This rather complicates the situation. People of Jesus' time were perfectly aware that there was a boundary between illness and possession by evil spirits, and we know that Jesus and his disciples were clearly aware of it, because we constantly find them distinguishing between the healing of the sick and the casting out of demons. The difference between then and now is that we draw the boundary in a different place. For some twenty-first century cultures and individuals, there is no such thing as possession by evil spirits, and everything that was interpreted as that in Jesus' time is taken to have been illness. There are also cultures and individuals today who believe that evil spirits can still possess people: they might place the boundary between illness and possession where Jesus and his contemporaries would have put it, or they might move it so that epilepsy and mental illness find themselves in the "illness" category, leaving quite rare events in the "possession" category. Such diversity over such a complex medical and theological issue is inevitable. So what is to be done? First of all we should expect the church to be following the patterns of action that we find in Jesus' ministry, and in the practice of the apostles: but we should also recognize that patterns of action change constantly in relation to changing patterns of action in which they are in network relationships. Changes in the ways in which we interpret illness will necessarily change how the church relates to illness; and changes in our understanding of possession by evil spirits will change how the church relates to such possession. We should probably expect the Christian approach to be as follows: Our patterns of action should be as close as possible to the patterns of action that we find in the ministries of Jesus and of the apostles, but we should expect change in relation to the occasions on which we practice the different patterns of action. So if in our culture epilepsy and mental illness are understood to be illnesses rather than possession by evil spirits, then the laying on of hands and prayer will be the appropriate pattern of action—alongside the best available medical care, of course; and on those few occasions when after careful enquiry illness has been found not to be the problem, and there might be good reason for believing that possession by evil spirits might be what is happening, then a casting out of evil might be appropriate. There will also be cultures in which presuppositions remain closer to those of Jesus' time. In that case, casting out of evil might be appropriate in more cases: but always alongside the best available medical care. If what the church perceives to be possession by an evil spirit might be epilepsy, then it should be treated as such, and similarly with mental illness. The world is now different from the way it was in Jesus' time, which means that the ways in which the coming of the Kingdom of God can be promised will be different. If someone is in difficulties of any kind, then the Kingdom of God will be most clearly signposted if every available route towards living the life of the Kingdom of God in our own time is attempted: and so the practice of high quality medicine, and alongside that whichever of the laying on of hands or exorcism appears to be the most appropriate, is what is to be done.

There might be a more general point to be made here. The church is the Body of Christ if its changing patterns of action are the changing patterns of action that constituted and constitute Jesus. Jesus' patterns of action changed during his ministry: we can tell this from the diversity that we find in the gospels, although because the gospels do not necessarily record events in the order in which they happened, it is sometimes difficult to tell precisely how Jesus' practices and ideas changed. This means that our patterns of action must change in ways that his might have done. For instance, it is reasonable to assume that Jesus shifted from understanding his mission to be purely to the Jews to a broader understanding that it was to be to everyone, so our patterns of action should change constantly from exclusion to inclusion. And we should also expect change to occur in relation to the changing patterns of action of the world around us across the two thousand years that separate us from Jesus and the apostles. The question will always be this: How can we most faithfully mirror in our own lives, and in our institutions and communities, the patterns of action that constituted and still constitute Jesus, and therefore constitute God and the Kingdom of God? We have seen that in relation to illness and spirit possession we might do that best by retaining the diverse patterns of action of Jesus and his first followers, and at the same time shifting the boundary that determines when each of the patterns of action is to be enacted. This might be an appropriate approach in other contexts.

## MARK 6:14–29

14 King Herod heard of it, for Jesus'[l] name had become known. Some were[m] saying, 'John the baptizer has been raised from the dead; and for this reason these powers are at work in him.' 15 But others said, 'It is Elijah.' And others said, 'It is a prophet, like one of the prophets of old.' 16 But when Herod heard of it, he said, 'John, whom I beheaded, has been raised.'

17 For Herod himself had sent men who arrested John, bound him, and put him in prison on account of Herodias, his brother Philip's wife, because Herod[n] had married her. 18 For John had been telling Herod, 'It is not lawful for you to have your brother's wife.' 19 And Herodias had a grudge against him, and wanted to kill him. But she could not, 20 for Herod feared John, knowing that he was a righteous and holy man, and he protected him. When he heard him, he was greatly perplexed;[o] and yet he liked to listen to him. 21 But an opportunity came when Herod on his birthday gave a banquet for his courtiers and officers and for the leaders of Galilee. 22 When his daughter Herodias[p] came in and danced, she pleased Herod and his guests; and the king said to the girl, 'Ask me for whatever you wish, and I will give it.' 23 And he solemnly swore to her, 'Whatever you ask me, I will give you, even half of my kingdom.' 24 She went out and said to her mother, 'What should I ask for?' She replied, 'The head of John the baptizer.' 25 Immediately she rushed back to the king and requested, 'I want you to give me at once the head of John the Baptist on a platter.' 26 The king was deeply grieved; yet out of regard for his oaths and for

l. Gk *his*
m. Other ancient authorities read *He was*
n. Gk *he*
o. Other ancient authorities read *he did many things*
p. Other ancient authorities read *the daughter of Herodias herself*

> the guests, he did not want to refuse her. ²⁷ Immediately the king sent a soldier of the guard with orders to bring John's head. He went and beheaded him in the prison, ²⁸ brought his head on a platter, and gave it to the girl. Then the girl gave it to her mother. ²⁹ When his disciples heard about it, they came and took his body, and laid it in a tomb.[268]

Words are action in changing patterns. Sometimes they have little effect on the networks of changing patterns of action around them: but sometimes they can cause ripples, waves, and disruptions, across multiple patterns of action. John's words had caused significant changes in the patterns of action that constituted the people who went to the Jordan to hear him and to be baptized. Each of those people had affected others around them: and so the brief sound waves that were John's words affected large portions of the society of his day. Most significantly for John himself, those words reached King Herod and his wife Herodias. They caused a mixture of reactions in Herod's brain: attractions and repulsions, statements and questions, and, above all, guilt. The changes in the patterns of action that constituted Herodias's brain appear to have been purely towards anger: a turbulence that generated a readiness to pounce.

Herod's daughter Herodias danced: a pattern of action designed to attract the eyes and brains of Herod and his guests, which it did. Herod's vow was merely sound waves: but numbers of other changing patterns of action that it came up against meant that it would have significant effects. His daughter ran to her mother; her mother's brain connected her daughter's sound waves with the anger already there; and an instruction—merely sound waves—was issued. More sound waves from Herod's daughter resulted in a soldier unlocking John the Baptist's cell door, taking an axe, raising it, and bringing it down on John's neck. He placed the separated head on a plate and took it into the dining room, where Herod's daughter received it and took it to her mother. These actions in patterns no doubt caused yet more of them—grief, disgust, guilt, satisfaction, mirth, fear, and more—in different family members and guests. All of it was changing action in patterns. And then John's disciples added more: they heard, they arrived, they took John's body, and they laid it in a tomb.

The changes in patterns of action brought about by this complex of action in patterns did not stop there. The complex changing patterns of action that constituted Herod's brain continued to be influenced by the events: and when he heard about Jesus' teaching and healing ministry, and what people were saying about it, he found himself aligning the changing patterns of action that constituted Jesus with those that constituted John. They were doing similar things, so they must be the same person. Because we are what we do, this was a reasonable conclusion to draw, so it was not surprising that those who heard Jesus' words, and saw his healing miracles and his casting out of evil, had drawn the conclusion that he might have been Elijah, whose return before the day of judgement had been prophesied,[269] or that he might have been another of the prophets, or a new prophet—or John the Baptist. Jesus was proclaiming the rule of God; he was defeating evil; he was healing the sick; he was calling for a new way of life, on the part of every individual, of the nation of Israel, and of other nations as well. Whether he was passing judgement in the same way that the former prophets and John the Baptist had done is not quite so obvious, because Jesus appeared to believe that unrepentant sinners were welcome in the Kingdom of God: but his call to repentance—to a complete change of mind, and to lives oriented towards the patterns of action of the Kingdom of God—was unmistakably in the tradition of the prophets. The changing pattern of action that constituted Jesus bore family resemblances to those of Elijah, the prophets, and John the Baptist.

The crowd who believed these things about Jesus were not wrong, just as Herod was not wrong to identify Jesus with John the Baptist. The prophets were what they did—they were their changing patterns of action: so if Jesus' changing patterns of action were sufficiently similar to theirs, then he was Elijah, or one of the other prophets, or John the Baptist. And Jesus' changing pattern of action would be that of John the Baptist in the sense that he, like John, would suffer a violent death at the hands of the nation's rulers: hence the length at which Mark records John's death and why it happened.[270]

To the extent that our changing patterns of action are those of our parents, we are our parents; to the extent that our words and thoughts and actions are those of people who have had a significant effect on us, we are those people; and to the extent that our changing patterns of action are those of Jesus, we are not just Christians, we are Jesus himself, active in today's world. The incarnation of God continues. And at the level of institutions: to the extent that the church is people whose changing patterns of action are those of Jesus, it is the Body of Christ: Jesus still at work in the world today.

We don't know how old Herod's daughter Herodias was, but however old she was she must have been deeply traumatized by the events of that evening. Herod and her mother Herodias had between them turned the day into a nightmare. First of all she had been told to dance in front of Herod and a roomful of his guests, and if she had a figure that attracted men's gaze, which we can reasonably assume that she had, then she would have felt everyone's eyes on her. Simply turning our eyes towards someone can have a profound effect on them, because this minor change in our pattern of action can send waves into someone's eyes and onto their retina that can cause considerable change in the patterns of action that constitute their brain. From a long way away, someone whose eyes swivel in our direction, even if they don't move their head, can impose a substantial effect on us. No doubt the reaction has evolved as a defense mechanism: our brains simply had to develop sensitivity to the direction in which another human being or a predatory animal was looking, even if the potential danger might be a long way off. The men sitting round Herod's dining room would have been quite close to the dancer, so she would have felt the full force of their eyes turned in her direction.

And then came Herod's scary vow. How should she respond to such a ridiculous promise? Did he really mean that he would give her half of his kingdom? Of course, it was not really his to give. He was king by permission of the Roman Empire, which might not have been too pleased to see that particular jurisdiction divided up in some incompetent manner. The daughter Herodias ran to her mother Herodias and simply took her instructions, the result of which was to be presented with a prophet's severed head on a plate. The event would surely have inflicted permanent damage. This was child abuse of an extreme kind. Actions have consequences. The changing patterns of action that impinge on us inevitably send the changing patterns of action that constitute who we are in all manner of new directions, all of them changing across the vast network of patterns of action that we are. No influence ever stops. Counselling might have helped the child, but the damage would never be undone: and no doubt this was not the only damage done by her rather strange parents.

Parents are faced with an impossible responsibility. Every one of our changing patterns of action, however brief, however apparently inconsequential, will affect our children for the whole of their lives. We cannot face that knowledge consciously all of the time: that would cause us to seize up as human beings. Much of the influence that passes from parent to child through our actions and words—all of it changing patterns of action—will enable the child to develop changing patterns of action of their own that will result in satisfying lives that will be good for themselves, for those they live among, and for the world around them. Some of what we do to them will have different effects. Consciously studying the changing patterns of action through which we relate to our children will help us to increase the creative influence and reduce the destructive—so it is fortunate that we have developed patterns of action that constitute feedback mechanisms in the brain: and perhaps it is these looping patterns in the patterns of action that constitute our brains that are at the heart of what it is to be human. And prayer for ourselves and for our children will also have an effect: both directly shaping the changing patterns of action that we are and that they are, and consciously engaging in the parent-child relationship the changing patterns of action that constitute God: patterns of action that forgive and renew in the sense that those patterns of action that we might term evil are received and transformed.

The same is true to a lesser extent of any human relationship: with relatives, friends, colleagues, acquaintances, and all of the institutions and their personnel that we have anything to do with. It is also true, and possibly to an even greater extent, of our relationship with the planet on which we all live. Every one of our patterns of action, however insignificant it might seem, will have permanent effects on every pattern of action around us, and so will ripple out through networks of patterns of action forever. We cannot live with that knowledge, so we don't. Most of it is never consciously processed: unless, of course, the effects of our patterns of action return to us via other patterns of action and inflict new change on the patterns of action that constitute who we are: that is, if the consequences of our actions come roaring back at us—at which point emotion can be intense, of joy, sorrow, guilt, fear, and so on. If the patterns of action that come at us are characterized by anger, and if they result in a pattern of action that we recognize as guilt, then hopefully self-conscious study of the network of changing patterns of action follows, and the result is a more creative interplay of changing patterns of action in the future, towards those closest to us, towards other people around us, towards ourselves, and towards the planet.

Children are of course particularly vulnerable to the damaging effects of destructive patterns of action around them. They have not had the opportunity to build the defenses against them that adults might have been able to generate: so here we must be particularly alive to the possibilities of abuse. It would appear that neither Herod nor his wife Herodias were.

Both Herod and those around him seriously considered the possibility that Jesus was John the Baptist raised from the dead.[271] There is an important sense in which they were correct. If reality is action in patterns, then we are what we do: so to the extent that Jesus' patterns of action were also those of John, Jesus was indeed John still active in Herod's territory. However, as Jesus' message and activity diverged from that of John, as it appears to have done, it became less true that Jesus was John risen from the dead: so although Herod might have been correct about the earlier period of Jesus' ministry, he was less correct in relation to the later period.

## MARK 6:30-44

> 30 The apostles gathered around Jesus, and told him all that they had done and taught. [31] He said to them, 'Come away to a deserted place all by yourselves and rest a while.' For many were coming and going, and they had no leisure even to eat. [32] And they went away in the boat to a deserted place by themselves. [33] Now many saw them going and recognized them, and they hurried there on foot from all the towns and arrived ahead of them. [34] As he went ashore, he saw a great crowd; and he had compassion for them, because they were like sheep without a shepherd; and he began to teach them many things. [35] When it grew late, his disciples came to him and said, 'This is a deserted place, and the hour is now very late; [36] send them away so that they may go into the surrounding country and villages and buy something for themselves to eat.' [37] But he answered them, 'You give them something to eat.' They said to him, 'Are we to go and buy two hundred denarii[q] worth of bread, and give it to them to eat?' [38] And he said to them, 'How many loaves have you? Go and see.' When they had found out, they said, 'Five, and two fish.' [39] Then he ordered them to get all the people to sit down in groups on the green grass. [40] So they sat down in groups of hundreds and of fifties. [41] Taking the five loaves and the two fish, he

q. The denarius was the usual day's wage for a labourer

> looked up to heaven, and blessed and broke the loaves, and gave them to his disciples to set before the people; and he divided the two fish among them all. ⁴² And all ate and were filled; ⁴³and they took up twelve baskets full of broken pieces and of the fish. ⁴⁴ Those who had eaten the loaves numbered five thousand men.[272]

The meaning of "apostle" is "the one sent as an agent": Jesus had sent them as missionaries; and the word continued to describe the twelve in the early church (with Matthias in the place of Judas, and then later on Paul quite justifiably adding himself to the company of apostles). These men—and they were all men—continued to regard themselves as explicitly sent by Jesus as his agents and to do his work. The Hebrew word from which the concept derived implied that the authority granted to the person who had been sent lasted only as long as the particular task lasted, and this would have been the twelve's understanding of the word, and the twelve's and Paul's understanding following Jesus' resurrection. The word denoted a particular pattern of action. It was not a status floating free from action, but was a description of a very particular pattern of action, and only those constituted by that pattern of action continued to be apostles.[273]

The apostles had been sent by Jesus to do some work, and they needed to debrief: and they all needed a rest. It was not to be. The attraction of Jesus' words and actions—the way that they drew people to him—was too great to allow any privacy. A crowd was already waiting when they all arrived: and Jesus "had compassion for them." The Greek word implies a movement within the body, which is what emotions are: electrical pulses and chemical changes. Everything is action in changing patterns: bodily movements; electrical pulses in the brain, which is itself changing patterns of action; the emotions—all of it is action in changing patterns. And all of it affects other changing patterns of action, within our own network, and in the networks around us. One of the results of Jesus' compassion was his teaching of the crowd, however tired he was. Another was his determination to feed them.

The apostles wanted to send the crowd to buy food. Market exchange was then, and is now, a significant and frequent pattern of action. Exchange takes place. And money itself is a pattern of action. If there is cash involved, as there was then, then it might have looked as if money was constituted by solid objects of a particular kind: by lumps of metal with pictures on them. But on their own, coins and banknotes are not money. Money is the patterns of action associated with those objects as much as it is the objects themselves. If a tax-collector demanded tax from a resident of that country, then they could pay the tax by handing over coins. We can pay our taxes by handing over banknotes or coins: although it would be more normal now for such transactions to be by bank transfer, or by deductions from wages or salaries, with the employer sending the money to the government—all of it electrical pulses in computers. It is our behavior that determines the character of money: our behavior as individuals, regulators, retailers, and institutions such as banks and building societies. Because money is constituted by our actions in changing patterns, we can change how money works: and we do, quite often, although not necessarily by conscious decisions. A huge change that occurred relatively recently was individual nation states pooling their currencies and establishing the Euro, with a European Central Bank trying to keep some kind of control over the currency: a fairly hopeless task because institutions and individuals in the market-place can together cause significant changes, largely because what happens in one country can affect every other, as we found out in 2008 when the actions in patterns of one or two financial institutions caused all manner of effects, including firms closing down and a lot of people having their posts declared redundant. Everything is connected, and particularly the ways in which money behaves, and the ways in which institutions and individuals behave in society.

It is market transactions that Jesus' disciples were recommending as a way to get the crowd fed. Jesus had other ideas. He was going to ensure the abundant passing around of food, so that not only would there be enough, but there would be plenty to spare as well. We are not concerned here with precisely "what happened," in the sense of whether food was created in the way in which the universe was created, with fairly stable patterns of action being created out of patternless action, or whether people in the crowd simply shared what they already had. The account does not suggest that a miracle took place, so we must leave the question open.[274] What concerns us here is Jesus' patterns of action, and those of his disciples, and those of members of the crowd.

Jesus "had compassion." This was not simply a feeling, although that would itself have been a changing pattern of action that both constituted Jesus and constituted God: it was rather an inner call to action that resulted in the action being carried out. In this case it led immediately to the series of patterns of action that Mark has recorded: actions carried out because Jesus "had compassion," and not to demonstrate his ability to perform miracles. The fact that the crowd exhibited no obvious surprise suggests that it was only the apostles who would have been aware of any miraculous character of the event.[275]

First of all food was brought to Jesus: a few loaves and a few fish. The people prepared themselves to eat, sitting on the grass in formations that echoed those of the Roman legions: a symbolism that would not have been missed by the crowd.[276] They were to be the army of the Kingdom of God. Jesus took the bread and the fish; he looked heavenwards—a pattern of action that analogically accompanies the turning of heart and mind, of the whole being, towards God; he blessed the food—that is, gave thanks for it, and dedicated it to a particular purpose—that of providing for the bodily needs of members of the crowd that had come to hear him; and he gave the bread and the fish to his disciples to share among the people. There was plenty to eat, and plenty to collect afterwards. Although Jesus' actions constituted a normal domestic blessing before a meal,[277] what the crowd had experienced was a pattern of action that constituted Jesus' last meal with his disciples before he died,[278] and that still constitutes the Eucharist and therefore the church—the taking of bread, the giving thanks, the breaking of the bread, and the sharing of the bread. This means that this crowd was the church. Early Christians made this connection, and so should we.[279]

What Jesus was creating here was an acted parable of the Kingdom of God; an active analogy of the rule of God. The Kingdom that Jesus promised and that he lived out would be one in which justice would be done, the hungry would be fed, needs would be met, gifts would be given and received, and the generous love of God would characterize all of the changing and diverse action that would constitute the Kingdom of God when it came. This Jesus achieved on that hillside in Galilee: and this Jesus would go on to achieve through the changing pattern of action that constituted the church, which is still his body doing these things. Not only was a promise of the Kingdom of God's coming given: the crowd experienced the Kingdom of God itself in the midst of their daily lives. They were the Kingdom of God. God is Action, the source of all action, and of particular changing patterns of action, among which we find the particular changing patterns of action that we find lived in Jesus of Nazareth, and that we shall find lived in the Kingdom of God when it comes. These patterns of action were in evidence on that day and in that place. The prophets had promised a Messianic banquet, and this was what Jesus was providing: so in his pattern of action he was the Messiah;[280] and just as God had provided manna to eat as the Israelites travelled through the wilderness following their escape from slavery in Egypt, so this new gathering of people was being fed as it journeyed with Jesus. Jesus was doing what God did, so in his actions on that hillside Jesus was God.[281] This is what incarnation is about: the action in changing patterns that constitutes God and the Kingdom of God already happening in the midst of people then and today. For the same patterns of action that occurred then still occur today. In every Eucharist—in every re-enactment of the Last Supper—we take bread, give thanks, break the bread, and share it, thus bringing into the midst of the congregation the patterns of action that constitute Jesus, God, and the Kingdom of God. Wherever food and other necessities of life are abundantly shared, and wherever people are spiritually fed as they travel through their own wildernesses, there too is the Kingdom of God:[282] not just a promise, but the Kingdom of God itself; and there too is Jesus, and there is God.

What are we to make of the fact that here it is definitely "men" who are mentioned? Were there women and children as well? In a similar event a little later simply the number of people present is mentioned: but here it is men only. The twelve apostles were all men. There might have been completely practical reasons related to safety for sending out only pairs of men to the villages to teach and heal, but we know that there were women who were followers of Jesus.[283] Might this be another matter over which Jesus slowly learnt obedience? Did he begin by internalizing the patriarchal norms of his society, and then found himself questioning them? The gospels are not necessarily ordered according to the chronology of events, so it is difficult to draw conclusions: but just as it appears that Jesus came to include unrepentant sinners, children, and Gentiles, in the Kingdom of God, so he might have come to understand that women were equally members of the Kingdom of God, and that that fact ought to be given expression in the context of his ministry.

As for the difference between men and women: In a context in which reality is action in changing patterns, we are not now asking about the being of men and the being of women. We are asking about complex networks of changing patterns of action that we might call someone's "identity": by which we mean the changing patterns of action that constitute who each one of us is. Some of those changing patterns of action we might call biological, some of them personal, some of them familial, some communal, some societal, some cultural: and all of them entangled with the changing patterns of action that constitute other people. There is nothing static. Everything is dynamic. The concept of definition assumes that there is some kind of static solidity to a being. If gender, sex, sexuality, and so on, refer to changing patterns of action, then definition too becomes dynamic: it is diverse changing patterns of action. This is what reality is: so this is what human reality is.

## MARK 6:45–52

> 45 Immediately he made his disciples get into the boat and go on ahead to the other side, to Bethsaida, while he dismissed the crowd. 46 After saying farewell to them, he went up on the mountain to pray.
>
> 47 When evening came, the boat was out on the lake, and he was alone on the land. 48 When he saw that they were straining at the oars against an adverse wind, he came towards them early in the morning, walking on the lake. He intended to pass them by. 49 But when they saw him walking on the lake, they thought it was a ghost and cried out; 50 for they all saw him and were terrified. But immediately he spoke to them and said, 'Take heart, it is I; do not be afraid.' 51 Then he got into the boat with them and the wind ceased. And they were utterly astounded, 52 for they did not understand about the loaves, but their hearts were hardened.[284]

Jesus made a rapid escape from the scene of the feeding of the five thousand, and ensured that his disciples did likewise. Perhaps what had occurred was looking uncomfortably military. What looked very like a legion (only men are mentioned, and they are seated as an army might have been seated) could have been interpreted as the beginning of an insurrection and crushed accordingly. Jesus' messiahship was not of that kind, and the Kingdom of God would not come by human military means. It was more accurately represented by the taking of bread, the giving thanks, the breaking, and the sharing among the crowd.[285]

## Mark's Gospel: An Actological Reading

"They did not understand." We don't understand either: and there is a sense in which we don't understand any of Mark's Gospel. Firstly, the gospel is written in a language that is not ours, even if we are Greek, because the Greek language has changed substantially during the intervening years. Secondly, Jesus and his disciples would have spoken Aramaic in domestic contexts, Hebrew in religious contexts, and Latin in relation to the Roman occupiers. Greek was also a language in circulation in the empire, so they might have known some of it, but it would not have been Greek in which the words recorded in the gospels would have been spoken. And thirdly, Mark's Gospel was written nearly two thousand years ago, in a world with ways of life and thought-forms that were very different from ours.

This was a world in which the sky was a dome that contained the sun, the moon, and the stars, and from which rain fell, and above which were the heavens where God dwelt. So prayer was addressed to the heavens, and going up a mountain brought you closer to God. So that is where Jesus went: to where he felt so much closer to the God that he called "Abba,"[z] [286] "Father": for as well as being God, in the sense of uniquely sharing changing of patterns of action that constituted God, he was a religious human being who longed for the coming of God's Kingdom, and sought to do his Father's will in order that the Kingdom of God might come.

The world in which Jesus, his disciples, and everyone else lived was one in which angels arrived, God's Holy Spirit filled people, evil spirits possessed people, there were heavenly battles between good angels and bad angels and spirits, and miracles happened. This is not to say that these things do not happen today—they do: but it is to say that these ways of understanding reality have been substantially supplanted by other means of explanation. It is in the different world of two thousand years ago that this passage from Mark's Gospel needs to be understood. None of this means that what we would call miracles were a regular occurrence, or that they were regarded as being in the same category as everyday events. People were well aware of what was normal and what was not, and they were clearly perturbed by miraculous events: but they did not dismiss them as impossible.

It is possible that Mark has here combined two separate stories, or that two stories coalesced in the oral tradition so that they already formed a single unit by the time Mark was writing. One narrative might have been about Jesus walking on the water—an epiphany in which he intended to pass by and not join them; and the other might have been about the stilling of the storm. We shall treat the story as if it was always a single narrative, which it might have been.[287]

The event recorded here in Mark's Gospel was a miracle. Jesus walked on the lake, and the disciples in the boat were appropriately terrified: not because there was someone walking on the lake, but because only disembodied spirits would not sink into the lake if they walked on it, so that is what they initially thought that they were looking at. It would not have occurred to them that a human being could walk on

---

z. Aramaic for *Father*

water. But that is what it was: it was Jesus. Again he told them not to be afraid; and again the wind ceased.

Whatever happened that night, this story would have been passed from generation to generation until it was written into Mark's Gospel, and it would have been preserved in the oral tradition for the same reason as the story in which Jesus was asleep in the boat during a storm. These stories were an encouragement to Christians during times of persecution, because they conveyed Jesus' presence: and this story in particular cohered with their experience that Jesus still came to them to calm their fears. The storm might be raging, but Jesus would come, and the storm would cease. Just as God had always been able to control the chaotic sea, so God was still in control, however out of control things might have appeared to be: and as it was Jesus who had exercised such control, he is now and forever God, and would continue to exert his control over chaos.[288]

None of this tells us what happened that night on the lake. In the end, of course, we cannot get behind the story to whatever events gave birth to it. Was it an early Christian preacher telling a story in the hope of encouraging the congregation to "take heart," a story that both the preacher and the congregation knew not to be based on eye-witness accounts of events in Galilee? Or did the event happen one night on the lake, and an account of it lodged in the memory, both because of the event's miraculous character, and because of the way in which remembrance of it was an encouragement to Christians facing persecution? We shall never know. The former possibility coheres with what we know of the thoughtforms and ways of life of both two thousand years ago and today. We write and read historical novels today, knowing that many of the events recorded in them never happened. Why should we not expect early Christians to have made up stories to express their convictions about who Jesus was? But what of the second option? We can see how Jesus' disciples could have believed such an event to be possible, and we can also recognize entirely appropriate behavior on the part of the boat's occupants when they saw someone walking on the water. This is not a fantastical story as far as the part played by the disciples is concerned: so the only question is whether we can envisage the patterns of action exhibited by Jesus constituting an event that we can envisage taking place. Of course, this is not to regard that as a criterion for deciding whether an event has taken place. The presuppositions that we bring to decision-making about the likelihood or otherwise of an account's veracity—essentially the question "If we had been there at that time what would we have witnessed?"—are entirely contingent, just like everything else. Everything is action in changing patterns, and there are no standpoints from which to judge the diversity: and this applies as much to our own thoughtforms as it does to the thoughtforms of two thousand years ago. We might know more about the construction of the cosmos, and that the sky is not a solid dome across which the sun, moon, and stars travel, but is rather an immense universe in which are scattered galaxies, nebulae, and much else: but that does not mean that we could construct a reliable list of events that could happen and of events that could not.

Proving and disproving things are patterns of action. We apply methods. For instance, we know that the sky is not a solid dome because we have sent probes beyond the moon, and now into space beyond our solar system. All of the evidence that we have amassed confirms a picture of the universe as immense, and no contradictory evidence has been discovered. And we can say that what we know about water and gravity means that we would expect it not to be possible for a human being to walk on a lake without sinking into it: but it would take only one counterexample to disprove a theory that it would be impossible for a human being to walk on the surface of a lake. And once we introduce an additional factor—for instance, that the person in question uniquely shares in changing patterns of action that constitute the God who created the universe—there is even less reason to commit ourselves to the position that it would be impossible for any human being ever to walk on the surface of a lake. There is no proof that unique events cannot happen.

All we can do is keep an open mind, which does not mean an inactive mind. Our minds are highly complex networks of changing patterns of action, and one of the substantial advantages of the considerable reasoning skills that human beings have evolved is that we are all perfectly capable of receiving new ideas—new changing patterns of action—and evaluating them in relation to our existing ideas, and at the same time using them to question ideas with which we have become comfortable. If we believe that such unusual events as a human being walking on a lake cannot happen, then we might wish to ask ourselves whether it might in fact be possible under unusual circumstances, and then whether those unusual circumstances might be possible; and if we believe that such unusual events can occur, we might want to consider the possibility that Jesus might have walked on the lake that night, and we might also continue to consider the possibility that he never walked on the lake, but that an early Christian preacher told a story about him doing so in order to encourage the congregation not to be afraid, and to know that in the midst of the threats that they faced Jesus would come to them.

What was it that the disciples did not understand about the loaves? Perhaps that the feeding of the five thousand should have taught them that miracles happen, so they should not have been surprised by Jesus coming to them across the lake. Perhaps that Jesus provided for them then, so they should have known that he would always provide them with what they needed. Perhaps that they had not understood the event as a promise of the Kingdom of God's coming, and as a sign of Jesus' relationship with the God whose kingdom it was. Perhaps if they had understood these things then they would not have been so terrified when Jesus came walking towards them on the lake.[289] Whatever it was that they did not understand, their "hearts were hardened": a changing pattern of action that we shall find echoed as we proceed through Mark's

Gospel.[290] They had not been able to take in the idea that something unique was happening around them: that the Kingdom of God was near, that Jesus was already living the life of the Kingdom of God, and that signs of its coming should be expected. Something new was breaking into human history. If this were to be at the heart of our thought-forms, then perhaps we would be better able to ensure that our hearts were not hardened against the possibility of unique events occurring. We might then be able to regard as entirely possible Jesus' feeding of five thousand and his walking on the lake, and the even bigger miracle that he comes to us still to provide for our needs, to calm our fears, and to bring about the Kingdom of God. For this is a fundamental pattern of action that constitutes Jesus: that he comes to us. He came then, a human being who uniquely shared and still shares patterns of action that constitute God; he came to the disciples on the lake; he has come to the church through two thousand years, through the scriptures, the sharing of bread and wine, prayer, and the fellowship of believers; he comes to us; he will continue to come to his disciples; and he will come into his Kingdom and rule as the servant of all. A cry of the earliest Christians was "Our Lord, come!"[u][291] This is what Jesus does, it is his changing pattern of action. He comes to us still.

In the Hebrew scriptures, God is the one who "trampled the waves of the Sea[y]," whose "way was through the sea," and "who makes a way in the sea, a path in the mighty waters":[292] so Jesus' pattern of action is a pattern of action that constitutes him as God.[293] As for his words: the NRSV English translation offers "It is I," whereas the more literal translation would be "I am," which suggests that Jesus was applying to himself the name of God that Moses experienced as he stood watching a bush that was burning but was not consumed.[294] Jesus' pattern of action—walking on the sea, and stilling the storm—was a pattern of action that constituted God; and the pattern of action of his spoken word was the pattern of action of a spoken word that constituted God. And once these parallels are recognized, more are revealed: the crowd eating the loaves was the Israelites eating manna in the wilderness; the hardening of the disciples' hearts was the hardening of Pharoah's heart;[295] and Jesus walking on the water was the Israelites walking across the Red Sea on dry land. A new Exodus was beginning: a new liberation; and they were all part of it.[296]

## MARK 6:53-56

> 53 When they had crossed over, they came to land at Gennesaret and moored the boat. 54 When they got out of the boat, people at once recognized him, 55 and rushed about that whole region and began to bring the sick on mats to

u. Gk *Marana tha*. These Aramaic words can also be read *Maran atha*, meaning *Our Lord has come*

y. Or *trampled the back of the sea dragon*

wherever they heard he was. ⁵⁶ And wherever he went, into villages or cities or farms, they laid the sick in the market-places, and begged him that they might touch even the fringe of his cloak; and all who touched it were healed.²⁹⁷

Mark's Gospel frequently cycles back to themes encountered before, but always with new elements, and particularly with an added sense of urgency and intensity. So here there is not just one woman touching the fringe of Jesus' cloak: here there are people lined up on mats in the marketplace. It is not just an individual brought by a group of friends who lower him through the roof: people "rushed about that whole region" to bring the sick to Jesus. And all of this because people "recognized him."

What is it that makes us who we are? First of all it is of course what we look like. Jesus' distant ancestor Abraham had come out of Ur of the Chaldees, in what is now Iraq, and travelled to what is now Israel: but it was not long before a now quite large extended family found itself in Egypt, and soon enslaved: so Jesus' ancestors from that time could have been from all manner of ethnic groups. Moses led the slaves out of Egypt, and a relatively settled period followed, with the nation of tribes led by wise religious "judges" and then by monarchs: and we know that at least one of Jesus' ancestors from that time, Ruth, was from Moab, in what is now Jordan. Then first the northern kingdom was taken into exile, and then the southern kingdom, and again Jesus' ancestors from that time could have been of a wide variety of ethnicities: and eventually some of the Jews trickled back into what is now Israel. Quite what Jesus would have looked like is difficult to tell, but probably something like today's Arabs, and shorter than people are today.

Reality might be action rather than being, but at least some of the action is relatively stable patterns. The patterns change all the time, but we still experience objects: that is, quite stable patterns of action; and we experience people with distinct identities: again, quite stable patterns of action. We change all the time, but there will be family likenesses between the patterns of action as they change from one moment to the next. Someone who knew us yesterday will still be able to identify us today; and someone who knew us twenty years ago might also be able to identify us today, although that might be more of a struggle, and whether recognition occurred would depend on how the light waves bouncing off the patterns of action that constitute who we are might have related to patterns of action in the brain of the person we met, and whether somewhere in among the network of changing patterns of action might be found a family likeness of some kind between a pattern of action that constituted an image generated by light bouncing off me in the past and the image created by the light bouncing off me today.

And so there might have been some who recognized Jesus as he got out of the boat at Gennesaret because they had seen him before. Perhaps they had met him in the carpenter's shop; perhaps in the early days of his ministry in a synagogue somewhere; or perhaps they were among the crowd that he fed with the five loaves and two fishes.

But it was not just facial recognition that we are discussing here. They might have recognized Jesus from the fact that some of his disciples had come to the town proclaiming the coming Kingdom of God, healing people, and casting out demons, and saying that Jesus of Nazareth would soon be coming. A group of people would then arrive, one of whom was clearly the Teacher: so that was Jesus. He would tell parables about the Kingdom of God, he would heal the sick, and he would cast out demons, and then he would move on. They recognized him from his patterns of action. Those patterns of action would always be different, from one day to another, and from one place to another, but there would be family resemblances between them. Each of us is changing patterns of action, and it is the family resemblances between the different patterns of action that constitute our identities, both for ourselves and for other people. The knowledge that I have that I am the same person that I was yesterday is the dense network of changing patterns of action that constitutes who I am in this moment and whom I know myself to have been yesterday: the knowing myself being constituted by changing patterns of action in my brain in this same moment.

It might be that I recognize someone from the past by the way that they walk, or by the sound of the voice that I hear. I was once recognized in New Zealand by someone who could not see me but who heard me calling to my wife. The only other time that we had ever met was on a group holiday in Germany. We are our patterns of action. Two of Jesus' disciples were walking from Jerusalem to Emmaus a few days after his crucifixion. They had heard others say that they had seen Jesus alive again, and they were wondering what that meant, when a stranger joined them. As they walked, they talked about Jesus and what had happened to him, and they discussed the prophecies in the Hebrew scriptures: and as it was getting dark when they arrived in their village they invited the stranger to stay overnight. It was as Jesus broke the bread, as he had done when he fed the five thousand, and as he did at his last meal before his death, that they recognized him.[298] We are what we do. Jesus was what he did. This was his identity.

And so in Gennesaret they recognized him: some no doubt from what he looked like; some from the gathering of disciples around the Teacher; and some from his actions: his story-telling, and his healing of the sick. In this person Jesus the Kingdom of God, and God too, had arrived in their midst, and they recognized their coming among them because of the changing patterns of action that they experienced.

## MARK 7:1-23

> 7 Now when the Pharisees and some of the scribes who had come from Jerusalem gathered around him, ² they noticed that some of his disciples were eating with defiled hands, that is, without washing them. ³ (For the Pharisees,

and all the Jews, do not eat unless they thoroughly wash their hands,[r] thus observing the tradition of the elders; [4] and they do not eat anything from the market unless they wash it;[s] and there are also many other traditions that they observe, the washing of cups, pots, and bronze kettles.[t]) [5] So the Pharisees and the scribes asked him, 'Why do your disciples not live[u] according to the tradition of the elders, but eat with defiled hands?' [6] He said to them, 'Isaiah prophesied rightly about you hypocrites, as it is written,

> "This people honours me with their lips,
>
> > but their hearts are far from me;
>
> [7] in vain do they worship me,
>
> > teaching human precepts as doctrines."

[8] You abandon the commandment of God and hold to human tradition.'

[9] Then he said to them, 'You have a fine way of rejecting the commandment of God in order to keep your tradition! [10] For Moses said, "Honour your father and your mother"; and, "Whoever speaks evil of father or mother must surely die." [11] But you say that if anyone tells father or mother, "Whatever support you might have had from me is Corban" (that is, an offering to God[v])[e]— [12] then you no longer permit doing anything for a father or mother, [13] thus making void the word of God through your tradition that you have handed on. And you do many things like this.'

[14] Then he called the crowd again and said to them, 'Listen to me, all of you, and understand: [15] there is nothing outside a person that by going in can defile, but the things that come out are what defile.'[w]

[17] When he had left the crowd and entered the house, his disciples asked him about the parable. [18] He said to them, 'Then do you also fail to understand? Do you not see that whatever goes into a person from outside cannot defile, [19] since it enters, not the heart but the stomach, and goes out into the sewer?' (Thus he declared all foods clean.) [20] And he said, 'It is what comes out of a person that defiles. [21] For it is from within, from the human heart, that evil intentions come: fornication, theft, murder, [22] adultery, avarice, wickedness, deceit, licentiousness, envy, slander, pride, folly. [23] All these evil things come from within, and they defile a person.'[299]

Tradition is a network of patterns of action that change constantly. Among those patterns of action might be ways of life, particular individual or social behaviors, laws

---

r. Meaning of Gk uncertain

s. Other ancient authorities read *and when they come from the market-place, they do not eat unless they purify themselves*

t. Other ancient authorities add *and beds*

u. Gk *walk*

v. Gk lacks *to God*

w. Other ancient authorities add verse 16, *'Let anyone with ears to hear listen'* about what should or should not be done, and interpretations of those laws. Tradition might be crystallized in written form, or it might not be.

The Jewish law, the law of Moses, as described in the first five books of the Hebrew scriptures, contains a wide variety of kinds of rules. What is at issue here in this passage from Mark's Gospel is one of the hygiene regulations and some of the rules for individual behavior that the law contains: or rather, how those hygiene regulations and rules for behavior had come to be interpreted and added to by religious teachers of the time.

It is of course entirely sensible to wash your hands before eating: a rule constantly reinforced during the pandemic raging at the time of writing, but also one relevant to good health in any context. Similarly with washing crockery and cooking vessels. But these were sensible advice that had been turned into religious tradition. It is this process to which Jesus objected: particularly as those who were criticizing his disciples seemed to him to have given up on those elements of the law that really mattered, as he would go on to explain, while turning their attention to traditions that did not matter anything like as much. When Jesus found scripture or tradition used against him, as had happened here, he would often respond with scripture: so here he quotes the prophet Isaiah in order to express his view of his questioners.

Jesus decides to criticize particularly the way in which religious people of his time were able to escape from a duty to care for their parents by declaring some of their wealth out of bounds. There was of course nothing wrong with establishing what we might call a restricted fund out of which money could be given for religious purposes. What Jesus was objecting to was first of all the use of an otherwise perfectly good mechanism to avoid caring for elderly parents, and secondly the way in which the Pharisees treated the oral legal tradition ("your tradition") as of equal status with the law in the Hebrew scriptures ("the commandment of God").[300] The latter was to be kept; the former only if consistent with the latter.

What follows is a challenge to the law and its traditional interpretations at least as significant as Jesus' healing on the sabbath. The law contained lists of animals, fish, and so on, that were not to be eaten. The origin of these lists might have been a perfectly sensible attempt to advise people that certain kinds of meat or fish went off quickly in a hot climate and so could poison them more easily than other kinds of food. However, sensible advice had become inflexible religious laws, meaning that food that might have been available to provide nutrition that people needed was simply not available to them. Jesus clearly thought this entirely wrong. He would always look for the reasons for laws and regulations, and in relation to this one he could not find any. What he was concerned about was what people did and what they said: the patterns of action that constitute who we are and how we treat other people. He therefore offered a contrast: what really mattered was what we do and say, whereas what we eat is only that—it passes through us.

The reason that this saying was remembered, along with Jesus' additional explanation to the disciples, is that it was not long after Jesus' resurrection and the beginnings of the church that Gentiles, non-Jews, began to join (—the fact that the Jewish purity rules had to be explained suggests that Mark was writing for a mainly or at least partially Gentile readership[301]). Some Jewish Christians believed that adherence to the law of Moses was still required, and that to be a follower of Jesus someone also had to be a good Jew, which included circumcision. Other Jewish Christians, including Paul, disagreed: and an incident recorded in the Acts of the Apostles suggests that Peter also came to see that Gentiles could be baptized as Christians without converting to Judaism, and that they were therefore under no obligation to keep the Jewish law.[302] Jewish Christians who believed that Gentiles could become Christians without obeying the Jewish law would have valued the account recorded here in Mark's Gospel, just as they would have been grateful for Jesus' reinterpretation of the sabbath as something offered to us as a gift rather than demanded as a requirement; and Gentile Christians would have been particularly encouraged by Mark's recording of Jesus' declaration that all food was fit to eat. A connected significance for Christians of Mark's time would have been the evidence of a mission to the Gentiles provided by the incidents reported later in this chapter, and in subsequent chapters: a mission consistent with Jesus' relativizing of the Jewish law. The fact that the last part of verse 19 might be the gospel-writer's comment on Jesus' actions and teaching does not alter the fact that the words clearly attributed to Jesus are clear that nobody could be defiled by eating particular kinds of food, and it was this that would have angered the interrogators from Jerusalem.[303]

In relation to the sabbath, Jesus was not breaking the law itself—he was simply moving outwards the boundary around what Jews were permitted to do during it; whereas in the incident reported here he was flatly contradicting the law. The law prohibited the eating of certain kinds of food, whereas Jesus was declaring all food to be permitted to be eaten. Jesus was not only criticizing the oral law by appealing to the written law: he was abrogating important elements of the "commandment of God." This was significant, perhaps in two different ways. Just as Jesus had responded to a complaint about his disciples not washing their hands by saying that it was far more important to keep such central prescriptions of the law as caring for parents, here Jesus is again emphasizing what really mattered as a contrast to what really did not. It really did not matter what people ate. What mattered was what they did. But perhaps more importantly, the Kingdom of God was near, in that Kingdom the Son of Man would rule with justice, and that Kingdom would see the fulfilment of God's promise that "I will put my law within them, and I will write it on their hearts; and I will be their God, and they shall be my people."[304]

Jesus framed his own prescription in terms of intentions from the heart, but what he then went on to describe were particular patterns of action: fornication, theft, murder, and so on. These were what mattered to God now, and they were what would always matter, so these were the aspects of the law that it was important to keep: laws about patterns of action to be avoided, because these were patterns of action inimical to those that constituted the Kingdom of God. Clearly, these were not all that "come from within": but they do come from within—from within the patterns of action that constitute who we are. It is these patterns of action that constitute who we are, and that are not patterns of action that constitute who God is, that constitute our defilement. As far as Jesus is concerned, the eating of particular foods could not possibly have such significance.[305]

There is a gradient to this passage. The first issue discussed—handwashing—was a sensible hygiene rule that had solidified into a religious tradition. Jesus contrasted with it one of the central laws of the Jewish law. The second issue was itself an important element of the Jewish law, and Jesus treated it in the same way as he had treated the hygiene rule, and again contrasted with it what he regarded as essential aspects of the law. By treating both the hygiene rule and the law about forbidden food in the same way, Jesus was making an important point: he was declaring them to be of the same status. Just as he had given himself the authority to decide what the sabbath was for, so here he was giving himself the authority to decide which aspects of the law of Moses mattered and which did not. He was behaving not only like a Messiah bringing a new law from God, but as God the lawgiver.[306] On the basis of a commitment that we might have made to understand Jesus as constituted by changing patterns of action that constituted God, and therefore as God, we might believe such behavior to be entirely appropriate: but we can perfectly understand why the matter might not have been viewed in quite the same way at the time.

A significant aspect of this passage is the close relationships between intentions, words, and actions. All of them do things: all of them are action in changing patterns. There are no different categories here: we might treat our words, our intentions, and our actions, as somehow different from each other, but the boundaries are social constructions: we have created them. The action in changing patterns that are our brains, the action in changing patterns that are our words, and the action in changing patterns that we call our actions, are all action in changing patterns, and they are all interconnected: words with intentions, actions with words, intentions with actions. And they are all actions in changing patterns that constitute who we are.

## MARK 7:24-30

> 24 From there he set out and went away to the region of Tyre.[x] He entered a house and did not want anyone to know he was there. Yet he could not escape notice, 25 but a woman whose little daughter had an unclean spirit immediately heard about him, and she came and bowed down at his feet. 26 Now the woman

x. Other ancient authorities add *and Sidon*

was a Gentile, of Syrophoenician origin. She begged him to cast the demon out of her daughter. ²⁷ He said to her, 'Let the children be fed first, for it is not fair to take the children's food and throw it to the dogs.' ²⁸ But she answered him, 'Sir,ʸ even the dogs under the table eat the children's crumbs.' ²⁹ Then he said to her, 'For saying that, you may go—the demon has left your daughter.' ³⁰ So she went home, found the child lying on the bed, and the demon gone.[307]

There cannot be anywhere in Mark's Gospel where it is clearer that Jesus is learning obedience. He is in mainly Gentile territory, in what is now Syria. From what the narrative says it looks as if he was there for a retreat: a time away from his normal ministry so that he could recharge and prepare himself for the grueling time ahead. But it was not to be: he was found out, and a Gentile woman came to see him. And Jesus was simply rude to her, and refused to cast the evil out of her daughter. A variety of spurious explanations for his behavior have been offered: perhaps that Jesus wanted to test the woman's faith, or that he was playing devil's advocate.[308] A simpler explanation is that Jesus' response to the woman's cry for help was simply racist. His mission was to the Jews, because it was to the Jews that the Kingdom of God was promised, and the Gentiles, not being God's chosen people, were not going to be part of it, and needed to be treated accordingly. It was a new Israel that Jesus envisaged. It was as simple as that. It might be objected that Jesus was simply explaining the boundaries of his mission as he understood them:[309] but that does not explain the insulting language that he used. What does explain it is the normal prejudice against Gentiles, against women, and thus against Gentile women, in the Judaism of Jesus' time. The woman gave as good as she got and appears to have jolted Jesus out of his racial prejudice.[310] He healed the woman's daughter, and credited the healing to the woman's response.[311]

Although there have already been hints that Gentiles are to be included in the Kingdom of God—in Jesus' healing of the man with a legion of evil spirits in Gentile territory, and in Jesus' challenging of the food laws—this passage marks a clear turning point: Jesus is learning that God's intention is inclusive rather than exclusive. Further signs of a turn to the Gentiles will follow this passage—travel through Gentile territory, and the miraculous feeding of a crowd that probably included Gentiles.[312] This incident, in which a Gentile woman educates Jesus, appears to be *the* turning point as far as Mark's Gospel is concerned. Jesus does not voluntarily turn towards the Gentiles: a woman from Syria turns him towards them.

Mark's Gospel is full of events, and his frequent use of the words *euthus* (immediately), *ērxanto* (he began) and *palin* (again) creates a sense of events following each other in quick succession. However, there is no reason to suppose that Mark has ordered his gospel in the same order in which events happened, and there is early evidence that he did not.[313] He might have had a plan for the order in which events are recorded, but it is not entirely obvious what that was. There is certainly no reason

---

y. Or *Lord*; other ancient authorities prefix *Yes*

to think that the gospel is in chronological order: and support for it not being can be found in the fact that before this event Mark has recorded healings in Gentile territory.

The most likely course of events might be that Jesus began as a disciple of John the Baptist, and that from that starting-point he developed a ministry that was initially entirely to the Jews. This was because he believed that the Kingdom of God was to be a renewed Israel, and it was his task to awaken the Jews to that and to tell them to turn their lives around in preparation for the promise being fulfilled. Jesus told parables to Jews, taught crowds of Jews, healed Jews, and cast demons out of Jews. He was only now in Gentile territory in order to get away from his hectic ministry for a while, and he had no intention of relating to Gentiles. But now he found himself having to do so: and he underwent a conversion experience. Jesus would always have believed that the Gentiles were also God's concern, but he would probably also have believed that the mission to the Jews would have to be completed before a mission to Gentiles could begin. A similar pattern of action was assumed among early Christians.[314] Perhaps the shift that has taken place is a recognition that Gentiles were being invited into the Kingdom of God before the Jews had all responded, and certainly that Gentiles were to be included in the healing action of the Kingdom of God before that Kingdom finally came.[315]

We have this woman to thank for Jesus' ministry among Gentiles, for the church following in his footsteps and welcoming Gentiles as equal members of the church, and possibly for associated conversion experiences as well. Might this event have been the bursting of a dam, enabling Jesus to say that no longer were there any boundaries? Having recognized that God's generous love was for Gentiles as well as Jews, might it not then have become obvious that God's generous love was as much for women as for men, and that women too were to be his disciples? And then the same for children: might they not be equal members of the Kingdom of God? And then the unrepentant sinners: for wasn't God's love absolutely generous—and in any case, how were boundaries to be set? Whose interpretation of the law should determine them? And had Jesus not in any case found himself questioning the validity of the law? Which order these conversions came in we cannot know: but come they all did.

This raises the same question that we raised in relation to Jesus being tempted by Satan. In what sense might Jesus have been without sin? All one can say is that he was not: at least, not during this incident recorded in Mark's Gospel. We now recognize racism as serious sin. Jesus was not just thinking something about the woman in front of him, and behaving towards her in the same way that he would have behaved towards a member of his own ethnic group. He offered her a racist insult. Perhaps he had forgotten his own very mixed heritage.

Jesus was a human being like the rest of us. The changing patterns of action that constituted him might have been those of God, but they were also those of a perfectly normal human being: hence his need for John's baptism, and his need for prayer, and presumably for confession. As the Letter to the Hebrews puts it, Jesus "learned obedience,"[316] perhaps to an extreme degree in relation to how we might slowly learn obedience to God's will—or perhaps not. But still this raises significant questions. In particular it raises the question as to God's relationship to Jesus' sin, and specifically to Jesus' racism. We might be committed to the idea of the changing patterns of action that constitute Jesus being the changing patterns of action that constitute God as well as the changing patterns of action of a perfectly normal human being: but that does not mean that there is not more to be said. It simply must be the case that God, as Action and the source of all action, might be the originator of patterns of action that we might call evil and sinful: hence Jesus' changing patterns of action might be of this nature. If so, then God constantly transforms them, absorbs the evil in them, and sends them back into the world cleansed and creative. Or perhaps we should say that although the changing patterns of action that constituted Jesus were those that constituted God, when up against the vast network of changing patterns of action that constituted other people and institutions of the time, they themselves turned bad, and that Jesus learned racism from people around him, and perhaps even from his parents. This would be understandable in a people desperately trying to hang on to its distinctive identity and culture in the midst of a vast empire and a cosmopolitan world. Either way, the changing patterns of action that constituted God were absorbing the evil that Jesus both suffered and perpetrated, and were transforming it into changing patterns of action that constituted the Kingdom of God: a Kingdom that would sweep away sin, evil, violence, injustice, and poverty.

It would have been very difficult for Jesus to grow up avoiding the racial prejudice that must have been all around him: prejudice that we can only recognize as sin. This means that we cannot avoid the conclusion that Jesus was entirely human to the extent that he committed sin and had to repent and seek forgiveness. This simply must mean that God experienced Jesus' sin: for is this not why the incarnation occurred at that time and in that place? To build a relationship between God and sinful humanity? How was God to do that without relating directly to human sin as that was experienced by and in God incarnate.

The same surely goes for all of the other prejudices with which Jesus grew up: the subordinate status of women; treatment of children as objects; and the distinction between the righteous and the unrighteous. Jesus went through several entirely human conversion experiences on the way to learning obedience to God in relation to the equality that characterizes the Kingdom of God, in which people of all ethnic groups will be welcome, in which women will be equal to men (if gender distinctions are to survive at all), in which children will be the first to enter, and also unrepentant sinners.

Of course, Jesus' followers have had to go through the same conversion experiences and more, over and over again. We find evidence of this happening in the Acts of the Apostles and in Paul's letters; and evidence of it happening again and again throughout the history of the church. It must keep on happening. God and the

Kingdom of God erect no boundaries, and Jesus learnt not to erect them. We too must continually learn not to erect them.

We shall be forever thankful to the Syrophoenician woman for converting Jesus to equality; and we must forever look back at the event at which Jesus' conversion experience happened, and learn over and over again that there are no boundaries to God's generous love, or to the Kingdom of God.

## MARK 7:31-37

> 31 Then he returned from the region of Tyre, and went by way of Sidon towards the Sea of Galilee, in the region of the Decapolis. ³² They brought to him a deaf man who had an impediment in his speech; and they begged him to lay his hand on him. ³³ He took him aside in private, away from the crowd, and put his fingers into his ears, and he spat and touched his tongue. ³⁴ Then looking up to heaven, he sighed and said to him, 'Ephphatha', that is, 'Be opened.' ³⁵ And immediately his ears were opened, his tongue was released, and he spoke plainly. ³⁶ Then Jesus^z ordered them to tell no one; but the more he ordered them, the more zealously they proclaimed it. ³⁷ They were astounded beyond measure, saying, 'He has done everything well; he even makes the deaf to hear and the mute to speak.'[317]

What was wrong with this man? Was it some minor problem that was easily fixed by Jesus doing what he did? Was Jesus not so much a miraculous healer but rather someone who understood people's physicalities and psychologies sufficiently to be able to heal them? Was the synagogue leader's daughter in a coma from which Jesus woke her? Was the man lowered through the roof in need of physical healing, or in need of an authoritative person telling him to get up? Was the woman who touched Jesus' cloak in need of being recognized as a member of society by someone with the authority to ensure that that happened? Is the physical reality that we are beginning to understand the only reality, or is there something else? Is there a God, and does God intervene in the world?

Before we respond to those questions, we might study the language of this passage. It is full of action. They brought, they begged, Jesus took the man aside, he put his fingers into the man's ears ("shoved his fingers into his ears" might be a better translation), he spat, he touched, he looked up to heaven, and he sighed: an inmost wrestling, presumably with the powers of evil responsible for the man's deafness.[318] And then Jesus said, "Be opened." And the passage is clear that it is what Jesus had done that mattered: a complex pattern of action that included spitting, touching, sighing, and speaking.[319] It is the patterns of action that are the center of attention here.

z. Gk *he*

Different conceptual frameworks offer different possibilities for responding to questions such as those above. In a Being framework that prioritizes beings, the unchanging, the unitary, and the static, we find ourselves with the kind of scenario that Plato developed, and that has largely controlled thinking about religion ever since. Because the fundamental reality is Being, the unchanging, the unitary, and the static, and the world that we live in is not those, we find ourselves living in two worlds: an invisible world of unchanging realities, and the world of changing beings in which we live. The former, because unchanging and unitary, has a reality that our world of diversity and change does not have. If there is to be any coherence in how we understand reality, then we have to find some way to reconcile the two different worlds, so we find ourselves assuming mediators between them: Plato's variety of Forms, subordinate to the Form of the Good or the One; the Word or Wisdom of God; the Holy Spirit; angels; good spirits, and therefore evil spirits. As our understanding of the world of changing beings has developed, we have found less need to employ such mediations in order to understand the world in which we live: and our trajectory is now firmly set towards abandoning those mediations and therefore the previously very real world of Being, the unchanging, and the unitary, where God was located. A perfect storm of secularization processes is now having a transformative effect on us. Not only does God not live above a physical dome in a seventh heavenly layer, but the invisible world of unchanging Being in which God had been relocated has now become an entirely unnecessary hypothesis. The Being conceptual framework has left us enclosed in our own world of changing beings, and unable to conceive of anything breaking into it, whether miracles, God, or a Kingdom of God. If religion survives, then it is disconnected from the rest of life because it is still trying to live in bits of the conceptual framework that our social and daily life has abandoned.

An Action conceptual framework, in which reality is action, change, movement, diversity, and generally the dynamic, offers somewhat different possibilities. The world of changing patterns of action in which we live is the real world, and any other world of changing patterns of action can be equally real. There need be no gulf between different worlds that needs to be bridged by mediators. If we identify God with Action rather than Being, that is, as the originator of all action rather than the originator of all being, then God can change and can be changing patterns of action without any contradiction with God's essential character being involved. No longer is there a conceptual problem with the changing patterns of action that constitute God relating to the changing patterns of action that constitute ourselves, the world, and the cosmos. God can be intimately involved in our lives in ways that are difficult to conceptualize in a Being conceptual framework; prayer can relate to the very heart of God, and God to our prayer; and our changing patterns of action can be our own changing patterns of action, God's changing patterns of action, and changing patterns of action highly influenced by the myriad changing patterns of action that constitute our environments and the people around us.

In particular, new possibilities are available for Christology: that is, how we understand the nature—or rather, the action—of Jesus Christ. In a Being conceptual framework, understanding how an unchanging God can become incarnate in a changing human person can be difficult to conceptualize. One of the outcomes of this difficulty is the idea that it is the Word of God—ambiguously God and not God—who becomes the human being Jesus, compromising both the incarnation and a trinitarian God. In an Action conceptual framework God is Action, the source of all action, and action in changing patterns, in which Jesus uniquely shares, and that he uniquely experiences: and as it is action and change that is reality, this sharing in God's changing patterns of action is a genuine incarnation—for changing patterns of action is what a human being is—and Jesus is genuinely God. Of course there are differences between the human Jesus and the God who is Action and the source of all action: but the identity, because constituted by changing patterns of action, is real.

In this context, Jesus' miracles begin to look rather different from the way they look in a Being conceptual framework. In an Action framework, Jesus' healings are networks of changing patterns of action in which the changing patterns of action that constitute Jesus, God, and the person healed, relate to each other. This does not mean that at this distance in time we can identify precisely what changing patterns of action were at work: but it does mean that we can conceive of God's intimate involvement in a relationship between Jesus and the person being healed that might not be simply about what we might call physical realities. Visible and understandable physical realities are constituted by particular changing patterns of action, but other changing patterns of action might be equally related to those.

With an Action conceptual framework there is one world—a world of changing patterns of action—and not the different unchanging and changing worlds that the Being framework delivers. It is in the Action framework that God, prayer, and Jesus' miracles, can begin to make new sense, and it is this framework that can begin to dissolve the now seriously hardening boundary between religion and our social and daily lives. And it is in the context of the Action framework that we can pray Jesus' prayer that the Kingdom of God should come on earth as it is in heaven.

"He has done everything well; he even makes the deaf to hear and the mute to speak." This probably means that Jesus is seen to be fulfilling prophecy, in this instance a prophecy in Isaiah:

> [5] Then the eyes of the blind shall be opened,
>    and the ears of the deaf unstopped;
> [6] then the lame shall leap like a deer,
>    and the tongue of the speechless sing for joy.
> For waters shall break forth in the wilderness,
>    and streams in the desert.[320]

The pattern of action found in the prophets is now being played out in their own town, so God must be at work.

## MARK 8:1-10

> 8 In those days when there was again a great crowd without anything to eat, he called his disciples and said to them, ² 'I have compassion for the crowd, because they have been with me now for three days and have nothing to eat. ³ If I send them away hungry to their homes, they will faint on the way—and some of them have come from a great distance.' ⁴ His disciples replied, "How can one feed these people with bread here in the desert?' ⁵ He asked them, 'How many loaves do you have?' They said, 'Seven.' ⁶ Then he ordered the crowd to sit down on the ground; and he took the seven loaves, and after giving thanks he broke them and gave them to his disciples to distribute; and they distributed them to the crowd. ⁷ They had also a few small fish; and after blessing them, he ordered that these too should be distributed. ⁸ They ate and were filled; and they took up the broken pieces left over, seven baskets full. ⁹ Now there were about four thousand people. And he sent them away. ¹⁰ And immediately he got into the boat with his disciples and went to the district of Dalmanutha.[a] [321]

What is this passage doing here? It looks remarkably similar to the account of a feeding of five thousand in a previous chapter. An obvious conclusion to draw is that as the story began to circulate among the early Christians, details got changed in the telling and retelling, so that by the time the story reached Mark as he wrote his gospel he thought that there were two incidents and so put both of them in. Or perhaps there were two distinct events, slightly different from each other.[322] And there do seem to be differences between the two narratives. Here there were "four thousand" in the crowd rather than five thousand, as in the previous account. The Greek original simply records the number: "There were four thousand." English translations tend to add "people" as that makes for better English, but it is not there in the original. Simply mentioning the number leaves us to guess whether it means "four thousand men," "four thousand adults," or "four thousand including children." In the feeding of the five thousand it is a very clear "five thousand men," the Greek word allowing no ambiguity about the gender.

The other significant difference between the two narratives is not found in the passage itself but in the previous passage. The Decapolis—the region of ten towns or cities—was on the eastern side of Lake Galilee and was more cosmopolitan than the western side where Jesus spent most of his ministry. This suggests that the crowd was more cosmopolitan and might have contained Gentiles as well as Jews. Either the event took place in cosmopolitan territory, or Mark has located it where he has

---

a. Other ancient authorities read *Mageda* or *Magdala*

in his gospel in order to suggest that in relation to this feeding of a multitude there were Gentiles as well as Jews present: not just Gentiles, and not just Jews, but both. A significant detail is that in the account of the feeding of the five thousand Mark used a Jewish word for the baskets that were filled with leftovers, whereas in this account a Gentile word is used.[323] The implication is clear.

If the event was in the Decapolis, and Jesus was feeding a crowd containing both Jews and Gentiles, then something was happening that would not normally have happened. Jews did not generally eat with Gentiles. The passage follows Jesus' encounter with the Syrophoenician woman, whose response to his rude rebuff converted him to an understanding that people of any and all ethnic groups, or from whatever other divisions of humanity we might think of, were all equally welcome in the Kingdom of God. If the passage is simply another version of the feeding of the five thousand, and it is Mark who is locating it in cosmopolitan territory, then he is making his own similar point: that the Kingdom of God is for everyone, whatever their ethnic origin, religious status, or anything else. Mark needed the church to believe that the inclusion of Gentiles alongside Jews was authorized by Jesus' practice, so even if there was little evidence that it was, Mark has ordered his material to provide the required legitimacy.[324] And perhaps the "four thousand," without "men" being added, was there to make the same point: that now the Kingdom of God has been thrown open to everyone, and is no longer the preserve of Jewish males. The church to which Mark belonged, and for which he was writing his gospel, would probably have contained both Jews and Gentiles. It might have benefited from Paul's evangelizing mission to the Gentiles, and it would have benefited from the apostles' and the Jerusalem church elders' understanding that God was welcoming Gentiles into the church on the same basis as Jews—a situation for which they made pragmatic regulations in order to ensure that no new burdens would be placed on Gentile Christians at the same time as ensuring that Jewish Christians would not be scandalized by Gentiles' freedom from the law: a law that many Jewish Christians continued to keep.[325] It would clearly have been helpful to the integration of both Jews and Gentiles in the same church for them to be able to find in Jesus' ministry an equal welcome of Gentiles and Jews in the Kingdom of God, and here Mark was ensuring that that message would be heard. From the Syrophoenician woman Jesus had learnt obedience to the equality of everyone in the eyes of God, and he put that new understanding into practice in his own ministry: so it was clearly essential for Jews and Gentiles to live at peace with each other in the church; and in particular it was essential for Jews and Gentiles to share in the Eucharist together.

We shall soon find Jesus sharing a last meal with his disciples during which he took bread, gave thanks, broke the bread, and shared it among his disciples. In the feeding of the five thousand, and now in this feeding of the four thousand, we find the same pattern of actions. Here we have Jews and Gentiles sharing together in this pattern of actions: an encouragement to Jewish Christians to share in the same Eucharist—the same remembrance of the last supper—as their Gentile fellow-Christians, and thus to break with the Jewish tradition of not eating with Gentiles.

This was clearly a live issue in the churches. An early mixing of Gentiles and Jews in the church appears to have taken place at Antioch: a church that was founded as the apostles and other Christians spread out from Jerusalem following Stephen's martyrdom and a growing general persecution of Christians. Paul, who had been one of those persecutors, having become a Christian, was an inveterate traveler, and when he found himself at Antioch he was horrified to find that Peter, having been firmly converted to the idea that Gentiles belonged in the same church as Jews, had now ceased to eat with Gentiles, having been put under pressure to do so by more conservative Jewish Christians. A public row broke out. This was a matter of absolute principle for Paul. The Lord's Supper, the Eucharist, was *the* focal expression of the church as the Body of Christ: a single body with many members. For Jews and Gentiles not to share together in the taking of bread, the giving thanks, the breaking, and the *sharing* of the bread, was to sunder the Body of Christ. It was absolutely essential for everyone to share together in this central pattern of action given to the church by Jesus himself. And later on, in a letter to the church in Corinth, Paul expressed considerable anger that the wealthy were bringing their own food to share with each other and were not sharing it with the poorer members of the church at the Lord's Supper. This was just as appalling a destruction of the church. They had simply not recognized "the Body": that is, that the church was the Body of Christ, a single body, and that a sharing together in the Lord's Supper was what constituted it. Mark would probably have been well aware of these conflicts, or at least of conflicts of a similar character. Perhaps the best explanation for his including both of the multitude feeding events in his gospel is that he was telling his congregation that Jesus not only fed a multitude of Jews, but also a multitude composed of both Jews and Gentiles, and that they ate together following Jesus' taking of bread, giving thanks, breaking it, and sharing it among them.[326]

Reality is action in changing patterns. The church is action in changing patterns: and at the heart of the reality of the church is the pattern of action that we find in Jesus at the feeding of the five thousand, at the feeding of the four thousand, and at the last supper: and as reality is action in patterns, the same pattern of action binds together the events of the feeding of the five thousand, the feeding of the four thousand, Jesus' last meal with his disciples, and the church's Eucharist: the doing of these actions in remembrance of Jesus. These events are all the same reality, undivided by the passing of time. So as we take bread, give thanks, break the bread, and share the bread, we are there,[327] among the four thousand, as they with Jesus do these same actions. As both Paul and Mark recognized, it was essential for Jews and Gentiles to share in this pattern of action together, and that this was what bound them together in the same church. It is therefore absolutely essential that in our own day every Christian, of whatever ethnic group, of whatever religious status—and so whether baptized or not—and of whatever denomination, should share together in this pattern of action:

the taking of bread, the giving thanks, the breaking of the bread, and the sharing of the bread.

An interesting question is this: As the patterns of action that constitute the feeding of the five thousand and the feeding of the four thousand are so similar, and if reality is action in patterns, then even if the two accounts are of different events, might we not regard them as substantially the same event? A change in the conceptual framework can dissolve dilemmas encountered in the previous one.

## MARK 8:11-13

> 11 The Pharisees came and began to argue with him, asking him for a sign from heaven, to test him. ¹² And he sighed deeply in his spirit and said, 'Why does this generation ask for a sign? Truly I tell you, no sign will be given to this generation.' ¹³ And he left them, and getting into the boat again, he went across to the other side.³²⁸

We are telling a narrative in which reality is action in changing patterns. Nothing stays still. Everything—or rather, every action in patterns, or every process—is action, movement, changing, dynamic. So where does this leave knowledge? And where does it leave truth? In John's Gospel, Pilate asks: "What is truth?" The question is left hanging in the air, waiting for us to answer it. For if what is the case one moment is not the case in another, then what is truth? And if what is the case in one place is not the case in another, then what is truth? And can we know anything? For whatever we think we have come to know we know no longer.

The obvious response is that if reality is action in changing patterns, then truth is action in changing patterns, and so is knowledge. Truth is as much of a process as is what it is truth about. It is a constant truth-seeking: the changing patterns of action that constitute our brains seeking a dynamic coherence, a harmony, with the changing patterns of action that constitute the changing patterns of action that constitute the events around us, and, crucially, with patterns of action in the past. And here we encounter a particular complexity. Because reality is dynamic, and everything—or rather, every pattern of action—changes all the time, and it is only those changing patterns of action happening in the present with which the changing patterns of action that constitute our brains can entangle themselves, what access to patterns of action in the past can we possibly have? Can we know the past in any sense? Can we know the truth about the past?

There is of course a sense in which the past is unreal, simply because it is not action in changing patterns. Events in the past are the patterns of action that constituted them moment by moment. They are forever fixed, static, and thus unreal. But it is those patterns of action that were changing at the time, and that influenced changing patterns of action at subsequent times, and therefore in our time as well. Here is our access to those patterns of action in the past: the changing patterns of action in the present. To take an example: We can engage with texts and places that resulted from the changing patterns of action that we now call the two world wars. The changing patterns of action that are our brains engage with these crystallized patterns of action to create new changing patterns of action in our brains that we might call memories or images of past events. The action of engaging with the crystallized patterns from the past we might call truth-seeking or knowledge-seeking: that is, truth or knowledge. It is the seeking out and complex intertwining of the crystallized patterns of the past with the changing patterns of action that constitute who we are that generate knowledge and truth. Knowledge we might understand as indicating what is going on in each of our brains in relation to those crystallized patterns, and truth as what is going on in multiple brains that are engaging with each other as they engage with the crystallized patterns. Lack of knowledge occurs where there is no engagement of the changing patterns of action that constitute who we are with either the changing patterns of action that constitute events around us or crystallized patterns from the past. Untruth can occur when the crystallized patterns with which our minds engage emerged without close reference to events at the time, or when our own changing patterns of action create their own crystallized patterns with no reference to crystallized patterns generated by events of their own time.

What were the Pharisees looking for when they asked for a sign from heaven? They were repeating a pattern of action that had occurred after the exodus from Egypt: even though Moses had already offered numerous signs, the Israelites still wanted more.[329] Moses had promised that God would send a prophet like himself. Early Christians understood Jesus to be that prophet, and Jesus might have understood himself to be the one promised, so it might have been no surprise to Jesus to have suffered from the same request for a sign.[330]

Let us assume good motives on the part of the Pharisees: that is, that they were genuinely interested in Jesus' relationship with God, and that they wanted some crystallized pattern—something permanent—with which they could engage. They wanted an event that would remain in the past. What they did not realize—or perhaps they did—is that Jesus was constantly providing them and everyone else with signs: changing patterns of action that represented the dynamic Kingdom of God that had come near and was fast approaching. The parables, the healings, the casting out of demons, and the miracles, were all signs: that is, they were action in changing patterns that were in some kind of harmony with the changing patterns of action that constituted the Kingdom of God—and Jesus' whole life, its actions and its words, were equally a sign: changing patterns of action that mirrored the changing patterns of action of the Kingdom of God, and therefore of God. Jesus did not need to provide a sign for the Pharisees because he *was* the sign, and he was constantly providing new signs: signs that were changing patterns of action—changing, moving, dynamic—and that were not the crystallized patterns that Pharisees could conveniently leave in the past.

Jesus' subsequent action is significant: "he left them"—the opposite of the many arrivals that we find in Mark's Gospel.[331] He left them so that he could arrive in a place, Bethsaida, where he could continue to heal so as to offer signs of the Kingdom of God: signs that were dynamic patterns of action; but he has also left them because they clearly had no intention of believing the good news of the Kingdom of God and of changing their way of life accordingly.

In John's Gospel we find the statement that Jesus is "the way, and the truth, and the life."[332] He is action in changing patterns, both then and now, and it is those changing patterns of action that are the way, meaning that Jesus is inviting us to join him in becoming changing patterns of action that represent the Kingdom of God. Jesus, constituted as he was and is by changing patterns of action that are the changing patterns of action that constitute God, is himself the truth, by which we mean those changing patterns of action. It is by engaging with those changing patterns of action that we do the truth, which is not some object that we can possess, but is rather a faithful engagement with the crystallized patterns from the past generated by the life of Jesus, and with the changing patterns of action that constitute who Jesus is today. And Jesus is the life—his changing patterns of action are simply what life is. There is no essential difference between the way, the truth, and the life: following the way, seeking the truth, and living the life, all express the engagement of the changing patterns of action that constitute who we are with the changing patterns of action that constitute who Jesus is and therefore who God is and what the Kingdom of God is: all of them changing patterns of action.

## MARK 8:14–21

> 14 Now the disciples[b] had forgotten to bring any bread; and they had only one loaf with them in the boat. 15 And he cautioned them, saying, 'Watch out—beware of the yeast of the Pharisees and the yeast of Herod.'[c] 16 They said to one another, 'It is because we have no bread.' 17 And becoming aware of it, Jesus said to them, 'Why are you talking about having no bread? Do you still not perceive or understand? Are your hearts hardened? 18 Do you have eyes, and fail to see? Do you have ears, and fail to hear? And do you not remember? 19 When I broke the five loaves for the five thousand, how many baskets full of broken pieces did you collect?' They said to him, 'Twelve.' 20 'And the seven for the four thousand, how many baskets full of broken pieces did you collect?' And they said to him, 'Seven.' 21 Then he said to them, 'Do you not yet understand?'[333]

b. Gk *they*

c. Other ancient authorities read *the Herodians*

What does it mean to understand? If we and everything around us are action in changing patterns, then if the changing patterns of action that constitute our brains manage to integrate some of the changing patterns of action in the world and people around us with some of the changing patterns of action that constitute our brains—patterns of action that we might call words, ideas, images, and concepts—then we might say to ourselves and to others "I understand": I understand that sentence, that situation, that event, that person, and so on. Sometimes we might misunderstand—we might manage to relate just one or two of the complex changing patterns of action that constitute our brains with just one or two of those multiple changing patterns of action that constitute another person, a situation, an event, or a sentence, whereas we might have been able to relate different and far larger selections of both sets of changing patterns of action instead. In relation to words spoken to us: Those words are changing patterns of action in the air that are the result of changing patterns of action in the speaker's brain that we might call the speaker's intended meaning. The moving air strikes our eardrums, electrical pulses occur in our brains, and those changing patterns of action entangle with other changing patterns of action to create yet more that we might interpret as the meaning of the words. The changing patterns of action that constitute the meaning that we understand might or might not be similar to those that constituted the intended meaning. They will never be the same. The complexity of the changing nature of complex patterns of action will ensure that: so the question comes down to one of similarity—and of course to a similarity that can never be evaluated in any way because to evaluate it would require our direct access to changing patterns of action in someone else's brain at some time in the past, which is an impossibility. Understanding is inevitably incomplete. We can never fully know the meaning intended by the speaker. Even less can we know the meaning intended by a writer of a text, because there the connection between the writer's intended meaning and the meaning that the reader understands will be far more tenuous. It is a connection that is pure pattern, a crystallization of the changing patterns of action that at some point in the past constituted the writer and their relationship with the pen, typewriter, or computer. This is the character of our understanding of Mark's intended meaning as he wrote his gospel: incomplete, because based on a most tenuous connection between the changing patterns of action that constituted Mark's brain and the changing patterns of action that constitute our brains in the present: which means that our understanding of the events that Mark records is radically incomplete, because now we have even more tenuous a connection: a combination of the tenuous connection between Mark's intended meaning and our own understanding, and the highly tenuous connection between the patterns of action that constituted the original events and the changing patterns of action that constituted Mark's brain. But this is true in relation to any and every historical event, to every event reported today, to every person we meet, and so on. The connections are always tenuous to a greater or lesser extent, so our understanding is always incomplete to a greater or lesser extent.

What we can say about our understanding of the text of Mark's Gospel, and of our understanding of the events to which it refers, is that the changing patterns of action that have entangled with the events, with the text, and with us, form an extremely dense network of changing patterns of action: more dense than would be the case in relation to any other set of events that long ago. And constantly entangling with that dense network of changing patterns of action—of all of them, from the original events to the changing patterns of action of our own brains—will be the changing patterns of action that constitute God. This does not mean that we will be able to understand that involvement, but it does mean that the network will be even more dense, and that throughout it, from the changing patterns of action that constituted and that constitute Jesus, through the events of his life, death and resurrection, through the changing patterns of action of Mark's brain, through the millions of interpreters of Mark's Gospel, to our reading of the gospel, changing patterns of action that constitute God are constantly entangled with all of the others: never on their own, and always along with those that constitute humanity and our world, and always contributing to the density of the connections. We can therefore read Mark's Gospel with some confidence that we are relating to God, to Jesus, and again to God: which does not mean that we shall understand those relationships, because the complexity of the dense network of changing patterns of action across twenty centuries would be impossible for any human brain to grasp: that is, it would be impossible for us to connect all of those changing patterns of action to the changing patterns of action that we might call our ideas, words, concepts, images and so on.

In relation to this passage: the disciples did not understand. They had connected Jesus' word "yeast" with the idea of "bread" because they had forgotten to bring any, whereas Jesus' intended meaning was nothing to do with bread and had everything to do with the ways in which the often onerous and exploitative actions of Herod, and the teachings of the Pharisees, infiltrated everyone's minds. And then there is a further misunderstanding, perhaps reflecting a separate conversation: The disciples had not understood the feedings of the five thousand and of the four thousand. But what was it that they are supposed to have understood? We can only guess, but what Jesus might have been getting at with his mention of the numbers of baskets of leftovers collected is that the disciples had not understood the generosity and overabundance of the Kingdom of God that those feedings of multitudes represented. Perhaps Jesus was being a little unfair. It must have been genuinely difficult to understand what was happening around them: after all, this was a unique person they were with, and it was unique events that they were experiencing, so it would not have been easy for the changing patterns of action that constituted their brains to relate to the changing patterns of action around them. As the next section of Mark's Gospel shows, the apostles did slowly gain a little more understanding:[334] their own changing patterns of action slowly related to more of Jesus' intended meanings and therefore to more of the changing patterns of action that constituted God and the Kingdom of God: but it was not until the resurrection and the gift of the Holy Spirit at the first Christian Pentecost that radical change occurred. And similarly for us: The more we are around the text of Mark's Gospel, the more we engage with other interpreters of the text, and the more we engage with the changing patterns of action of the God who has been intimately involved with the dense network of changing patterns of action that constituted the original events, Mark's mind, and twenty centuries of interpretation, the greater will be our understanding of Mark's Gospel: but it will still be the case that only encounter with the patterns of action that constitute the risen Christ still among us by the Holy Spirit will change the patterns of action that constitute who we are in ways similar to those experienced by Jesus' first disciples, and that will enable us to live in our own times the patterns of action that constitute the Kingdom of God.[335]

## MARK 8:22-30

> 22 They came to Bethsaida. Some people[d] brought a blind man to him and begged him to touch him. 23 He took the blind man by the hand and led him out of the village; and when he had put saliva on his eyes and laid his hands on him, he asked him, 'Can you see anything?' 24 And the man looked up and said, 'I can see people, but they look like trees, walking.' 25 Then Jesus[e] laid his hands on his eyes again; and he looked intently and his sight was restored, and he saw everything clearly. 26 Then he sent him away to his home, saying, 'Do not even go into the village.'[f]
>
> 27 Jesus went on with his disciples to the villages of Caesarea Philippi; and on the way he asked his disciples, 'Who do people say that I am?' 28 And they answered him, 'John the Baptist; and others, Elijah; and still others, one of the prophets.' 29 He asked them, 'But who do you say that I am?' Peter answered him, 'You are the Messiah.'[g] 30 And he sternly ordered them not to tell anyone about him.[336]

If we understand Mark's Gospel as a three-act drama, then this is where Act two begins. The journey to Jerusalem has begun; Jesus predicts what will happen when he gets there; and attention shifts from educating the crowd to educating the disciples.[337] Existing patterns of action fall into the background, and new ones emerge.

This healing miracle mirrors the healing of the deaf and dumb man recorded after the feeding of the five thousand.[338] There is no mention of the faith of the person who is

d. Gk *they*
e. Gk *he*
f. Other ancient authorities add *or tell anyone in the village*
g. Or *the Christ*

healed, and spittle is used. The difference is that during this event a man comes to see, whereas during the previous similar event someone comes to hear and speak. Mark has probably placed this incident at this point in his gospel to close a section in which the disciples do not understand—they do not see—and at the beginning of a section in which they begin to understand: to see.[339] The two incidents exhibit similar patterns of action, and this one a pattern of action similar to the pattern of action that is the disciples' experience.

But what precisely happened during this event? Was this what we might call a natural healing, that is, a healing that relied on Jesus' understanding of a physical cause of the man's blindness which it was possible to heal by the method employed, or was there something miraculous, out of the ordinary, something not purely related to the normal laws of physics, chemistry, and biology? That might look like a fairly simple question, even if we know that at this distance in time, and with the limited amount of information available to us in the text, it would be impossible to answer it: but the question itself might not in fact be as simple as it looks. This is because the laws of physics, chemistry, and biology are not necessarily the universal and consistent things that we might think they are. It has been clear for a long time that the laws of sciences such as economics are limited in their application, and would be better understood as approximate models of the real world rather than laws that the real world obeys: but it now appears that what we think of as the laws of physics are of a similar character. They might be more generally applicable in most contexts than any laws of economics, but any law of physics is in fact only an approximation to how the universe works, and any such law is only applicable at all in certain contexts. The laws that Newton discovered apply fairly accurately in most contexts and in relation to what we would normally regard as objects and actions related to them, but at the micro-level, and at the level of the universe as a whole, those laws fail, and different laws are required: and at the micro-level we find that we need laws with the notion of probability rather than predictability at their heart. The universe is action in changing patterns, and although there will be contexts in which patterns of action remain relatively stable for most of the time, we cannot assume that patterns of action will not change. They have done, they do, and they will. If God is Action, the source of all action, and in particular the source of the creative changing patterns of action that gave birth to the universe, and if Jesus is God incarnate, and therefore constituted by changing patterns of action that constitute God as well as being constituted by the changing patterns of action of his complete humanity, then it should be no surprise that in the midst of his activity we might find the kind of creative law-changing patterns of action that were in evidence at the creation of the universe. Whilst we need and expect the patterns of action that sustain the universe, the planet, the ecosystem, and our own lives, to remain relatively stable—for if they did not then the universe would collapse back into chaotic action—we should also expect patterns of action to change, particularly in the context of patterns of action that constitute the God who is the author of action, and of the changing patterns of action, that gave birth to the universe in which we live, and that continue to sustain it as its patterns of action continue to change. Jesus' healing of the blind man might therefore be not simply some law-breaking activity of God, or a chemical and biological process that conforms to what we experience as the normal laws of chemistry and biology, but rather an example of the laws of chemistry and physics changing in the context of the changing patterns of action that constitute God.

We have encountered multiple healings as we have read Mark's Gospel: evil spirits have been cast out, Simon's mother-in-law has been healed of a fever, a man has been healed of leprosy or some other skin disease, a man with paralysis has walked away carrying his bed, a man's withered hand has been healed, a woman has been healed of constant blood loss, a girl has been brought back to life, a man has been cured of his deafness, and multiple healings have taken place when Jesus has arrived in new places to proclaim the Kingdom of God's coming: and now a blind man is healed. Why keep adding all of these different stories of healings? There is evidence that at least some of what we find in Mark's Gospel, and perhaps all of it, was gathered by Mark as he listened to Peter's preaching and reminiscences, so maybe there are numerous similar healing stories because Peter had been present at the events and spoke of what he knew.[340] Additional material might have reached Mark through the broader oral tradition circulating in the church, and perhaps early written collections of events of Jesus' ministry. Mark might also have included so many of the stories because each one had a role to play where Mark placed it. What is significant about this particular story is the process, from not being able to see, to seeing rather less than clearly, to seeing clearly. What follows is Jesus' discussion with his disciples about who people think he is. A number of possibilities are offered, all of them understandable. Jesus might well have started out as a disciple of John the Baptist, doing and saying similar things to John: but their ways parted, either before or after John was imprisoned, with Jesus coming to understand that the invitation to enter the Kingdom of God was unconditional, whereas John probably continued to demand repentance, baptism, and a genuine moral transformation. Now that John was dead, it was not surprising that Jesus had taken on John's mantle. And similarly with Elijah, who was then and still is regarded as the prophet now in heaven who will be sent as the new age dawns. It would have been clear to many that Jesus was Elijah. And similarly with the other prophets: those who, at various points in Israel's history, announced the coming of God's Kingdom. The disciples were correct: Jesus *was* these people, because his changing patterns of action mirrored the changing patterns of action that constituted who they were. This is what all of us are: changing patterns of action—so if the changing patterns of action that constituted Jesus could be identified with those that constituted John the Baptist, Elijah, and the other prophets, then that was who Jesus was.

But then, like the second stage of the healing of the man's blindness,[341] Jesus asks a rather more direct question of his disciples, and Peter states that Jesus is the Messiah:

an identification that people who thought that he was a prophet were not making.[342] The root meaning of the word is "the anointed one," and so "the one whom God has anointed," and because the Kings of Israel were anointed during what was looked back to as a golden age in the nation's history, in Jesus' time "Messiah" was taken to mean the one who would be anointed as King of Israel and rule a newly independent nation.[343] So Peter might have meant by "Messiah" that Jesus was the hoped-for rescuer of Israel, and presumably a military leader who would free the Jews from Roman occupation. It is not clear whether Jesus accepted this verdict: only that he said that it was not to be discussed with anyone else. If Jesus believed that Peter had got it right, and if both of them were assuming that the Messiah would function rather like King David, who united the tribes in a single kingdom and defended its borders, then insisting on silence was clearly wise—otherwise crucifixion might have occurred sooner than it did. But if Jesus intended to redefine what "Messiah" meant—as he was about to do, and which the meaning of "the anointed one" of course permitted—then he would still have wanted to prevent any further discussion, because the public understanding of "Messiah" would have been of a military leader of some kind, and Jesus would have been understood in that light however much he might have wished to redefine the role of the Messiah, particularly as this conversation happened at Caesarea Philippi where there was a temple to one of Rome's divinities: Caesar.[344] We can now see another reason for Mark recording the healing of the blind man immediately before Peter's declaration about Jesus. The man is not to tell everyone about what has happened as that would have made it difficult for Jesus to continue his preaching and actions about the Kingdom of God; and the disciples were told not to discuss with anyone else their ideas about who Jesus was for the same reason: that to do so might have prevented Jesus' own plans for his journey to Jerusalem, and would in any case have misrepresented his own idea of the Messiah's task. Accordingly the titles "Christ" and "Messiah" largely disappear from Mark's account until they take center stage at Jesus' trial, and "Son of Man" returns as Jesus' preferred self-designation.[345]

The Messiah, as understood by Jesus, was constituted by changing patterns of action, the character of which Mark will unfold as his gospel continues. These changing patterns of action were those on which Jesus would now model his own, so that he would indeed now become the Messiah: but they were not the patterns of action that many would have associated with a Messiah.[346] The disciples could perceive dimly, so an additional healing of their ideas was required.

They were "on the way": a phrase frequently found in Mark's Gospel. Jesus was constantly on the move, as were his disciples: an essential pattern of action for Jesus, for his followers then, and for his followers now.[347]

# MARK 8:31–9:1

> 31 Then he began to teach them that the Son of Man must undergo great suffering, and be rejected by the elders, the chief priests, and the scribes, and be killed, and after three days rise again. ³² He said all this quite openly. And Peter took him aside and began to rebuke him. ³³ But turning and looking at his disciples, he rebuked Peter and said, 'Get behind me, Satan! For you are setting your mind not on divine things but on human things.'
>
> 34 He called the crowd with his disciples, and said to them, 'If any want to become my followers, let them deny themselves and take up their cross and follow me. ³⁵ For those who want to save their life will lose it, and those who lose their life for my sake, and for the sake of the gospel,[h] will save it. ³⁶ For what will it profit them to gain the whole world and forfeit their life? ³⁷ Indeed, what can they give in return for their life? ³⁸ Those who are ashamed of me and of my words[i] in this adulterous and sinful generation, of them the Son of Man will also be ashamed when he comes in the glory of his Father with the holy angels.' 9 ¹And he said to them, 'Truly I tell you, there are some standing here who will not taste death until they see that the kingdom of God has come with[j] power.'[348]

This is the third mention of the "Son of Man" in Mark's Gospel. The first was when in the context of the healing of the man lowered through the roof Jesus declared the Son of Man to have authority to forgive sins, and the second was when he declared the Son of Man to have authority over the sabbath. Now we hear that the one who has authority to forgive sins and has authority over the sabbath—and therefore over the law—is to suffer, be killed, and rise again. We have already asked the question as to whether Jesus employed "Son of Man" to refer to himself, to the figure in the Book of Daniel who would approach the Ancient of Days, or to both. We might now be in a position to recognize that this question is looking in the wrong direction. It is asking about beings: that is, does "Son of Man" mean the being Jesus of Nazareth, or the being who comes to the Ancient of Days, or both? Perhaps we should be asking about patterns of action. Jesus has defined the Son of Man as the one who declares the forgiveness of sins and who exercises authority over the law: both patterns of action that constitute God. If a heavenly figure exhibits this pattern of action, then he is the Son of Man; and if Jesus of Nazareth exhibits this pattern of action, then he is the Son of Man. The Son of Man is a particular pattern of action: clearly a changing pattern of action, but a distinctive pattern of action nevertheless.

And now the definition of the Son of Man is being deepened by the completion of the complex pattern of action that constitutes him. We have already encountered his

---

h. Other ancient authorities read *lose their life for the sake of the gospel*
i. Other ancient authorities read *and of mine*
j. Or *in*

authority to forgive, his authority over the law, and his authority to cast out demons; and we have already recognized that his mission might encompass suffering and death: but now "after three days rise again" is added to the list.[349] Where this complex pattern of patterns of action is found—declaring forgiveness; exercising authority over the law; and suffering, being rejected, being killed, and rising again—there is the Son of Man. So Jesus of Nazareth is the Son of Man if he is constituted by these patterns of action; and the heavenly figure is Son of Man if he exhibits these patterns of action. The identity is the patterns of action, and the patterns of action are the identity. And if Jesus is constituted by changing patterns of action that are changing patterns of action that constitute God, then not only are declaring forgiveness and exercising authority over the law patterns of action that constitute God, but suffering, being rejected, being killed, and rising again, are also patterns of action that constitute God. The Messianic Son of Man of the Book of Daniel is still the anointed one who will reign in God's Kingdom, but only after the rejection, suffering, and death, that Jesus here predicts: a possibility already recognized in the merging of the suffering servant of God and the Son of Man in apocalyptic literature that would have been circulating in Jesus' time.[350]

Peter has just declared Jesus to be the Messiah: the one who will rescue Israel. He has not heard Jesus disown that title, and so he still regards it, along with his presuppositions about its meaning, as applicable to Jesus. Those presuppositions will have been about patterns of action, and probably military ones. Now Jesus has promised rather different patterns of action: suffering, being rejected, being killed, and rising again. These don't fit Peter's understanding of the Messiah, and he presumably tells Jesus that he is wrong: that these are not the patterns of action that define the Messiah, or the Son of Man for that matter, because what Peter has understood about the Son of Man so far is that he is defined by the exercise of authority. What Peter has not done, and Jesus has done, is to identify the Son of Man with the Suffering Servant of the Book of Isaiah:

> [3] He was despised and rejected by others;
>> a man of suffering[u] and acquainted with infirmity;
> and as one from whom others hide their faces[v]
>> he was despised, and we held him of no account.
> [4] Surely he has borne our infirmities
>> and carried our diseases;
> yet we accounted him stricken,
>> struck down by God, and afflicted.
> [5] But he was wounded for our transgressions,
>> crushed for our iniquities;

u. Or *a man of sorrows*
v. Or *as one who hides his face from us*

> upon him was the punishment that made us whole,
>> and by his bruises we are healed.
> ⁶ All we like sheep have gone astray;
>> we have all turned to our own way,
> and the Lord has laid on him
>> the iniquity of us all.
> ⁷ He was oppressed, and he was afflicted,
>> yet he did not open his mouth;
> like a lamb that is led to the slaughter,
>> and like a sheep that before its shearers is silent,
>> so he did not open his mouth.
> ⁸ By a perversion of justice he was taken away.
>> Who could have imagined his future?
> For he was cut off from the land of the living,
>> stricken for the transgression of my people.³⁵¹

This is the pattern of action that Jesus "must undergo" because it was prophesied and was therefore what God required of him.³⁵² The prophets had suffered, and they had said that the Servant of God must suffer, so as he was the Servant of God, Jesus must suffer.³⁵³ Only when the Kingdom of God came would the suffering end.

We do not hear Peter's rebuke of Jesus, but we do hear Jesus' response: an understanding of the Messiah as doing the kinds of things that Israel's kings did in its heyday is not Jesus' understanding. Jesus can foresee suffering, rejection, death, and resurrection, so if he is the Messiah then it is those that are the patterns of action that define the Messiah. And Jesus is clear: it is these patterns of action that are patterns of action that constitute God, and not the patterns of action that Peter has in mind.

Jesus is here explicit: suffering, rejection, being killed, and rising again, are "divine things": literally "things of God": and because they are patterns of action, they are actions of God. In the suffering, rejection, being killed, and rising again of the Son of Man, it is God who is suffering, being rejected, being killed, and rising again. These are patterns of action that constitute God. God is not somehow beyond these human experiences, and they are not experiences with which God somehow sympathizes: they are patterns of action intrinsic to God. They are "things of God."

No theologian has put this more clearly than Geoffrey Studdert Kennedy:

> The true God is naked, bloody, wounded, and crowned with thorns, tortured, but triumphant in His love . . . with bloody brow and pierced hands, majestic in His nakedness, superb in his simplicity, the King Whose crown is a crown of thorns. He is God.³⁵⁴

> In His suffering manhood they saw God, and learned to love and worship.³⁵⁵

Having rebuked Peter, Jesus called his disciples and anyone else who could hear, and he challenged them to exhibit patterns of action that mirrored the "things of God" of which he had been speaking to Peter.[356] Again it is all about patterns of action. If we are to be followers of Jesus, then we must "deny ourselves," take up our crosses, follow Jesus, and lose our lives. These are of course changing patterns of action: they will be different for every individual, and for each individual they will be different at different times: but always it will be a radical and costly following of Jesus.[357] This raises the question as to how we are to judge whether or not we are fulfilling what Jesus demands of his followers. Where are the boundaries? As this particular person, at this time, and in this place, am I denying myself, taking up my cross, following Jesus, and losing my life—for if I do not do those things then I shall lose my life. What is required is that we lose our lives specifically for the sake of Jesus and of the good news of the coming Kingdom of God, and the words that follow provide something of a test as to whether we are fulfilling that requirement. If we find ourselves being ashamed of Jesus and of his words when we are in challenging situations, then he will be ashamed of us, because our being ashamed will be an indication that we have not denied ourselves, taken up our crosses, followed Jesus, and lost our lives. Shame is an emotion intimately related to patterns of action: if in a situation that demands that we speak of Jesus and of his words—and presumably specifically his words about the coming Kingdom of God—and we do not do so, then we shall feel shame. It happens in that order. None of this makes decisions for us, of course. Patterns of action change, and all of them relate to a vast network of patterns of action that constitute our lives, the people around us, and the situations and events among which we find ourselves: but if we notice the emotion of shame, then we might need to study our patterns of action, and ask ourselves whether we are denying ourselves, taking up our crosses, following Jesus, and losing our lives; and if necessary we shall have to choose to die because we are followers of Jesus. Among the earliest Christians there will have been those who literally carried their crosses on the way to crucifixion as Jesus had done.[358] Since then, death has come by other means, but death nevertheless: and still it happens. These patterns of action, like the suffering, rejection, being killed, and rising again of Jesus, are "things of God"; so if denying ourselves, taking up the cross, following Jesus, losing our lives, suffering, being rejected, being killed if necessary, and rising again, both in the present and in the future, are patterns of action that constitute us, then we too shall be doing "things of God." This is the "following me" that Jesus demands.[359] "Life" here represents two very different patterns of action: one the patterns of action that constitute us as human beings; and the other our relationship with those patterns of action that constitute God. What Jesus is saying here is that there is such a thing as an impossible pattern of action: once the pattern of action that constitutes God has been lost, there is no pattern of action that would retrieve it.[360] Human life might go on: but the life that mattered would not. It is only the proclamation of the good news of the Kingdom of God, accompanied by a willingness to lose the pattern of action that constitutes our human life, that will ensure that we continue to experience the patterns of action that constitute God—for the obvious reason that proclamation of the good news, and willingness to suffer death, *are* patterns of action that constitute God.

This passage is the "hinge" of Mark's Gospel: before it, Jesus' messiahship is hidden, but now it is revealed, and Jesus is revealed as a suffering Messiah. Such a suffering Messiah might not have been the Messiah expected, but Mark has now shown that the Messiah had to suffer: a revelation that was probably designed to inspire a church suffering persecution to remain faithful to Christ.[361]

We find ambiguity again at the end of this passage. By employing "Son of Man," was Jesus referring to himself or to someone else? Presumably to himself: he was the Son of Man who would come and would take authority to reign in God's Kingdom: a rule that would inevitably imply judgement.[362] And we find yet more ambiguity in the last line of this passage: Was Jesus simply wrong?[363] Or did he mean something different by "the kingdom of God coming with power" from what either his disciples or we might mean by it? Did he mean that the Kingdom of God had already arrived because the future King was already present? Or that the transfiguration, that Mark is about to record, is the Kingdom coming with power?[364] Or that Jesus' death would defeat evil and so would itself constitute the kingdom of God coming with power?[365] Did he mean that the "one like a son of man" would be presented to the Ancient One and would receive authority to rule?[366] But then how would that generation "see" it? Did Jesus perhaps mean the resurrection? Or did he mean that those gathered around him would perceive that he had been vindicated, had been presented to the Ancient One, and had begun his rule over the Kingdom of God?[367] If so, then the disciples had already experienced that pattern of action in Jesus' casting out of demons, his announcement of forgiveness, his healing of the sick, and his raising of the dead. What they would experience before they died would be even more significant signs of Jesus' ruling in the Kingdom of God: the transfiguration, which will follow this saying in Mark's Gospel, and which three of the disciples "saw"; the resurrection; and the gift of the Holy Spirit to the church.[368]

## MARK 9:2-8

> 2 Six days later, Jesus took with him Peter and James and John, and led them up a high mountain apart, by themselves. And he was transfigured before them, 3 and his clothes became dazzling white, such as no one[k] on earth could bleach them. 4 And there appeared to them Elijah with Moses, who were talking with Jesus. 5 Then Peter said to Jesus, 'Rabbi, it is good for us to be here; let us make

k. Gk *no fuller*

three dwellings,[l] one for you, one for Moses, and one for Elijah.' ⁶ He did not know what to say, for they were terrified. ⁷ Then a cloud overshadowed them, and from the cloud there came a voice, 'This is my Son, the Beloved;[m] listen to him!' ⁸ Suddenly when they looked around, they saw no one with them any more, but only Jesus.[369]

What happened? If I had been standing on that mountain not long before Jesus' crucifixion, what would I have seen and heard? What are the options? Here are several of them:

1. I would have seen and heard what is recorded in Mark's Gospel;

2. I would have seen Jesus sitting with his disciples in the usual way, talking with them, but one or more of Peter, James and John would have looked transfixed for a while as they saw in their mind's eye Jesus transfigured. I would then have heard Peter saying what he is recorded as saying, and one or more of them would have told of the voice that they had heard—a voice that I would not have heard;

3. I would have experienced nothing out of the ordinary at all. A Christian preacher told this story to express Jesus' glory, and to explain to the congregation that as God's Son he was greater than both Moses and Elijah;

4. and 5, and 6. I would have experienced nothing out of the ordinary because I would have been there at the wrong time. This was something that happened after Jesus' resurrection. The three options listed above are all possibilities.

The first thing to say is that none of these complex patterns of action are impossible. There are no natural laws that are universally applicable, so what we might regard as out of the ordinary will always be possible. Reality is action in changing patterns, and there is nothing impossible about the action in changing patterns represented by any of the six options. So let us study the different options in more detail:

1. *Anyone on the mountain at the time would have seen and heard what is recorded in Mark's Gospel.* God is Action and the source of all action, and God is also constituted by particular changing patterns of action, one of which, as the creation story in the Book of Genesis recognizes, is the creation of light: itself a particular changing pattern of action. Given Jesus' unique status as constituted by changing patterns of action that were and are God's changing patterns of action, we should not be surprised that God's creation of light broke into that event on the mountain. Were Moses and Elijah standing there? Each of them was changing patterns of action at a particular point in time: so the question here is whether the changing patterns of action that constituted Elijah and Moses could become changing patterns of action within an event during Jesus' lifetime. If any and every changing pattern of action is present to God, then there is no reason why not: and it would have been entirely appropriate for these changing

l. Or *tents*
m. Or *my beloved Son*

patterns of action to come together before what was to be history's focal complex changing pattern of action: the crucifixion and resurrection of God in the person of Jesus. The prophet Malachi had prophesied that Elijah would appear at the day of judgement to call for repentance,[370] and in the Torah, the Jewish law, a prophet like Moses was predicted,[371] so their appearance would not have been a complete surprise. Peter's reaction, referencing the Jewish Festival of Booths, is perhaps no surprise, and it might be true that its inclusion argues for the event having happened as recorded, as might the very precise time interval of "after six days" at the beginning of the account, and Peter's use of the term "Rabbi" for Jesus.[372] And the voice from heaven is no more of a surprise than it would have been following Jesus' baptism. In the context of this unique event, out-of-the-ordinary God-created sound-waves were and remain an appropriate additional changing pattern of action. An additional confirmatory factor is that Peter offered to build three tents, which might suggest that he was experiencing physical presences:[373] patterns of action similar to those that constituted Peter and his companions.

*2. Any or all of Peter, James, and John, saw and heard these things in their minds. An observer would have noticed nothing, apart from Peter's words, which would have been inexplicable until the vision to which they were a response had been reported.* This option might appear to us to be more of a possibility than the first one, but it is not. In both cases we are discussing out of the ordinary changing patterns of action. We might think that this second option feels less out of the ordinary than the first one, but, if so, we are only talking about a matter of degree, and not a difference in kind. The changing patterns of action that constitute God constantly relate to the changing patterns of action that constitute us and our brains, and for this revelation of the character of Jesus, and of his significance, to have been given to his closest disciples, should be no surprise. The prophet Malachi had prophesied that Elijah would appear at the day of judgement to call for repentance,[374] and in the Torah, the Jewish law, a prophet like Moses was predicted,[375] so their appearance would not have been a complete surprise, and the disciples' minds might have been expecting them to accompany a transfiguration of Jesus. Similarly, the cloud might have been expected, as God had led Israel through the wilderness by means of a cloud;[376] and the physical transformation was a pattern of action that echoed the shining of Moses' face after he had spoken with God.[377] Peter's response to what he had seen in his mind's eye (a phrase that I use advisedly) is no surprise either, as the Jewish Feast of Tabernacles looked back to the Exodus, and forwards to a time when God would dwell with his people and other nations would dwell with them as well.[378] The disciples are no less likely to have heard a voice that other people would not have heard than they were to have seen things that other people would not have seen. What we see and hear is changing patterns of action in our brains, and none of it is cordoned off from the action in changing patterns that constitute God. That God should relate to us in different ways at different times is only to be expected, but precisely how God's influence relates to the patterns of action intrinsic to our brains remains a mystery.

3. *A Christian preacher told this story to express Jesus' glory, and to explain to the congregation that as God's Son he was greater than both Moses and Elijah.* Jesus told stories to communicate the Kingdom of God, so if we are to be followers of Jesus then we too shall tell stories. The Kingdom of God was a uniquely new changing pattern of action, and so inexpressible in the normal categories of the time—for to use the ideas and categories around at the time would have been to betray the new and unique character of the Kingdom of God: hence the parables. In the same way, Jesus was a uniquely new changing pattern of action, and so equally inexpressible in the normal categories around at the time, and so just as in need of the narrative form in order to express who he was. As Christian preachers telling stories about Jesus would have been regarded as a completely legitimate following of Jesus' own practice, it would not be wrong to assume that this and an unknown number of other passages in Mark's Gospel had their birth in Christian sermons rather than in Jesus' own life.

4, and 5, and 6. *This was something that happened after Jesus' resurrection. The three options listed above are all possibilities.* An observer standing on a mountain after Jesus' resurrection might have seen this event as it is recorded; it might have been something that happened in the minds of Jesus' disciples; and it might have been a story told by a preacher to convey the glory of the risen Christ. Against the suggestion that this is a post-resurrection event is the factor that in all of the resurrection accounts Jesus is either absent and then present, or he is present and not recognized, or both, whereas here he is present, and recognized throughout.[379]

There is no way to decide between these options. They are all perfectly possible. We might regard this as a problem because there are clear differences between the options, and those differences could legitimately be regarded as significant for Christian life and faith. However, there is a sense in which it really does not matter what precisely gave birth to the narrative at this point in Mark's Gospel. This is for two reasons. First of all, it is the pattern of the text that impinges on the changing patterns of action that constitute our brains, and that pattern is the same whatever lies behind it. If we happened to know in detail the characters of the multiple changing patterns of action that resulted in Mark writing what he wrote, then that knowledge would no doubt affect how we interpreted the text, but those changing patterns of action are probably forever hidden from us. We therefore have to recognize that all we have is the text, deductions that we might make from other parts of Mark's Gospel, and contributions from other documentary evidence, none of which will discount any of the options that we have discussed. So we have to say that it cannot matter what precisely gave birth to the narrative. Secondly, it does not matter because the changing patterns of action expressed by the different options all bear family resemblances to each other. Whether an observer on the mountain would have seen the event unfold as recorded, or it happened in the disciples' minds' eyes, or the story was invented later by a preacher, the patterns of action conveyed to the hearers and readers of the account are that 'he was transfigured before them': before Peter, James, and John; before the early hearers of the story, however it was given birth; before Mark; before the church for which he wrote his gospel; and before every reader of Mark's Gospel. And Jesus is still transfigured before us.

All of the options that we have discussed are possibilities; the text still speaks of Jesus' transfiguration; that transfiguration is a statement that Jesus is the one who will complete the work of Moses and Elijah by bringing in the Kingdom of God, and that he will be given authority to rule the nations; we are still terrified and make entirely inappropriate responses; we still hear that Jesus is God's beloved son; we still look around and see the normal world around us and Jesus still with us; and we still know that the Kingdom of God is still to come, however near it might be, and whatever Jesus might have meant by the promise that "there are some standing here who will not taste death until they see that the kingdom of God has come with[j] power."[380] As we engage with this passage in Mark's Gospel, we are engaging with changing patterns of action that constitute Jesus and that constitute God, they engage with us, and they change us. As we seek truth—as we truth-seek—in this passage, we shall be discovered by truth.

## MARK 9:9-13

> 9 As they were coming down the mountain, he ordered them to tell no one about what they had seen, until after the Son of Man had risen from the dead. [10] So they kept the matter to themselves, questioning what this rising from the dead could mean. [11] Then they asked him, 'Why do the scribes say that Elijah must come first?' [12] He said to them, 'Elijah is indeed coming first to restore all things. How then is it written about the Son of Man, that he is to go through many sufferings and be treated with contempt? [13] But I tell you that Elijah has come, and they did to him whatever they pleased, as it is written about him.'[381]

Jesus had already told them not to tell anyone that he was the Messiah, and now they were not to tell anyone about the transfiguration: but there is now a difference, because there is an end-point to the secret: the resurrection.[382] However, for the time being silence is to be kept. Either this was what Jesus demanded of them, or it was a story that circulated after Jesus' death to explain why nobody had known that he was the Messiah before the early Christian church had decided that he was. And there was clearly a mystery about the resurrection as well. Everywhere a not knowing. In one sense the disciples did know what rising from the dead could mean, as since the time of the Maccabean resistance to Greek occupation many Jews had believed that those who died fighting the occupiers, or who were killed because they would

j. Or *in*

not deny their Jewish faith by eating pork or worshipping the Greek gods, would be raised to a new life at the end of the present age. The Pharisees continued to believe this, but the Sadducees did not: hence the disputes about the issue that we find in the gospels—in which Jesus is clearly on the side of the Pharisees—and also in the Acts of the Apostles, in which Paul was still very much the Pharisee that he had always been.[383] What would have been strange to Jesus' disciples was the idea that someone might rise from the dead within the present age rather than at the end of it. That is what they could not understand.[384]

What is time? Is it like a ruler along which we move from date to date? Or perhaps like a river flowing towards us from the future? That is, does it somehow exist, and we move through it, or it moves towards us? Or perhaps it is more like a train laying a railway line in front of it as it travels. Perhaps time is created as we leave the present moment. The problem with ideas like these is that the ruler, the river, and the railway line, exist in time, so if they are not themselves to be something other than time then an infinite regress is implied. So might time be what Immanuel Kant says it is: an intuition in our minds that we apply to sense data in order to make sense of it?

All such discussions assume that Being and beings are the foundational reality: beings travelling through time (which exists in time), time flowing towards a being (that is in time), a being creating time as it moves (through time), a mind in time intuiting and applying time. A different possibility emerges if we begin with action as the foundational reality. Then it is changing patterns of action that define time, and time becomes a subsidiary matter rather than the primary framework within which beings exist and move. This makes sense of the ways in which we now know time to behave. Two planes flying round the planet in different directions will arrive back at the same place at slightly different times because of the effects of relativity. Time is relational (that is, related to action) *and* it is a framework (a context for action), for action and its patterns *constitute* time, a pattern of action happening in time being a pattern of action happening in relation to other patterns of action. So perhaps there is no time as such. Every use of the word "time" means something different because the word is always in a new context. Everything is action in changing patterns.

To return to Immanuel Kant: We are changing patterns of actions, and those are influenced by a vast network of changing patterns of actions. One of our patterns of action is the sorting of sense data—the changing patterns of action that impinge on our senses—so that they become usable experience. "Time" is how we describe some of the patterns in which action occurs in our brains. Everything is an open and evolutionary system, within it memory is actions in changing patterns, and part of the patterning is an ordering, one "after" another. This pattern of patterns constitutes our identities, and intrinsic to it is a sense of time, constituted by the ordering of memories into a series, related by "before" and "after."

God is Action and the source of all action as well as being constituted by particular changing patterns of action; and those patterns of action entangle with the changing patterns of action that constitute who we are, so we might say that our time—our diverse and changing time—enters God's experience. This does not mean that God is in time in any sense, but it does mean that the time that we experience is no stranger to God and God is no stranger to experienced time. So Elijah and his times are changing patterns of action to which God continually relates, and those changing patterns of action are mirrored in John the Baptist:[385] and because our identities are our changing patterns of action, we can say that John the Baptist is Elijah, and that his being Elijah is God's action in changing patterns as well as his own. The connections between patterns of action are primary, and any ordering in relation to other patterns of action, and so in relation to time, is a secondary matter.

The resurrection of the dead is changing patterns of action that are God's changing patterns of action that have already happened in Jesus and that will happen, always in new and different ways. What will be true is true already, and any understanding of time must fit around that.

So why are the sentences in this passage in the order in which we find them? There was an expectation that Elijah would come before the end of the age to put everything in order ready for the Son of Man's coming: that is, for the coming of the figure who was to come to the Ancient of Days, as predicted in the Book of Daniel. However, there are also passages in the scriptures that speak of the suffering of God's Servant, whom Jesus identifies with the Son of Man, and therefore with himself. But how is that to happen if everything will already have been put right by Elijah before the Son of Man arrives? What Jesus seems to be saying here is that the expectation mentioned by the disciples is not entirely correct. The expectation was that Elijah would come "to restore all things," and then the Son of Man would come. John the Baptist was Elijah because the changing patterns of action that constituted John mirrored those that constituted Elijah. John had come to restore all things, but he had been murdered; and now the Son of Man had indeed come, only to suffer and die as well.[386] This was the new pattern of action.[387] The ordering in time was the same, but the patterns of action were now different. The end of the age was to be constituted by suffering and death before it would see the resurrection of the dead. It is Elijah's life and now John's that together define time, and it is these events—suffering, death, and resurrection—these changing patterns of action, that now define time as well. Time is changing patterns of action: it is diverse and changing like everything else; and it is the changing patterns of action that constitute Jesus that are now the basis of time itself.

## MARK 9:14–29

> 14 When they came to the disciples, they saw a great crowd around them, and some scribes arguing with them. 15 When the whole crowd saw him, they were immediately overcome with awe, and they ran forward to greet him.

¹⁶ He asked them, 'What are you arguing about with them?' ¹⁷ Someone from the crowd answered him, 'Teacher, I brought you my son; he has a spirit that makes him unable to speak; ¹⁸ and whenever it seizes him, it dashes him down; and he foams and grinds his teeth and becomes rigid; and I asked your disciples to cast it out, but they could not do so.' ¹⁹ He answered them, 'You faithless generation, how much longer must I be among you? How much longer must I put up with you? Bring him to me.' ²⁰ And they brought the boy[n] to him. When the spirit saw him, immediately it threw the boy[n] into convulsions, and he fell on the ground and rolled about, foaming at the mouth. ²¹ Jesus[o] asked the father, 'How long has this been happening to him?' And he said, 'From childhood. ²² It has often cast him into the fire and into the water, to destroy him; but if you are able to do anything, have pity on us and help us.' ²³ Jesus said to him, 'If you are able!—All things can be done for the one who believes.' ²⁴ Immediately the father of the child cried out,[p] 'I believe; help my unbelief!' ²⁵ When Jesus saw that a crowd came running together, he rebuked the unclean spirit, saying to it, 'You spirit that keep this boy from speaking and hearing, I command you, come out of him, and never enter him again!' ²⁶ After crying out and convulsing him terribly, it came out, and the boy was like a corpse, so that most of them said, 'He is dead.' ²⁷ But Jesus took him by the hand and lifted him up, and he was able to stand. ²⁸ When he had entered the house, his disciples asked him privately, 'Why could we not cast it out?' ²⁹ He said to them, 'This kind can come out only through prayer.'[q] [388]

This is the only healing miracle in the section of Mark's Gospel that begins with the healing of the blind man that preceded Peter's declaration of Jesus' messiahship and ends with the healing of blind Bartimaeus immediately prior to the entry into Jerusalem, and it is typical of this section in the sense that it is more about the education of Jesus' disciples than it is about Jesus' relationship with "the crowd."[389] A new overall pattern of action is now center stage.

There is so much that is strange about this passage: but first of all the part that is relatively easy to decide. The boy has epilepsy, understood then as possession by a demon: and there is a sense in which they were not wrong to believe that.[390] And a further understood element: Jesus coming down the mountain to find a faithless generation at the bottom of it echoes Moses coming down the mountain with the ten commandments to find the Israelites indulging in idol worship.[391] Another repeated pattern of action.

The first aspect of the story that does need to be discussed is Jesus' complaint. It is simply misplaced. The man who brought his son to Jesus has already exhibited faith.

n. Gk *him*
o. Gk *he*
p. Other ancient authorities add *with tears*
q. Other ancient authorities add *and fasting*

If he had not believed that Jesus could heal his son then he would not have brought him. The fact that the disciples had not healed the boy was neither here nor there. And presumably the crowd had faith in Jesus as well. They were in awe of him, and they clearly expected Jesus' disciples to exercise the authority that Jesus had given to them to heal the sick and to cast out demons: so whether this boy needed a demon casting out, or an illness healed, the crowd does not appear to have been lacking in faith. Jesus' exasperation is inexplicable. A certain amount of annoyance that the disciples hadn't been able to solve the problem was perhaps in order, but it wasn't the disciples that Jesus was complaining about: he was complaining about all of them. Perhaps, as can so easily happen, a simple failure in a particular task had triggered a frustration that had been building up inside Jesus, and it was those who had at least tried to effect a cure who just happened to be in the way when it was expressed. The patterns of action that constituted Jesus were human patterns of action, whatever else they might have been.[392] Or was it perhaps the opposite that Jesus was complaining about? That the disciples had been sure that they would be able to cure the boy themselves, rather than depending on God to heal him? Jesus' statement later in the account, that prayer was required, would support this interpretation.[393]

And then he tells the father that it's all up to him: "If you are able!" It is no surprise that the father was experiencing a mixture of belief and unbelief.[394] Jesus' disciples had been given authority to heal, and they had not managed to heal his son. "I believe; help my unbelief!"—which of course Jesus did by healing his son. Belief is not a thing to be possessed, but a process: one in which the boy's father was engaged, but which perhaps Jesus' disciples were not:[395] that is, we have in this passage two rather different patterns of action: one that is always on the move, never still; and one that assumed that faith is something that can be achieved. Faith is never achieved.

Just as inexplicable as Jesus' accusation of unbelief, and his expression of exasperation, is the last line of the passage: "This kind can come out only through prayer." But presumably the disciples had prayed: so what was that about?

Perhaps what we are seeing here is a fairly common phenomenon: someone gets overworked and overtired, which perhaps Jesus was; something rather frustrating happens (Jesus' disciples were unable to heal the boy): so frustration tips over into unjustified complaint in entirely the wrong direction. And then perhaps there comes a recognition that the reaction has been over the top, so the search is on for something to say in defense of the rather poor behavior, which often turns out to be somewhat inappropriate, as in this case.

God he might have been, but Jesus was entirely human, and no more clearly so than here. Emotions are changing patterns of action in the brain and throughout the body, and those patterns of action that we regard as more rational can't always damp them down: so they emerge, and have significant effects, and sometimes devastating ones, on the changing patterns of action around us. There is nothing unusual about this. It is of considerable theological benefit to us that early Christians remembered such bad behavior on Jesus' part, and that Mark wrote it into his gospel: benefit because it makes it crystal clear that there was nothing unusual about Jesus' humanity. He really was a human being like the rest of us. But he was also God, so what does this tell us about God? It tells us that the human life that God has lived among us is a properly human life, that the changing patterns of action that constitute God, and that constituted and still constitute Jesus, cannot be separated in any way from the changing patterns of action that constituted him as a human being, and that God is therefore subject to the emotions and the bad behavior that we have seen evidenced in this story. This should be no surprise. Human nature comes as a package: so if God lives a human life, then God experiences the whole package, and not just bits of it.

Might this passage raise the same questions that we find raised by passages in the Hebrew scriptures that describe a belligerent God: a God who ordered genocide so that his favorite tribes could occupy the land of the peoples they murdered; and a God who ordered his prophets to kill hundreds of the prophets of rival gods?[396] It is no surprise that this God turns people off, and at the same time is used to justify all manner of terrible behavior in the present. What we cannot do is sift out this appalling material in the Hebrew scriptures—or this story about Jesus—and keep the rest. What justification could there be for removing particular lines from Mark's Gospel? If reality is action in changing patterns, then we have to recognize that the changing patterns of action that are God, and that are Jesus' real humanity, are completely entangled with each other. Disentanglement is impossible.

The only conclusion to draw is that in this passage in Mark's Gospel we have a window into the character of God, for in Jesus God has become human and has revealed God's humanity: a complex humanity, with a distinctive shadow side to it—a side that we surely have every right to describe as sinful. This is who God is: a God who shares in the changing patterns of action that we call human emotions. That is where any debate of this issue must start: not hiding what might appear to be an unfortunate conclusion from ourselves, but understanding that this must be as much a root of Christian theology as anything else.

So how are we now to understand God's righteousness? How are we to understand the love of God? In the same way that we have begun to understand Jesus' righteousness, love, and perfection. Jesus "learnt obedience": so God learns obedience. God is Action and the source of all action, and God is constituted by changing patterns of action: and a crucial changing pattern of action is that which we call "learning obedience": learning obedience to love, to righteousness, to justice . . . . This was the pattern of Jesus' life, and it is a changing pattern of action that constitutes God. The evil is absorbed by the good, the murderous by the life-giving, the prejudiced by equal regard, the possessive by generosity, and so on. In God this is an eternal process, the absorption of evil by good; it is what we see in Jesus, who takes us by the hand and lifts us up, and we are able to stand; and if we are to be Jesus' followers then it will be our changing pattern of action as well. We shall know ourselves in relationship with a God who constantly learns obedience, and whose love and righteousness constantly absorbs the evil changing patterns of action that constitute God, and those that constitute ourselves and our world. It is to this God that we pray "deliver us from evil" because we know that God knows the experience of being delivered from evil. God learns obedience; Jesus learns obedience; and we, Jesus' followers, are called to learn obedience.

## MARK 9:30–37

> 30 They went on from there and passed through Galilee. He did not want anyone to know it; 31 for he was teaching his disciples, saying to them, 'The Son of Man is to be betrayed into human hands, and they will kill him, and three days after being killed, he will rise again.' 32 But they did not understand what he was saying and were afraid to ask him.
>
> 33 Then they came to Capernaum; and when he was in the house he asked them, 'What were you arguing about on the way?' 34 But they were silent, for on the way they had argued with one another about who was the greatest. 35 He sat down, called the twelve, and said to them, 'Whoever wants to be first must be last of all and servant of all.' 36 Then he took a little child and put it among them; and taking it in his arms, he said to them, 37 'Whoever welcomes one such child in my name welcomes me, and whoever welcomes me welcomes not me but the one who sent me.'[397]

This is Jesus' second prediction of his suffering and death. The new element is the betrayal, expressed in the present tense as if it is something that is occurring at that moment. A pattern of action is already established, and, as it will happen, it has happened.[398] A consistent pattern of action has emerged: Jesus predicts his suffering and death; his disciples do not understand; and Jesus then focuses his teaching on a particular person, in this case a child.[399]

Whether at this stage Jesus identified himself with the "one like a son of man," who in the Book of Daniel comes to the Ancient of Days, is an open question. The situation will not be any clearer when he speaks of the Son of Man at his trial, where he might still be referring to himself or someone else. However, what is clear is that Jesus did identify himself as the Son of Man who would suffer and die in Jerusalem and then rise again. Whether this was simply something that was going to happen, or a task that he was obligated to carry out, is again difficult to decide: possibly both. It is not surprising that his disciples did not understand. If they knew about the Son of Man at all then they might have had in mind the figure in the Book of Daniel, in which case suffering and dying did not really fit. And the fact that they were arguing about who was the greatest among them means that they had not understood very much at all about Jesus, nor about what it meant to follow him. Jesus was God in the midst of them: a God for whom serving others was an essential pattern of action. As far as Jesus was concerned, to serve others by proclaiming the coming Kingdom of God, healing the sick, casting out demons, spending nights in prayer, and generally giving himself in the service of others, was the changing pattern of action that informed every other pattern of action that constituted who he was: and this was who he was because this was who God is: Action and the source of all action, and changing patterns of action, of which the one that informs all of the others is a constant generous outpouring of love towards the universe and everyone and everything in it: a total serving of others.

It is this changing pattern of action to which Jesus was called, so it was the changing pattern of action to which his disciples were called as well. It was therefore obvious that "whoever wants to be first"—presumably in the sense of exhibiting changing patterns of action closer to Jesus' patterns of action than anyone else's—"must be last of all and servant of all." That is what Jesus would be: closer in his changing patterns of action to those that constituted God than anyone else, because the network of changing patterns of action that constituted who he was was focused on a changing pattern of action that was the constant serving of others: a changing pattern of action that would be the pattern of action that constituted the Kingdom of God that was already active in Jesus, and would be the changing pattern of action when the Kingdom of God finally came. It was that servanthood to which Jesus' disciples were called, and consistent with it were nonviolent patterns of action that challenged oppressive powers, because that was the only way to confront them without compounding the violence.[400] Jesus was seated as he taught them this: a pattern of action that emphasizes the authority of the teacher, and the importance of what is being taught.[401]

The following line might not look quite as connected to the subject of greatness and servanthood as we might expect, but if we rephrase "whoever welcomes one such child in my name welcomes me . . ." to read "whoever welcomes one such child as if they were me welcomes me . . ." then we can see the connection. Jesus is comparing himself to a child. He had already compared himself to a servant, and he would do so again, thus allocating to himself a position well down the status ladder. Here he is doing something similar, because in Jesus' time children were not ascribed the same status and rights as they are now.[402] To welcome is a particular changing pattern of action—it means to acknowledge another, to give oneself to another, to be changed by the other. Jesus' followers are to welcome children because they share changing patterns of action with Jesus: so in welcoming a child, we welcome Jesus, whose changing patterns of action they share, and we also welcome God, whose changing patterns of action both Jesus and the child share. God is Action, the source of all action, and is constituted by changing patterns of action, some of which we now know to be the changing patterns of action that constitute a child.

Because Mark's Gospel is the shortest, and because the authors of Matthew's Gospel and of Luke's Gospel look as if they have used Mark's Gospel as a basis for their own work, and adapted and added to it to suit their own theological purposes, we normally assume that Mark's Gospel was written before the other two, and that the others were indeed based on it. However, there are occasional passages that pose problems, and this is one of them. In the context of a discussion about who was the greatest, it is not surprising that Jesus indicates a child: but there is quite a conceptual leap between "Whoever wants to be first must be last of all and servant of all" and "Whoever welcomes one such child in my name welcomes me." The parallel passage in Matthew's Gospel runs like this:

> **18** At that time the disciples came to Jesus and asked, 'Who is the greatest in the kingdom of heaven?' ² He called a child, whom he put among them, ³ and said, 'Truly I tell you, unless you change and become like children, you will never enter the kingdom of heaven. ⁴ Whoever becomes humble like this child is the greatest in the kingdom of heaven. ⁵ Whoever welcomes one such child in my name welcomes me.'[403]

To invite the disciples to become like children—vulnerable, inquisitive, trusting, and so on—is perhaps a more appropriate way to reinforce the message that "whoever wants to be first must be last of all." We can understand why the further sentence about welcoming a child might have been added, even though it constitutes something of a change of direction. Either Matthew's Gospel has added to Mark's Gospel in order to create a better connection between a discussion of greatness and the line about welcoming children, or Mark's Gospel has used Matthew's Gospel, or a written source that Matthew then used, and has left out the connecting sentence.[404] It is difficult to know which. The lesson to draw is not any particular theory about how the different gospels were constructed, but rather a recognition that the gospel texts that we read today are the result of a highly complex network of changing patterns of action, the nature of which is forever hidden from us.

In numerous places in Mark's Gospel we find Jesus sending the disciples, but here we have the single example of Jesus being sent by God.[405] Sending is a pattern of action that constitutes God, so Jesus is sent, and Jesus sends: and it is not insignificant that it is in the context of this passage about a child that Jesus' having been sent is mentioned. Jesus has been sent not as powerful and in order to obtain some kind of status, but as vulnerable and in order to serve, to suffer, and to die. That is the character of the "being sent" that the disciples are to emulate.

## MARK 9:38–50

> 38 John said to him, 'Teacher, we saw someone[r] casting out demons in your name, and we tried to stop him, because he was not following us.' 39 But Jesus said, 'Do not stop him; for no one who does a deed of power in my name will be able soon afterwards to speak evil of me. 40 Whoever is not against us is for us. 41 For truly I tell you, whoever gives you a cup of water to drink because you bear the name of Christ will by no means lose the reward.
>
> 42 'If any of you put a stumbling-block before one of these little ones who believe in me,[s] it would be better for you if a great millstone were hung around your neck and you were thrown into the sea. 43 If your hand causes you to stumble, cut it off; it is better for you to enter life maimed than to have two hands and to go to hell,[t] to the unquenchable fire.[u] 45 And if your foot causes you to stumble, cut it off; it is better for you to enter life lame than to have two feet and to be thrown into hell.[t] 47 And if your eye causes you to stumble, tear it out; it is better for you to enter the kingdom of God with one eye than to have two eyes and to be thrown into hell,[t] 48 where their worm never dies, and the fire is never quenched.
>
> 49 'For everyone will be salted with fire.[v] 50 Salt is good; but if salt has lost its saltiness, how can you season it?[w] Have salt in yourselves, and be at peace with one another.'[406]

What was it that concerned Jesus' disciples about the person casting out demons in Jesus' name? Presumably the sense of loss of both control and status.[407] If they were the only ones able to exercise the authority that Jesus had given to them to heal the sick and to cast out demons, then theirs was a privileged status. Why would they want to share it with anyone else? One person's privilege requires everyone else to be not so privileged. And what if the person now casting out demons started to gather larger crowds than they could gather? And perhaps to do it differently? No longer would they be in control of events, and to lose control is always scary.

What does it mean to control events? It means that changing patterns of action that constitute our brains can impose patterns of action on the people and the world around us, and can impose changes on patterns of action. Only if the person casting out demons was part of their group would the disciples be able to have that effect.

Jesus' response was entirely pragmatic. Specifically, someone who casts out demons in Jesus' name cannot then speak evil of Jesus; and more generally, "Who is not

---

r. Other ancient authorities add *who does not follow us*

s. Other ancient authorities lack *in me*

t. Gk *Gehenna*

u. Verses 44 and 46 (which are identical with verse 48) are lacking in the best ancient authorities

v. Other ancient authorities either add or substitute *and every sacrifice will be salted with salt*

w. Or *how can you restore its saltiness?*

against us is for us." Each of us is changing patterns of action, and one person's changing patterns of action will have an effect on those of everyone around them. They will either enhance them or oppose them, and such enhancement and opposition will be at opposite ends of a spectrum of possibilities strung between the two. The further from one end, the nearer to the other. "Whoever is not against us is for us."

There is a constant tension in Mark's Gospel.[408] Jesus chose just twelve men, and there were women too, and then a wider group, and also a larger group of disciples, resulting from an unconditional welcome of sinners, and therefore without boundaries. Jesus' mission was initially restricted to the Jews, and then it was about a Kingdom of God into which all of the nations would be welcomed. We experience the same today in the permanent tension between the church and the Kingdom of God. The tension has a long history, reaching back to Israel regarding itself as God's chosen people, and taking that as permission to dispossess other tribes: but then in the prophets understanding itself as God's servant with a mission to all nations. In this passage—"whoever is not against us is for us"—we find the community without boundaries, the unconditional welcome, the Kingdom of God.[409]

Another saying is added, either by Jesus or by the gospel-writer, because it is of a similar theme, bound to the previous sentences by the idea of the "name of Christ." To bear the name of Christ means to be his follower, which means that the changing patterns of action that constitute who we are will become progressively more similar to those that constitute Jesus. A name is simply a word: a particular changing pattern of action in the air, or a pattern that crystallizes the changing pattern of action that gave rise to a written word. The name will affect the changing patterns of action that constitute the brain of the speaker or writer, and the brains of the hearers or readers, and will bring along with it the changing patterns of action that constitute the person whose name is being communicated. So to bear Christ's name will be to find ourselves entangled in the changing patterns of action that constitute Jesus. To give a cup of water will be a changing pattern of action that affects the changing patterns of action that constitute the recipient, and if the recipient bears the name of Jesus then the giving of the cup of water will affect the changing patterns of action that constitute Jesus himself. The giver of the cup of water will also find themselves tangled up in the changing patterns of action of the recipient and of Jesus, and therefore of the Kingdom of God and of God. Perhaps that itself is the reward that not only will not be lost, but that will also be received; or perhaps what is envisaged is the reward of entry into the Kingdom of God when that comes.

Who are "these little ones" whom we are forbidden to cause to stumble? Perhaps children are intended, or perhaps disciples of Jesus.[410] Either way, it would be better if it had not happened. Similarly, with the receiving of a child in the previous section:

whether a child or a disciple of Jesus was intended, it is the receiving that matters. Further potential judgements are offered, along with ways to avoid them. I hope that the literary form is hyperbole. Here "Cut it off" is applied to anything that causes us to stumble, rather than to anything that might cause others to stumble. To match the active prescription, hell is described in dynamic terms. This is not a state: it is action in changing patterns.

What are we to make of Jesus' forays into descriptions of the torture that people thrown into hell will suffer? First of all, this sounds more like John the Baptist than it sounds like the Jesus who made it clear that unrepentant sinners were welcome in the Kingdom of God, that the sins of a man who had been let down through the roof by his friends could be declared forgiven, and, according to Luke's Gospel, that the thief who was crucified next to him would be with him in Paradise.[411] So one possibility is that these words were from the beginning of Jesus' ministry when he was a disciple of John the Baptist, or was emerging from that discipleship: that is, before the conversion experiences that Jesus might have undergone in relation to unrepentant sinners and in relation to Gentiles. After all, all of our lives are changing patterns of action, so nobody should be expected to remain entirely consistent in their views or behaviors throughout their lives: indeed, we should fully expect people not to do so, and to be surprised if they did.

Another possibility is that the imagery might have been meant to be taken as seriously as the commands to cut off hands and feet and to remove eyes: that is, not at all seriously. Or perhaps Jesus might have meant precisely what he was saying. We shall never know: which leaves us having to make our own decisions about how to take these words. Perhaps the possibility that best understands the passage as a whole is that which recognizes that all of it—the cutting off of hands and feet, the removal of eyes, and the descriptions of hell—should be regarded as a single unit of the same literary style, so that if the first part has an element of irony about it, then we must assume that the second part does as well. Jesus was teaching in such a way as to leave an impression: his words and actions were designed to affect the changing patterns of action that constitute who we are, so they needed to be chosen and organized so as to lodge firmly among those changing patterns of action. To employ extreme imagery was a way to do that. Serious matters required serious language.[412] So what was he trying to say? Perhaps that if anything in our lives held us back from following Jesus into the Kingdom of God—here understood as God's eternal kingly rule[413]—then we should cast it off: and that if we did not, then a judgement would follow: but the character of the judgement would be as different from unquenchable fire as the disposing of that in our lives that was holding us back from the Kingdom of God was different from cutting off our hands.

Either the gospel-writer has brought together at the end of the passage a number of short sayings, each of which might have been delivered in a different context, or he might have found the sayings already together in Peter's conversations with him, in the broader oral tradition preserved by the church, or in written form. Jesus' earliest disciples would have relied completely or partially on remembering his teaching, so his teaching would have been designed to make that easy to do: hence the use of parables, and also very short sayings which he might have repeated on different occasions. In the oral tradition the patterns of action that constituted the spoken words would have changed as the sayings passed from context to context and from person to person. There would still have been family resemblances with Jesus' patterns of action, but change would always have occurred. It is when the sayings took written form that a solidification or crystallization would have occurred: patterns of action becoming pure pattern representing the pattern of action at that time and place. This process would have occurred as Mark wrote, or as whatever written records that he was using were written. It is as his work was copied and then translated that the pure pattern of the text gave birth to new patterns of action in people's minds: again bearing family resemblances with the patterns of action that constituted Jesus' teaching the disciples and the crowd, but constantly changing. And the same is true of our reading: as our eyes scan the text, that pattern of action changes the patterns of action that constitute our brains, and the patterns of action that constitute who we are are changed, so that those too begin to exhibit family resemblances with the patterns of action that constitute who Jesus is. It is in this way that reading the gospels constantly creates conversion experiences.

All of these sayings employ the imagery of salt: a precious commodity then; although the first short saying is not in fact about salt at all: it is about a judgment that would be a cleansing, presumably of disciples of Jesus in the present day—maybe referring to persecution that they would suffer—and perhaps also on entry into the Kingdom of God. The second saying might refer to his disciples' need for persistence in their faith in him, and in their vocation as proclaimers of the Kingdom of God. Enthusiasm for a task once lost is not always easy to recover. As for the third short saying, what Jesus meant by "have salt in yourselves" is not easy to work out. Salt was a preservative, so perhaps the meaning is the same as that of the second short saying. The disciples are to persevere, and if they persevere in the task of proclaiming the Kingdom of God then there will be peace in the community: a pattern of action that we often see when people work together to pursue a common task.[414]

## MARK 10:1-12

> 10 He left that place and went to the region of Judea and[x] beyond the Jordan. And crowds again gathered around him; and, as was his custom, he again taught them.
>
> 2 Some Pharisees came, and to test him they asked, 'Is it lawful for a man to divorce his wife?' ³ He answered them, 'What did Moses command you?' ⁴ They said, 'Moses allowed a man to write a certificate of dismissal and to divorce her.' ⁵ But Jesus said to them, 'Because of your hardness of heart he wrote this commandment for you. ⁶ But from the beginning of creation, "God made them male and female." ⁷ "For this reason a man shall leave his father and mother and be joined to his wife,[y] ⁸ and the two shall become one flesh." So they are no longer two, but one flesh. ⁹ Therefore what God has joined together, let no one separate.'
>
> 10 Then in the house the disciples asked him again about this matter. ¹¹ He said to them, 'Whoever divorces his wife and marries another commits adultery against her; ¹² and if she divorces her husband and marries another, she commits adultery.'[415]

The "teaching" theme established during the last half of chapter 8 and most of chapter 9 continues in chapter 10, initially with both Pharisees and Jesus' disciples as the audience, but then increasingly just the disciples, as in the previous chapter; and a general theme is continued from chapter 9: the teaching focuses on the patterns of action that constitute the Kingdom of God rather than those that constitute the world in which Jesus and his disciples are living.[416]

We have already found the Pharisees attempting to set traps for Jesus, and this might be another. They might have been aware of increasing equality among Jesus' male and female followers, as well as of his forays into Gentile territory with the news of a Kingdom of God that was no longer to be the sole preserve of Israel. Perhaps they were hoping that Jesus would say that women could divorce their husbands, or that he would simply contradict Moses' provision for divorce following the issuing of a certificate. He did neither. He asked what Moses had commanded, and they responded with Moses' permission to divorce as long as the man issued a certificate of divorce to his wife. But Jesus was looking for something deeper. Both Jesus and the Pharisees believed Moses to have written the book of Genesis, so Jesus' quotation of the statement "a man leaves his father and his mother and clings to his wife, and they become one flesh"[417] was also a valid response to the question "What did Moses command?" This was no attempt at liberalization—this was a radicalization of the law: a going back to

---

x. Other ancient authorities lack *and*

y. Other ancient authorities lack *and be joined to his wife* the roots.[418] Jesus was opposing a pattern of action established by God at the creation to one that had emerged later, and it is clear which he regarded as having priority.

Jesus' motive would first of all have been to avoid the trap, but it might also have been to address a severe injustice: that a man could simply send his wife away, knowing that she would be without financial support in the world of male breadwinners into which she would have to go.[419] If her own family would not take her back, which might have happened because of the stigma of divorce, and also because their own resources might already have been stretched, then the divorced wife would have been both penniless and homeless. She might have got away with the dowry that she took into the marriage, but she might not: and if she did, it would soon be gone. By appealing to the creation story, Jesus was ensuring an equality of women and men in the only way possible under the circumstances in which the debate took place: and he made it clear that it was equality of treatment that was his concern by adding the final prohibition: that just as a man should not divorce his wife, so a wife should not divorce her husband.

Everyone involved in the debate would probably have assumed that adultery was grounds for divorce, although presumably not for the death penalty prescribed in the law:[420] but whereas rabbinic teaching at the time was that a woman could commit adultery against her husband, but a man could only commit adultery against another man and not against his own wife, Jesus was clear that a man could commit adultery against his wife in the same way that a woman could commit adultery against her husband.[421] However, because women divorcing their husbands was not then a live option, it is possible that some of this material was added later by a gospel-writer, or by a church wishing to clarify the situation in a Gentile context—possibly in Rome[422]—in which women were able to divorce their husbands.[423] Christian ethics has always been changing patterns of action, constantly informed by the changing patterns of action that constitute God relating to the changing patterns of action that constitute society, the economy, and the world around us, and in particular the changing patterns of action that constitute the minds of Christians across time and space.

If reality is action in changing patterns, what can we now make of the idea that a man and a woman become "one flesh" when they marry. My flesh is the changing patterns of action that constitute who I am, and my wife's flesh is the changing patterns of action that constitute who she is. Any relationship between two people will intertwine their changing patterns of action, which will change them, and will keep on changing them, so that integration will occur between the changing patterns of action of the two individuals. In the context of a long-term and intimate relationship, this intertwining, constant mutual changing, and integration, will be intense: so the two individuals will become increasingly "one flesh." The process will never be complete, because both will continue to change, and they will continue to change each other, so we would expect oscillations in the intensity of the unity of the flesh: and further influences on the changing patterns of action of one or both of the partners might one day disrupt any existing integration, might reduce the mutual changing, and might set up a rejection process in one or both of the partners, so that the level of integration declines. Married or cohabiting partners might become less "one flesh" than they were. But often the process of what we might call "onefleshment" will result in increasing integration, so that the two individuals come to think and feel with each other in often surprising ways, including the sometimes uncomfortable transference of mood from one to the other and back again: a distinct sign of an intense onefleshment.

Sexual intercourse will in many cases be a vital element in the becoming one flesh. On its own it does not constitute it, but for many couples it will be a significant intertwining of the changing patterns of action that they are, and this intertwining will enhance every other intertwining, enabling an ever deeper integration to occur. And whenever it happens, giving birth to children, and bringing them up together, will be a further intertwining of the changing patterns of action that constitute who we are, and will result in a wider relating of changing patterns of action as parents and children grow into a family, constituted by individuals with changing patterns of action that constitute who they are, and also by changing patterns of action that constitute the entire family as a unit that then relates to the changing patterns of action that constitute other families, other individuals, and the world around the family.

None of this applies only to the male and female couples that Jesus was talking about. A same sex couple will also experience onefleshment: a deep integration of changing patterns of action, whether or not genital activity is involved; and the more intimate a group of friends are with each other, the more "one flesh" they will become. In the context of Jesus' own time, the option of publicly declared same sex relationships would not have been on his agenda; but it is on ours, so we must attempt to draw lessons from what Jesus says about onefleshment in a marriage between a woman and a man. And in our own culture, divorce is a significant and frequent reality, so we must address that as well in the light of Jesus' words and actions.

First of all in relation to divorce: Jesus' concern was clearly with the gender imbalance of contemporary arrangements, and with the penury, homelessness, and stigma to which a divorced wife could be subjected. In most cultures today the situation is very different. Divorce is far less likely to result in penury, homelessness, and stigma, and there will be circumstances in which a woman might regard divorce as preferable to staying with her husband. During the early days of the Christian church we find Paul recognizing that there might be circumstances in which a married couple might separate, and although he did not then countenance remarriage, he had arguably taken an important step away from Jesus' "let no one separate . . . ."[424] The world changes. Everything changes. Reality is action in changing patterns, so for anything to stay the same is in fact for it to change, because the patterns of action that constitute it will be relating to constantly different changing patterns of action, and so will be forced to change, unless an impermeable boundary can be fixed between whatever it is and the rest of the world: but then to all intents and purposes it would cease to exist in the world, because it would no longer relate to the changing patterns of action that constitute the world around it. For Jesus' prohibition of divorce, and his decision that divorce should be counted as adultery, to remain the same today, would be to make them into something different.[425] Instead of being a protection for women, they could constitute entrapment in misery and penury. Today, the prevention of poverty might require divorce rather than forbid it. Many churches have of course come to this conclusion, and arguably they ought to have been ahead of society on divorce law reform rather than lagging behind, as has frequently happened. To recognize that divorce might sometimes be necessary is not in any sense to deny that marriage is in principle for life. Onefleshment is real, and to "put asunder" a marriage will often cause severe distress to the couple, to their children, to their wider family, and to other people around them. It can still cause penury, homelessness, and stigma. The onefleshment that was so important to Jesus should still be important to us, however different our world might be from his. And of course the equality in marriage that Jesus wanted to see should be something that Christians should pursue in theory, and in practice, and in every culture.

The same is true of same sex relationships. In our own time, Jesus would have recognized the onefleshment of same sex couples, and he would have wanted to see equality within every relationship. He would also have wanted same sex couples to see their relationships as in principle lifelong; and in these changed times he would have recognized that divorce might sometimes be preferable to staying together.

Doing Christian ethics is never easy. Jesus spoke and acted in a particular context, and what he said and did were changing patterns of action that were deeply entangled in the changing patterns of action of the people and the world around him. People are now very different, and the world is now very different, and for us to try to transfer Jesus' commands and prohibitions into the present day as a package would be to disconnect them from the world. Interpretation is required: that is, translation into a new context that will connect the patterns that constitute Jesus' words with the new and constantly changing patterns of action that constitute the world of today. The task then is to ask how the intentions behind the words—intentions perhaps best understood by studying Jesus' actions as well as his words—can be turned into changing patterns of action in today's world. I come to the tentative conclusion (—and it can only be tentative, because everything will continue to change) that Jesus' words should be taken with the utmost seriousness, that Christians should still regard marriage, whether between a man and a woman, or between two people of the same gender, as in principle lifelong, but that in today's world justice and compassion might mean that in some cases divorce might be preferable to a couple staying together; that in today's world same sex marriage is as valid and important as marriage between a man and a woman; that all marriages should be in principle lifelong; and that equality between the members of a marriage partnership is essential.

## MARK 10:13-16

> 13 People were bringing little children to him in order that he might touch them; and the disciples spoke sternly to them. ¹⁴ But when Jesus saw this, he was indignant and said to them, 'Let the little children come to me; do not stop them; for it is to such as these that the kingdom of God belongs. ¹⁵ Truly I tell you, whoever does not receive the kingdom of God as a little child will never enter it.' ¹⁶ And he took them up in his arms, laid his hands on them, and blessed them.[426]

Jesus has already told them that if they receive a child in his name—that is, as if the child was him—then they received both him and the Father who had sent him; and he has made it clear that any abuse of children is abhorrent and subject to judgement. Already children have been given a massively higher status than would normally have been ascribed to them in Jesus' time. And now Jesus is saying that the Kingdom of God belongs to children, and that if anyone is to enter the Kingdom of God then they must receive it as a child: they must become children in order to receive the Kingdom, presumably meaning that they cannot earn their way into God's Kingdom, but must receive it as a gift, just as a child cannot earn their own keep but must receive from adults everything that they need.[427] Jesus then gave the children his blessing.

Women and men were equally Jesus' followers; unrepentant sinners were welcome in the Kingdom of God; Gentiles were as welcome as Jews; and now not only were children welcome in the Kingdom of God, but if anybody else was to enter it then they had to become like children: they must become the changing patterns of action that constitute children—patterns of action that we might call vulnerability, dependency, trust, and sinful innocence. There are no longer boundaries around the Kingdom of God. Admission does not require ascription to a creed, the keeping of laws, belonging to an organization, baptism, or anything else: and it is the vulnerable and those of low social status who will enter first.

So we have two interpretations to consider: Either it is simply God's will that the vulnerable should enter the Kingdom of God first, so children should be welcomed; or everyone should receive the Kingdom of God as dependent and vulnerable individuals.[428] However, if reality is action in patterns, then these interpretations merge. It is the patterns of action that constitute a child that characterize the Kingdom of God.

All of this raises significant questions for the church. Children are not the church of tomorrow: they are as much members of the church today as anyone else is. So why is it that we so often exclude them from the central action that constitutes the church? When we come to discuss Jesus' last meal with his disciples, we shall find him taking bread and wine, giving thanks, breaking the bread, and sharing the bread and wine with his disciples. If that event was a Passover, then it was a celebration of the Israelites' escape from Egypt: a celebration in which there has always been a part played by a child. If there were children at that last meal before Jesus died, then it is inconceivable that they would not have received the bread that was passed round. Yet churches routinely exclude children from this central action that constitutes the church, and those churches that do to some extent treat children as full members by including them in the administration of communion insist that they should be seven years old, that they should be baptized, and that they should have attended a series of classes so that they can learn what the event means. There are of course churches in which any child who holds out their hand will have bread placed in it, but that will often be in contravention of the institution's rules. Yet all of those children have already been declared by Jesus to be owners of the Kingdom of God: according to Jesus, the Kingdom belongs to them. Adults must become like children, and should not expect children to become like adults; and because it is the pattern of action that is the welcoming of another that is crucial, there can be no boundaries around the category of people who can be welcomed.

This raises the significant question as to whether just anybody should be able to participate in the church's re-enactment of the Last Supper. Any adult, whether Christian or not? But what exactly do we mean by "Christian" here? If the category is not to be defined by some list of characteristics that we have chosen, then we surely have to say that someone is a Christian in the context of the Eucharist if in that moment they hear Jesus' call to become one of his disciples as they share bread and wine together at his invitation. Of course, many people who do not regard themselves as Christians will not want to do that: but if someone who does not generally regard themselves as a Christian, and might not be regarded as one by other people, wishes in that moment to participate in the changing pattern of action that constitutes someone as Jesus' disciple at the Last Supper and in today's Eucharist, then that is sufficient. They are behaving as a child behaves—reaching out their hand at Jesus' invitation: and they must receive bread and wine. It is those of us who might wish to refuse someone the bread and wine who need to examine ourselves: we must ask whether we ourselves are coming to the event as children come to it—vulnerable, dependent, trusting, sinfully innocent: because if we are not then we must repent and become like children.

But what of someone who might come to receive communion and who by coming will scandalize members of the congregation? Clearly someone who presents a danger to others will need proper controls to be put in place, and there are ways of doing that while still welcoming them as equal participants with everyone else; and someone who might pose a challenge to one or more members of the congregation must still be able to participate along with everyone else. This is not to minimize the reality of evil: it is to recognize that Judas was among those who at the Last Supper received bread and wine from Jesus. Nobody was excluded then, and nobody must be excluded now.

To raise a question that perhaps has not been fully addressed in explicit form until now: What precisely is the Kingdom of God that we are to receive as children? Like every other reality, it is changing patterns of action: the changing patterns of action that we see in Jesus, and which are changing patterns of action that constitute God, whose rule the Kingdom of God is. These changing patterns of action will constitute the whole of reality when the Kingdom of God comes in its fulness at the end of the age, but we do not have to wait until then. The Kingdom of God is among us, according to Jesus—it was among them then in Jesus himself, and it is among us now in Jesus: that is, in the Spirit of Jesus, which is the changing patterns of action that constitute Jesus and that remain as creative in our time as they were in his. And wherever we see changing patterns of action with the character of those that constitute the Kingdom of God, there is the Kingdom of God today, and we belong to it, and it belongs to us, as the changing patterns of action that constitute who we are entangle with the changing patterns of action that constitute the Kingdom of God. There is no-one excluded, either now or in the future. Everyone's changing patterns of action are invited to participate in the changing patterns of action that constitute the Kingdom of God; and according to Jesus, those changing patterns of action that most easily integrate with those that constitute the Kingdom of God are those that constitute children. The Kingdom of God already belongs to them. Jesus' parables are not exactly descriptions of the Kingdom of God, but they are indications of its character, so we can gain some idea of what Jesus meant by the term "Kingdom of God" by studying those parables: but here he is providing us with a clearer understanding of the Kingdom of God: it belongs to children, and we must become like children if we are to enter the Kingdom and discover what it's about.

As for the text itself: As it travelled through the highly complex oral and perhaps written tradition,[429] and before it was crystallized in written form in Mark's Gospel or before that, might it have been shaped by controversy in the church as to whether infants should be baptized? We have here a familiar tension: Should membership of the church be restricted to those who can confess the Christian Faith and choose to be baptized, or should the boundaries be wider than that and include Christians' households, as appears to have happened when the Philippian jailer was baptized?[430] Or should the church be understood to be constituted by everyone whose pattern of action bears a family resemblance to the pattern of action that constitutes Jesus, and in particular by everyone who does what Jesus asked us to do? Whether or not the text was shaped by a particular controversy, it now mandates the welcome of children, requiring us to grant children full membership of the church alongside adults; and it mandates the Christian not only to confess that Jesus is a Messiah who functions as the servant of Jew and Gentile, and of men, women, and children, but more importantly calls us to imitation of Jesus' nonviolent bringing in of the Kingdom of God by welcoming that Kingdom as children.[431]

## MARK 10:17–31

> 17 As he was setting out on a journey, a man ran up and knelt before him, and asked him, 'Good Teacher, what must I do to inherit eternal life?' 18 Jesus said to him, 'Why do you call me good? No one is good but God alone. 19 You know the commandments: "You shall not murder; You shall not commit adultery; You shall not steal; You shall not bear false witness; You shall not defraud; Honour your father and mother."' 20 He said to him, 'Teacher, I have kept all these since my youth.' 21 Jesus, looking at him, loved him and said, 'You lack one thing; go, sell what you own, and give the money[z] to the poor, and you will have treasure in heaven; then come, follow me.' 22 When he heard this, he was shocked and went away grieving, for he had many possessions.
>
> 23 Then Jesus looked around and said to his disciples, 'How hard it will be for those who have wealth to enter the kingdom of God!' 24 And the disciples were perplexed at these words. But Jesus said to them again, 'Children, how hard it is[a] to enter the kingdom of God! 25 It is easier for a camel to go through the eye of a needle than for someone who is rich to enter the kingdom of God.' 26 They were greatly astounded and said to one another,[b] 'Then who can be saved?' 27 Jesus looked at them and said, 'For mortals it is impossible, but not for God; for God all things are possible.'
>
> 28 Peter began to say to him, 'Look, we have left everything and followed you.' 29 Jesus said, 'Truly I tell you, there is no one who has left house or brothers or sisters or mother or father or children or fields, for my sake and for the sake of the good news,[c] 30 who will not receive a hundredfold now in this age—houses, brothers and sisters, mothers and children, and fields, with persecutions—and in the age to come eternal life. 31 But many who are first will be last, and the last will be first.'[432]

What is my life? It is the changing patterns of action across a lifespan that I and others identify as constituting this particular person with this particular name. The changing patterns of action that constitute me constantly relate to a vast network of changing patterns of action made up of the changing patterns of action that constitute individual people and individual things, and that between them, along with ourselves, constitute forms of life, as Wittgenstein put it. Within those forms of life fit the languages that we use (which, like everything else, are changing patterns of action that relate to vast networks of changing patterns of action), the traditions and assumptions of our cultures, and such institutions as ownership, money, and so on. We are constantly influenced by changing patterns of action around us, and we in our turn constantly influence them.

z. Gk lacks *the money*
a. Other ancient authorities add *for those who trust in riches*
b. Other ancient authorities read *to him*
c. Or *gospel*

The changing that occurs in patterns of action, whether in what we refer to as physical objects, in such institutions as the sciences, or among the changing patterns of action that constitute our brains, will usually be of an evolutionary kind: change will be constant and ubiquitous, but not significantly disruptive. But then sometimes something different can occur. A set of changes in the patterns of action that constitute an object, an institution, or a person, can cause significant disruption around that particular network of patterns of action, sparking major change in the patterns of action around it, so that disruptive change takes place across vast numbers of changing patterns of action. At the limit, patterns can disappear, returning action to an original chaotic, patternless state. Something like this happened when the core of a nuclear power plant in Chernobyl went into meltdown; and this is also what happened during the financial crisis of 2008: although fortunately in that case new changing patterns of action enabled the institutions to avoid a collapse into entirely chaotic action. In relation to the sciences we call the process a paradigm shift: a science might be changing patterns of action, with non-disruptive change happening all over the institution of the science. Then opposing changes might happen in patterns of action that relate to each other: for instance, new evidence might disprove a long-held theory—that is, the changing patterns of action of an experiment disrupt the fairly stable pattern of action that constitutes a theory that had previously meshed coherently with the changing patterns of action that constituted experiments. More such events can cause considerable turbulence in the science, until a descent into chaotic action, unordered by theory, is arrested by new theories emerging: that is, new patterns of action that can cohere with the changing patterns of action that constitute current experiments. Eventually one of those new theories might cohere with more and more of the changing patterns of action that constitute the science. The paradigm will have shifted.

When this process happens to an individual person, we speak of a conversion experience. The multitude of changing patterns of action that constitute ideas in the brain, processed sense data, memories, and so on, will normally change in a non-disruptive fashion, with the patterns of action that constitute beliefs, commitments, and behaviors, adapting relatively smoothly to the changing patterns of action that constitute sense data, and generally to the changing patterns of action that constitute other people, the environment, and in particular the words and concepts that impinge on the brain from outside it. But sometimes the mutual changing of patterns of action becomes less coherent; changing patterns of action that constitute experience of the world and of other people causes disruptive change in the changing patterns of action that constitute the brain; and memories emerging from the subconscious can cause similar effects. The action that constitutes the brain can become less patterned, risking a collapse into totally chaotic and patternless action. It is at that point that new changing patterns of action might emerge in the brain: new ideas, new beliefs, new commitments and convictions, that can relate to the new changing patterns of action to which the previous ideas, beliefs, commitments, and convictions could not relate without disruptive change occurring in the patterns of action that constitute the brain. Old ideas and beliefs will simply have disappeared, their action having been repatterned to enable new patterns of action to emerge that can change coherently with the changing patterns of action impinging on the brain. A whole new way of life can open up: a turning around, a new direction: conversion. Any direction is possible, and in relation to religion a conversion can be towards new religious convictions, or away from religious convictions into atheism or agnosticism.

Jesus' disciples had been through conversion experiences, some more quickly than others no doubt, but all of them conversions. Jesus meeting them on the shores of Lake Galilee had caused completely new directions for their lives. Whether they had left everything permanently is open to question, because occasionally we find them fishing, and Peter still had a home and a mother-in-law living in it, and so presumably a wife as well,[433] so what might have happened is that for part of each year Jesus would send them all off to proclaim the Kingdom of God's coming, to heal the sick, and to cast out demons, and they would then go home for a while to carry on with their lives. So it might have been for relatively short periods of time that they "left everything":[434] but that would still have been a real leaving behind of everything; and perhaps as Jesus' ministry progressed, the amounts of time that they spent with him might have increased. And perhaps eventually they really did leave everything to follow him: although one both hopes and expects that they would have continued to provide for their dependents in a world in which nobody else would have been able to do so.

Jesus makes a promise: that those who followed him and left everything would receive abundantly in this life. There is a sense in which this has been the experience of members of the church throughout the centuries, for just as Jesus counted his followers as his family, so Christians find that the changing patterns of action that constitute a family can often be found as much in the church as among blood relatives. "Persecution" is added to what Jesus' followers would be given: perhaps added by Mark to express the experience of the church for which he was writing.[435]

But it was not just this life to which Jesus was referring. He offered those who followed him "eternal life": a changing pattern of action that reflects the changing patterns of action that constitute the Kingdom of God, and that entangles with the changing patterns of action that constitute who we are both now and in the future: and one of the patterns of action that will characterize the Kingdom of God will be reversal: whatever is "first" will be "last," and vice versa. This pattern of action was evident in Jesus' life and in his teaching; it is a pattern of action that he was commending to his followers;[436] it is a pattern of action that constitutes who God is and what God does; and it is a pattern of action that is still sometimes in evidence in the world and in the church: and where it is evident, there is Jesus, there is eternal life, there is the Kingdom of God—whether now or in an age to come, and whether on Earth or elsewhere: and there is God.

So are conversions irresistible? Clearly not. Jesus holds a discussion with a rich young man who has seen something in Jesus, and for whom a conversion experience is clearly beginning to occur. We must assume that his question is genuine: he really does want the eternal life that he believed Jesus had to offer. Jesus' heart went out to him with a love that simply wanted the best for this young man.[437] He wanted him to experience the Kingdom of God for himself, then and there. Here was someone whose life was shaped by devotion to the God whom Jesus knew as Father, and Jesus could see how this man's life would be eternal life if he joined his band of disciples and proclaimed the coming of the Kingdom of God. The young man heard the call, and he could feel the tug of a paradigm shift from regarding keeping the law as all that was required to understanding that a giving of himself and all that he had would set him free, and that the Kingdom of God was to be received as a gift and not by a keeping of the law. The young man was facing a radical shift from one pattern of action to another:[438] but then he closed his mind—that is, he created a boundary between the changing patterns of action that constituted his brain, and the changing patterns of action beckoning to him from Jesus' words and actions. The future would not be different from the past. He was shocked. A disruption had begun, and he had halted it, and the uppermost changing pattern for him was now that of grief: a sense of loss for the new life, the eternal life, that might have been.

Jesus generalized the experience for those who were listening. People heavily invested in their current forms of life—people for whom change would be significantly disruptive, and for whom the kind of life that was beckoning them might be very different from their present lives, and disruptive of their relationships with other people and with the world around them—would find it hard to live the life of the Kingdom of God today, and in particular to give themselves for its proclamation.

But that is not to say that the rich are excluded from the Kingdom of God. They too will be welcomed and accepted. They too will hear the words "You are accepted"; and they will experience the overwhelmingly generous embrace of God that is eternal life. We might not be able to see how the rich would ever be able to accept the paradigm shift required of them if they are to live the life of the Kingdom of God today, but that does not mean permanent exclusion from the Kingdom of God. Jesus bore no hatred towards the rich young man. As well as a sharing of the man's wealth among the poor, Jesus simply wanted something better for him.[439] Once we are forced to shed our forms of life at death, everything is possible for God: and there might have been a time before this rich young man died when he again encountered Jesus or his followers, again heard the call, and responded differently.

The lesson for us is this: Jesus invites us to significant disruption: to the first being last and the last first; to massive changes in our forms of life, individually and as a society; and to new scientific and institutional paradigms. We can resist and walk away: but for God "all things are possible," and, in particular, eternal life, the life of the Kingdom of God, will be a reality for everyone. The question for all of us is whether we wish to hear Jesus' call to live today the patterns of action that constitute the Kingdom of God into which we shall be welcomed in God's generous future.

We have encountered two fundamental patterns of action so far in this chapter: giving, and committing. The Kingdom of God is a gift that we are to receive as children receive; and absolute commitment is required. These patterns of action would appear to be entirely incompatible. They are: but "for God all things are possible."[440]

## MARK 10:32-45

> 32 They were on the road, going up to Jerusalem, and Jesus was walking ahead of them; they were amazed, and those who followed were afraid. He took the twelve aside again and began to tell them what was to happen to him, 33 saying, 'See, we are going up to Jerusalem, and the Son of Man will be handed over to the chief priests and the scribes, and they will condemn him to death; then they will hand him over to the Gentiles; 34 they will mock him, and spit upon him, and flog him, and kill him; and after three days he will rise again.'
>
> 35 James and John, the sons of Zebedee, came forward to him and said to him, 'Teacher, we want you to do for us whatever we ask of you.' 36 And he said to them, 'What is it you want me to do for you?' 37 And they said to him, 'Grant us to sit, one at your right hand and one at your left, in your glory.' 38 But Jesus said to them, 'You do not know what you are asking. Are you able to drink the cup that I drink, or be baptized with the baptism that I am baptized with?' 39 They replied, 'We are able.' Then Jesus said to them, 'The cup that I drink you will drink; and with the baptism with which I am baptized, you will be baptized; 40 but to sit at my right hand or at my left is not mine to grant, but it is for those for whom it has been prepared.'
>
> 41 When the ten heard this, they began to be angry with James and John. 42 So Jesus called them and said to them, 'You know that among the Gentiles those whom they recognize as their rulers lord it over them, and their great ones are tyrants over them. 43 But it is not so among you; but whoever wishes to become great among you must be your servant, 44 and whoever wishes to be first among you must be slave of all. 45 For the Son of Man came not to be served but to serve, and to give his life a ransom for many.'[441]

Mark records three predictions by Jesus of his suffering and death in Jerusalem, of which this is the third and the most detailed in relation to the pattern of action that would occur. Whether the details were filled in afterwards, or Jesus foresaw in detail what awaited him, we shall never know: but what is clear from the string of verbs—"condemn," "hand over," "mock," "spit," "flog," "kill," and "rise again"[442]—is that he could see the pattern of action that would unfold once he arrived in Jerusalem. Jesus was on his way to Jerusalem where the events that he was predicting would take place, and the disciples who were travelling with him clearly believed that the Kingdom of God about which Jesus had said so much was about to dawn. They appear to have had in their minds a vision of that Kingdom that was all to do with ruling others, and little to do with suffering and service; and so desperate were James and John to have the prime seats in the new Kingdom, perhaps in order to pre-empt a leadership bid by Peter,[443] that they were willing to incorporate into their understanding of how the Kingdom of God would come about the suffering and death that Jesus had predicted for his disciples, on the understanding that resurrection would follow and that they would rule with Jesus.

Here we are discussing some very different changing patterns of action. To suffer and to die are common human patterns of action. It is these that Jesus was predicting for himself, which means that these changing patterns of action are changing patterns of action that constitute God: although whether Jesus would have understood his role in that way is of course open to question. These were changing patterns of action that Jesus was also predicting for his followers:[444] and we know from the Acts of the Apostles that James suffered execution for being a Christian.[445] Other apostles suffered the same, although we do not know how many of them. Christian martyrs through the ages are particularly honored because they have experienced these particular patterns of action that constituted Jesus and that constitute God, and to that extent have become God.

We are also discussing the changing pattern of action that we call resurrection: rising from the dead. As we have recognized, many Jews expected this to occur at the end of the age when the Messiah came to rescue God's chosen people from oppression. What was not expected was a single individual rising from the dead before that time. It is this that Jesus' disciples experienced at Jesus' resurrection, and that we shall discuss when we arrive at the end of Mark's Gospel. Here we have Jesus' prediction of the event: and if he made that prediction, then it might have been as a result of his reading of the Book of Hosea:

> 6 Come, let us return to the Lord;
>> for it is he who has torn, and he will heal us;
>> he has struck down, and he will bind us up.
>
> ² After two days he will revive us;
>> On the third day he will raise us up,
>> That we may live before him.[446]

A further pattern of action that we are discussing is that of ruling over others: the imposition of a changing pattern of action that constitutes one person on the network of changing patterns of action that constitute other people. This is what James and John were seeking from Jesus: in the Kingdom of God that would follow their arrival in Jerusalem, perhaps given birth through their suffering, death, and resurrection, they wanted Jesus to grant them the right to rule. This was entirely understandable. For a long time Israel had been ruled by other nations: now it was the turn of God's chosen people to rule, and they wanted to be part of it.

Jesus fobbed them off. Perhaps he did not know himself how the Kingdom of God would be inaugurated, what the resurrection of the dead would be like, who would rule in the Kingdom of God, and so on. What he did know was that God would decide how it would happen: that is, what changing patterns of action would constitute the Kingdom of God. Perhaps it would be tax collectors, prostitutes, unrepentant sinners, Gentiles, and children, who would rule in God's Kingdom, and not even experiencing the kind of suffering and death that Jesus would experience could earn the privilege for James and John: a privilege that was not even on offer in the terms in which they seem to have meant it.[447] The "glory" that Jesus was after was that of servanthood, which was rather different from the kind of glory that James and John clearly had in mind.[448]

It is no surprise that James' and John's request gave rise to a certain amount of controversy. Jesus had already told them that the first would be last and the last first. This was to be the pattern of action that would constitute the Kingdom of God, so he expected it to be in action already among his followers. It was service to others that was the highest calling: a calling thoroughly recognized and fulfilled in his own life. In the fourth gospel we find Jesus at his last meal with his disciples before his death washing his disciples' feet, which would have been the work of a slave or a servant, and not the work of a Rabbi.[449] The event is not recorded in Mark's Gospel: instead we have these sayings, one of which is in quite extreme language: the statement that the one who wishes to be great must be a servant, and that "whoever wishes to be first among you must be slave of all"—a slave, not a servant, and so someone with no freedom to do as they wish, their only task in life being to serve. This is how Jesus saw himself: as a slave in the service of God and of other people; and it is that vocation to which he was calling his disciples, and to which he calls us. Self-giving is Jesus' pattern of action, it must be the pattern of action of his followers, and it is what Jesus expected of James and John.[450]

And then comes a most significant line: "For the Son of Man came not to be served but to serve, and to give his life a ransom for many." The first part of the sentence repeats the message that has already been given: the second part explains what Jesus saw as the most important example of his serving of others—or does it? Matthew's and Luke's Gospels repeat this section of text from Mark's Gospel, as they do with much of the gospel, but Luke leaves out this line. Perhaps he thought that it would not be understood by his Gentile readers; or perhaps he thought that Jesus had not said it and that it had been added to Jesus' words as Jesus' teaching travelled through the oral tradition; or perhaps that Mark had added the sentence himself as his own understanding of Jesus' death. Either way, we have to admit a sliver of doubt as to whether these were Jesus' words.

## MARK 10:32–45

Let us suppose that Jesus spoke these words. He was probably beginning to see the suffering and death that awaited him in Jerusalem in the light of the "suffering servant" described in Isaiah 53,[451] and it is not impossible that his actions were purposely designed to create a fulfilment of the prophecy in his own person:[452]

> 3 He was despised and rejected by others;
>> a man of suffering[u] and acquainted with infirmity;
>
> and as one from whom others hide their faces[v]
>> he was despised, and we held him of no account.
>
> [4] Surely he has borne our infirmities
>> and carried our diseases;
>
> yet we accounted him stricken,
>> struck down by God, and afflicted.
>
> [5] But he was wounded for our transgressions,
>> crushed for our iniquities;
>
> upon him was the punishment that made us whole,
>> and by his bruises we are healed.
>
> [6] All we like sheep have gone astray;
>> we have all turned to our own way,
>
> and the LORD has laid on him
>> the iniquity of us all.
>
> [7] He was oppressed, and he was afflicted,
>> yet he did not open his mouth;
>
> like a lamb that is led to the slaughter,
>> and like a sheep that before its shearers is silent,
>
> so he did not open his mouth.
>
> [8] By a perversion of justice he was taken away.
>> Who could have imagined his future?
>
> For he was cut off from the land of the living,
>> stricken for the transgression of my people.[453]

This passage might originally have been written about King Zedekiah who suffered terribly when Babylon took him and much of the population of the country into exile, but it has been subsequently understood as a description of experiences that would be suffered by a particular servant of God, or by servants of God in general. Perhaps Jesus understood the passage as predicting his own suffering and death, and his own death as some kind of necessary payment—a ransom—that would release people from imprisonment.[454] But to whom did he think the ransom would be paid? The idea of Jesus'

---

u. Or *a man of sorrows*
v. Or *as one who hides his face from us*

death as a ransom has had a long history in Christian theology, and all of it is problematic, as is Jesus' own use of the idea. If the ransom is to be paid to God, then God is an angry God who needs to be placated by a sacrifice. Jews would have understood this. But it leaves us with God requiring someone else to suffer rather than those who had committed the sins that needed to be forgiven. We are left with the toxic combination of injustice and abuse. Perhaps Abraham going to Mount Moriah to sacrifice his only son Isaac at God's command was in Jesus' mind: but such horrendous child abuse can hardly be a model for the relationship between Jesus and the God whom he called Abba, Father.[455] Is there any way of rescuing the idea of Jesus' death as a ransom?

If Jesus is changing patterns of action that are changing patterns of action that constitute God, then it is God who is the ransom being discussed here. It is God who is suffering and dying and who is the ransom: the pattern of action that is the necessary requirement for reconciliation between God and humanity. It is not a necessary sacrifice in the sense that God requires something from humanity before forgiveness can happen, because God can simply forgive, as Jesus made clear during an earlier incident in Mark's Gospel:[456] but it was necessary because if God is to share the life of humanity, and thus create reconciliation—a constant intertwining of the changing patterns of action that constitute God with the changing patterns of action that constitute humanity—then God must experience human death; and for reconciliation to occur, God must experience the most extreme human changing patterns of action, and so has chosen to experience humiliating suffering and death by crucifixion. The suffering and death of Jesus are now patterns of action at the heart of God, enabling God to be reconciled with us and us with God—something that would have been impossible if that had not happened—so now and forever God is reconciled to humanity in all of its suffering and death.[457]

And perhaps in this context we can make new sense of the idea that Jesus "bore our sins in his body on the cross°." [458] As a human being like the rest of us, Jesus was enmeshed in human sin: there was no escape. All of us belong to a vast network of action in changing patterns, much of which is sin, and all of which is implicated in sin in some way. For Jesus not to have shared in the human experience of sin to the full, and in the guilt and shame that accompanies it, would have rendered his humanity impossible. The changing patterns of action that constituted who he was would have had no connection with the changing patterns of action that constitute sinful human life in sinful human society. It was all of this that Jesus carried with him throughout his life and as he died. This is the deep love of God: willingly to participate in human sin that is utterly inimical to God, and to do that through extreme suffering and death. God spared God nothing. It is in that sense that Jesus gave his life as a ransom. God asked it of God, and God did it.

o. Or *carried up our sins in his body to the tree*

Here we face a mystery. We find it difficult to understand any of this, and no set of words can describe what takes place in the heart of God. But if we are to speak of God at all, then we have to construct a narrative; and if we are Christians then that narrative must have at its heart the incarnation: God living a human life. At the end of that human life was intense suffering and death by crucifixion. That too is God living a human life, our human life, at its most extreme. Reconciliation is now achieved.

However important the theological meaning of this final verse might be, the context shows that it belongs in a passage in which Jesus was teaching his disciples that the Kingdom of God was the pattern of action represented by the verb "to serve."[459] He was asking his disciples—including us if we are his followers—to be the pattern of action represented by the verb "to serve." Only in that way can we be his followers and live in our own time the life of the Kingdom of God.

## MARK 10:46–52

> 46 They came to Jericho. As he and his disciples and a large crowd were leaving Jericho, Bartimaeus son of Timaeus, a blind beggar, was sitting by the roadside. 47 When he heard that it was Jesus of Nazareth, he began to shout out and say, 'Jesus, Son of David, have mercy on me!' 48 Many sternly ordered him to be quiet, but he cried out even more loudly, 'Son of David, have mercy on me!' 49 Jesus stood still and said, 'Call him here.' And they called the blind man, saying to him, 'Take heart; get up, he is calling you.' 50 So throwing off his cloak, he sprang up and came to Jesus. 51 Then Jesus said to him, 'What do you want me to do for you?' The blind man said to him, 'My teacher,[d] let me see again.' 52 Jesus said to him, 'Go; your faith has made you well.' Immediately he regained his sight and followed him on the way.[460]

This is the last healing miracle recorded by Mark, and it is placed just before the account of Jesus' entry into Jerusalem at the beginning of the week of his death: so the obvious question is why Mark might have placed it in this prominent position. One answer is that it balances the healing of a blind man at the beginning of the central "teaching" section of the gospel; another is that there are echoes in this story of what was to follow; and another is that after the secrecy related to Jesus' Messiahship, that status can now be openly acknowledged.[461] The genealogy at the beginning of Matthew's Gospel tells us that Jesus was a descendent of David, the king who had united the nation and inaugurated a time that Jews regarded as a golden age of prosperity and peace; and as Jesus entered Jerusalem, the crowd clearly believed that he had come to inaugurate a repeat of the "kingdom of our ancestor David." Bartimaeus called Jesus "Son of David," subverting Jesus' desire for messianic designations not to be used, and determining the position of this healing miracle.[462] A further reason for placing

---

d. Aramaic *Rabbouni*

this story here is that Jesus had called Israel's ruling classes "blind guides,"[463] and they were about to capture him and hand him over to the Roman occupiers to kill him. Bartimaeus's blindness was cured: theirs was not.

Jesus was not looking for opportunities to heal people with disabilities: his mind was fixed on going to Jerusalem. Just as Jesus' disciples had tried to prevent parents from bringing their children to Jesus, so the crowd now tried to prevent Bartimaeus from attracting Jesus' attention: but Bartimaeus was insistent, Jesus heard him, and Jesus called him. This is not just a healing miracle: it is a "calling" story alongside the callings of Jesus' first disciples, and with a very different outcome from Jesus' encounter with the rich young man.[464] Like the first disciples, and many others during the years of Jesus' active ministry, Bartimaeus heard the call; he had faith—he trusted; and he followed Jesus "on the way": a reference both to the journey onwards to Jerusalem, and to a continuing following in the way of Jesus:[465] an expression used for being a disciple of Jesus that we find reflected in John's Gospel's description of Jesus as "the way, and the truth, and the life."[466] Bartimaeus is represented here as the ideal disciple: that is, his pattern of action is that of the ideal follower of Jesus. Jesus opens his eyes, he knows who Jesus is, he persists against opposition, he responds, he is "saved," and he "follows" Jesus "in the way";[467] and the fact that Bartimaeus's name is recorded in Mark's Gospel suggests that he did indeed follow in the way of Jesus and became a member of the church.[468]

Bartimaeus regained his sight. In a previous account we find a blind man receiving his sight gradually, perhaps an active metaphor for the common experience of a slow realization of who Jesus was.[469] Here sight is given immediately: there was no time for slow realization, as Jesus was about the reach the climax of his work: his death and resurrection. Jesus was "Son of David" and "Teacher" to Bartimaeus: but now Bartimaeus can see clearly who Jesus is—although the reader is left to decide what it is that Bartimaeus now sees in Jesus.

For centuries, the image of blind people gaining sight has been employed as an analogy for someone coming to know the truth, and in particular coming to know the truth about Jesus—we often say "seeing the truth": a recognition that sight has often functioned as an analogy, or a metaphor, for knowledge. The hymn "Amazing Grace" contains the line "I . . . was blind, but now I see," referring to conversion to faith in Christ, and to the conversion of the slave trader and hymnwriter John Newton in particular. Professor John Hull and others have rightly questioned this usage. Those who lose their sight, or who have never been able to see, understandably have no wish for their condition to be treated as an analogy for ignorance, lack of compassion, lack of faith, or life before conversion to Christ. The ways in which we see things—that word again: so let's rephrase it—The ways in which we understand things change over time: the patterns of action that constitute individuals' brains, and society's presuppositions and prejudices, change all the time in relation to each other, but sometimes change in parts of the vast network of patterns of action can be slower than in other parts of it. Whilst we are now less likely to employ the concept of blindness to express ignorance, lack of faith, lack of compassion, or life before conversion to Christ, we still find ourselves reading passages about Pharisees being "blind guides," we still read Bartimaeus's healing as a metaphor for conversion to Christ, and no doubt we shall continue to sing the hymn "Amazing Grace": but we might slowly cease to do so.

In the story that Mark tells, we have multiple changing patterns of action interweaved with each other: those that constituted Jesus, those that constituted Bartimaeus, those that constituted Bartimaeus's voice, those that constituted Jesus' disciples, those that constituted the crowd, those that constituted the road to Jerusalem, those that constituted Jesus' call to Bartimaeus, those that constituted Bartimaeus coming to Jesus, those that constituted the throwing off of his coat, the complex changing patterns of action that constituted the giving of sight, those that constituted Jesus' declaration about Bartimaeus's faith, and those that constituted Bartimaeus's following Jesus in the way. The people, the words, the actions, and everything else, were action in changing patterns, so the whole event, which included the changing patterns of action of the individuals involved, was changing patterns of action: so it would not be wrong to describe the people involved as continuous events participating in an event. And engaging with every changing pattern of action that constituted the event were the changing patterns of action that constituted God. Separation is impossible: so God too is a continuous event that belongs to the event of the healing of Bartimaeus.

In Mark's mind, as he carefully penned the words of his gospel, there would have been a multitude of jostling changing patterns of action related to what he had been told about Jesus. Perhaps there were written accounts on his desk as well, passed on to him by previous writers. Whatever it was that he had available, it was now Mark's task to put it all in order. Perhaps the last of the eyewitnesses of these events had already died, and perhaps not, but either way what mattered was to ensure that memories were not lost so that the new generation of Christians could know what Jesus had said and done, and why it was that people had followed him then, and were following him still. Mark was engaged in a highly creative changing pattern of action that would have been influenced by the crystallized patterns of action represented by texts in front of him, if there were any; by the changing patterns of action that constituted the brain's memories of the many things that Mark had been told by Peter, by Paul, and by other early Christians that he knew and had known; by the changing needs of the Christian community for which Mark was writing his gospel;[470] and by the changing patterns of action of Mark's mind as he sorted and ordered his material—for instance, ordering the three chapters that we have just read into three examples of the same structure: a healing, a prediction of Jesus' suffering, the disciples' misunderstanding, discipleship instruction, and finally some climactic event—Peter's confession, teaching about divorce, and "The Son of Man came not to be served, but to serve, and to give his life as a ransom for many": a summary of the meaning of the predicted suffering.[471] To summarize: the text of Mark's Gospel constitutes a pure pattern in which is crystallized the changing patterns of action that constitute Jesus, the church, and Mark himself.[472]

And engaging with all of those changing patterns of action that gave birth to the text of Mark's Gospel would have been the changing patterns of action that constituted the Holy Spirit, or the Spirit of Jesus: changing patterns of action that constituted God and that were relating in perhaps a unique way to the changing patterns of action of Mark's mind as he wrote a text about the changing patterns of action that constituted God living a human life among us. Like Jesus himself, Mark's Gospel was and is both human and divine, in the sense that it is entirely a human book about events in the human world, and thus as fallible as any other book, and that the changing patterns of action that constituted God were entangling with the changing patterns of action of Mark's mind as he wrote his gospel. Was this God-engagement unique in any sense? Yes, in the sense that Mark was recording changing patterns of action that constituted God living a human life: but whether qualitatively unique—that is, different in kind from God's engagement with other writers' minds—or quantitatively different—that is, perhaps different in the intensity of God's engagement with the writer's mind, but not different in kind—will have to remain an open question.

## MARK 11:1-11

> 11 When they were approaching Jerusalem, at Bethphage and Bethany, near the Mount of Olives, he sent two of his disciples ² and said to them, 'Go into the village ahead of you, and immediately as you enter it, you will find tied there a colt that has never been ridden; untie it and bring it. ³ If anyone says to you, "Why are you doing this?" just say this, "The Lord needs it and will send it back here immediately."' ⁴ They went away and found a colt tied near a door, outside in the street. As they were untying it, ⁵ some of the bystanders said to them, 'What are you doing, untying the colt?' ⁶ They told them what Jesus had said; and they allowed them to take it. ⁷ Then they brought the colt to Jesus and threw their cloaks on it; and he sat on it. ⁸ Many people spread their cloaks on the road, and others spread leafy branches that they had cut in the fields. ⁹ Then those who went ahead and those who followed were shouting,
>
> > 'Hosanna!
> >
> > > Blessed is the one who comes in the name of the Lord!
> >
> > ¹⁰ Blessed is the coming kingdom of our ancestor David!
> >
> > > Hosanna in the highest heaven!'
>
> 11 Then he entered Jerusalem and went into the temple; and when he had looked around at everything, as it was already late, he went out to Bethany with the twelve.[473]

Jesus has arrived in Jerusalem, and the patterns of action will be those of Jesus' relationships with the religious and civic authorities rather than those of his relationships with the crowd or with his disciples, although both of those will continue to have roles to play. The patterns of action will be increasingly those of conflict, culminating in Jesus' death, followed by an enigmatic gesture towards his resurrection. Between the confrontational dialogues and the passion narrative the trajectory of the action will be interrupted by chapter 13: the Marcan apocalypse.[474] Whether or not Jesus offered this prediction of the birth-pangs of the Kingdom of God at this point in his ministry, its position in Mark's Gospel is entirely appropriate, because both the apocalypse and the passion narrative represent patterns of action that constitute intense suffering that precedes the coming to birth of God's Kingdom.

Presumably Jesus, or someone previously sent by him, had already discussed the arrangements for borrowing the donkey, in much the same way as parish churches will sometimes arrange to borrow a donkey for Palm Sunday processions.[475] And then it happened: a triumphant entry into Jerusalem, with branches being laid on the ground, and hosannas being sung: although as with many patterns of action, multiple interpretations are possible. The structure of Mark's Gospel assumes that this event happened a few days before Passover, but there are also arguments that it occurred before the Feast of Dedication, for then the hosannas and branches would have been a recognized element of the festival, and so would not have been regarded as out of the ordinary: and interestingly, if it was the Feast of Dedication to which Jesus was coming, then because the festival commemorated the rededication of the temple by Judas Maccabaeus after its desecration, Jesus' cleansing of the temple, which was to follow the next day, would have had a clearer meaning than if it had occurred a few days before the Passover.[476] Whichever festival it was, Jesus appears to have been purposely acting out the words of the prophet Zechariah:

> Rejoice greatly, O daughter Zion!
>> Shout aloud, O daughter Jerusalem!
>
> Lo, your king comes to you;
>> triumphant and victorious is he,
>
> humble and riding on a donkey,
>> on a colt, the foal of a donkey.[477]

The implications of "your king" in the prophecy would not have been lost on either Jesus or the crowd. Jesus had purposely replicated a pattern of action expressed in the prophecy, so it was no surprise that the crowd—presumably of Galilean pilgrims[478]—believed that God's rescuer had arrived, and that he would free them from oppression by the Romans and by his puppet monarch Herod, and presumably would free them as well from the ruling classes in Jerusalem: the priests and the rest. Was this what was in Jesus' mind? Bartimaeus had not been asked to desist from calling him "Son of David," and riding into Jerusalem on a donkey clearly put an end to any ambiguity as to whether Jesus was willing to be regarded as a messianic figure.[479] It is difficult to believe that Jesus did not at this point understand himself to be God's Messiah, the promised founder of the rule of God. He was wrong. That is not what happened. God did not establish the Kingdom of God on Earth in Jerusalem on that day. The Romans continued to rule, as did Herod and the priests, and the people were still oppressed. Jesus was betrayed by one of his followers, presumably out of disappointment that the promise expressed by that triumphant entry had not been fulfilled, and perhaps out of a virtuous desire to defend the people from the kind of vicious backlash that was bound to occur if any kind of armed insurrection had actually taken place. And so Jesus was crucified, and on the cross he expressed his anguish that he, and the mission to which he had committed his life, had been abandoned by God.

Are there two distinct streams running through Jesus' teachings and actions? His explicit statements about being a servant point in one direction; this event points in another; and in the light of the entry into Jerusalem, there are other events that we must now count as ambiguous, such as Jesus' reaction to Peter's declaration that he was the Messiah. Was Peter's statement an encouragement to Jesus to think of himself as the one who would enter Jerusalem as king, and that if he played that part then God would drive out the oppressors and establish the Kingdom of God to which all of his teachings, healings, and castings out of evil had looked towards? Maybe Jesus really did believe that if he rode into Jerusalem as king then God would establish the Kingdom of God, Jesus would be king, and that he would rule as servant of the people. Or perhaps if there was any messianic intention in Jesus' mind then it was an intention to reframe the concept of a Messiah: perhaps the emphasis was on the "humble" in the Zechariah passage, and in Jesus' mind the Messiah was now merged with the servant who would suffer. And perhaps Jesus simply did not know how his messianic vocation would work out, so that the ambiguity of the event echoed an unknowing in the mind of Jesus.

The problem with the interpretation that the entry into Jerusalem would result in the Kingdom of God's establishment is that Mark's Gospel records Jesus as predicting his death, in detail, and stating that his life would be offered as "a ransom for many."[480] So maybe Jesus believed that he would arrive in Jerusalem as king; that he would be crucified; that after three days he would be raised from the dead—and that then the Kingdom of God would be established, and he would rule as servant of the people, his life having been given as their ransom. But then why the cry from the cross that God had abandoned him? Whichever interpretation of Jesus' entry into Jerusalem and of what followed we choose, we shall be left with questions that we cannot answer: and as we attempt to answer them, a lot will depend on the weight that we give to different elements of the text. If emphasis is placed on this passage, then Jesus might have thought that he was arriving as king, and that God would establish the Kingdom of

God in which Jesus would rule as a servant of the people. It is not without interest that such events as Jesus' response to Peter's declaration that he was the Messiah makes immediate sense in the context of this interpretation, and that the only passages in Mark's Gospel that pose difficulties are Jesus' predictions of his suffering, death, and resurrection: and it is easy to see how Christians might have believed that Jesus must have predicted what eventually happened to him, and so wrote predictions into the oral tradition. But if emphasis is placed on the predictions of suffering and crucifixion, then the entry into Jerusalem was Jesus reinterpreting messiahship in that direction. The passage from Zechariah goes on:

> He[x] will cut off the chariot from Ephraim
>> and the warhorse from Jerusalem;
> and the battle-bow shall be cut off,
>> and he shall command peace to the nations;
> his dominion shall be from sea to sea,
>> and from the River to the ends of the earth.[481]

Any kingship intended was of an entirely humble and peaceable kind.[482]

Would there be a problem if Jesus had not in fact predicted his own suffering and crucifixion? Would it matter that Jesus might have been wrong, and that he might have been very wrong about God's intentions, about his own mission, and, in the end, about God? No, it is not a problem that Jesus might have been wrong about all of this. If he was God living a human life, then he was God living a contingent human life, because that is the only kind of human life that there is. The changing patterns of action that constituted who he was were those that constituted God, but they were also those that constituted human actions, words, and ideas: and those ideas could have been wrong. And if this was so, then those changing patterns that constituted some very wrong ideas about what God would do both were and still are changing patterns of action that constitute God. God knows what it is to be wrong: for how else could God be reconciled to human beings who know what it is to be wrong? And similarly, would there be a problem if Jesus both predicted his suffering and death, and believed himself to be the Messiah entering Jerusalem to rule in the Kingdom of God, and was not sure how to fit those two convictions together? After all, this might be the best explanation of the ambiguity of the entry into Jerusalem. Again there would be no problem. It would be entirely human to hold what might feel like contradictory convictions at the same time, hoping that reconciliation might occur.

All of this is action in changing patterns: the events themselves; the words spoken about them; the thoughts thought about them; the writing of text about them; every interpretation of the text; and the being wrong, if that is what happened. All of it is changing patterns of action, with each one affecting multiple other changing

---

x. Gk: Heb *I*

patterns of action, so that the changing patterns of action that constituted the original events continue to affect the changing patterns of action that constitute who we are two thousand years later. The only hiatus is the text of Mark's Gospel. Mark's writing of the text was action in changing patterns as changing patterns of action that constituted his brain, and in particular those that constituted memories of words about Jesus that he had heard, and those that might have been generated as he read pieces of parchment on which text about the events had come to him, changed the changing patterns of action that constituted his hand moving the quill pen on the parchment on which his gospel was taking shape. "Shape" is here the operative word: the text was pure pattern: a crystallization in pure pattern of multiple changing patterns of action; a crystallization awaiting the changing patterns of action of the reader, without whom it was not real, it did not exist, because there was no action. But now we can read and interpret the text, bringing back to life the changing patterns of action that gave birth to the text: changed again of course by our reading and interpreting, but still communicating the events of Jesus' life, including the entry into Jerusalem. But what of what was in Jesus' mind? That above all is what gave birth to the event of the entry into Jerusalem, so above all it was that mind's changing patterns of action that gave birth to what followed, and to the oral tradition, and to Mark's Gospel, and therefore to our reading and interpreting. The fact that we cannot now truth-seek what was in Jesus' mind in the way that we can in relation to the entry into Jerusalem itself does not mean that what was in Jesus' mind is lost to us. It is forever present, forever real, forever changing the changing patterns of action that constitute who we are, just as is Jesus riding on a donkey into Jerusalem and the complex changing patterns of action that unfolded during the days following.

What is the significance of this event? What does it signify? To what is it a sign: or rather, to what changing patterns of action does it lead us? For each one of us, and for each institution, church or otherwise, that engages with this event and with what followed, the changing patterns of action that constituted the last week of Jesus' life constantly change the changing patterns of action that constitute who we are. There is no static significance: no significance that we can pin down and define, except momentarily, and then the words in which we define will have changed their meaning, sending us on a new journey of significance. And it is of course impossible to separate out the significance of this event from every other changing pattern of action that constitutes who we are.

Significances change significances across a vast network of changing patterns of action, so separating out the significance of any particular event in the past is completely impossible, for an individual, for a community, for a society, or for an institution. And so the actions and teachings of Jesus, and the entry into Jerusalem, and the crucifixion, as we read them in Mark's Gospel, and as we have heard them from people who have taught us in the past, or who have discussed them with us in the present, and perhaps as we have watched them interpreted in passion plays, entangle with the changing patterns of action that constitute our brains, and so with our understandings of the world, of the sciences, of the events of history, and of ourselves; and so entangle with the action in changing patterns that constitute who we are and what we do. Nothing is lost; everything relates to everything; and Jesus' entry into Jerusalem constantly changes who I am, what I think, and what I do.

## MARK 11:12-26

> 12 On the following day, when they came from Bethany, he was hungry. [13] Seeing in the distance a fig tree in leaf, he went to see whether perhaps he would find anything on it. When he came to it, he found nothing but leaves, for it was not the season for figs. [14] He said to it, 'May no one ever eat fruit from you again.' And his disciples heard it.
>
> 15 Then they came to Jerusalem. And he entered the temple and began to drive out those who were selling and those who were buying in the temple, and he overturned the tables of the money-changers and the seats of those who sold doves; [16] and he would not allow anyone to carry anything through the temple. [17] He was teaching and saying, 'Is it not written, "My house shall be called a house of prayer for all the nations." But you have made it a den of robbers.'
>
> 18 And when the chief priests and the scribes heard it, they kept looking for a way to kill him; for they were afraid of him, because the whole crowd was spellbound by his teaching. [19] And when evening came, Jesus and his disciples[e] went out of the city.
>
> 20 In the morning as they passed by, they saw the fig tree withered away to its roots. [21] Then Peter remembered and said to him, 'Rabbi, look! The fig tree that you cursed has withered.' [22] Jesus answered them, 'Have[f] faith in God. [23] Truly I tell you, if you say to this mountain, "Be taken up and thrown into the sea," and if you do not doubt in your heart, but believe that what you say will come to pass, it will be done for you. [24] So I tell you, whatever you ask for in prayer, believe that you have received[g] it, and it will be yours.
>
> 25 'Whenever you stand praying, forgive, if you have anything against anyone; so that your Father in heaven may also forgive you your trespasses.'[h] [483]

The "tourism Jesus" at the end of the last passage suggests a connecting verse inserted by Mark to separate the entry into Jerusalem and the cleansing of the temple so that he could insert the cursing of the fig tree.[484] It is therefore perfectly possible that the

e. Gk *they*: other ancient authorities read *he*

f. Other ancient authorities read '*If you have*

g. Other ancient authorities read *are receiving*

h. Other ancient authorities add verse 26, '*But if you do not forgive, neither will your Father in heaven forgive your trespasses.*'

cleansing of the temple in fact took place immediately after the procession into Jerusalem. But we are reading Mark's Gospel in the order in which we find it, so we shall read the story of the cursing of the fig tree before we read about Jesus' cleansing of the temple. There are reasons for keeping together the different aspects of the longer passage, because the two parts of the fig tree narrative form the outer layers of a sandwich with the cleansing of the temple in the middle, so presumably Mark saw a connection between the fig tree passages and the account of the temple incident. He probably saw the fig tree incident as an acted parable related to Jesus driving the stallholders out of the temple. What was to follow the cursing of the fig tree in his gospel no doubt has a variety of meanings, but one of them must be that Jesus was declaring a judgment on the temple because it had usurped the place of God and of the Kingdom of God in the hearts and minds of Israel.[485] Jesus prevented the sacrificial system from functioning for a short while by preventing people from purchasing animals for the required sacrifices. Alongside Jesus' likely prediction of the destruction of the temple, Jesus' symbolic cleansing of the temple courtyard would have been understood as the work of the Messiah, the one sent by God to establish the Kingdom of God. The one who was to rule in the Kingdom of God had arrived in Jerusalem, and now he would begin his work of judgement. In this context the "mountain" to be cast into the sea was the hill on which the temple stood. When the Kingdom of God comes, there will no longer be any need for a temple, and certainly not for a temple that had become a source of national identity and pride, and was actively oppressing the poor,[486] rather than a place for the nations to gather. So the temple had to go: briefly and symbolically that day, and permanently if the disciples' faith was strong enough.

The temple had not borne fruit and so was cursed: the fig tree had not borne fruit and so was cursed. The connection is clear. So there would be reasons for discussing the different aspects of the longer passage together: but because each part of the narrative has its own sources, and each part exhibits plenty of potential for theological reflection, we shall deal with them separately, although because of the connections the entire passage is printed at the top of this section and at the top of the next.

Whether or not the fig tree incidents began as a parable and became a pair of events in the oral tradition, we shall treat them as events in which Jesus cursed a tree and it then withered.[487] This reveals a petulant Jesus. As the text says, it wasn't the season for figs, so it was hardly surprising that there weren't any: but Jesus cursed the tree anyway, and the curse worked. Jesus' miracles were usually entirely positive and salvific: Jesus healed the sick, cast out evil, raised the dead, fed hungry people, and calmed storms. They were acted parables, revealing the character of the Kingdom of God. The cursing of the fig tree was entirely negative and destructive. If it happened,[488] then there would appear to be just one possible explanation: later in the year leaves on the tree would have offered the hope that there would have been fruit as well, but Jesus knew that there would be no figs during the week before Passover and so decided to use the tree as an acted parable for a temple religion that promised good fruit but produced none. He then cursed the tree to represent the destruction that his actions in the temple would also represent.[489] If the event did not happen, then it is difficult to work out where the story came from: Why would Christians have invented it? And why would they have communicated it to each other for long enough for it to end up in Mark's Gospel? The sayings that follow the disciples pointing out the withered tree are entirely characteristic of Jesus, and we can see why Mark has included them here: but they do not need the cursing and withering of the fig tree. Perhaps all we can say is that the story of the fig tree came from somewhere—perhaps from the same source as some of the fantastical miracle stories that we find in the apocryphal gospels probably written towards the end of the New Testament period; that Mark found the story among his sources; and that before and after the cleansing of the temple seemed to be the best place for it, perhaps because Jesus' cursing of the tree seemed to Mark to be akin to his driving out of the traders, and, like that event, it represented God's judgment on Jerusalem and its religious institutions:[490] that is, here were two changing patterns of action that changed in similar ways the changing patterns of action that constituted Mark's brain.

The sayings that follow present their own challenges: not because they are fantastical, but because they are demanding. "Have faith in God" is often a difficult command to obey. According to the Letter to the Hebrews, "faith is the assurance of things hoped for, the conviction of things not seen,"[491] so Jesus is asking us to be sure that God can bring about the changing patterns of action that we hope for, even though now we might see no evidence of that happening. We never see Jesus moving mountains, and it might be that he never intended his disciples to do so. What he was asking was that they should be sure that if they asked something of God then that thing would happen. Here the responsibility is clearly ours: but that means, of course, that because doubt is inevitable, what we hope for will never come about. Was Jesus making it clear to his followers that they were not in fact able to bring about the Kingdom of God, and that God would have to do it? Was he asking them to behave as the man who had brought his epileptic son, and to say "I believe: help my unbelief"?[492] and to recognize that it was generally true that "for mortals it is impossible, but not for God; for God all things are possible"?[493]

But what does it mean to 'believe that'? To "believe in" is to trust, so to believe in God is to trust in God, which means to recognize God's existence, in the sense that there is Action, the source of all action, and particular changing patterns of action that constitute God; and it means to believe that God is trustworthy: that the changing patterns of action that constitute God have the welfare of others in view—which goes to show that "believing that" is integral to "believing in." So what does it mean to "believe that"? It means that one of the changing patterns of action that constitute our brain would be the same in the presence of reliable evidence that whatever it was was the case. If someone I trust tells me that something in particular has happened, then even if I have no other evidence that it has happened, I can still believe that it has happened. I can have in my mind the same changing pattern of action that I would have if I had some direct evidence that the event had taken place. So to believe that Jesus is risen from the dead is to have in our minds the same changing pattern of action that we would have had in them if on the first Easter Day we had been with Mary Magdalene in the garden when she saw Jesus alive.[494] But this is surely impossible. Again we have to say "I believe: help my unbelief,"[495] and to recognize that it is generally true that "for mortals it is impossible, but not for God; for God all things are possible."[496] Instead of hoping against hope, we must believe against unbelief; and we must recognize that in relation to Christian faith, belief is a gift and not something that we can achieve.

The final line about forgiveness, which demands that we forgive if we wish to be forgiven, appears to have been a common theme for Jesus. We find it in the prayer that we find him teaching his disciples in Matthew's and Luke's Gospels, and also in a parable about a servant who is forgiven a large debt and is then severely punished when he does not forgive a small debt owed to him.[497] But what *is* forgiveness? Is it simply saying to someone that they are forgiven? That is probably required: and it is never just words, because our words are actions in patterns that change the changing patterns of action that constitute the person whom we forgive, and that inevitably change the changing patterns of action that constitute who we are as well. But that is not all that forgiveness is: it is a starting again, a new relationship with the person whom we feel has wronged us. It means absorbing the wrong and ensuring that the changing patterns of action that we are, and that engage with the changing patterns of action that constitute the other person, will enhance their life and not diminish it, and will not carry back to them any of the wrong that they might have done, or any of the effects that that wrong might have had on us. This does not mean that sin is not real, or that harm is not real, for there are multiple changing patterns of action that can damage the coherence and the creativity of the changing patterns of action that constitute who we are. Forgiveness is ensuring that the harm goes no further: it stays with us. What Jesus is saying is this: God offers us forgiveness: that the evil that we do, the changing patterns of action that diminish rather than enhance both us and the people around us, that harm rather than do good, and with all of which the changing patterns of action that constitute God entwine: all of it is absorbed by God and transformed, so that none of the evil emerges in the changing patterns of action that constitute God's relationship towards us. For evil it is a one way journey, into God. But if we do not forgive others in this way—that is, if we do not absorb the evil patterns of action, transform them, and ensure that no evil travels back across the changing patterns of action that constitute our relationships with others—then God's forgiveness will be withdrawn, and we shall be left with untransformed changing patterns of action. The evil will stay with us, just as we have allowed the evil to stay with the person whom we have failed to forgive.

But what of Jesus' saying that what is not possible for us is possible for God? Is God not capable of forgiving when we are not? What if the wrong was so horrendous, towards others or towards ourselves, that we simply cannot forgive? Perhaps then what is not possible for us is possible for God: but under normal circumstances the command to forgive is absolute. It is what Jesus expected of his disciples, and it is what he expects of us still.

One aspect of these various sayings is particularly important, and it is an aspect that is not immediately obvious in an English translation: the "you" in verses 21, 24, and 25 is in the plural. It is together that we are to exercise faith, together that we are to pray, and together that we are to forgive. Jesus was addressing his words to the community of his disciples, so today the words are addressed to the church, and not simply to individuals within it. It is not individual faith, prayer, and forgiveness that Jesus is asking for here, although those individual patterns of action will no doubt be a consequence of the communal patterns of action that Jesus demands. What is required is patterns of action that constitute the church as a whole forgiving, exercising faith, and praying.[498]

# MARK 11:12-24

12 On the following day, when they came from Bethany, he was hungry. [13] Seeing in the distance a fig tree in leaf, he went to see whether perhaps he would find anything on it. When he came to it, he found nothing but leaves, for it was not the season for figs. [14] He said to it, 'May no one ever eat fruit from you again.' And his disciples heard it.

15 Then they came to Jerusalem. And he entered the temple and began to drive out those who were selling and those who were buying in the temple, and he overturned the tables of the money-changers and the seats of those who sold doves; [16] and he would not allow anyone to carry anything through the temple. [17] He was teaching and saying, 'Is it not written, "My house shall be called a house of prayer for all the nations." But you have made it a den of robbers.'

18 And when the chief priests and the scribes heard it, they kept looking for a way to kill him; for they were afraid of him, because the whole crowd was spellbound by his teaching. [19] And when evening came, Jesus and his disciples[e] went out of the city.

20 In the morning as they passed by, they saw the fig tree withered away to its roots. [21] Then Peter remembered and said to him, 'Rabbi, look! The fig

e. Gk *they*: other ancient authorities read *he*

tree that you cursed has withered.' ²² Jesus answered them, 'Have[f] faith in God. ²³ Truly I tell you, if you say to this mountain, "Be taken up and thrown into the sea," and if you do not doubt in your heart, but believe that what you say will come to pass, it will be done for you. ²⁴ So I tell you, whatever you ask for in prayer, believe that you have received[g] it, and it will be yours.

²⁵ 'Whenever you stand praying, forgive, if you have anything against anyone; so that your Father in heaven may also forgive you your trespasses.'[h] [499]

Again we have printed the entire "sandwich," and here we shall discuss Jesus driving the traders out of the temple.

Why did Jesus do that? Had the traders set up their stalls in the only temple court to which Gentiles were permitted access, thus preventing them from praying in the temple? Was Jesus' understanding that Gentiles and Jews were equally members of the Kingdom of God the motive for him emptying the court so that Gentiles could use it for prayer? Was Jesus consciously acting as God's judgement on the temple for representing a national exclusiveness rather than being a place to welcome the nations? Was this the opening act of the revolution that would establish the Kingdom of God?

Let us suppose first of all that Jesus was simply trying to clear traders out of the outer court that Gentiles were allowed to enter so that they could enter it and pray uninterrupted by the commotion of a market. Jesus quoted from the prophet Isaiah, and the whole of the passage runs like this:

> ³ Do not let the foreigner joined to the LORD say,
>> 'The LORD will surely separate me from his people';
> and do not let the eunuch say,
>> 'I am just a dry tree.'
> ⁴ For thus says the LORD:
> To the eunuchs who keep my sabbaths,
>> who choose the things that please me
>> and hold fast my covenant,
> ⁵ I will give, in my house and within my walls,
>> a monument and a name
>> better than sons and daughters;
> I will give them an everlasting name
>> that shall not be cut off.
> ⁶ And the foreigners who join themselves to the LORD,
>> to minister to him, to love the name of the LORD,

    f. Other ancient authorities read *'If you have*
    g. Other ancient authorities read *are receiving*
    h. Other ancient authorities add verse 26, *'But if you do not forgive, neither will your Father in heaven forgive your trespasses.'*

> and to be his servants,
>> all who keep the sabbath, and do not profane it,
>>> and hold fast my covenant—
> ⁷ these I will bring to my holy mountain,
>> and make them joyful in my house of prayer;
> their burnt-offerings and their sacrifices
>> will be accepted on my altar;
> for my house shall be called a house of prayer
>> for all peoples.
> ⁸ Thus says the Lord God,
>> who gathers the outcasts of Israel,
> I will gather others to them
>> besides those already gathered.ᵈ ⁵⁰⁰

This is radically inclusive. The law had declared eunuchs to be social outcasts—they were not to be admitted to "the assembly of the Lord"⁵⁰¹—and here was Isaiah not only including them but honoring them. And similarly with "foreigners": they too were now to be included. Isaiah is envisaging a new era that will follow the exile into which so many Israelites had been taken: an era in which there would be a new inclusion. Jesus clearly wanted to see that taking place in the temple on that day. He had learned to include Gentiles alongside Jews as equal members of the Kingdom of God; he had healed them; and he had fed them. He had provided Gentiles with signs of the Kingdom of God's coming: and now he wanted foreigners to be made joyful in the house of prayer which would from then on be for everyone, and not just for the few.

But this passage from Isaiah is not the only biblical text that would have come into the minds of those who were in the temple that day. A second passage would have been from the prophet Malachi:

> See, I am sending my messenger to prepare the way before me, and the Lord whom you seek will suddenly come to his temple. The messenger of the covenant in whom you delight—indeed, he is coming, says the Lord of hosts.⁵⁰²

And yet another text would have come to mind:

> Has this house, which is called by my name, become a den of robbers in your sight? You know, I too am watching, says the Lord.⁵⁰³

Jeremiah's objection had been to regarding possession of the temple rather than righteous behavior as a guarantee of God's favor. Jesus might not have been suggesting that the traders' temple court transactions were necessarily corrupt: his "den of robbers" accusation might have been a more general complaint that the Jewish authorities had

---

d. Heb *besides his gathered ones*

abandoned justice and were instead relying on possession of the temple. Jeremiah predicted the destruction of the temple of his time, which is what happened. Jesus was making the same prediction.[504] He was modelling his pattern of action on Jeremiah's.

And yet more passages from the Hebrew scriptures would also have come to mind: "Because of the wickedness of their deeds, I will drive them out of my house. I will love them no more; all their officials are rebels";[505] and "there shall no longer be traders[r] in the house of the Lord of hosts on that day":[506] that is, on the day on which God would both judge Israel and restore its fortunes. John the Baptist had come to prepare the way, and now "the Lord," the Messiah, "the one like a son of man," had arrived and would establish his kingdom.[507] Jesus was deliberately replicating the patterns of action found in these prophecies, and so was claiming to be the Messiah who would bring judgement on the temple and establish the Kingdom of God in which the Messiah would rule in place of the corrupt Jerusalem authorities, and in which a new and perfect temple would represent God's rule.[508]

So was this the opening act of the revolution that would bring about the Kingdom of God in which Jesus would be king, in which he and his disciples would rule, and in which the Messiah would fulfil his task of bringing in all the nations?[509] A more recent parallel might be the Boston Tea Party, when in 1773 American revolutionaries tipped an entire cargo of tea belonging to the British East India Company into Boston Harbor as a protest against what they saw as unjust British tax legislation. This event is regarded as the beginning of the American War of Independence. Perhaps Jesus saw his cleansing of the temple as the revolutionary act that would begin the process that would establish the Kingdom of God. Might the chief priests and the scribes have understood that if Jesus was left to carry on like this then he might not have unseated the Romans, but he might have ended up unseating them: hence the discussions that took place to plan Jesus' death? Jesus might have remained unsure about the direction that his messiahship would take now that he was in Jerusalem—he might in this incident have been understanding himself as both King in the Kingdom of God, and as High Priest of a new covenant, or he might have understood himself as a suffering servant of God representing in an acted parable God's judgement on a corrupt religious institution that was refusing to include the Gentiles in the old covenant—but either way he looked like a threat to the established order.[510] As Jesus was dying, some of those who were watching the crucifixion joked that he had said that he would destroy the temple and rebuild it in three days, but that he could not even save himself: but then the curtain temple was torn in two, destroying the priests' monopoly on access to God, thus attacking the very heart of the temple religion.[511]

We know that Jesus' disciples had at least one sword with them in the Garden of Gethsemane when Jesus was arrested, because we hear that the high priest's slave had his ear cut off;[512] and Luke's Gospel tells us that there were two swords, and that Jesus had commented "It is enough!"[513] Unfortunately, we don't know whether he meant

r. Or *Canaanites*

"No more discussion of that kind" or "Two swords is enough." A lot hinges on what Jesus meant. If the incident in the temple was the opening act of a revolution, then it fits with the entry into Jerusalem as king, and it fits with Jesus' response to Peter's declaration that he was the Messiah. But it really does not fit with Jesus' predictions of his death and resurrection.

All we can say is that we have to assume that in the end it does not matter what Jesus meant by his response to Peter, by the entry into Jerusalem on a donkey, by the incident in the temple, and by Jesus' disciples carrying swords in the Garden of Gethsemane. It cannot matter because we cannot know whether or not Jesus intended to start a revolution in an attempt to drive out the Romans and establish the Kingdom of God, presumably with God's assistance. All we have available to us now is the text of Mark's Gospel, which tells us of a Jesus who entered Jerusalem on a donkey, and who threw market traders out of the temple. This is the story that must be told: and as the pure pattern of the text changes the changing patterns of action that constitute our brains, and therefore the changing patterns of action that constitute families, communities, societies, and the world, so the changing patterns of action crystallized in the text will continue to change us and to reveal to us Jesus, who was changing patterns of action that were and are changing patterns of action that constitute God.

Was Jesus religious? He prayed: he prayed a lot. And he clearly knew the scriptures of his religion, and was practiced in interpreting them, often in quite radical ways. But his attitude to the law that was central to Judaism remains something of an enigma. In Matthew's Gospel we find Jesus saying this: "Do not think that I have come to abolish the law or the prophets; I have come not to abolish but to fulfil."[514] But what does Jesus mean by "fulfil"? Does he mean that he intends to keep the law as written and as traditionally interpreted? To keep it as written but as newly interpreted? Or to transform it into a perfect law that he will then keep? The last of those options might cohere best with Jesus' practice: for instance, with his healings on the sabbath, and with his statement about all food being clean. Although we cannot tell how Jesus' convictions evolved during the three years or so of his ministry, it is perfectly possible that he began as a disciple of John, and with John's rigorous attitude to the law, but that he then came to see the law as oppressive and discriminatory, and therefore to be radicalized, in the sense of being returned to its roots. Those roots, as we shall see, came down to love of God and love of neighbor: these, and not the old law, were to be the law of the new Kingdom of God. It is not insignificant that when Jesus came to Jerusalem he did not choose to attend one of the regular sacrifices: instead he cleared the courtyard of its moneychangers and stallholders, which would have resulted in the temporary closing down of the temple's activity. A new Kingdom of God for all the nations was about to be born: the very opposite of the exclusively Jewish religious institution of the temple.[515]

So was Jesus religious? Perhaps not in the traditional sense of the word, and not in a sense that the Jews of his time would have understood. His relationship with God was perhaps too intense to be described as religious: and perhaps it was even more intense than Jesus himself realized. For Jesus, God was Abba, Father: and it was this God who would bring about the Kingdom of God that was already near and of which Jesus' teachings and healings were evidence. This combination of personal and cosmic religion might best be described as occupying the two ends of a spectrum running between intimacy with God and living already in the midst of an apocalyptic eschatology: an utterly disruptive last things that would give birth to the utterly new. Most of us live our religion in calmer stretches somewhere around the center of the spectrum. Maybe it was Jesus' living of a changing pattern of action that represented a unique kind of religion that mystified and wrong-footed the chief priests and scribes just as much as his actions in the temple had done. This was not the kind of religion to be expected from someone everyone called Rabbi: and when you put together the triumphal entry and the incident in the temple, things were looking distinctly risky for those whose positions relied on the toleration of an occupying force that had an interest in avoiding social instability.

The chief priests and scribes were now determined to kill Jesus because they could see how attractive the people were finding his promise of a Kingdom of God: but not just yet, so Jesus was able to leave the city, presumably to stay with his friends Martha, Mary, and Lazarus.

## MARK 11:27-33

> 27 Again they came to Jerusalem. As he was walking in the temple, the chief priests, the scribes, and the elders came to him 28 and said, 'By what authority are you doing these things? Who gave you this authority to do them?' 29 Jesus said to them, 'I will ask you one question; answer me, and I will tell you by what authority I do these things. 30 Did the baptism of John come from heaven, or was it of human origin? Answer me.' 31 They argued with one another, 'If we say, "From heaven," he will say, "Why then did you not believe him?" 32 But shall we say, "Of human origin"?'—they were afraid of the crowd, for all regarded John as truly a prophet. 33 So they answered Jesus, "We do not know." And Jesus said to them, "Neither will I tell you by what authority I am doing these things."[516]

By what authority did Jesus teach, heal, and cast out evil? Who had given him permission to do those things? —which comes down to the question: Who constantly enabled him to do those things? And underlying this question was probably the one that bothered them most: Did Jesus think of himself as a prophet, or perhaps as the Messiah?[517] Bartimaeus's public declaration that Jesus was "Son of David," and the ride into Jerusalem on a donkey, had begun to dissolve the secrecy that Jesus had previously commanded, but still there had been no clear declaration by Jesus himself as to how he understood his role and status.[518] That would not happen until his trial, so rather than give a straight answer to his questioners, Jesus chose to ask a question in return. The question put his questioners in a quandary. They could have said that they had asked the question first, and that if Jesus answered it then they would answer his: but they chose not to do that, presumably because they would still have been left trying to find a response to Jesus' question about the authority for John's baptizing. If he had answered their question, what would Jesus have said? He might have responded in terms similar to those that he had employed before: "The Son of Man has authority . . ."; or he might have responded as we find him doing in Luke's Gospel: "If it is by the finger of God that I cast out the demons, then the Kingdom of God has come to you."[519] But he did not. He left them to decide for themselves where his authority came from.

The question is still a real one: Where does authority come from? And in practical terms: Where should each of us look for authority? In the context of the conceptual framework that we are employing here: Where are the changing patterns of action that should shape and change the changing patterns of action that constitute who we are, and that constitute our families, communities, societies, and institutions? Jesus was clear enough: He sought to do the will of God: that is, he looked for the changing patterns of action that constituted God, and he modelled his own changing patterns of action on those: and he did that to a superlative extent. In relation to Jesus, we have here a dual process: Jesus was and is God incarnate: the changing patterns of action that constitute Jesus are those that constitute God—although, as we have discovered, Jesus, like the rest of us, had to "learn obedience" to those God-originated changing patterns of action. And at the same time Jesus consciously sought out the changing patterns of action that constituted God, and consciously modelled his own changing patterns of action on those. He did this through prayer: the changing patterns of action that constituted his brain consciously seeking and entangling with the changing patterns of action that constituted God, so that his own thought-forms and bodily actions would more closely mirror the changing patterns of action that constituted God. He did this through the scriptures of his own religion: so we find him consciously modelling his life on the servant of God in Isaiah, and seeking out the roots of the law in the commands to love God and neighbor; and we find him doing this by listening to the people he encountered: perhaps the most extreme case of this being the Syrophoenician woman. God was where Jesus looked for his authority: and if the chief priests, the scribes, and the elders had not recognized his—had not recognized that Jesus' words and actions consciously reflected the changing patterns of action that constituted God—then no amount of Jesus telling them was going to persuade them.

If Jesus' authority was from God, then where did Jesus' disciples find their authority? Jesus was their Rabbi, their Teacher: the title that people frequently gave to him. He was their authority: and because Jesus' changing patterns of action were those that constituted God, God was their authority. Jesus taught his disciples to pray; they too would have known the scriptures, at least to some extent; and they too would have learnt from others. The conversations that took place among themselves were not always of the highest quality, but they became so once Jesus got involved in them.

So where should *we* look for authority? Where should *we* look for the shaping and changing of the changing patterns of action that determine who we are, and of what we think, say, and do? The meaning of being a Christian is that we look to Jesus as our authority: that it is the changing patterns of action that determined who Jesus was, and who he is, that should determine the changing patterns of action that constitute who we are, and what we think, say, and do: and, if we are Christians, then the changing patterns of action that constitute who Jesus was and is are the changing patterns of action that constitute who God was and is.

So we too will pray in the way that Jesus taught his disciples to pray. There is more clear instruction on prayer in Matthew's Gospel and in Luke's Gospel than there is in Mark's Gospel, so that is where we should look for the patterns of action that should constitute our praying. And we too should study the scriptures. We should read the Hebrew scriptures, because that is where both Jesus and his disciples discovered the changing patterns of action that constitute God; and it is the reading of those scriptures that shaped and changed the changing patterns of action that constituted who they were, and what they thought, said, and did: so by reading those same scriptures we shall discover the changing patterns of action that constituted Jesus and his first disciples; and through our reading of the Hebrew scriptures, the changing patterns of action that constitute who we are, and what we think, say, and do, will be shaped and changed by the changing patterns of action that constituted who Jesus and his first disciples were, and what they thought, said, and did. The reading of the New Testament, the specifically Christian scriptures, is another matter. That is precisely what we are doing here through our actological explorations in Mark's Gospel. In the gospels we find text that has crystallized the changing patterns of action that constituted Jesus and his first disciples; and in the Acts of the Apostles, the epistles, and the Revelation, we find text that has crystallized the changing patterns of action that constituted the early Christians. As we read them, the texts change the changing patterns of action that constitute who we are, and what we think, say, and do: so what we are, and what we think, say, and do, are shaped and changed by the changing patterns of action that constituted Jesus, his first disciples, and the first Christians. This is how authority works for the Christian. It is Jesus who is our authority, which means that it is God who is our authority, and the New Testament is a pure pattern by which we access that authority and through which it has its effect.

At the beginning of Mark's Gospel we found John predicting that Jesus would baptize us with the Holy Spirit; and in chapter 13 we shall find a promise that the Holy Spirit will teach us what to say in contexts of persecution. We find much more on the

Holy Spirit in the other gospels, in the Acts of the Apostles, and in the letters of the New Testament. The Holy Spirit, who is the Spirit of Jesus, or the Spirit of Christ, is simply the changing patterns of action that constitute God still active among us and within us across the history of creation, and in particular across Christian history. Because the Holy Spirit is the changing patterns of action that constitute God, the Holy Spirit is God, just as Jesus was and is God: hence the church's development of the doctrine of the Trinity: that God is one, and that God is the Father who creates; that God is Jesus, the Son of God and the Word of God incarnate; and that God is the Holy Spirit: God active in the world today—and perhaps it is through an Action, action, movement, change, diversity, and generally dynamic conceptual framework that the Trinity will make more sense today than it might through a Being, beings, rest, unchanging, unitary, and generally static conceptual framework: and perhaps, too, such a dynamic conceptual framework might always have been able to make more sense of God as Trinity. Not only do we access Jesus and therefore God as our authority through prayer and through reading the scriptures, nor is it only through these patterns of action that Jesus and therefore God shape and change the changing patterns of action that constitute who we are and what we think, say, and do: it is also the Holy Spirit—the changing patterns of action that constitute who God is constantly enmeshed in the changing patterns of action that constitute the world and ourselves—that is our access to authority, and that shapes and changes the changing patterns of action that constitute who we are and what we think, say, and do.

So Jesus and therefore God is our authority: and through prayer, by reading of the Hebrew and New Testament scriptures, and by the Holy Spirit at work within and around us, we access that authority, and that authority is active in our lives. And just as Jesus and his disciples found their authority in people who taught them obedience, such as the Syrophoenician woman, so we shall find that other people function as channels of authority. Our authority is ultimately God in Jesus: but our secondary authorities are now fourfold: prayer, the scriptures, the Holy Spirit, and other people. It is because this complex combination of complex changing patterns of action constitute our authority that we say that the church is our authority, for it is these changing patterns of action that constitute the church: but they are not restricted to it or constrained by it. Whoever prays, whoever reads the Hebrew and New Testament scriptures, whoever is changed by the Holy Spirit active within themselves and in the world around them, and whoever is changed by the people around them, finds that God is active as their authority, changing the changing patterns of action that constitute who they are and what they think, say, and do. We might therefore say that for Christians there is a fivefold secondary authority: prayer, the scriptures, the Holy Spirit, other people, and the church: but "secondary" is the essential word here. For the Christian, Jesus is our authority: the changing patterns of action that constitute who he was and who he is. That is where the Christian's authority is to be found.

# MARK 12:1-12

> 12 Then he began to speak to them in parables. 'A man planted a vineyard, put a fence around it, dug a pit for the wine press, and built a watch-tower; then he leased it to tenants and went to another country. ² When the season came, he sent a slave to the tenants to collect from them his share of the produce of the vineyard. ³ But they seized him, and beat him, and sent him away empty-handed. ⁴ And again he sent another slave to them; this one they beat over the head and insulted. ⁵ Then he sent another, and that one they killed. And so it was with many others; some they beat, and others they killed. ⁶ He had still one other, a beloved son. Finally he sent him to them, saying, "They will respect my son." ⁷ But those tenants said to one another, "This is the heir; come, let us kill him, and the inheritance will be ours." ⁸ So they seized him, killed him, and threw him out of the vineyard. ⁹ What then will the owner of the vineyard do? He will come and destroy the tenants and give the vineyard to others. ¹⁰ Have you not read this scripture:
>
>> "The stone that the builders rejected
>>
>> has become the cornerstone;^i
>
> ¹¹ this was the Lord's doing,
>
>> and it is amazing in our eyes"?'
>
> ¹² When they realized that he had told this parable against them, they wanted to arrest him, but they feared the crowd. So they left him and went away.[520]

As usual, there are multiple possibilities for the origin and intended meaning of this parable. Might the story have been based on a local incident during which some vineyard tenants killed the owner's son? —for if the landowner had been a proselyte with only one son, then the vineyard might indeed have passed into the ownership of the tenants. Or did Jesus tell the story with reference to himself? Did he tell it with reference to John the Baptist? Did he mean by it that the Kingdom of God would be given to Gentiles rather than to the Jews? Did early Christians tell the story with reference to Jesus?[521] Whichever is the case—and there might of course be multiple roots for the story that we have in Mark's Gospel—the parable is a crystallization of patterns of action that constituted Jesus' mind, and of patterns of action constituted by John's death, Jesus' death, the gift of the church and the Kingdom of God to Gentiles, and more besides.

A clear reference is to a prophecy in Isaiah in which God plants a vineyard:[522]

> 5 Let me sing for my beloved
>
>> my love-song concerning his vineyard:
>
> My beloved had a vineyard
>
>> on a very fertile hill. . . .

---

i. Or *keystone*

² He dug it and cleared it of stones,
    and planted it with choice vines;
he built a watch-tower in the midst of it,
    and hewed out a wine vat in it;
he expected it to yield grapes,
    but it yielded wild grapes.
³ And now, inhabitants of Jerusalem
    and people of Judah,
judge between me
    and my vineyard.
⁴ What more was there to do for my vineyard
    that I have not done in it?
When I expected it to yield grapes,
    why did it yield wild grapes?
⁵ And now I will tell you
    what I will do to my vineyard.
I will remove its hedge,
    and it shall be devoured;
I will break down its wall,
    and it shall be trampled down.
⁶ I will make it a waste;
    it shall not be pruned or hoed,
    and it shall be overgrown with briers and thorns;
I will also command the clouds
    that they rain no rain upon it.
⁷ For the vineyard of the LORD of hosts
    is the house of Israel,
and the people of Judah
    are his pleasant planting;
he expected justice,
    but saw bloodshed;
righteousness,
    but heard a cry![523]

So in Jesus' parable God is the vineyard-planter, and Israel is the vineyard. Presumably the tenants are the current leaders of Israel: the "chief-priests, scribes and elders" of the previous passage. They and their predecessors had persecuted and killed the prophets sent by God to call Israel to righteousness: "their share of the produce." But who is God's son in this story? It is unlikely that Jesus would have implied that John the Baptist was God's son by thinking that the son in the parable stood for John. Jesus would have regarded John as being one of the servants sent to collect the rent. But would Jesus have referred to himself as God's son, even by implication? Jesus would not normally have called himself the Son of God—he called himself by the ambiguous title "Son of Man," and he attempted to silence evil spirits that recognized him as Son of God: but it is not impossible that he would have understood himself as the son of the vineyard owner in relation to a series of assaults and killings perpetrated by the tenants. So we have to assume that either Jesus included the vineyard owner's son in the parable as a veiled reference to his own growing understanding of his unique relationship with his Father,[524] or that early Christians either created this parable, or adapted a similar parable by Jesus, to tell a story that they wanted to tell. Any of these would have been entirely possible. Jesus told parables, so his followers would not only have felt it to be appropriate to create parables of their own, but they might have felt obliged to do so as an essential element of their discipleship: it was Jesus' changing pattern of action, so it had to be a changing pattern of action that constituted early Christian activity. Parables were Jesus' teaching method, so it had to be a teaching method of the early church: which of course leaves us with the question as to how many of the parables in the gospels were told by Jesus, and how many of them were created by early Christians. We shall never know the origin of this parable, and can only keep an open mind.

In relation to the story itself: Why on earth would a vineyard owner whose servants had already been killed by the tenants send his only son, on his own, to collect the rent? Simply because that fitted the story that had to be told. Perhaps for Jesus, and certainly for the early Christians, God had sent his Son, knowing that he would be killed by the "chief-priests, scribes and elders." There is no sense here that the son's death was regarded as some kind of ransom. God was sending his son to call Israel to righteousness: to provide their "share of the produce." It is irrelevant that no real vineyard owner would send his son following the assaults and deaths of his servants: if Jesus told this parable, and he was hinting that he himself is God's Son—a hint that might have led to the High Priest asking Jesus if he was the Son of the Blessed at his interrogation—then the death of the son matters, because it is that that results in the destruction of the vineyard's tenants, and the handing of the vineyard to others.[525] We might have expected that at this point the vineyard owner would have followed the Isaiah prophecy and simply destroyed the vineyard: but he does not. It is the tenants that God "destroys." The vineyard is handed to "others."

The parable was indeed told "against them": that is, against the "chief-priests, scribes and elders" who were to hand Jesus over to the Roman authorities who would then crucified him. A possible context for the creation of the parable might therefore be the early persecution of Christians that resulted in Stephen's martyrdom, and in which Saul's—Paul's—campaign to imprison Christians was clearly an important element.[526] Christians were convinced that the Jesus whom the "chief-priests, scribes and elders" had handed over had now been vindicated as Son of God—he was now the "cornerstone"—and the Son having been rejected by Jewish leaders, the Kingdom of God had now been handed to "others": to Christians.

Or perhaps the context was a slightly later time by which Gentiles were members of the church. The Isaiah prophecy might then have a double meaning: the "stone" that had been rejected and had now become the "cornerstone" is both Jesus, the Son of God rejected by the tenants—the "chief-priests, scribes and elders"—and also the Gentiles. Jesus, rejected by the Jewish leaders, had been vindicated as God's Son, and the Gentiles, rejected by Israel, which had failed to realize its mission to be God's servant to the nations, had now been given the Kingdom of God and were equally members of the church. They had become its "cornerstone."

The parable is incomplete in itself. The vineyard owner's son is dead, so a resolution is still required. This is provided by the quotation from Psalm 118[527] in which a vindication is promised. Either Jesus added this quotation to the parable to express a conviction that he would be vindicated as the Son of Man and would be presented to the Ancient One; or Christians added it to express their conviction that Jesus was risen, had ascended, and was already ruling in the Kingdom of God; or Christians added the quotation to express the fact that Gentiles had become the cornerstone of the church. Perhaps all three: and in particular, if Jesus had become convinced that he was the Messiah—the Son of Man who would be vindicated and would be presented to the Ancient One—then there is every reason to believe that Jesus could have spoken these words to express his growing conviction that the Son of Man was Son of God.[528]

But is this a parable? And if it is not, does that make it more likely that it was told by early Christians rather than by Jesus? A significant reason for believing that this passage might have been constructed by early Christians, and not by Jesus, is that all of the details clearly matter to its meaning. The parables that we might legitimately regard as Jesus' own parables of the Kingdom—those in chapter 4—have a central message represented by the punchline. The details of the story might or might not be relevant. Here the details clearly matter. A story is being told. What we have here might best be described as a drama: a series of changing patterns of action that resemble the changing patterns of action of God's history with Israel: the creation of the vineyard resembling God's establishment of Israel in the promised land; the vineyard owners' servants being assaulted and killed resembling Israel's treatment of the prophets; the vineyard owner's son being killed by the tenants representing the Jewish leaders getting Jesus killed; and the handing of the vineyard to others representing the transfer of the Kingdom of God from Israel, represented by its leaders, to Christians, Gentiles, or both, with Jesus being finally vindicated as the cornerstone of the new Kingdom of God.

Just as Israel's relationship with God was changing patterns of action—the travels and actions of the patriarchs; the exodus from Egypt; the establishment of the kingdom by David and his successors; the prophets and the exiles; the return to the promised land; and a glorious future to be inaugurated by the Messiah, a Davidic figure who would ensure the future peace and prosperity of Israel: so for the church the relationship with God was changing patterns of action. It was all of those that constituted Israel's relationship with God, but then there were more: Jesus' birth, life, ministry, suffering, death, and resurrection; the coming of the Holy Spirit; the growth of the church; and the future return of Jesus to establish the Kingdom of God. Just as Israel told stories constituted by changing patterns of action that resembled the changing patterns of action that constituted God's relationship with Israel—as in the parable of the vineyard in Isaiah—so the church told stories constituted by changing patterns of action that resembled the changing patterns of action that constituted God's relationship with the church. We need more such stories, and today we need the stories to be constructed from changing patterns of action that might connect more easily with the changing patterns of action that constitute modern minds than might stories about vineyard owners who send successive servants to be persecuted and killed by tenants, and then sends his only son to be treated in the same way. What is required is a deep and reflective understanding of the changing patterns of action that constitute God's relationship with the created order, with the human race, and with Jesus, and then stories constructed out of changing patterns of action that resemble those. This will be no easy task.

## MARK 12:13-17

> 13 Then they sent to him some Pharisees and some Herodians to trap him in what he said. [14] And they came and said to him, 'Teacher, we know that you are sincere, and show deference to no one; for you do not regard people with partiality, but teach the way of God in accordance with truth. Is it lawful to pay taxes to the emperor, or not? [15] Should we pay them, or should we not?' But knowing their hypocrisy, he said to them, 'Why are you putting me to the test? Bring me a denarius and let me see it.' [16] And they brought one. Then he said to them, 'Whose head is this, and whose title?' They answered, 'The emperor's.' [17] Jesus said to them, 'Give to the emperor the things that are the emperor's, and to God the things that are God's.' And they were utterly amazed at him.[529]

The nouns here are all about changing patterns of action. For each of us our identity, in terms of the groups to which we might belong, our gender, our skin color, our height, our health, our beliefs, our prejudices, and so on, is constituted by changing patterns of action of particular kinds. A Pharisee was a person who was committed to keeping the Jewish law, and who believed in the resurrection of the dead. The patterns of action that constituted a Pharisee's brain cohered with the patterns of action that constituted the activity required by the law in relation to religious ritual, personal ethics, hygiene rules, and so on; and to the changing pattern of action that constituted God's raising of the dead. A Herodian was someone enthusiastic for the reign of King Herod, perhaps someone in his service, and also perhaps someone who wanted to see Herod as the substantive ruler of the country rather than being a puppet of the Roman occupiers. This is how we would describe the changing patterns of action that constituted the ideas in a Herodian's brain. Jesus is here described as "Teacher." This was his identity as far as the Pharisees and Herodians were concerned. The changing patterns of action that constituted who they were were entangled with the changing patterns of action that constituted Jesus to the extent that they questioned him and he responded: but perhaps their words were not simply questions seeking information: perhaps they were being ironic—that is, a particular combination of conflicting changing patterns of action in the brain giving rise to words and facial expressions that between them communicated a questioning attitude that they were inviting their listeners to share.

Turning to the other nouns in the text: "Deference" is a changing pattern of action that is likely to be changed, perhaps significantly, by the changing patterns of action that constitute someone else. Someone who does not show deference is someone constituted by changing patterns of action that repel those changing patterns of action that constitute people who might wish to draw other people into conformity with their own changing patterns of action. The Pharisees and Herodians had recognized that Jesus did not show deference: his changing patterns of action were the changing patterns of action that constituted and that constitute God, and although there were multiple entanglements with the changing patterns of action that constituted other people, Jesus was not drawn in to the changing patterns of action that constituted other people. He made his own decisions as to what to do and what to say: that is, God, and his own humanity, were the origin of the patterns of action that constituted Jesus, in general and in detail. Similarly in relation to partiality. Someone who shows partiality is someone who chooses that their changing patterns of action should influence and be influenced by one person's changing patterns of action rather than by those of another. Truth we have previously understood as "truth-seeking." Hypocrisy is related. It is a truth-seeking that is then contradicted by someone's changing patterns of action. Taxes are money paid to a government. We have already discussed money as a changing pattern of action: so taxes are also changing patterns of action with a particular engagement with the changing patterns of action that constitute a country's government: in this case the Roman government. A test was and is a changing pattern of actions that discovers whether a particular changing pattern of action can be found when a search is conducted of the changing patterns of action that constitute an object, or in this case a person. A denarius was a unit of money, and so although the coin brought to Jesus was a relatively stable pattern of action that we might call a coin, the denarius was a more complex changing pattern of action that included patterns of action related to the buying of goods, the settling of debts, and the payment of taxes.

The design on the face of a coin, like the coin itself, is pure pattern, and so is like text. It crystallizes the changing patterns of action that constituted the person or machine that made the coin, and the pattern then changes the changing patterns of action that constitute individuals and institutions as the coin is spent and received over and over again. And the title is like all text: a pure pattern that crystallizes the changing patterns of action that created it, and that in this case would have included changing patterns of action that constituted the emperor.

Ownership is an institutional changing pattern of action: a complex bundle of changing patterns of action that binds the changing patterns of action that constitute an object of some kind to the changing patterns of action that constitute a person or an institution. Jesus is saying that the denarius belongs to the emperor, and also, by extension, that anything else that the emperor owned by way of laws imposed on Israel—laws that were pure pattern, and that were changing the changing patterns of action that constituted the daily life of individuals and institutions at the time—belonged to the emperor, and were to be given to the emperor. In contrast, the things that belonged to God—objects, commitments, love, honor, obedience, and much more: changing patterns of action entangled by ownership in the changing patterns of action that constituted God—were to be given to God.

It is difficult to see why Jesus' hearers were amazed by his response. For Jesus to point out that what belonged to the emperor should be given to the emperor, and that what belonged to God should be given to God, was hardly a novel idea. Perhaps the amazement was due to the fact that Jesus had wandered well off the territory defined by the questioner. They had simply asked about taxes imposed by Rome, perhaps hoping that Jesus would incriminate himself in relation to Roman law by saying that taxes ought not to be paid; or perhaps that he would make himself unpopular with those who wanted to be rid of the Romans by simply saying that of course taxes should be paid. He did say that (which might be why the account was retained in the tradition, because it would have legitimized Christians paying taxes to the Roman Empire),[530] but only after revealing his questioners' complicity in the tax-paying. They were using the emperor's money, and like all money it gained its value by enabling people to pay their taxes. This meant that simply by possessing a coin with the emperor's face and title on it, Jesus' questioners were implicating themselves in the tax-paying in relation to which they were hoping to trip up Jesus. They were also implicating themselves in some very unjewish practices. Images of human beings were generally unacceptable, and the coin that they presented to Jesus not only had the Emperor's image on it, but it also declared him to be son of a divine Caesar and a Roman high priest. Jesus was asking his questioners to ask themselves what belonged to Caesar, and was asking them to decide whether taxes should be paid in coins that were blasphemous in the extreme;

and at the same time he was hinting that he was no friend of Roman coinage, and that it should indeed be given back to Caesar, which is where it came from.[531]

But perhaps what really did amaze them was that Jesus had taken their question as an opportunity to remind them that what God owned should be given to God. By this Jesus would have been understood to mean obedience to the law, that both God and neighbor should be loved, that vows should be fulfilled, that prayer and other religious duties were to be offered to God, that the scriptures were to be read, and so on. This was not the only time that Jesus turned challenges into opportunities for those who challenged him to examine themselves. A classic case was the woman who had been caught in adultery.[532] If Jesus had declared that she should be stoned, as the law directed, then he would have betrayed compassion, and compromised the equal value that his teaching about marriage, and his calling of women as disciples, had attributed to women; but if he had not declared that the woman should be stoned then he would have contradicted the law. He told the person present who had never sinned to throw the first stone at the woman. None of them did. They all walked away, leaving Jesus to tell the woman not to sin again. Everyone who had spent those few minutes with Jesus would have been radically changed by the encounter.[533]

Perhaps the same will have happened here. Those who thought that they had found a question that Jesus could not possibly answer without getting himself into trouble one way or another had found themselves challenged about the direction of their own lives. The changing patterns of action that constituted who they were had entangled with those that constituted Jesus and that constituted God. They were never the same again.

This event would have been remembered for an obvious reason: Christians' ultimate loyalty was to Jesus, but they lived, as Christians still live, in a complex political world in which multiple authorities demand our allegiance. What Jesus' response to the question about paying tax to Caesar offered to Christians then, and offers to Christians now, is a statement of the legitimacy of giving allegiance to civic authorities, even if that might appear to compromise religious requirements.[534] The pattern of action that is obedience can relate to a variety of institutional and personal patterns of action. We are not told how to manage the complexity that results from that, but what this passage does tell us is that managing the complexity is an obligation.

## MARK 12:18-27

> 18 Some Sadducees, who say there is no resurrection, came to him and asked him a question, saying, ¹⁹ 'Teacher, Moses wrote for us that if a man's brother dies, leaving a wife but no child, the man[j] shall marry the widow and raise up children for his brother. ²⁰ There were seven brothers; the first married and,

j. Gk *his brother*

when he died, left no children; $^{21}$ and the second married her and died, leaving no children; and the third likewise; $^{22}$ none of the seven left children. Last of all the woman herself died. $^{23}$ In the resurrection$^k$ whose wife will she be? For the seven had married her.'

24 Jesus said to them, 'Is not this the reason you are wrong, that you know neither the scriptures nor the power of God? $^{25}$ For when they rise from the dead, they neither marry nor are given in marriage, but are like angels in heaven. $^{26}$ And as for the dead being raised, have you not read in the book of Moses, in the story about the bush, how God said to him, "I am the God of Abraham, the God of Isaac, and the God of Jacob"? $^{27}$ He is God not of the dead, but of the living; you are quite wrong.'[535]

Jews had not always believed that God would raise the dead. This was a belief that had emerged during the Maccabean period: Jews fighting to remove the Greeks from their land were fortified in their adherence to their faith under severe persecution by the belief that if they died for their faith then God would raise them from the dead. The Pharisees and many other Jews still believed that. The Sadducees did not. Jesus was closer to the Pharisees on this: hence the attempt by the Sadducees to prove him wrong on this particular issue.[536] To do this they exercised some logic on an element of the law designed to ensure that a childless widow would not be destitute: the requirement that the dead husband's brother should marry her. The argument would have applied to any woman who had had two husbands, or to a man who had had two wives: Who would be married to whom when the dead were raised?

Jesus' response was an obvious one. The life into which the dead would be raised would not be like the life that we live now,[537] so two people married in this life would not be married in the next. But that raises the question as what we might mean by the resurrection of the dead, or by any concept of a life after this one. In this life we are constituted by the changing patterns of action that constitute who we are across our entire lifespans from birth to death. In relation to marriage, the changing patterns of action that constitute who we are are significantly shaped and constantly changed by the changing patterns of action that constitute who our spouse is. We are literally inseparable. There is no way of ever separating the ways in which two members of a married couple change each other and have changed each other. So if the entire experience of being married to someone is somehow lost at the resurrection of the dead, then it is not us who are raised to a new life: it is someone else—a new person.

Clearly, if there is a life different from this one for each one of us, then the changing patterns of action that we are now must continue to constitute the person that we shall be then. This is particularly true of our memories. The changing patterns of action that we are now are significantly shaped, and constantly changed, by our memories: by changing patterns of action in the brain that relate to events in the past: that is, complex patterns of action that change large numbers of changing patterns of

k. Other ancient authorities add *when they rise*

action that we are and that we shall be. If those memories do not survive into a future life, then that future life is not our future life. And many of those memories will relate to people we have known, and in particular to people to whom we have been married, or who have otherwise been life partners, or partners for many years. There is a sense that we are who we are married to: we really are one flesh—and if we are not that one flesh in some future life, then again it is not us who are raised from the dead.

Paul wrote about the "spiritual body"[538] that we would have following the resurrection of the dead. This was first of all an attempt to express the mystery of what would follow this life, but it was also a recognition that individual people must be somehow embodied—a boundary of some kind is required, however porous it is to the influence of others' changing patterns of actions and the changing patterns of action of the world around us; and also a recognition that there would be something divine about us that would not be true of this life. Our changing patterns of action would have been through a cleansing and a transformation, so that they will more nearly reflect the changing patterns of action that constituted and constitute Jesus, and therefore the changing patterns of action that constitute God.

Just as a creature who lived in a two dimensional world would not be able to conceive of a world of three dimensions, and just as we cannot envisage a world of five, six, or seven dimensions, so we cannot envisage some new kind of life in which reality would be constituted by changing patterns of action that would be both different from and the same as they are in this life: if they were not the same then we would not be the same people, and if they were not different then we would be in this life and not the next. And what of the gap between our deaths and whatever comes next: a gap constituted by the change from this life to one in many ways utterly different, whether or not that gap is temporal as well, if time continues to function in the same way as it does now? Perhaps all we can say is that God will remember us: that the changing patterns of action that we are now will be taken in among the changing patterns of action that constitute God in order to be cleansed and transformed and then created new as a person who will be both a new creation and the people that we are now. This is not a life that we can envisage now, but if it is constituted by changing patterns of action that reflect the changing patterns of action that we are now then there would be no reason for saying that a resurrected life cannot be real or that it cannot be us who are raised from the dead. Our bodies might be turned to ash or they might decay in the ground, but there will be new spiritual bodies that will embody the new people that we shall be.

And we shall be "with Christ": not only in the sense that somehow there will be a relationship with the Jesus who has already been raised from the dead and who will reign as God's servant in the Kingdom of God in which we shall then live, but also because the changing patterns of action that we shall then be will have been shaped by being taken into God, and they will be so transformed that they will conform to the changing patterns of action that constitute Jesus and therefore God, and that constitute God and therefore Jesus.

The second response that Jesus gives to the Sadducees is a somewhat subtle argument. A literal translation of Mark's text would be "I the God of Abraham, the God of Isaac, and the God of Jacob." There is no verb, just as there is no verb in the Hebrew text that Jesus quoted.[539] Jesus is making the theological point that God is the God of Abraham, of Isaac, and of Jacob, so they cannot be simply dead to God, but must be somehow alive.[540] It is not so much God's timelessness that is assumed here, but rather what we might call God's alltimeness. God is Action and the source of action, and is particular changing patterns of action, and if these are to relate to the changing patterns of action that constitute who we are, then God exists in time: God changes, which is a time-dependent characteristic of patterns of action—or perhaps time is change-dependent. Either way, God lives in all time, as it is God's creation, and so God was the God of Abraham, Isaac and Jacob back then, and he is their God still. Everyone, constituted by the changing patterns of action that they were, are, and will be, is present to God: our changing patterns of action and God's constantly relate to each other across time. God is "not God of the dead, but of the living."

## MARK 12:28-34

> 28 One of the scribes came near and heard them disputing with one another, and seeing that he answered them well, he asked him, 'Which commandment is the first of all?' [29] Jesus answered, 'The first is, "Hear, O Israel: the Lord our God, the Lord is one; [30] you shall love the Lord your God with all your heart, and with all your soul, and with all your mind, and with all your strength." [31] The second is this, "You shall love your neighbor as yourself." There is no other commandment greater than these.' [32] Then the scribe said to him, 'You are right, Teacher; you have truly said that "he is one, and besides him there is no other"; [33] and "to love him with all the heart, and with all the understanding, and with all the strength," and "to love one's neighbor as oneself,"—this is much more important than all whole burnt-offerings and sacrifices.' [34] When Jesus saw that he answered wisely, he said to him, 'You are not far from the kingdom of God.' After that no one dared to ask him any question.[541]

Much rabbinic thought had gone into how to rank the commandments so as to determine priority in the case of conflict between them, so the scribe's question would not have been unfamiliar to Jesus, and his response would have been well within the rabbinic tradition.[542] The questioner might well have been genuinely interested in what Jesus might have had to say on a matter of current debate. A further possibility is that this was another trick question, inviting Jesus to fall into a trap. He had "answered well" so far, but might a scribe be able to find a question that Jesus could only answer by incriminating himself in some way? Asking about the commandment that was "first of all" could have been a good choice. When Moses was on Mount Sinai, "God spoke all these words":[543] and "all these words" were the ten commandments. And then there were the hundreds of other commands in the law that many believed to be equally important. After all, if God had said all of those words, and Moses had written them down, then were they not all equally important? It would have been a brave rabbi who decided that they knew which one God regarded as "first of all," particularly if they were to choose from among the ten commandments that were the first to be given on Sinai.[544] So Jesus chose his response from elsewhere in the law. He chose from the Book of Deuteronomy: "Hear, O Israel: The LORD is our God, the LORD alone.[n] You shall love the LORD your God with all your heart, and with all your soul, and with all your might"[545]—a commandment that stands alone in its context. And then, making it clear that he was not compromising the primacy of the command to love God, he chose from Leviticus: "you shall love your neighbour as yourself."[546] Jesus had responded to the difficult question with what as far as we know was a unique combination of texts, while remaining entirely within the boundary of Jewish orthodoxy.[547] What might have been significant for the early Christians in this exchange, and was perhaps the reason for the passage being retained in the oral tradition, and eventually written into Mark's Gospel, was the relativizing of anything to do with the ritual law in the scribe's response to Jesus. Even though early Jewish Christians, and Gentile Christians to a lesser extent, continued to regard the Hebrew scriptures as authoritative, none of them felt any need to take any notice of the laws about ritual: a position granted legitimacy by the scribe's response to Jesus.[548]

If there had been any intention on the part of the questioner to trap Jesus when the question was asked, then it appears to have been dissipated by Jesus' reply. Either the questioner already believed that some of the commandments were more important than others, or Jesus' response had led him to that belief. Either way, Jesus recognized in the questioner someone who had understood something of the character of the Kingdom of God, so he said so. The Kingdom of God had come near in Jesus, and the questioner had come near to the Kingdom of God.[549] The gap between them was closing.

Jesus had answered all of the questions asked, none of them had tripped him up, and in relation to this final question both Jesus and the questioner appear to have ended up on the same territory. Perhaps the reason for nobody else being willing to ask Jesus questions was that others in the crowd were becoming concerned that they too might be drawn closer to Jesus and his Kingdom, and for others to recognize that that was what was happening to them might have been problematic for them.

n. Or *The Lord our God is one Lord*, OR *The Lord our God, the Lord is one*, OR *The Lord is our God, the Lord is one*.

Some of the most interesting changing patterns of action relate to how minds are changed within groups of people. While studying how groups function within organizations, Serge Moscovici discovered that a small minority of people who thought differently from the majority about something can manage to persuade the majority to think as they did. The process seems to work like this. If a minority express a consistent and easily comprehensible view that is different from the view of the majority, and if issues related to the debate, but not essential to the minority's core message, remain open for discussion, then the minds of many members of the majority will be engaged in the debate, and one or two of them might begin to agree with the minority position. However, if their social standing within the group requires a level of conformity with the majority view, then they will not declare their conversion to the minority view. Slowly more individuals might be persuaded by the minority, until a majority have come to believe what was the minority view: but still nobody realizes that that has happened, because none of the conversion experiences have been declared. It then takes just one brave member of the former majority to reveal their change of mind for others to make their own declarations, and very quickly it becomes clear that what was the minority view is now a view held by the majority of the group. It often looks as if a whole group of people has suddenly changed its mind, or even that an entire society has done so, but that is not what has happened. Minds have been changing slowly, but perceived social pressure has prevented the constant slow process of conversions from becoming known. A clear recent example of such a process in many parts of the world is conversion to the legitimacy of same sex partnerships and marriages. In many communities this has appeared to be a rapid process, but it never has been. Minds have been changing slowly, but in multiple families, groups, and communities, it has taken longer for the conversions to be declared than it has taken for them to happen.

We can find evidence of undeclared conversion experiences in the gospels. Nicodemus, a Pharisee, came to Jesus "by night."[550] He was attracted to Jesus' message and wanted to discuss it. We find him later in the gospel arguing with other Pharisees that Jesus should be given a hearing,[551] and we hear of him again at Jesus' burial.[552] It is true that we only hear of him in John's Gospel, so it is not impossible that he is an invented representative of Jesus' secret followers: but that would be to make the same point—that there were those who had been converted to Jesus' Kingdom of God, and to understanding something of who Jesus was, but that the pressure imposed on them by their positions in society had prevented those conversions from being declared.

Later in Mark's Gospel we shall encounter Joseph of Arimathea, who collects Jesus' body and places it in a tomb. He was someone who "waited expectantly for the Kingdom of God,"[553] and to do what he did he must have recognized something of the uniqueness of Jesus in relation to that Kingdom of God: but we only hear of him this once. There is no secrecy about his discipleship in Mark's Gospel, or in Matthew's or Luke's, who are here relying on Mark's account. In John's Gospel, Joseph of Arimathea is described as "a disciple of Jesus, though a secret one because of his fear of the Jews."[554] Enmity between "the Jews" and Jesus' disciples is a common theme in John's Gospel, and it is possible that the gospel-writer has made Joseph's discipleship a secret one in order to serve his own agenda: but it is also possible that some of the wealthier and better-connected of Jesus' followers might have been less than public about their discipleship. It was not very likely that the majority of Jews were about to become followers of Jesus, and now that Jesus had been crucified, Jesus' better-connected disciples might have been even more keen to keep their enthusiasm for the coming Kingdom of God, and for Jesus' proclamation of it, as quiet as possible.

The process that takes place in groups of people is somewhat analogous to what can happen within the sciences. Fairly settled changing patterns of action can be disrupted by new evidence that does not fit the existing theories, so turbulence results, new theories—new changing patterns of action in scientists' brains—and eventually a new paradigm emerges that best explains both the old and the new evidence. Stability returns, until the process happens again. Something similar can happen within an individual mind. We might begin with a fixed view about something: a view that coheres with all of the other areas of our thought and action. The changing patterns of action that constitute the vast network of our brains and of its activity fit together fairly harmoniously. But then we encounter something new and different, and aspects of our thought-forms begin to shift. Turbulence emerges as different parts of our thought and action contradict each other. The changing patterns of action become unstable, and subject to rapid and unpredictable change, until eventually a new changing pattern of action begins to invade the entire network and bring it to a new stability. A conversion has occurred. It might look rapid, but it was not. It was happening slowly, but could only be recognized as the complete change that it was once the turbulence that was bringing it to birth had subsided. This appears to be what happened to Saul on the road to Damascus.[555] He did not suddenly turn from persecuting the church to being the most powerful advocate of the gospel. His mind might have been changing since he watched Stephen being martyred, and the increasingly obsessive pursuit of Christians might have been a last ditch attempt by his former self to take control: but that only made the final shift to a new paradigm even more disruptive. The changing patterns of action that had constituted Saul had been so changed that a new name was required: Paul.

We are left wondering what happened to the scribe whom Jesus declared to be "not far from the kingdom of God." How did the changing patterns of action that constituted who he was continue to be changed by his encounter with Jesus? We shall never know.

To return to Jesus' response to the questioner: What precisely do we mean by "love your neighbor"? "Love" is clearly a particular changing pattern of action: but of what kind? For the Christian, a useful place to start might be Paul's first letter to the Christians at Corinth:

> 4 Love is patient; love is kind; love is not envious or boastful or arrogant ⁵ or rude. It does not insist on its own way; it is not irritable or resentful; ⁶ it does not rejoice in wrongdoing, but rejoices in the truth. It bears all things, believes all things, hopes all things, endures all things.[556]

So to love our neighbor we need to exercise these changing patterns of action in relation to our neighbor—that is, towards anyone with any relationship with us: we must be patient and kind, and not envious, boastful, arrogant, or rude. We must not insist on our own way, and must not be irritable or resentful or rejoice in wrongdoing. We must rejoice in the truth, bear all things, believe all things, hope all things, and endure all things. So love is changing patterns of many different changing patterns of action. We must "love our neighbors as ourselves," which suggests that we must exercise these changing patterns of changing patterns of action towards ourselves as well as towards our neighbors. We must be patient with our neighbors, and patient with ourselves.

Perhaps more interesting is the question of how we are to obey the command to love God: less common in the New Testament than passages about God's love for us, or our love for the neighbor.[557] The piling up of the parts of the human being—"with all your heart, and with all your soul, and with all your mind, and with all your strength"—is a recognition that God loves the whole of us, and that an equally comprehensive love is therefore called for in response:[558] but still we are not told what love is. So the question must be whether Paul's description of love applies here as well. If so, then we must exercise all of these changing patterns of action towards God; being patient; being kind; not being envious, boastful, arrogant, or rude; not insisting on our own way; not being irritable or resentful; not rejoicing in wrongdoing; rejoicing in the truth; bearing all things; believing all things; hoping all things; enduring all things. God's relationship with us is complex—it is a changing pattern of changing patterns of action: so a wide variety of changing patterns of action on our part is likely to be appropriate. We must be patient with our neighbor, with ourselves, and with God. Love is not always going to be an easy changing pattern of action to exercise, and it might in general be quite difficult to exercise it, in relation to our neighbor, to ourselves, and to God. But it is love that is commanded, so that is what we must do: and we must then be patient with ourselves, and kind to ourselves, when we fail to love.

# MARK 12:35-37

> 35 While Jesus was teaching in the temple, he said, 'How can the scribes say that the Messiah[1] is the son of David? ³⁶ David himself, by the Holy Spirit, declared,
>
>> "The Lord said to my Lord,
>>
>>> 'Sit at my right hand,
>>>
>>>> until I put your enemies under your feet.'"
>
> ³⁷ David himself calls him Lord; so how can he be his son?' And the large crowd was listening to him with delight.[559]

Whether "How can the scribes say . . ." was the beginning of a discussion instigated by Jesus, or Jesus' response to a question that he had been asked but that is now lost, is not at issue here. (If Jesus' words were a response to a question, then the question might have been lost because it was the response and not the question that was of interest to Christians.) And neither are we interested in the main purpose of Jesus' words at the time, which was presumably to extricate himself from a potential trap,[560] and to make it clear that the Messiah had a God-given sonship and not one dependent on having David as an ancestor, and so was not to be aligned with a nationalistic or military expectation.[561] What is at issue for us is what Jesus called himself, what others called him, and what we might call him.

"The Lord said to my Lord" is a quotation from Psalm 110, where "Lord" is two different words. The first is "YHWH," the name of God, and the second is "*Adonai*," "lord." The complication is that orthodox Jews never pronounce the name of God, and when they find the tetragrammaton—the four letters—in the text, they say "*Adonai*": so when a Jew reads this passage in the Psalms we hear "Adonai said to Adonai," which is somewhat confusing, and will be the reason for the Greek "*kurios*" being used twice in the verse in Mark's Gospel: "The Lord said to my Lord." What the first verse of the Psalm originally meant was "God says to my Lord [the King of Israel] . . .": but Jesus, perhaps following a common interpretation of his own time, interprets the second "Lord" as the Messiah, the one who would rescue Israel from oppression and usher in a time of peace and prosperity.[562] This is an understandable interpretation in the context of the rest of Psalm 110:

> 1 The LORD [YHWH] says to my lord [*Adonai*],
>> 'Sit at my right hand
>>> until I make your enemies your footstool.'
> ² The LORD [YHWH] sends out from Zion
>> your mighty sceptre.
>> Rule in the midst of your foes.

1. Or *the Christ*

[3] Your people will offer themselves willingly
on the day you lead your forces
on the holy mountains.[q]
From the womb of the morning,
like dew, your youth[r] will come to you.
[4] The Lord [YHWH] has sworn and will not change his mind,
'You are a priest for ever according to the order of Melchizedek.'[s]
[5] The Lord [*Adonai*] is at your right hand;
he will shatter kings on the day of his wrath.
[6] He will execute judgement among the nations,
filling them with corpses;
he will shatter heads
over the wide earth.[563]

Jesus' argument assumes that King David was the author of the psalms: a common assumption then, and one made until relatively recently, because a collector of the Psalms had added "Psalm of David" at the top of rather a lot of them. The identification of the psalmist enables Jesus to argue that David called the Messiah "Lord," so the Messiah could not be David's son. Presumably this was not an original argument. There might have been Jews from other tribes that resented members of the tribe of Judah being possessive about the Messiah, so attempts to abolish the connection between the Messiah and King David, who had come from the tribe of Judah, might have been quite common.

So which tribe was Jesus from? The genealogy at the beginning of Matthew's Gospel places him in a direct line of descendants from both Judah and David,[564] as does that in Luke's Gospel;[565] and Paul regards Jesus as having been descended from David.[566] Perhaps what Jesus was saying was that even though he was descended from David, "Son of David," with its military overtones, did not express the kind of messiahship that he saw himself performing, and to recognize that the Messiah was lord over David allowed the Messiah to take a role that was not in any way determined by David's.[567] Or perhaps the argument recorded here is evidence that it was known that Jesus was not from the tribe of Judah, and that he was not a descendant of David: so if he was to be the Messiah then he had to prove that the Messiah was not necessarily descended from David. Perhaps the crowd's delight was because they wanted to be able to interpret Jesus as the Messiah, as Peter had done, and it was good news that one of the common arguments against that possibility could be easily disposed of.

q. Another reading is *in holy splendour*
r. Cn: Heb *the dew of your youth.*
s. Or *for ever, a rightful king by my edict*

## MARK 12:35–37

The difficulty is that Bartimaeus had called Jesus "Son of David," and he had not been asked not to do that. As often, we have encountered a significant level of ambiguity.

It might or might not be significant that at Jesus' entry into Jerusalem on a donkey, the term "Son of David" was not used. It was the "kingdom of our ancestor David" that was being welcomed, and Jesus was welcomed as the one coming "in the name of the Lord."

Did Jesus see himself as the Son of David? Did he see himself as the Messiah? Did he see himself as the Son of God—a title given to the kings of Israel: "You are my son: today I have begotten you"?[568] Did he see himself as the Son of Man mentioned in the Book of Daniel?

> 13 As I watched in the night visions,
> I saw one like a human being[b]
>     coming with the clouds of heaven.
> And he came to the Ancient One[c]
>     and was presented before him.
> [14] To him was given dominion
>     and glory and kingship,
> that all peoples, nations, and languages
>     should serve him.
> His dominion is an everlasting dominion
>     that shall not pass away,
> and his kingship is one
>     that shall never be destroyed.[569]

All we can find in Mark's Gospel in relation to these titles is ambiguity. When Jesus used the term "Son of Man" it was usually ambiguous because it could mean "a human being" as well as the figure in Daniel's vision (which in the New Revised Standard Version is translated as "human being"); and when Jesus used the term at his trial in connection with some of the other lines in Daniel's prophecy, he could have been referring either to himself or to someone else "coming with the clouds of heaven." Jesus himself did not use the term "Son of God," and when others used it of him he asked them not to do so; and when Peter called Jesus the Messiah he was asked not to tell anyone else. The titles by which Jesus was generally known were "Lord," again a somewhat ambiguous title, because it generally meant "master" even though it could also be used of God; and Jesus was also called Rabbi, Teacher: a title with which he appeared to be entirely comfortable, because that is what he was. All we can conclude

---

b. Aram *one like a son of man*
c. Aram *the Ancient of Days*

from the evidence is that Jesus seemed to be happy to leave people guessing as to whether they should use various titles for him. As with the title "Son of David," there is ambiguity everywhere. Perhaps Jesus wanted to leave everyone to make up their own minds as to who he was.

Would Jesus have called himself "God'? He was a Jew, and so would surely have regarded that as blasphemy. Did he have any idea that that is who he was? As a tutor once put it to me: "Did Jesus think that he was the second person of the Trinity?" Again, the answer is probably no: again because he was a Jew and might not have been able to think like that. However, by employing ambiguously the term "Son of Man"; by not contradicting Peter when he called him "Messiah"; and by accepting the term "Son of God" from the demons, Jesus offers evidence that he might have been aware of an identity that was somewhat out of the ordinary. Whether he had got further than that in conceptualizing what that meant we shall never know.

## MARK 12:38–44

> 38 As he taught, he said, 'Beware of the scribes, who like to walk around in long robes, and to be greeted with respect in the market-places, [39] and to have the best seats in the synagogues and places of honour at banquets! [40] They devour widows' houses and for the sake of appearance say long prayers. They will receive the greater condemnation.'
>
> 41 He sat down opposite the treasury, and watched the crowd putting money into the treasury. Many rich people put in large sums. [42] A poor widow came and put in two small copper coins, which are worth a penny. [43] Then he called his disciples and said to them, 'Truly I tell you, this poor widow has put in more than all those who are contributing to the treasury. [44] For all of them have contributed out of their abundance; but she out of her poverty has put in everything she had, all she had to live on.'[570]

Matthew's and Luke's Gospels contain a variety of "Woe to you" sentences aimed at the religious leaders of the time to balance the "Blessed are you" beatitudes addressed to Jesus' followers. In Mark's Gospel we have a brief warning to Jesus' disciples, and perhaps to his hearers more generally, to "beware of the scribes." Jesus regarded himself as a servant, and appears to have modelled his life on that of the servant of Israel described in Isaiah: the very opposite of what he saw in the religious leaders of the time. What did Jesus expect to happen to them? Condemnation greater than whose? Than everyone else? Whereas for the rich, admission to the Kingdom of God was almost impossible, it was possible for God: so was it not possible for God to forgive and welcome scribes who did not understand that they were meant to be servants rather than masters?

And what did Jesus mean by "devour widows' houses"? Whatever he meant, this would have been yet another example of Jesus' understanding of the ways in which the poor were oppressed by the social, legal, and religious systems of the time, and in particular of his understanding of how vulnerable certain groups were within society: children, women, and widows.

The story of the widow and her coins might have been a parable before it became a narrated incident as it travelled through the church's tradition, and it might have been remembered as an encouragement to Christians to give everything for Christ,[571] and as a subversion of traditional values, with Jesus valuing the poor widow above the wealthy:[572] but what matters to us here is the action and its meaning. The account of the widow contributing two copper coins can be read in two very different ways. Was the contribution to the temple treasury a freewill offering, or was it an enforced contribution? If it was a freewill offering, an expression of the widow's thankfulness to God, then Jesus was praising her for her generosity. The last line could be translated "her whole life," rather than "all she had to live on,"[573] so perhaps Jesus was offering her to his disciples as an example of the self-giving required of them. But if the contribution was enforced, by being a legal requirement, a social convention, or a religious obligation, then it was utterly unjust and oppressive. Widows were economically extremely vulnerable, especially if they did not have adult children, or other family members, to care for them, and to expect this widow to contribute to the temple what small amount of money she had was unconscionable, especially when everyone else was contributing the small proportions of their wealth that they could easily afford.

We find similarly ambiguous passages about economics in the other gospels. Jesus told a parable[574] in which a man hands over to three slaves different amounts of money—five talents, two talents, and one talent—and when he comes back he expects them to have made a profit. Those given larger amounts have done so, but the one who had been given the smallest amount had buried it so that he could be sure of giving back to his master what he had been given. As the slave said, he "was afraid." The master ordered the single talent to be given to the slave who had already turned five talents into ten, and he ordered the deprived slave to be thrown "into the outer darkness, where there will be weeping and gnashing of teeth." The parable has frequently been interpreted to mean that we should use well the "talents" that we have been given—that is, the skills and other capabilities that we have been given by birth or by upbringing. A different and perhaps more likely interpretation is that the parable is about how the economy works. Those who already have more than others will always find it easier to increase their wealth, whereas those who have little will always be afraid of losing what little they have, and so will not be able to take the risks required to increase their wealth: risks that the wealthy can handle far more easily. This interpretation is reinforced by the last line of the passage: "For to all those who have, more will be given, and they will have an abundance; but from those who have nothing, even what they have will be taken away."

Jesus spent his life among the people of Galilee: a region at some distance from Jerusalem, an agricultural and fishing area, that was vulnerable to the vagaries of the weather, and oppressed by Rome's occupying forces and tax collectors, and by local landlords who extracted extortionate rents. It was easy to end up in debt, and thus effectively enslaved: hence Jesus' parables about debt, and what is probably the original version of the prayer that Jesus taught his disciples: "And forgive us our debts, as we also have forgiven our debtors."[575]

Because Jesus wanted to see the Kingdom of God established "on earth as it is in heaven,"[576] he was intensely interested in the way that society and the economy worked. The Kingdom of God was a changing pattern of action that conformed to the changing patterns of action that constituted God: a changing pattern of action often deeply opposed to the changing patterns of action that constituted the society and economy of the time. The Kingdom of God that Jesus represented in his teaching, his healing, and his casting out of evil, was entirely directed towards the wellbeing of everyone: of unrepentant sinners, prostitutes, tax-collectors, Gentiles, women, widows, children, the poor, and everyone else, which included the rich, who needed to dispose of their wealth in the direction of the poor. Jesus knew that only God could bring about the Kingdom of God, but he wanted to see signs of its coming to birth in the society in which he lived: hence his teaching, healing, casting out of evil, and the choosing of a group of followers who would live the life of the Kingdom of God together, however imperfectly. Jesus' comments on the widow's contribution to the temple treasury fit into this pattern of action, as does the parable of the talents. Where the changing patterns of action that constituted the economy of the time were opposed to the changing patterns of action that constituted the Kingdom of God, Jesus had no choice but to say that.

We have discussed two examples of Jesus pointing out how far the economy of his own day was from the Kingdom of God: but did he also offer accounts and parables that positively reflected the changes that needed to take place if the economy was to reflect the changing patterns of action that constitute the Kingdom of God? Not in Mark's Gospel, but in Matthew's and Luke's Gospels, yes. In Luke's Gospel, to balance the criticism of a system that required a widow to contribute all that she had, we find Jesus commending a tax-collector for offering to give half of his wealth to the poor, and to pay back fourfold anything that he had collected fraudulently. Jesus' verdict: "Today salvation has come to this house."[577] And in Matthew's Gospel, to balance the parable of the talents, we find a vineyard-owner paying to every worker—those who had worked the whole day, and those who had worked only for an hour—the same wage. This was patently unfair, but that is not the point. As the vineyard-owner puts it at the end of the story: "Am I not allowed to do what I choose with what belongs to me? Or are you envious because I am generous?" And Jesus adds, as he often does: "So the last will be first, and the first will be last.ᶻ" ⁵⁷⁸ This was the positive character of the Kingdom of God: equal treatment of every individual, whatever their contribution: so equal treatment of unrepentant sinners, prostitutes, tax-collectors, Gentiles, women, widows, children, the poor, and everyone else, including the rich: and it would be the unrepentant sinners who would enter the Kingdom of God first, and the wealthy only with difficulty.

## MARK 13:1-8

> 13 As he came out of the temple, one of his disciples said to him, 'Look, Teacher, what large stones and what large buildings!' ² Then Jesus asked him, 'Do you see these great buildings? Not one stone will be left here upon another; all will be thrown down.'
>
> 3 When he was sitting on the Mount of Olives opposite the temple, Peter, James, John, and Andrew asked him privately, ⁴ 'Tell us, when will this be, and what will be the sign that all these things are about to be accomplished?' ⁵ Then Jesus began to say to them, 'Beware that no one leads you astray. ⁶ Many will come in my name and say, "I am he!"ᵐ and they will lead many astray. ⁷ When you hear of wars and rumours of wars, do not be alarmed; this must take place, but the end is still to come. ⁸ For nation will rise against nation, and kingdom against kingdom; there will be earthquakes in various places; there will be famines. This is but the beginning of the birth pangs.'⁵⁷⁹

Chapter 13 is "eschatological": an account of terrestrial and cosmic events of the "last times" that will prepare the way for the coming of the Kingdom of God. It has a distinctive ethos, but there is nothing here that is out of character with the rest of Mark's Gospel, all of which can be understood as eschatological, and as a recognition that Jesus' life, death, and resurrection was a fulfilment of prophecy and a preparation for the final coming of the Kingdom of God.⁵⁸⁰

But what was the origin of this particular passage? Was it written before the Romans burned and then levelled the Jerusalem temple in the year 70 CE? —and was it therefore a prediction of that event?⁵⁸¹ Or was it written after that event and was shaped by it? Either way, it is perfectly possible that Jesus predicted the destruction of the temple. Mark records him as sitting opposite the temple, and talking to just a few of his disciples: details that might suggest that this is precisely how the words recorded here, or at least some of them, were first spoken.⁵⁸² Jesus might first of all have recognized that there might one day be a revolution against Roman rule, and that the outcome would be Jerusalem's destruction: but perhaps more importantly, he might have expected the destruction as God's punishment for Israel's unfaithfulness, and

---

z. Other ancient authorities add *for many are called but few are chosen*
m. Gk *I am*

particularly for that of its leaders. According to the prophets, the previous destruction of the city and its temple had been the result of the nation's unfaithfulness, and particularly that of its religious and national leaders: and given Israel's current lack of recognition of the need for repentance in preparation for the Kingdom of God's coming, it was only natural to assume that another destruction was looming. A pattern of action that had occurred in the past was about to repeat itself.[583]

And perhaps a more positive meaning can be found in the promised destruction of the temple. We have seen Jesus predicting that the Son of Man would give his life as a ransom. If this was the future that Jesus now saw for himself, then the pattern of action that he was describing would make the constant sacrifices of the temple redundant. A new order was about to begin, a new covenant, a new Kingdom of God—and the old order, with its continuous sacrifices and numerous laws, must make way for it.[584]

But why did the prophets regard the many defeats of Israel and the accompanying destructions as God's action? Was the nation not his chosen people? Why would he indulge in such destruction of what he had carefully nurtured, preserved, rescued from slavery in Egypt, and defended from its enemies? Because this was the only explanation that made sense. Two options faced the prophets: Either Israel's defeats were the result of the gods of surrounding nations being stronger than Israel's God, or the defeats were God's doing. Only the latter explanation was acceptable, so that is what the prophets chose to say: and if God's causing of the destruction of Jerusalem and its temple, the defeat of Israel's army, and the taking of Israel into exile, was not to be a wanton and irrational act, then it could only be a just punishment for Israel's sin. This was the tradition within which John the Baptist prophesied, and it was the tradition within which Jesus predicted the destruction of the temple. Here was a pattern of action that constituted God's relationship with his people: a changing pattern of action, as no defeat or destruction was ever the same as another, but still an identifiable pattern of action that was about to be repeated yet again: a pattern of action constituted by suffering and vindication: a pattern of action that Jesus would encounter during his own suffering, death, and resurrection; that Israel would experience as the temple was destroyed and God's Messiah brought about the Kingdom of God; and that Christians would encounter as they experienced persecution and then eternal life in the Kingdom of God.[585] God was in control of the present, which meant that God's promised future would come about.[586]

Jesus' disciples wanted to know when this would happen, and, as often happened, Jesus did not directly answer the question. Instead, we find a warning that the disciples were not to believe reports that Jesus had returned. Following Jesus' death and resurrection, the early Christians believed that Jesus would return to found the Kingdom of God that he had said so much about, and here we find that event assumed. Either Jesus predicted his own return, or this passage was influenced by the early Christian belief that he would return, or Jesus was promising that he would be presented to the Ancient One, that his rule would begin and the temple would be destroyed, and that at a later date, at the dissolution of all things, God's Kingdom would be established on earth as in heaven.[587] As always, we cannot know which. As for what follows, there is no reason to suggest that Jesus did not say it. Apocalyptic literature written between the Hebrew scriptures and the New Testament is full of such predictions of the end of the era, and there is an early example of this kind of literature in the Book of Daniel. The combination of a sudden end, signs predicting its coming, and not knowing when it will happen, are not inconsistent in this context:[588] and there is no reason to assume that Jesus would have regarded the destruction of the temple as an isolated event rather than as one element in a complex changing pattern of patterns of action that would announce the coming of God's Kingdom, to be followed by a subsequent final completion of the Kingdom of God on earth as in heaven. Trying to get a clear timeline out of the text would be both impossible and unnecessary. What matters is the changing pattern of action: the pattern of action that constitutes the old order being defeated by the new pattern of action that is the Kingdom of God, that all adds up to a complex changing pattern characterized throughout by the inevitable suffering of a coming to birth. And so whether the people claiming "I am he" that Jesus warned his disciples about referred to individuals claiming to be the Messiah (of which there were many[589]), and so usurping the position that would be his following his presentation before the Ancient One, or whether Jesus was referring to individuals claiming to be Jesus himself already returned at the end of the age, matters little. Jesus' beginning his rule as king in the Kingdom of God following his crucifixion, and his return to the Earth as king, would both be the pattern of action that would constitute him as God and as ruling in the Kingdom of God, so to pretend to be either the Messiah or Jesus would be to pretend to a pattern of action that no-one else had the right to claim as theirs.

Apocalyptic literature of the kind that we find in this and subsequent passages would have made sense to Jesus, because if the Kingdom of God was to be brought to birth then there was no reason to think that the birth would be painless. Birth was not. Jesus is here likening the sufferings of the birth of the Kingdom of God to the excruciatingly painful contractions that precede the birth of a child. He is also saying that the pain accompanying a human birth is as nothing compared with what will accompany the "birth pangs" of the Kingdom of God. The wars, earthquakes, and famines, of which there would be plenty of examples following Jesus' crucifixion,[590] would be just the beginning: the first twinges of the birth, which meant that Christians were not to expect the Kingdom of God to be completed soon.[591] There would be a changing pattern of action the like of which had never before been experienced. A more elaborate expression of that changing pattern of action can be found in the Book of Revelation, which also relies to some extent on previous apocalyptic literature, including the Book of Daniel. All of this literature is text, and so is pure pattern: a crystallization of the changing patterns of action in the minds of the writers, and, in the case of Mark's Gospel, in the mind of Jesus. He would be the servant king in the Kingdom of God that God would establish, but that Kingdom's birth would be a painful business, and it is likely that Jesus saw his own suffering and death as an essential contribution to the "birth pangs." Christians too saw their own sufferings as contributing to the suffering required before the birth could happen; and Paul explicitly identified his own sufferings as helping to "complete" the total of suffering that had to take place.[592] There are no time-barriers here. Prophecy is the crystallization in text or spoken word of a future pattern of action that would mirror patterns of action in the past or present.[593] God has made it known, so it will happen, and that knowledge enables Christians to know that their sufferings are within the will of God, and that they will be vindicated.

Some communities will find it easier than others to identify with the changing patterns of action described here. If the community for which Mark was writing was a first-century Palestinian Christian community around Galilee, then the wars and rumors of wars might have been the escalating revolts against Roman occupation that occurred during the sixth decade of the common era;[594] and any community suffering persecution, famine, war, earthquakes, or any of the other horrendous experiences that afflict the world from time to time, or that are imposed on it by people able to do that, will be able to identify with the language in this chapter of Mark's Gospel, and with the changing pattern of action described: a changing pattern of action that we might label "birth pangs of the Kingdom of God." Looking back, we can identify this changing pattern of action in Jesus' suffering and death, in the suffering of the early Christians, in any Christian church suffering persecution, and in any community suffering the terrible experiences that Jesus describes. Quite how we are to understand all of this as the action of a compassionate God I have no idea. Why would God choose to bring about the Kingdom of God through such horrendous suffering? Why not simply bring about the Kingdom of God without requiring that it should be preceded by terrible suffering? We don't know: but that really does appear to be what is happening. We face the same dilemma as the prophets: either the birth pangs are God's doing, or God watches as it happens and is powerless to stop it. The conclusion that we have to draw is that all of this suffering, past, present, and predicted for the future, is a changing pattern of action that constitutes God, as well as one that constitutes the world in which we live: in which case we have to say that it is a changing pattern of action that God transforms as the Kingdom of God comes to birth, and that those who have suffered the most terrible events in their lives will be transformed along with those events so that the changing patterns of action that constitute who they are will be transformed into the changing patterns of action that constitute the Kingdom of God. We also have to say that this whole process occurs within God as much as it occurs for each individual, family, community, society, planet, and cosmos. The birth pangs will end, the Kingdom of God will come to birth, death and suffering will be no more, and what there has been will be transfigured just as it is transfigured in God. The complex pattern of patterns of action represented in this chapter, and that will be experienced, perhaps over and over again, will finally give birth to the complex pattern of changing patterns of action that constitute the Kingdom of God, that constitute Jesus, and that constitute God, and in which we and all reality will participate.

## MARK 13:9-13

> 9 'As for yourselves, beware; for they will hand you over to councils; and you will be beaten in synagogues; and you will stand before governors and kings because of me, as a testimony to them. １⁰ And the good news[n] must first be proclaimed to all nations. ¹¹ When they bring you to trial and hand you over, do not worry beforehand about what you are to say; but say whatever is given you at that time, for it is not you who speak, but the Holy Spirit. ¹² Brother will betray brother to death, and a father his child, and children will rise against parents and have them put to death; ¹³ and you will be hated by all because of my name. But the one who endures to the end will be saved.'[595]

Mark has presumably placed this material just before the account of Jesus' suffering because he wants his readers to understand their own experiences of suffering as an inevitable accompaniment of being a disciple of the Jesus who suffered:[596] but again we have to ask to what extent the content of the passage is the result of the experience of the church for which Mark was writing his gospel, and of the church generally from Stephen's martyrdom onwards, and to what extent it is based on a prediction that Jesus made. Either way, it is what happened; and either way it is not inappropriate that, in contrast to other apocalyptic literature, this chapter of Mark's Gospel is addressed to the hearers as an exhortation, and is not simply a statement of what will occur.[597]

From the beginning of the church until today, Christians have been persecuted. Rather than understand this as the action of a God who punishes sin, as the prophets saw the various defeats of Israel, Christians have understood their sufferings as contributing to the birth-pangs of the Kingdom of God, as uniting them with Jesus in his sufferings, and as foreseen by the prophets and therefore known to be God's will.[598] Christians have been handed over to councils, have been beaten in synagogues, and have stood before governors and kings to answer for their faith, and people have betrayed other members of their families when their own lives have depended on them doing so, or when they have simply believed that other family members deserve to suffer for their views. It is rare for Christians to have been hated by "all," but there have presumably been occasions when that has happened. The promise that to remain faithful is the route to being saved, to eternal life, and so on, has frequently fortified Christians, and indeed members of other faiths, as they have faced persecution and death. These changing patterns of action have been replicated across human history in multiple contexts, and whenever they have occurred they have mirrored Jesus' own

n. Gk *gospel*

experience of suffering and death. Everywhere there are changing but repeated patterns of action.[599]

But something a bit different interrupts the flow of the passage, which would have made perfect sense, and indeed better sense, if "When they bring you to trial" had immediately followed "as a testimony to them." The interruption is "And the good news must first be proclaimed to all nations." "First" before what? Before the persecution that has just been described? Or before the signs of the Kingdom of God's birth: wars, earthquakes, famines? Before the destruction of the temple?[600] Or is there now an assumption that persecution is one of the signs of the Kingdom of God's birth, so that the good news must be preached "to all nations" before the birth pangs arrive? If this is what Jesus meant, then he was wrong. Wars, earthquakes, famines, and persecutions have happened ever since Jesus spoke these words, and the gospel had not been preached to all nations by the time the temple was destroyed, or presumably by the time Jesus had begun to rule in the Kingdom of God. So perhaps some of the context of the sentence has gone astray, and what it meant was that "the good news must be proclaimed to all nations" before the Kingdom of God came fully to birth: or perhaps that "the good news must be proclaimed among all nations," which could suggest a mission to the Jews before the birth-pangs and the coming of the Kingdom of God, with the Gentiles then welcomed into the Kingdom once it was established.[601] Or perhaps the "must" in the sentence is an imperative rather than a condition to be met.[602] Whatever our interpretation of Jesus' meaning, the text raises the question as to whether a proclamation to or among all nations has now happened. There cannot now be a nation to which the good news has not been proclaimed in some way or other. If the command or requirement (and it could be either or both) means that every member of every nation must have the good news proclaimed to them before the Kingdom of God is established, then that has not happened, and it is difficult to see how it can. Whatever is meant, an obligation is laid on Christians to proclaim the good news, which presumably means that it must be proclaimed today as well as then.

Jesus' own ministry was a proclamation of the good news. He taught people in the synagogues and in the open air, he healed the sick, and he cast out demons. The apostles and other early Christians employed the same methods. For centuries, these were the changing patterns of action by which the good news was proclaimed. Then the technology began to change. Folios replaced scrolls, making it easier to transport books from place to place: so the gospels were written, recopied, and carried from place to place, and Paul's letters were delivered and were later collected. Then once the printing press was invented, the gospels, the letters, and the whole of the Hebrew scriptures as well as the New Testament could be circulated widely. Printed text proclaimed the good news in a wide variety of forms; radio and television followed; and now the internet and social media. Still the good news is proclaimed through the spoken word indoors and outdoors, still people are prayed for and healed, and occasionally evil will be cast out: but the world has changed, so to employ such traditional methods is not to proclaim as effectively as the methods did in the past. Proclamation requires a speaker and also a hearer who can interpret what they hear, and interpretation will always run more smoothly if the medium of communication is familiar, the concepts through which the good news is explained are familiar, and actions that accompany or substitute for the spoken or written words are comprehensible: that is, the changing patterns of action must in principle cohere with the changing patterns of action that constitute the recipient of the proclamation. Proclamation is always a complex changing pattern of action that connects the changing patterns of action that constitute both the proclaimer and the hearer, and it must be adapted to that specific task, which requires a deep understanding of the changing patterns of action that constitute the hearer, and also a deep understanding of the changing patterns of action that constitute the proclaimer—and, of course, a really deep understanding of the changing patterns of action that constitute the Kingdom of God that is being proclaimed. Proclamation therefore becomes a highly complex changing pattern of changing patterns of action. The task is never complete. If in one generation the good news is proclaimed to all nations, then in the next generation it will have to be done again. Everything changes, so new proclamation will always be needed, and that proclamation will not be the same as last time. There is a sense in which the life of Jesus and his death and resurrection never change because they are in the past: but their interpretations will constantly change; and because the patterns of action that are the life, death, and resurrection of Jesus are changing patterns of action that constitute God, they will constantly change other changing patterns of action that constitute God, and those will then change the changing patterns of action that constitute the proclamation of the good news. Whether "the end" that is to come is the destruction of the temple or the end of the age, Jesus' disciples must not stop proclaiming.[603]

The sentence "When they bring you to trial . . ." follows "as a testimony to them," but it also follows "And the good news must first be proclaimed to all nations," and it fits into both contexts—which is perhaps why Mark decided to put that apparently out of place line where he has. Jesus tries to reduce the anxiety that anyone faced with answering for their faith before "governors and kings" would be bound to experience by promising that it would be the Holy Spirit who would speak, and not the disciple. This is simply a promise: that in those circumstances, the changing pattern of action that is God active in our midst will engage with the changing patterns of action that constitute our brain so that it will be the Holy Spirit who speaks: although it cannot strictly be true that it will not be us speaking as well, because it will be. There is plenty of experience of a sense of being given the right words to say in a difficult situation, and the practice of prayer turning into a Spirit-given language, as in the Acts of the Apostles and in Paul's letters, and plenty of experience today of speaking in tongues that then need to be interpreted if spoken in a public gathering, and sometimes in known languages not known to the speaker.[604] Within a conceptual framework of Action, action, change, diversity, movement, and the generally dynamic, it is far easier to conceive of it being both the Holy Spirit who speaks, and at the same time ourselves who speak, than it would be if we were operating with a Being, beings, unitary, unchanging, rest, and generally static ontology. It is the meeting and entanglement of changing patterns of action that enable both the Holy Spirit and the speaker to speak, and for one voice to be heard.

Jesus would be crucified, would rise again, and would be presented to the Ancient One; a new order, a new pattern of action that had already become visible in Jesus, the Kingdom of God, would become a cosmic reality; and the old order would begin to crumble—a change that would be accompanied by the destruction of the Jerusalem temple, by Jesus' disciples telling the good news of the Kingdom of God in every nation,[605] by Christians sharing in the birth pangs of the new age, and by the Holy Spirit enabling Jesus' followers to begin to live the life of the Kingdom of God. Eventually Jesus would return and the Kingdom of God would come on Earth as in heaven.

## MARK 13:14–23

> 14 'But when you see the desolating sacrilege set up where it ought not to be (let the reader understand), then those in Judea must flee to the mountains; 15 someone on the housetop must not go down or enter the house to take anything away; 16 someone in the field must not turn back to get a coat. 17 Woe to those who are pregnant and to those who are nursing infants in those days! 18 Pray that it may not be in winter. 19 For in those days there will be suffering, such as has not been from the beginning of the creation that God created until now, no, and never will be. 20 And if the Lord had not cut short those days, no one would be saved; but for the sake of the elect, whom he chose, he has cut short those days. 21 And if anyone says to you at that time, "Look! Here is the Messiah!"º or "Look! There he is!"—do not believe it. 22 False messiahs[p] and false prophets will appear and produce signs and omens, to lead astray, if possible, the elect. 23 But be alert; I have already told you everything.'[606]

The temple had already been desecrated by the introduction of images during a former occupation, and here was a prophecy that it would happen again.[607] Why should the reader understand? Perhaps the desecration had occurred by the time Mark wrote his gospel. Whether or not that was the case, Jesus foresaw that such a desecration would not come alone: it would be accompanied by suffering for those living in and around Jerusalem, and perhaps for those living further afield. Perhaps Jesus foresaw Roman legions' banners arriving on the temple mount, which would have been understood as a sacrilege of the sacred space;[608] or perhaps that had already happened:

o. Or *the Christ*
p. Or *christs*

Either way, rapid escape was required. Perhaps if Jesus was foretelling the event then he was warning those who were still his followers to preserve themselves as a movement rather than stay to defend Jerusalem and its temple, which were bound for destruction, and in particular that they were not to follow the revolutionary leaders who would only lead the Christian community to oblivion.[609] Or perhaps the prophecy was remembered by early Christians because they had already experienced the siege and destruction of Jerusalem, and had escaped because Jesus had told them to do so; and perhaps they also remembered it because they had suffered further persecution that had caused them to leave their homes, maybe quite rapidly. There is no suggestion that what is predicted would happen only once. What Jesus is describing here is a changing pattern of action that had happened, that would happen, and that would finally happen as the Kingdom of God was brought to birth.[610]

"If the Lord had not cut short those days . . . ." This raises the obvious question: If God was able to cut short the time of predicted suffering, then why would the time not be cut to zero? And the passage raises in an acute form the more general question: If God was able to cut this particular period of suffering short, and would in fact do so, then why does God not cut all suffering to zero? We are not here discussing a God unable to intervene in the world's suffering: here is a God both able and unwilling to relieve suffering. What are we to make of this? And even more problematic: Who is the "elect" for whom the cutting short is to occur? Jesus' followers? Would they be the "stump" that remained after the felling of the tree of Israel?[611] Then what of the rest? Does their suffering not count with God? Presumably those who are not members of "the elect" will benefit from the shortening of the period of suffering, but God would not be taking account of their suffering when the length of the period during which suffering will be taking place is being calculated.

There has been plenty of choosing of those to whom God will show particular favor. The obvious example is God's choosing of Israel as his servant, with the task of serving the nations. This was no choosing for privilege, but was rather selection for hard work. Jesus did some choosing, too. He chose society's outcasts for the Kingdom of God; and for his apostles—those whom he would send—he chose some often rather flawed individuals from across the less privileged end of his society. But when it comes to the choosing that Christians have done, the choosing has often been of religious conformists—those conforming to religious rules of behavior, and to statements of religious faith; and it has been a choosing for privilege—for salvation, for heaven rather than hell, for God's presence, for a privileged position when Jesus returns, and similar privileges, rather than for service to the poorest of the world. Who are the "elect" that Jesus has in mind here? His disciples? Unrepentant sinners? We shall probably never know: at least, not in this life.

How much does it matter that this passage looks as if it has been modelled on other apocalyptic literature: for that is what it is—apocalyptic literature that "unhides" what is to happen. Similar literature is to be found in the books of Daniel and of

Revelation, the latter appearing to have been at least partially inspired by the former. In such literature we often find suffering, and an elect rescued from the suffering. There is so much that seems out of place here. So does it help to decide that this passage might have been a construction by early Christians who were writing what we might regard as a historical novel, and who decided that the Jesus they were writing about was going to say these words that mirrored existing apocalyptic literature? No, it does not help, because it raises this question: Why decide that Jesus did not say this particular passage rather than the others that we might prefer him to have said? What right do we have to choose which passages accurately, or at least fairly accurately, record what Jesus said and did, and which passages do not? For if we do the choosing, then we shall be choosing on the basis of our own presuppositions, and not on any objective basis. It is surely preferable to reckon that Jesus said these words, and then to work out why.

The obvious explanation is that Jesus was an apocalyptic prophet as well as everything else that he appears to be. He was a healer, a teacher, someone who cast out evil, and someone who looked forward to a coming Kingdom of God that was already near, and he chose a group of disciples to help him to spread the good news of the Kingdom of God. He was someone who appears to have changed his mind: he might have begun as a disciple of John the Baptist, so that early in his independent ministry he could have taken a rigorous attitude to the keeping of the law, but then he came to appreciate God's unconditional welcome, perhaps taught by the Syrophoenician woman among others—hence the gathering of unrepentant sinners, tax-collectors, prostitutes, and so on, and the equal value that he gave to Gentiles, women, and children, somewhat against the social norms of his times. He became something of a revolutionary: literally so in relation to the word "revolution": "the last shall be first, and the first last." At the heart of Jesus' message and activity from the beginning was the Kingdom of God. Early on he required repentance and belief from those who wished to enter the Kingdom, but as his ministry developed, the welcome became more generous, and in the end unconditional: even the rich might be able to enter, for that would be possible for God. Like any birth, the birth of the Kingdom of God would be painful: there would be birth-pangs, one of which would be the destruction of the temple and the intense suffering that would precede and accompany that. It is not impossible that the apocalyptic material that we find in this part of Mark's Gospel represents the apocalyptic prophet that Jesus might have been at the beginning of his ministry. Jesus' earlier requirement of repentance and belief before admission to the Kingdom of God could be achieved would have resulted in an "elect"; Jesus had learnt from John the Baptist that there would be a judgement—"the axe is lying at the root of the trees; every tree therefore that does not bear good fruit is cut down and thrown into the fire";[612] and apocalyptic ideas were clearly quite widespread—we find the idea that there is a certain amount of suffering to be completed in Paul's letter to the church in Colossae: "I am now rejoicing in my sufferings for your sake, and in my flesh I am completing what is lacking in Christ's afflictions for the sake of his body, that is, the church."⁶¹³ And perhaps as Jesus approached his own suffering and death he revisited his earlier apocalyptic ideas, and interpreted them in relation to his own suffering and to the suffering that would follow for his disciples.

Jesus' mind was like anyone else's: highly complex changing patterns of action—indeed, highly complex changing patterns of changing patterns of action. There would have been plenty of diversity, and plenty of change: for that is the character both of the human mind and of God. Into this complex and changing mixture the apocalyptic ideas in this chapter of Mark's Gospel fit just as well as the rest of it.

## MARK 13:24-27

> 24 'But in those days, after that suffering,
>    the sun will be darkened,
>    and the moon will not give its light,
> ²⁵ and the stars will be falling from heaven,
>    and the powers in the heavens will be shaken.
> ²⁶ Then they will see "the Son of Man coming in clouds" with great power and glory. ²⁷ Then he will send out the angels, and gather his elect from the four winds, from the ends of the earth to the ends of heaven.'⁶¹⁴

Jesus would often quote the Hebrew scriptures in order to say what needed to be said.⁶¹⁵ The text of the scriptures was a crystallization of patterns of action that had happened, were happening, and would happen, and by revisiting them and reusing them Jesus was reawakening and repurposing not only the text but also the patterns of action that had given birth to it. The events of the past, of the present, and of the future, were all action in patterns, and if patterns of action were repeated then they belonged together, however distant they were from each other in space and time. And the same goes for the events found together in this passage: some of them are terrestrial, and some cosmic, but they are all events related to the End, to the coming of the Kingdom of God, so they belong together. There are no boundaries between them.⁶¹⁶

This is particularly the case here, where we find future events following the contemporary events in previous passages, and events both cosmic and terrestrial. The prophet Daniel, probably writing during the Babylonian exile, saw in a vision "one like a son of man" coming to the "Ancient of Days": that is, to God. In the context of that vision, the human figure probably stands for Israel, or for a future king of Israel, finally vindicated as God's chosen people following God's final defeat of the nations that had defeated and exiled it. Whereas Jesus' previous use of "Son of Man" was probably purposely ambiguous, meaning either himself or this heavenly figure, or possibly both, here we find the term used clearly in the sense in which Daniel used it.

The establishment of the Kingdom of God is what is happening here. The birth pangs will continue, with the sun darkening, the moon disappearing, the stars falling, and the cosmos shaken—and then the climax will occur and the "elect" will be gathered into the Kingdom of God.

The addition of additional birth pangs is understandable in this context, but what does Jesus mean by then adding a clear reference to the Daniel prophecy?

> [13] As I watched in the night visions,
> I saw one like a human being[b]
>    coming with the clouds of heaven.
> And he came to the Ancient One[c]
>    and was presented before him.
> [14] To him was given dominion
>    and glory and kingship,
> that all peoples, nations, and languages
>    should serve him.
> His dominion is an everlasting dominion
>    that shall not pass away,
> and his kingship is one
>    that shall never be destroyed.[617]

The figure who comes to God is sometimes interpreted as Israel, now vindicated and appointed to rule the nations, and sometimes as a kingly Messiah figure who will rule both Israel and the other nations. Either way, Jesus is now using this prophecy to express the establishment of the Kingdom of God that will follow the birth pangs. More detail is added relating to the angels gathering the "elect"—a common apocalyptic theme, and one that is particularly clear in Revelation—but essentially Jesus' prophecy is Daniel's prophecy repurposed.

The real question here is whether Jesus believed that he was the "Son of Man" described in Daniel's prophecy. We shall never know: but what we do know is that it is perfectly possible, and maybe even likely, that Jesus simply could not make up his mind as to whether he was the Son of Man in Daniel 7. He knew himself to be a Teacher, a healer, and someone with God's authority to cast out demons: but did he know that he was God living the life of a human being among us? A lot hinges on whether he predicted his resurrection. Let us suppose that he did. What would that have meant to him? Would it have meant what then transpired? A few appearances to his disciples, followed by two thousand years of Christian experience of his continuing presence? Probably not. There were two options offered by the Hebrew scriptures: a general resurrection of the dead prophesied by the vision of the dry bones being

b. Aram *one like a son of man*
c. Aram *the Ancient of Days*

given new life in the Book of Ezekiel,[618] and the heavenly vindication prophesied by Daniel. Jesus was predicting his own resurrection, and not the general resurrection, so we have to conclude that when he predicted his resurrection he would have understood that to be a heavenly resurrection: a "coming with the clouds of heaven . . . to the Ancient One." Given Jesus' employment of the term "Son of Man," and his quotation of the Daniel prophecy both here and at his trial, we might reasonably conclude that Jesus predicted his own resurrection, and that he looked forward to being presented to God and appointed to rule the nations. Jesus would also have been aware of the prophecy in Hosea:

> After two days he will revive us;
>> on the third day he will raise us up,
>> that we may live before him.[619]

It would be on the third day that Jesus would be presented before the Ancient One and would begin his rule of the Kingdom of God.

But how can we square this with the resurrection appearances? In relation to Mark's Gospel there is no need to do so. There aren't any. This is not to say that they did not happen, for it is of course perfectly possible that they did: but it is to say that the meaning of the resurrection is primarily the vindication of Jesus as God living among us by his being presented before God on the third day after his death. The appearances are secondary matters, and the accounts of the ascension are constructions designed both to explain the end of the regular appearances and to function as a narrative that expresses the meaning of the resurrection as Jesus' presence with God. It is not insignificant that the hymn that Paul quotes in his letter to the Philippians expresses precisely this pattern of action:

> [5] Let the same mind be in you that was[i] in Christ Jesus,
> [6] who, though he was in the form of God,
>> did not regard equality with God
>> as something to be exploited,
> [7] but emptied himself,
>> taking the form of a slave,
>> being born in human likeness.
> And being found in human form,
> [8]  he humbled himself
>> and became obedient to the point of death—
>> even death on a cross.
> [9] Therefore God also highly exalted him
>> and gave him the name

---

i. Or *that you have*

that is above every name,

> [10] so that at the name of Jesus
> every knee should bend,
> in heaven and on earth and under the earth,
> [11] and every tongue should confess
> that Jesus Christ is Lord,
> to the glory of God the Father.[620]

There are no resurrection appearances here. The pattern of action is precisely that of the Daniel prophecy:

> [13] As I watched in the night visions,
> I saw one like a human being[b]
> coming with the clouds of heaven.
> And he came to the Ancient One[c]
> and was presented before him.
> [14] To him was given dominion
> and glory and kingship,
> that all peoples, nations, and languages
> should serve him.
> His dominion is an everlasting dominion
> that shall not pass away,
> and his kingship is one
> that shall never be destroyed.[621]

We find the same pattern of action in the Letter to the Hebrews:

> [14] Since, then, we have a great high priest who has passed through the heavens, Jesus, the Son of God, let us hold fast to our confession.[622]

Again, no resurrection appearances. The resurrection here is Jesus' arrival in heaven. This is what will be "seen."[623]

This is the changing pattern of action that Jesus predicted: He would suffer and be killed, and on the third day he would be presented before God, and would rule in the Kingdom of God to which the nations of the world would be subject. He would be the servant king that he had always said would be required, and his followers from all of the nations, and not just from among the Jews, would be gathered into the church so that there the rule of God might be "seen" and the good news of a final fulfilment might continue to be proclaimed until the final establishment of the Kingdom of God.[624]

b. Aram *one like a son of man*
c. Aram *the Ancient of Days*

So has this resurrection happened? The conviction of the writers of the hymn that Paul quoted, and of the Letter to the Hebrews, is yes, it has; and if the early Christians generally believed this to be the case then it would explain a great deal of what they said, wrote, and did. And if this is the case, then the resurrection appearances were not the resurrection, but revelations of it that would enable the disciples to proclaim that the Kingdom of God had already begun, and that Jesus was its servant king.

If this interpretation is anything like correct, then all of chapter 13 up to this point is about a pattern of action soon to follow Jesus' death—persecution of Jesus' followers, and the desecration and then destruction of the temple—and not about the final collapse of the physical order and Jesus' return: although the passages to follow might be.[625]

## MARK 13:28-37

> 28 'From the fig tree learn its lesson: as soon as its branch becomes tender and puts forth its leaves, you know that summer is near. 29 So also, when you see these things taking place, you know that he[q] is near, at the very gates. 30 Truly I tell you, this generation will not pass away until all these things have taken place. 31 Heaven and earth will pass away, but my words will not pass away.
> 
> 32 'But about that day or hour no one knows, neither the angels in heaven, nor the Son, but only the Father. 33 Beware, keep alert;[r] for you do not know when the time will come. 34 It is like a man going on a journey, when he leaves home and puts his slaves in charge, each with his work, and commands the doorkeeper to be on the watch. 35 Therefore, keep awake—for you do not know when the master of the house will come, in the evening, or at midnight, or at cockcrow, or at dawn, 36 or else he may find you asleep when he comes suddenly. 37 And what I say to you I say to all: Keep awake.'[626]

The "he" that will be near is the Son of Man: so why the third person pronoun, and not "I"? Perhaps again we have to ask about the order of events during Jesus' ministry. Might Jesus have begun his ministry thinking that it was his task to announce the coming of the Kingdom of God, which would entail "one like a son of man" coming to the Ancient of Days and taking authority over the nations? And might he not have known whether that "one like a son of man" would be him or someone else? —hence the ambiguous use of "Son of Man," which could refer either to a human being—that is, himself—or to the heavenly figure in the Book of Daniel. And might Jesus later on have thought it more likely that "the one like a son of man" might be himself? If so, "when you see these things taking place, you know that he is near, at the very gates" might be from an earlier period in Jesus' ministry, or it might be from a later period

q. Or *it*

r. Other ancient authorities add *and pray*

and an expression that continued to allow a level of doubt as to whether Jesus was Daniel's Son of Man.

And what could Jesus have meant by "this generation will not pass away until all these things have taken place"? It is "this generation." If it had been "that generation" then Jesus might have meant that the generation that saw the beginnings of the signs would not pass away until the Kingdom of God had come.[627] But the text says "this generation," so Jesus was referring to the people listening to him. It might be true that there were wars and earthquakes during that generation, but the sun carried on shining, the moon did not disappear, the stars did not fall, the Kingdom of God did not arrive, and they did not see the Son of Man coming in clouds with great power and glory. It does not solve the problem to assume that Jesus' resurrection was already the beginning of the end times that Jesus was predicting,[628] as that is not among "these things" that Jesus here describes; and neither does it solve it to say that some of the signs were already happening in Jesus' time,[629] because the plain meaning of "these things" is all of the things that Jesus had predicted.

So how is the problem to be solved? One solution is to assume that Jesus was simply wrong. That is not a problem. He was a human being like the rest of us, and just as he would have shared in the sin that the whole of the human race experiences, so he would have shared in its limited knowledge and understanding. However much the changing patterns of action that constituted Jesus were also changing patterns of action that constituted God, they were also changing patterns of action that constituted Jesus as a human being: so he experienced limited knowledge and limited understanding, which means that God experiences limited knowledge and limited understanding as well. Such limitations will of course be absorbed into the complete knowledge and understanding that constitutes God, but it must also remain true that God knows the experience of limitation—just one of the countless aspects of the reconciliation brought about by the incarnation: that is, by the changing patterns of action that constitute Jesus being changing patterns of action that constitute God.

However, there is another solution to the problem, and one for which we have already prepared: If "all these things" is the desecration and destruction of the temple, and the suffering of Christians before and during that time, as the disciples' question as to the timing of "these things" at the beginning of the chapter suggests, then "these things" would take place within the lifetime of some of those who were listening to Jesus.[630] This is by far the simplest explanation of the text as a whole, and so is the one that we should assume.

And what of the next sentence? The obvious assumption to make is Wittgenstein's: that words belong to forms of life, which means that they are inextricably connected to forms of human life on this planet. But what Jesus is saying here is that that is not necessarily the case. He envisages the arrival of a new heaven and a new earth—a promise repeated in the penultimate chapter of the Book of Revelation[631]—and that in that new Kingdom of God his words will survive. But might this not be true of us as well? Indeed, must it not generally be true that everything about all of us must somehow survive into the Kingdom of God if we are to be welcomed into it? —otherwise it will no longer be us. We have already discussed the complexity of this problem in relation to Jesus' "when they rise from the dead, they neither marry nor are given in marriage, but are like angels in heaven":[632] for if it is to be us in the Kingdom of God when it fully comes then our relationships must somehow survive into that new era. Perhaps what matters in that sentence is the "somehow." God has raised Jesus from the dead so that he is already the one like a son of man who has been presented to the Ancient of Days and given authority to reign as servant king. That resurrection is a promise that we too shall be raised from the dead with the "spiritual bodies" that Paul discussed in his first letter to the church in Corinth.[633] For those new bodies to be the same people as we are, God will have to transform the changing patterns of action that constitute who we are, and will also have to ensure continuity between the changing patterns of action that constitute who we are now and those that will constitute who we shall be, including sufficient of the memories that constitute so much of our identity, otherwise it will not be us who are raised from the dead. The changing patterns of action that constitute our relationships will also have to be both transformed and somehow continuous.

Our words are a different matter. Most of them "pass away" immediately they are spoken or written. There will only be a few that will continue to change the changing patterns of action that constitute who we are, and those will have to be both transformed and continuous if they are to be changing patterns of action that constitute our spiritual bodies.

All of this is clearly true of Jesus. The changing patterns of action that constituted who he was are both transformed and continuous in the spiritual body that is already his and that was revealed to his disciples during the resurrection appearances recorded in three of the four gospels. But here an additional statement is being made: that his words will not pass away, presumably referring to all of them; so perhaps we might also have to say that there will be a sense in which all of the changing patterns of action that constituted who Jesus was are both transformed and continuous in the Kingdom of God. The changing patterns of action that constituted who Jesus was are uniquely changing patterns of action that constitute God, so it is not too speculative a thought to believe that whereas for each of us a sufficient selection of the changing patterns of action that constitute who we are will be continuous with the changing patterns of action that constitute our spiritual bodies, for Jesus there will be a completeness about that continuity that we shall not experience. The changing patterns of action that constituted Jesus' humanity are now changing patterns of action that constitute God, and if that humanity is to be eternally changing patterns of action that constitute God, and is to constitute God's reconciliation with us, then nothing will be lost of that humanity. Not only all of Jesus' words, but every changing pattern of action that constitute who he was and is will be transformed in the Kingdom of God. And if that is possible for Jesus, then might it not be possible for us as well?

The second part of the passage might be thought to contradict Jesus' statement that "this generation will not pass away until all these things have taken place." Perhaps "this generation will not pass away . . ." belongs to a period in his ministry when Jesus believed that the final coming of the Kingdom of God was imminent, and that "about that day or hour no one knows, neither the angels in heaven, nor the Son" belongs to a period when he was less sure of the date of its coming, and when he had begun to see himself as God's Son in some sense. Or perhaps "this generation will not pass away until all these things have taken place" refers to the words of the previous verses, and "about that day or hour no one knows" refers to the verses to come which are about a different subject. This could make sense. The previous verses can be interpreted as being about the destruction of the temple, and the suffering prior to that happening, whereas the subsequent verses might be about a final end of the age, Jesus' return, and the complete victory over evil of the Kingdom of God.[634]

Whether Jesus was here referring to the destruction of the temple or the end of the present age, it is Jesus' uncertainty—the uncertainty of the "son," a title that Jesus now seems to apply to himself[635]—that was the experience of the early Christians, particularly as the first generation began to die and the Kingdom of God had not arrived; and to know that Jesus shared in their human ignorance[636] might have been an encouragement to persist in hope without knowing how long they would have to wait. For subsequent generations of Christians, including our own, the pattern of action must be the same: to "keep awake"—a changing pattern of action, because the world changes, but still an identifiable pattern of wakefulness: of being alert, and ready for the new heaven and new earth in which Jesus would be the servant king.

The whole purpose of the apocalyptic chapter 13 of Mark's Gospel, both when it was first spoken, and as it was passed from person to person in the church and then written down, either before Mark wrote, or as he wrote, is to inspire a pattern of action: the pattern of action represented by wakefulness—a committed scanning of the horizon, looking for the Kingdom of God's arrival—and by faithfulness in the midst of persecution and suffering: the kind of persecution and suffering described in this chapter.[637] Whenever we notice a pattern of action represented by one of the signs described in this chapter, our own changing patterns of action will be redirected into a new longing for the Kingdom of God to come,[638] and towards living lives composed of patterns of action that are those of the Kingdom of God. We might not know the time of the Kingdom of God's final arrival, and indeed we shall never know that until the event happens, but in the meantime we shall be constantly addressed by this chapter, constantly reawakened by it, and constantly summoned both to a continuous discipleship and to a permanent pattern of action: "Keep awake!"[639]

## MARK 14:1-11

**14** It was two days before the Passover and the festival of Unleavened Bread. The chief priests and the scribes were looking for a way to arrest Jesus[s] by stealth and kill him; ² for they said, 'Not during the festival, or there may be a riot among the people.'

3 While he was at Bethany in the house of Simon the leper,[t] as he sat at the table, a woman came with an alabaster jar of very costly ointment of nard, and she broke open the jar and poured the ointment on his head. ⁴ But some were there who said to one another in anger, 'Why was the ointment wasted in this way? ⁵ For this ointment could have been sold for more than three hundred denarii,[u] and the money given to the poor.' And they scolded her. ⁶ But Jesus said, 'Let her alone; why do you trouble her? She has performed a good service for me. ⁷ For you always have the poor with you, and you can show kindness to them whenever you wish; but you will not always have me. ⁸ She has done what she could; she has anointed my body beforehand for its burial. ⁹ Truly I tell you, wherever the good news[v] is proclaimed in the whole world, what she has done will be told in remembrance of her.'

10 Then Judas Iscariot, who was one of the twelve, went to the chief priests in order to betray him to them. ¹¹ When they heard it, they were greatly pleased, and promised to give him money. So he began to look for an opportunity to betray him.[640]

The Jewish leaders faced a genuine quandary. They must have been seriously concerned that a crowd, and possibly Jesus as well, had understood the entry into Jerusalem on a donkey as a fulfilment of Zechariah's prophecy:

> Rejoice greatly, O daughter Zion!
> > Shout aloud, O daughter Jerusalem!
> Lo, your king comes to you;
> > triumphant and victorious is he,
> humble and riding on a donkey,
> > on a colt, the foal of a donkey.[641]

It was a reasonable assumption that an armed mob might attack the Roman garrison, that the revolt would be quickly crushed, and that there might be serious consequences both for Jerusalem's inhabitants and for themselves. Jesus had to be stopped, if necessary by arranging for him to be killed. The problem was that he was popular, so arresting him would be difficult, and could provoke the very thing that they were trying to

---

s. Gk *him*

t. The terms *leper* and *leprosy* can refer to several diseases

u. The denarius was the usual day's wage for a labourer

v. Or *gospel*

prevent. Judas's visit must have been an answer to their prayers. Tim Rice's lyrics for the musical "Jesus Christ Superstar" probably have it right: Judas too could foresee violence on the horizon. He had been a committed follower of Jesus, and as much as anyone he wanted to see the Kingdom of God inaugurated: but he could see that Jesus' entry into Jerusalem on a donkey was going to have the opposite effect—Roman liquidation of Jesus, of his followers, and possibly of many others as well. Jesus had to be stopped, and Judas had probably worked out that the Jewish leadership would have wanted that to happen as well: hence his offer to arrange for Jesus to be arrested away from the crowd and at night, and maybe also to provide an account of some of Jesus' discourses that might serve to condemn him.[642] It is possible that Judas hoped that Jesus would simply be arrested and removed from Jerusalem:[643] but he must have been aware that those he went to see would have wanted a more permanent solution.

In the meantime, Jesus was in Bethany, outside Jerusalem, sitting with someone who had probably been a social outcast but appears to have been one no longer, possibly because his skin disease (which might or might not have been leprosy) had been healed, maybe by Jesus. And then what looked like a completely irrational event occurred: a bizarre and wasteful act of worship. It was not. Consistently with the entry into Jerusalem, this was an act that could be interpreted as the anointing of the Messiah, "the anointed one"; and consistently with the anointings of the kings of Israel, it was also the anointing of a future king of Israel.[644] But that isn't mentioned, either by Mark, or by the characters in the narrative. A very different conversation takes place. Whether this is a conversation that evolved during the oral transmission of this account in order to provide an edifying message for what had become an event that no longer fitted the Christian story, or whether the conversation took place in the context of the event, we cannot now know. Jesus had predicted his own death, and he could well have given the pouring out of the ointment the meaning of a preparation for his burial, maybe to draw attention away from the obvious interpretation that the woman was anointing someone she thought was about to become King of Israel: but whatever the reason, the saying was probably maintained in the tradition because it showed that a prior anointing had rectified before the event the absence of a proper anointing of Jesus' corpse before its burial.[645] That a pattern of action occurs is far more important than when it does. And Jesus might have latched onto someone's comment about the expense of the ointment for the same reason: to distract attention from obvious but dangerous meanings of the anointing. It was clearly a lot safer to discuss the needs of the poor than to discuss openly with probably quite a large group of people the question as to whether the Kingdom of God was about to be established in Jerusalem and Jesus was to be its king. But perhaps this discussion of the expense of the ointment has another purpose as well: the woman has spent money in order to prepare Jesus for his burial, whereas Judas will receive money for facilitating Jesus' death:[646] so a pattern of action and its inversion. And perhaps all of it fits together, and we have here an incident that in many ways provides the key that binds together the complex and changing pattern of action that has constituted Jesus from his entry into Jerusalem, and will constitute it until and after the Kingdom of God is established. Patterns of action carry meaning—indeed, they are meanings—and this event was the anointing of the Messiah who was about to die and be buried and who would be King of Israel: all of that in this breaking of a jar of ointment over Jesus' head.[647]

Jesus had become increasingly convinced that the Kingdom of God was not only near but was about to be inaugurated, and was also increasingly convinced that he was to be its servant king. Hence the entry into Jerusalem, riding on a donkey. He was also aware that his death might be required as a vital part of the birth pangs of the Kingdom of God, and he believed that if that was what had to happen then God would raise him from death to be presented as the "one like a son of man" who would then rule over the nations in a new heaven and a new earth. There was thus a degree of uncertainty in amongst the conviction of who he was and what his destiny would be. As the events of the next few days unfold, we shall see that Jesus' death was indeed required as an essential prelude to his reign.

Even if some of this is mistaken, all of it is perfectly understandable: the characters, the events, and the accounts in Mark's Gospel. We can reasonably conclude that we have here expressed what might have been the changing patterns of action that constituted Jesus during this last week of his life, that might have constituted how Jesus' followers told and understood these events, and that might have constituted Mark's mind as he crystallized changing patterns of action into the pattern of the text of his gospel. The significant question that we now have to answer is whether and how the changing patterns of action that constituted Jesus during these events were the changing patterns of action that constitute God: the ambition to be king; the uncertainty; the knowledge that death might or might not be required; and particularly the knowledge that other lives would be at risk, because Jesus must have been aware of that possibility. The question comes down to this: Who was Jesus? Was he an eschatological prophet: a unique human being destined to reign in the Kingdom of God; or was he, and is he, God.

The first thing to say is that if God is to live a human life—if the changing patterns of action that constitute a human being are to be changing patterns of action that constitute God—then that human life will have to be a particular human life. It could have been any human life. Presumably it could have been the life of a carpenter living in Nazareth, whose father had died while he was still young so that he had to run the family firm from an early age, who married and had children, who was a pillar of the local synagogue and community, and who died in old age having lived an ordinary, useful, and fulfilled life. It could have been the life of the wife of a carpenter who had children and grandchildren, and died in old age having lived an ordinary, useful, and fulfilled life. Or it could have been the life of someone living with disability and poverty who died young and uncared for. It could have been any kind of human life, in any place, and at any time. The question is whether there has to be anything particular about the life that God lives, and whether there has been anything particular about that human life.

A conclusion that we might come to in response to this question is that there might be something particularly appropriate, and perhaps even necessary, about the human life that God lives being the life of the human being who will be the servant king in the Kingdom of God: the "one like a son of man" who will be presented to the Ancient of Days. Thus the whole experience, the whole changing pattern of changing patterns of action that constitute the human person, not only are throughout that human life changing patterns of action that constitute God, but finally and eternally they become the changing patterns of action that constitute God in a way in which no other individual human being's can. At precisely this point Mark's Gospel makes the connection: Previously the "good news" has been the good news of the Kingdom of God, but from now on the "good news" is to be accompanied by the memory of the woman's anointing of Jesus. This implies that the good news is now as much about Jesus himself as it is about the Kingdom of God.[648] The patterns of action are now aligned: the patterns of action that constitute Jesus are the patterns of action that constitute the Kingdom of God, and are the patterns of action that constitute God. That is not all that there is to be said: but that is to be said.

We shall never understand this: of course we shall not. The question is whether through creating such a theological narrative we might in some flawed but still legitimate way be able to indicate truth about God, about Jesus, and about the Kingdom of God. In terms of the changing patterns of action that constitute who we are: Is this a truth-seeking narrative? The reader must judge.

## MARK 14:12-25

12 On the first day of Unleavened Bread, when the Passover lamb is sacrificed, his disciples said to him, 'Where do you want us to go and make the preparations for you to eat the Passover?' [13] So he sent two of his disciples, saying to them, 'Go into the city, and a man carrying a jar of water will meet you; follow him, [14] and wherever he enters, say to the owner of the house, "The Teacher asks, Where is my guest room where I may eat the Passover with my disciples?" [15] He will show you a large room upstairs, furnished and ready. Make preparations for us there.' [16] So the disciples set out and went to the city, and found everything as he had told them; and they prepared the Passover meal.

17 When it was evening, he came with the twelve. [18] And when they had taken their places and were eating, Jesus said, 'Truly I tell you, one of you will betray me, one who is eating with me.' [19] They began to be distressed and to say to him one after another, 'Surely, not I?' [20] He said to them, 'It is one of the

twelve, one who is dipping bread[w] into the bowl[x] with me. ²¹ For the Son of Man goes as it is written of him, but woe to that one by whom the Son of Man is betrayed! It would have been better for that one not to have been born.'

22 While they were eating, he took a loaf of bread, and after blessing it he broke it, gave it to them, and said, 'Take; this is my body.' ²³ Then he took a cup, and after giving thanks he gave it to them, and all of them drank from it. ²⁴ He said to them, 'This is my blood of the[y] covenant, which is poured out for many. ²⁵ Truly I tell you, I will never again drink of the fruit of the vine until that day when I drink it new in the kingdom of God.'[649]

Whether Jesus' last meal with his disciples was a Passover meal is disputed, mainly because there is no mention of a Passover lamb, and Joseph of Arimathea's actions after Jesus' death suggest that the Passover was about to start.[650] If the meal was the night before the Passover lambs were slaughtered, as John's Gospel suggests, and as Mark might be interpreted as assuming, then the Passover would still have been in the minds of both Jesus and his disciples: so the fact that it might not have been a celebration of the Passover might not be very relevant. Or perhaps this was a Passover meal and there was no lamb because the lambless Passover meal was yet another rejection of the temple cult, and another statement that a new inclusive covenant was being established.[651] Whichever was the case, it is the pattern of action that matters, and not the date on which it was held and whether or not it was a Passover meal.

If the meal was a celebration of the Passover, then they were celebrating the central act of remembrance for Jews: a celebration of the angel of death leaving their own homes untouched as he slaughtered the first-born children of the Egyptians—a slaughter that led directly to the Israelites' escape from slavery. On that occasion, lambs had been slaughtered and eaten, and the blood smeared on the doorposts to alert the angel of death to the presence of Jews, so Jesus and his disciples would probably have eaten lamb, and also unleavened bread, because their ancestors had had to leave Egypt in such a hurry that the bread dough for baking the next day had not had time to rise. The traditional Passover meal, then and now, involved a variety of symbols, such as bitter herbs to represent the slaves' bitter lives in Egypt; and wine—a celebration of the life of abundance to which the former slaves were heading.

Presumably Jesus had already made arrangements for the meal to be celebrated in the room to which he directed his disciples: his history of confrontation with the authorities, and his awareness that they wished to kill him, probably necessitating the surreptitious method by which the disciples were directed to the room.[652] And then the first event recorded is Jesus' prediction of Judas's betrayal, during which it becomes clear that Jesus has now recognized that his own death might be required as an essential element of the sufferings that would precede the establishment of the

w. Gk lacks *bread*

x. Other ancient authorities read *same bowl*

y. Other ancient authorities add *new*

Kingdom of God. "For the Son of Man goes as it written of him . . . ." Here Jesus combines prophecies: "Truly I tell you, one of you will betray me, one who is eating with me . . . It is one of the twelve, one who is dipping bread into the bowl with me" reflects words in Psalm 41: "Even my bosom friend in whom I trusted, who ate of my bread, has lifted the heel against me";[653] "one like a son of man" is the one whom Daniel pictures being presented to the Ancient of Days[654] and who will rule in God's Kingdom; and the death is that of the servant of God who will suffer and die in fulfilment of a prophecy in Isaiah, which it is worth quoting in full here:

> 53 Who has believed what we have heard?
>> And to whom has the arm of the LORD been revealed?
>
> ² For he grew up before him like a young plant,
>> and like a root out of dry ground;
>
> he had no form or majesty that we should look at him,
>> nothing in his appearance that we should desire him.
>
> ³ He was despised and rejected by others;
>> a man of suffering[u] and acquainted with infirmity;
>
> and as one from whom others hide their faces[v]
>> he was despised, and we held him of no account.
>
> ⁴ Surely he has borne our infirmities
>> and carried our diseases;
>
> yet we accounted him stricken,
>> struck down by God, and afflicted.
>
> ⁵ But he was wounded for our transgressions,
>> crushed for our iniquities;
>
> upon him was the punishment that made us whole,
>> and by his bruises we are healed.
>
> ⁶ All we like sheep have gone astray;
>> we have all turned to our own way,
>
> and the LORD has laid on him
>> the iniquity of us all.
>
> ⁷ He was oppressed, and he was afflicted,
>> yet he did not open his mouth;
>
> like a lamb that is led to the slaughter,
>> and like a sheep that before its shearers is silent,
>> so he did not open his mouth.
>
> ⁸ By a perversion of justice he was taken away.

> u. Or *a man of sorrows*
> v. Or *as one who hides his face from us*

> Who could have imagined his future?
> For he was cut off from the land of the living,
>   stricken for the transgression of my people.
> ⁹ They made his grave with the wicked
>   and his tomb[w] with the rich,[x]
> although he had done no violence,
>   and there was no deceit in his mouth.[655]

Here is the source of Jesus' previous statement that "the Son of Man came not to be served but to serve, and to give his life a ransom for many,"[656] and of Jesus' growing conviction that the Son of Man would have to suffer and die before being presented to the Ancient One and being given authority to rule. The changing pattern of action that would be his in a few hours' time was now decided: by God, by Judas, by the Jewish leaders, and probably by Jesus himself.

Jesus' statement that it would have been better for his betrayer not to have been born is probably precisely that: a statement of fact. Jesus could see that Judas's mind would be thrown into such turmoil by betraying him that he would live the rest of his life in despair, or would die by suicide. The latter is what happened.

The account of Jesus' last meal with his disciples is brief, and concentrates almost entirely on the actions related to the bread and wine, no doubt because it was these patterns of action that gave birth to the church's Eucharist and that constantly underpinned its validity as an effectual sign, a sacrament.[657] Jesus took bread, gave thanks for it, broke it, and gave it to his disciples: the same four verbs as at the feeding of the five thousand and the feeding of the four thousand.[658] And he took wine, gave thanks for it, and gave it to his disciples. It is these four-fold and three-fold patterns of action that constituted the central complex changing pattern of action of Jesus' last meal with his disciples before he died; and it is this complex changing pattern of action that constituted the early Christians' regular remembrance of Jesus. In what might or might not be an earlier account of the last supper, Jesus follows the action with "Do this in remembrance of me,"[659] but the words do not appear in Mark's Gospel. Either Jesus said them, or he was thought to have said them because that is what the Christians were doing: but perhaps he did not say them, because his disciples' repetitions of Jesus' actions with the bread and wine were not intended, by Jesus or the disciples, to be backward-looking, but rather forward-looking: a looking forward to the disciples' renewed following of Jesus, to their own taking up of the cross, perhaps literally, and to the Kingdom of God in which bread and wine would again be shared.[660] Either way,

w. Q Ms: MT *and in his death*
x. Cn: Heb *with a rich person*

this complex changing pattern of action quickly became the Christians' central act of worship, and, as reality is changing patterns of action, it is no exaggeration to say that this complex changing pattern of action constitutes the church. Where this complex changing pattern of action happens, there is Jesus—for this is his complex changing pattern of action; and where this complex pattern of action happens, there are Jesus' disciples gathered. We get a glimpse of this development in one of the resurrection narratives of Luke's Gospel. Two disciples, possibly a married couple, are walking home from Jerusalem to Emmaus a few days after Jesus' crucifixion. They are joined by a stranger who shows them how Jesus' death fulfilled the prophecies; they invite him to stay with them; and he breaks the bread and disappears: and they recognize that it was Jesus.[661] Whether the story originated in a resurrection appearance, in the experience of the early Christians—they knew Jesus to be present as the bread was broken, or both, is not the issue here. The story reveals the centrality of the taking of bread, the giving thanks for it, the breaking of it, and the sharing of it, to early Christians' remembrance of Jesus. This pattern of action simply was, and is, and always will be, the presence of Jesus among his followers.[662]

Whether it was Jesus or early Christians who introduced the words "Do this in remembrance of me" into Paul's narrative of the last supper, this is what the complex changing pattern of action was for early Christians: a remembrance—not in the sense of simply bringing to mind images and words of Jesus, but rather in the sense of Jesus' presence. Each of us is changing patterns of action: that is who we are; so for a gathering of Christians to take bread, give thanks, break the bread, and share it among themselves, was and is to *be* Jesus. And so when today anyone takes bread, gives thanks for it, breaks it, and shares it, Jesus is present, because this is the complex changing pattern of action that he was and that he still is.

But what of Jesus' words "Take: this is my body" and "This is my blood of the covenant, which is poured out for many"? Jesus would have spoken in Aramaic, so there would have been no expressed verb: "This my body."[663] Once we dispense with the verb "to be," new interpretations are open to us. Within a Being, beings, unchanging, rest, unitary, and generally static conceptual framework, we might ask such questions as "How can the bread be Jesus' body?" and "How can the wine be his blood?" Within an Action, actions, change, movement, diversity, and generally dynamic conceptual framework, we have different questions to ask: "How can the breaking of the bread be Jesus' body?" And "How can the pouring of the wine be the blood of the covenant poured out for many?" Within a Being conceptual framework we are likening objects to objects: bread to body, wine to blood: but within an Action conceptual framework we are likening actions to actions, and so we are relating the breaking of the bread to the breaking of Jesus' body, and the pouring of the wine to the pouring out of his blood by which a new covenant is established:[664] hence the essential action of the soldier who plunged a spear into Jesus' side.[665] It is actions that matter, not things, and the words that Jesus spoke only matter in the sense that they draw attention to the actions, and are themselves actions in patterns. The actions can never be "caged" by the words.[666]

So here is the remembrance of Jesus—the changing pattern of action that constitutes Jesus still present in our midst: the breaking of the bread is the breaking of his body; and the pouring of the wine is the pouring out of his blood; so as we do his complex changing patterns of action—the taking of the bread, the giving thanks for it, the breaking of it, and the sharing of it; and the pouring of the wine, the giving thanks for it, and the sharing of it—the changing pattern of action that constitutes Jesus is happening among us, and he is here. To eat with someone in Jesus' time was to constitute a relationship with them, so doing these actions today does not simply express a relationship with Jesus: it creates a relationship with Jesus.[667] Before Jesus said "this is my body," he said "Take." Jesus' death was not to be a pattern of action somehow distant from them. They were to benefit from it, and to participate in it.[668]

According to much of the Jewish law, the covenant between God and Israel was established and maintained by the pouring of blood, and we also find examples of covenants being established by people eating and drinking together.[669] Whether Jesus intended the pouring of his blood to establish a new covenant between God and a new Israel constituted by Christians, and potentially Gentile Christians as well as Jewish Christians, or to re-establish the old covenant, is not clear: but Christians have always interpreted Jesus' death as establishing a new relationship between God and us, which surely it does: because the changing pattern of action that constitutes Jesus' death constitutes a human death, but it is also a changing pattern of action that constitutes God. Here is the foundation of the new relationship: God has suffered a human death, so human death is eternally the experience of God. A new and intimate covenant has been established that enables genuine community between God and humanity.

The Christian celebration that is rooted in the last supper has many names: the Eucharist (Thanksgiving), the Mass, the Lord's Supper, the Holy Communion. Each name represents a different understanding of what is happening, and all of them to some extent represent the event as the complex changing pattern of action that constitutes who Jesus was at the last supper, and so who Jesus is as we do the four-fold and three-fold patterns of action today. The patterns of action might be somewhat different from place to place, from time to time, and from tradition to tradition, but they are still identifiable as the same changing patterns of action. It is this that constitutes the church.

When many churches celebrate the Eucharist, the Mass, the Lord's Supper, the Holy Communion, the words that Jesus used at the last supper are repeated, often with the addition of "Do this in remembrance of me," but generally not with "Truly I tell you, I will never again drink of the fruit of the vine until that day when I drink it new in the kingdom of God," which is in Mark's account. Why is that? A fairly obvious reason is that the congregation is about to "do this in remembrance," so to stop there seems obvious: but to do that loses something important. Jesus was looking forward to the Kingdom of God that would be established by the events about to unfold: by his suffering and death, which he might now have understood to be both necessary and inevitable; by his resurrection—his being presented to the Ancient of Days; and by his being given authority to rule. Then he will be able to drink wine again with his disciples. Jesus here sets us a most complex and a most important question: How will it be that we shall share wine with him in the Kingdom of God? What matters is that that is the question. The question is not "Will we share wine with him?." It is "How will it be that we shall share wine with him?." The Kingdom of God will be defined by the changing patterns of action that will constitute it, so the "spiritual bodies" that Paul discusses will be constituted by changing patterns of action just as our bodies here are, but differently, as Jesus' resurrection body was changing patterns of action but differently. Of all of the changing patterns of action that constitute who Jesus was, and therefore who he is, the complex changing pattern of action that constituted the last supper is surely central. It is inconceivable that this complex changing pattern of action will not happen in the Kingdom of God. Jesus will indeed take bread, give thanks, break the bread, and share it among everyone in the Kingdom of God, and so with everyone; and similarly with the wine. This complex changing pattern of action must continue. We really ought to be saying all of these words during our celebrations of the Eucharist: "This is my blood of the covenant, which is poured out for many. Truly I tell you, I will never again drink of the fruit of the vine until that day when I drink it new in the kingdom of God." And a further reason that we should be saying these words is this: If we are together doing this pattern of action at every Eucharist, then because this pattern of action constitutes who Jesus is, Jesus is real and present to us in this pattern of action: so Jesus is eating and drinking with us, and the Kingdom of God has already come. We still await the fulfilment of the Kingdom of God on earth as in heaven, but whenever the Eucharistic pattern of action takes place, the Kingdom of God is here in that moment.[670]

## MARK 14:26-31, 66-72

26 When they had sung the hymn, they went out to the Mount of Olives. 27 And Jesus said to them, 'You will all become deserters; for it is written,

"I will strike the shepherd,

and the sheep will be scattered."

28 But after I am raised up, I will go before you to Galilee.' 29 Peter said to him, 'Even though all become deserters, I will not.' 30 Jesus said to him, 'Truly I tell you, this day, this very night, before the cock crows twice, you will deny me

three times.' ³¹ But he said vehemently, 'Even though I must die with you, I will not deny you.' And all of them said the same. . . .

⁶⁶ . . . While Peter was below in the courtyard, one of the servant-girls of the high priest came by. ⁶⁷ When she saw Peter warming himself, she stared at him and said, 'You also were with Jesus, the man from Nazareth.' ⁶⁸ But he denied it, saying, 'I do not know or understand what you are talking about.' And he went out into the forecourt.[c] Then the cock crowed.[d] ⁶⁹ And the servant-girl, on seeing him, began again to say to the bystanders, 'This man is one of them.' ⁷⁰ But again he denied it. Then after a little while the bystanders again said to Peter, 'Certainly you are one of them; for you are a Galilean.' ⁷¹ But he began to curse, and he swore an oath, 'I do not know this man you are talking about.' ⁷² At that moment the cock crowed for the second time. Then Peter remembered that Jesus had said to him, 'Before the cock crows twice, you will deny me three times.' And he broke down and wept.[671]

The two events to be discussed here—Jesus' prediction of Peter's denial, and the denial itself in the courtyard outside the house where Jesus' trial was taking place—are divided in chronology, and in Mark's Gospel, but they belong together, so we shall discuss them together. And they follow Judas's promise to betray Jesus, and precede the actual betrayal. These are patterns of action that Jesus suffered alongside the patterns of action of physical suffering and death, and were perhaps as painful as those. The fact that they were predicted in the scriptures—"strike the shepherd, that the sheep may be scattered"[672]—would have been little comfort.[673]

Jesus was well aware of the character of his followers. They were a diverse group of men and women, all with flaws: and it is perhaps likely that when Jesus gave to Simon the name Peter, which means a rock, he was being purposely ambiguous. To some extent it was a joke, in that he would already have been aware that Peter was what we might today call flaky. Impetuously loyal, and the next moment unreliable. It is no surprise that it was Peter who got out of the boat to meet Jesus as he walked on the water towards them, and then was terrified by the waves and began to sink.[674] Jesus' prediction of his impending denial required no supernatural powers. Peter's promise of absolute loyalty, even if it would require him to die with Jesus, was entirely predictable, as was the denial. The denial followed during the same night, and it was perhaps more extreme than we might realize, because the word "began to curse" would normally take a direct object, suggesting that Peter in fact cursed Jesus, but Mark was unwilling to make that explicit.[675] Dying as a follower of Jesus would have to wait, but tradition tells us that it happened.

But that was not all that there was to Peter. The name "Peter" might have been spoken with a wry smile, but perhaps Jesus could also see that Peter had the potential to lead his band of followers after he was dead. If the Kingdom of God was not

c. Or *gateway*
d. Other ancient authorities lack *then the cock crowed*

established on Earth immediately after his death, even if it was established in heaven, then the vision would need to be kept alive, so Peter will have been on Jesus' agenda as he prayed in the Garden of Gethsemane. Jesus might have seen that none of the others would have been capable of providing the leadership that would be required in no doubt challenging circumstances, so Peter it would have to be. The Acts of the Apostles proves Jesus to have been right. Peter was still flaky, as we discover in Paul's letter to the church in Galatia,[676] but along with Jesus' brother James he not only provided the brave leadership required, but he also handled the changing context and nature of the church as well as anyone could have been expected to do.

What does it mean to be a follower of Jesus today? If reality is changing patterns of action, then what we are discussing here is the changing patterns of action that constitute the following of Jesus, and not some state of being. Let Peter be our model.

First of all, Peter knew who Jesus was: not in the sense of knowledge somehow possessed, but in the sense of a constantly changing understanding of the changing patterns of action that constituted who Jesus was. Jesus was a preacher of the Kingdom of God's coming; then he was the Messiah, but not in the traditional sense of the word; and now he was to be the slaughtered servant of God.

Trust as a changing pattern of action is clearly essential. At least Peter got out of the boat; and at least he promised to die with Jesus, even though his courage failed when it came to it. He continued to trust as he led the church during its first couple of decades. As the circumstances change, and as we change, so our trust in Jesus will change: but it will still be identifiable as the changing pattern of action that we call trust.

And we shall fail, we shall know that we have failed, and we shall be reconciled with Jesus and forgiven: all changing patterns of action that Peter experienced during the short period between the night of Jesus' trial and a few days later: patterns of action that we shall experience constantly throughout our lives. Peter wept when he remembered Jesus' prediction of his denial: and John's Gospel records an incident a few days later when Peter sees Jesus on the seashore and leaps out of the boat to meet him. Three times Jesus elicits from Peter statements of his love for him to match the three previous denials—that is, Jesus invites Peter to be the changing patterns of action that Paul describes as love in his first letter to the church in Corinth:[677] and each time Jesus commands Peter to "feed my sheep": to care for the church. That is what Peter went on to do.[678]

Wherever and whenever we live, our following of Jesus will be very different from Peter's. Being a Christian will be a unique changing pattern of action for each of us, influenced by every changing pattern of action that constitutes who we are, and the people and the world around us. Our contexts, our histories, our relationships, and much more, will shape and change the changing patterns of action that constitute our following of Jesus. But that following will bear a family resemblance to the changing pattern of action that constituted Peter's following of Jesus, and to the myriad of changing patterns of action that constituted and that still constitute followers of Jesus during the past two thousand years and today.

Still the church needs leaders. Again, we live in a world radically different from Peter's. An organization that began as a group of followers of Jesus who had experienced his resurrection, and who were united by the changing pattern of action that constituted the Eucharist and by their hope for the immediate return of Jesus and the coming of the Kingdom of God, then spread, largely through Paul's efforts, and in order to remain something like united and functioning through time it had to develop relatively stable structures: not fixed structures, but patterns of action that would continue to change as the world and the church continued to change. Still today the church needs relatively stable structures if it is to function as a single body: for that is what it is, the body of Christ: the changing patterns of action that constitute Jesus active in the world today. As Paul made clear in more than one of his letters, the body of Christ is made up of many limbs, all of which need each other and all of which have to work together to be the body of Christ:[679] that is, to be the changing patterns of action that constitute who Jesus still is. And still those relatively stable structures must change if the church is to be Christ's body in the world: for just as Jesus constantly changed during his ministry, so he still continues to change, because he is still God living a human life in the Kingdom of God, and God is Action, the source of all action, and changing patterns of action.

And still we shall fail, as Peter did. Across history, individual Christians and the church as a whole have denied Jesus. We have not believed; we have not trusted; and we have not followed him. And still Jesus meets us, invites us to love him—to be the changing patterns of action that constitute the love of which Paul wrote in his letter to Christians in Corinth[680]—and calls us again to love his church and the world that together will inherit the Kingdom of God when it comes on earth as well as in heaven.

But what of that single line that interrupts Jesus' prediction of his disciples' abandonment of him? "But after I am raised up, I will go before you to Galilee." A new gathering will follow the scattering.[681] This really is an interruption, because Peter's declaration of loyalty that follows this sentence would follow naturally from "and the sheep will be scattered." Either Jesus said this line at this point, or he said it at another point in time and Mark has put it here to make it clear that Jesus would not view his disciples' abandonment of him as the end of the story; or perhaps the line has some other origin. Wherever it came from, and wherever it belongs, this sentence is another promise of the resurrection, and perhaps the prediction that is the most explicit in relation to the detail. It is a promise that the disciples will meet Jesus again in Galilee. Matthew's Gospel records such a meeting,[682] although Mark's does not.

The resurrection appearances are the most mysterious events promised and recorded in the gospels. There is so much wrong with the accounts of them, and yet if they had not occurred then it would be difficult to understand the survival and momentum of the church. The appearances were not the resurrection, they were not the presentation of the Son of Man before the Ancient of Days, and they were not the establishment of the Kingdom of God in which Jesus reigns as servant king: but they are the changing patterns of action that constitute those events breaking into the changing patterns of action that constitute the world in which we live, and so they function as a permanent but still changing witness to the events themselves. They are not what matters most, but they matter, and perhaps Mark has located this sentence here to explain that they matter more than the entirely understandable denial of Jesus by one of his closest followers: a three-times denial in contrast to the three times that Jesus was to pray to be spared the crucifixion, and the three times that he knew that he must go through with it.[683] And it is not insignificant that at the empty tomb the young man who tells the women the good news of Jesus' resurrection specifically mentions Peter by name as one of those to whom they are to pass on the news.[684] In the courtyard outside the High Priest's house Peter's following of Jesus had ended, but it would begin again.[685]

## MARK 14:32-52

32 They went to a place called Gethsemane; and he said to his disciples, 'Sit here while I pray.' [33] He took with him Peter and James and John, and began to be distressed and agitated. [34] And he said to them, 'I am deeply grieved, even to death; remain here, and keep awake.' [35] And going a little farther, he threw himself on the ground and prayed that, if it were possible, the hour might pass from him. [36] He said, 'Abba,[z] Father, for you all things are possible; remove this cup from me; yet, not what I want, but what you want.' [37] He came and found them sleeping; and he said to Peter, 'Simon, are you asleep? Could you not keep awake one hour? [38] Keep awake and pray that you may not come into the time of trial;[a] the spirit indeed is willing, but the flesh is weak.' [39] And again he went away and prayed, saying the same words. [40] And once more he came and found them sleeping, for their eyes were very heavy; and they did not know what to say to him. [41] He came a third time and said to them, 'Are you still sleeping and taking your rest? Enough! The hour has come; the Son of Man is betrayed into the hands of sinners. [42] Get up, let us be going. See, my betrayer is at hand.'

43 Immediately, while he was still speaking, Judas, one of the twelve, arrived; and with him there was a crowd with swords and clubs, from the chief priests, the scribes, and the elders. [44] Now the betrayer had given them a sign, saying, 'The one I will kiss is the man; arrest him and lead him away under

---

z. Aramaic for *Father*

a. Or *into temptation*

guard.' ⁴⁵ So when he came, he went up to him at once and said, 'Rabbi!' and kissed him. ⁴⁶ Then they laid hands on him and arrested him. ⁴⁷ But one of those who stood near drew his sword and struck the slave of the high priest, cutting off his ear. ⁴⁸ Then Jesus said to them, 'Have you come out with swords and clubs to arrest me as though I were a bandit? ⁴⁹ Day after day I was with you in the temple teaching, and you did not arrest me. But let the scriptures be fulfilled.' ⁵⁰ All of them deserted him and fled.

51 A certain young man was following him, wearing nothing but a linen cloth. They caught hold of him, ⁵² but he left the linen cloth and ran off naked.⁶⁸⁶

There is nothing surprising about the disciples going to sleep. They might have drunk rather a lot of wine, and it was late at night. Their "flesh" was weak, and their "spirit" willing—"flesh" and "spirit" representing different patterns of action that together constitute us as human beings:⁶⁸⁷ different, but both of them physical. What was perhaps surprising is that so many other people were wide awake: Jesus, and the armed group that arrived to arrest him.

Jesus tells Peter to pray that he won't come to the "time of trial." This is the same word that he used in the prayer that he taught his disciples: "Do not lead us into the time of trial."ʲ ⁶⁸⁸ The word *peirasmos* had diverse meanings. It could mean the deep suffering that would have to be endured as the Kingdom of God came to birth: a time of testing for the people of God; or it could mean a personal time of trial: hence the diverse translations of the word as "temptation" and "time of trial." So what was Jesus asking Peter to pray for? In his own prayers Jesus was asking God to take from him the "cup" that would be his own "time of trial": a time of deep suffering that he was desperate to avoid and yet knew that that might not be possible. Perhaps the explanation for the combination of Jesus' prayer for himself and his telling Peter to pray that he would "not come into *peirasmos*" is that he believed that the Kingdom of God was soon to be born, that the sufferings would soon begin, that he could not avoid suffering and death, but that Peter should pray to be spared. Or perhaps he simply meant that Peter should pray not to be tempted to abandon him or deny him, because he knew that he would either give in to the temptation or would die if he resisted it.

But what of Jesus' own prayer as he struggled with whether to go through with the suffering that he could see coming his way? As we have often discovered, Jesus' prayer is a pattern of action that mirrors a pattern of action to be found in the psalms:

> ²⁰ Deliver my soul from the sword,
> my lifeʸ from the power of the dog!⁶⁸⁹

> ⁹ Be gracious to me, O LORD, for I am in distress;
> my eye wastes away from grief,

j. Or *us into temptation*
y. Heb *my only one*

> my soul and body also.
> ¹⁰ For my life is spent with sorrow,
>   and my years with sighing;
> my strength fails because of my misery,ᵃ
>   and my bones waste away.⁶⁹⁰

If the psalms could not have been taken to prophesy Jesus' distress, then it might have been more difficult for early Christians to believe that Jesus experienced the anguish and doubt that afflicted him in the Garden of Gethsemane; and the fact that Peter was asked to accompany Jesus in prayer, and failed to do so, might have been first of all an inspiration to pray in the midst of suffering, and secondly a comfort when they failed to do so. Jesus demanded of Peter the pattern of action that he exemplified, and the same demand was experienced by the church.⁶⁹¹

Presumably even at this late stage it might still have been possible to escape from Jerusalem, return to Galilee, and live a quiet life as a rabbi and occasional healer. The question here is how we are to interpret this agonizing on the part of Jesus. He was a human being uniquely constituted by the changing patterns of action that constituted God, and he was now struggling with the changing patterns of action that constituted God. All of his praying, from one end of his life to the other, was like this of course: it was relationships between many different changing patterns of action that constituted God: but here, perhaps for the first time, and certainly in its most extreme form, we find prayer that represents genuine conflict within the changing patterns of action that constitute God. God—for that is who Jesus was and is—was going to die. Jesus, facing death, was face to face with his father, his Abba,⁶⁹² and so God was face to face with God. Human death was to be eternally God's experience. Perhaps in that sense the conflict is not so surprising. God was living a human life, so the changing patterns of action that constituted Jesus' humanity were changing patterns of action that constituted God: so the horror of approaching death was already a changing pattern of action that constituted God. The struggle was within God, and so is within God eternally. Additional explanations of this event, and of Jesus' suffering and death, are of course possible, and are commonly expressed—that the agonizing was a recognition of the righteous wrath of God that demanded Jesus' death as a ransom for sinful human beings; that the Satan whom Jesus had beaten off in the wilderness after his baptism was now closing in; and so on⁶⁹³—but the primary narrative has to be that here is the most extreme struggle imaginable, indeed not even imaginable, within God; for God in Jesus was about to suffer human death: that characteristically human pattern of action that ends a human life and is utterly inimical to the creative changing patterns of action that constitute God. There was no voice from heaven in response to Jesus' prayer⁶⁹⁴—there was only silence—because it was God who was praying in the garden while the disciples slept.

a. Gk Syr: Heb *my iniquity*

Judas and the mob sent by the Jerusalem leadership arrived, so there was no longer a decision to be made. Jesus had known that it would come to this, as he had for a long time identified himself with the servant of God about whom Isaiah had written. And now this scripture was to be fulfilled: Jesus was to be

> like a lamb that is led to the slaughter,
> > and like a sheep that before its shearers is silent,
> > so he did not open his mouth.[695]

Jesus did open his mouth, but he was now in others' hands, and knew the likely outcome: so God was a prisoner, and subject to the wills of others; and God was terrified of the suffering to come, even though, and perhaps because, the scriptures had to be fulfilled.[696]

Why the armed resistance from the disciples? In Luke's Gospel we hear them discussing the two swords that they had with them. Jesus says "That's enough!," leaving us unclear as to whether he meant "Two swords is enough: we don't need more than that," or "I don't want to hear any more about swords." But why did they have swords at all? Did they think that they had to protect Jesus from arrest for sufficiently long to give God and the angels time to intervene and establish the Kingdom of God that night, starting in Gethsemane? Possibly. Maybe they thought they really could begin an armed insurrection against the Roman authorities, but that seems rather doubtful. Perhaps the most likely explanation is that they simply did not know what they were doing. They were simply confused. Their minds couldn't find any pattern that could hold together the entry into Jerusalem, the incident in the temple, the last supper, and Jesus' arrest. And perhaps Jesus couldn't either. Maybe Jesus too was being swept along by a jumble of ideas about the Kingdom of God, the Son of Man being presented before God and given authority to rule the nations, the sufferings that would precede that, and what was happening to him now in this garden outside Jerusalem. Given the evidence, there is no reason to think that it all hung together somehow in Jesus' mind or in the minds of his disciples.

And still all of this was changing patterns of action that constituted Jesus, and that constituted God, and therefore constitute God eternally. This bundle of events, ideas, words, and so on—this confused human experience—is eternally the experience of God.

Jesus was right. The disciples abandoned him. And so did a young man who ran away naked. Was this Mark? Quite possibly. What was he doing there, dressed like that? One can only speculate. Perhaps he was the son of one of Jesus' disciples and had therefore been at the last supper. We don't know how old this "young man" was, but if he had been the youngest child at a Passover meal then he would have asked the traditional questions to elicit the meaning of the celebration. It is not impossible that he was the son of the owner of the house in which the last supper took place, that he was getting ready to go to bed, that he heard a noisy crowd leaving the house, and that he grabbed something to wear and followed them to see what would happen. Pure speculation, but it would fit the facts. If so then this event would have been seared into his mind, and it would have been unthinkable to leave it out of his gospel. And if the speculation is anything like accurate, then we can assume that Mark and other members of his family remained followers of Jesus, looking forward to his return and to the establishment of the Kingdom of God; that Mark accompanied Paul on some of his journeys; and that as the first generation of Christians started to die, he talked to Peter, and perhaps to his parents if they were still alive, and wrote down what they told him about Jesus' life and ministry, and particularly what they told him about the last week of Jesus' life. But he would not have needed to be told about the incident in the Garden of Gethsemane. He was there, and maybe party to everything that happened, including Jesus' struggle with what was to come.

Might there be additional meanings? Might the linen cloth represent a baptismal garment, and the young man a disciple who abandons Jesus? And might his reappearance during the account of the empty tomb represent the disciple's renewed faith?[697] Might there be multiple layers of meaning here, representing multiple patterns of action, all bearing family resemblances with that pattern of action in the Garden of Gethsemane? Possibly, but not necessarily. It might just have been something that happened.[698]

## MARK 14:53–65

> 53 They took Jesus to the high priest; and all the chief priests, the elders, and the scribes were assembled. 54 Peter had followed him at a distance, right into the courtyard of the high priest; and he was sitting with the guards, warming himself at the fire. 55 Now the chief priests and the whole council were looking for testimony against Jesus to put him to death; but they found none. 56 For many gave false testimony against him, and their testimony did not agree. 57 Some stood up and gave false testimony against him, saying, 58 'We heard him say, "I will destroy this temple that is made with hands, and in three days I will build another, not made with hands." 59 But even on this point their testimony did not agree. 60 Then the high priest stood up before them and asked Jesus, 'Have you no answer? What is it that they testify against you?' 61 But he was silent and did not answer. Again the high priest asked him, 'Are you the Messiah,[b] the Son of the Blessed One?' 62 Jesus said, 'I am; and
>
>> "you will see the Son of Man
>> seated at the right hand of the Power,"

b. Or *the Christ*

and "coming with the clouds of heaven.'"

⁶³ Then the high priest tore his clothes and said, 'Why do we still need witnesses? ⁶⁴ You have heard his blasphemy! What is your decision?' All of them condemned him as deserving death. ⁶⁵ Some began to spit on him, to blindfold him, and to strike him, saying to him, 'Prophesy!' The guards also took him over and beat him.[699]

Was Jesus purposely fulfilling prophecy?

> like a sheep that before its shearers is silent,
>> so he did not open his mouth.[700]

According to John's Gospel, Jesus did say "Destroy this temple, and in three days I will raise it up."[701] A note is added to say that Jesus was referring to his body: that his body would be destroyed, and then after three days raised to life. However, this passage does make us wonder whether Jesus might really have said something like "I will destroy this temple that is made with hands, and in three days I will build another, not made with hands." The fact that different witnesses' testimonies did not agree during this probably informal gathering to collect evidence, first of all to persuade significant Jewish authorities that Jesus deserved to be charged with blasphemy, and secondly that a more political charge should therefore be put to Pilate,[702] suggests that there were different accounts circulating as to what Jesus had actually said. Trying to recover now Jesus' actual words about the destruction and rebuilding of the temple would be pointless because it would be impossible.[703] In a largely oral culture, it must always have been difficult to know what someone had said, and even if aspects of someone's public statements had been remembered with some degree of accuracy, the precise grammar and wording will often have been completely lost. This must be true of every word of Jesus that we find in the gospels. We can never assume accuracy of reporting, particularly as what we have in the Greek New Testament is already a translation, because Jesus spoke Aramaic. A handful of words in Aramaic and Hebrew have survived, so perhaps we can regard those as words that Jesus actually spoke: but in relation to everything else, we have to keep an open mind. If Jesus' words about the temple were differently remembered so close to the time at which he said them, then we certainly cannot hope to be clear now about what he said.

Does it matter? No, it does not. Far more important than any of Jesus' words was and is the changing pattern of action that constituted Jesus's life, death, and resurrection. But perhaps we cannot trust any of that reporting either? Yes, we can. The witnesses at Jesus' trial were able to agree that Jesus had spoken about the destruction and rebuilding of the temple, even though they could not agree on the details of what was said, so we can assume that Jesus did speak about the destruction and rebuilding of the temple. Similarly, we can assume that what we find recorded in the first three gospels is based on eyewitness accounts, even if the detail of what was remembered and is now recorded might not be entirely accurate. The fourth gospel is another matter: that looks like a historical novel, with speeches constructed to convey the theological position of the writer: but the first three gospels look like genuine attempts to record for future generations the oral memory of the earliest Christians. The changing patterns of action of Jesus' words and actions had changed the changing patterns of action that constituted the brains and lives of the people around him, and those changing patterns of action had changed the changing patterns of action that constituted people around them, and thus to Mark's mind, and to the pen that crystallized the changing pattern of action in his mind into the pure pattern of the text that we read and interpret today. As we interpret, the changing patterns of action that constitute us are changed by the changing patterns of action that constitute the whole of that history: and so we too are changed by Jesus himself. A lot of the detail might have dissipated along the way, and a lot of changing patterns of action from elsewhere will have entered the flow of changing patterns of action, but still there will be changings of our changing patterns of action influenced by the changing patterns of action that constituted Jesus and that constitute God.

And then, perhaps because at the first attempt to make a charge stick witnesses had not agreed,[704] the High Priest composed a question that would have related to the authority that Jesus might have been claiming if he had threatened to destroy the temple. The High Priest's straight question—perhaps based on Judas's accounts of Jesus' private conversations with his disciples—elicited the response "I am": a stark contrast to Peter's declaration that he was not a disciple of Jesus.[705] Was this the moment of revelation for Jesus? The moment when it all came together? Now that he was facing death, did the Messiah, the Son of Man, the suffering servant, and the Son of God—a name of the kings of Israel, because Jesus was now to be the servant king of the Kingdom of God—finally come together in his mind, so that he knew himself to be all of these? And perhaps he now saw that although the meanings of these terms exhibited differences across the many different passages in which they were to be found in the scriptures, they all referred to a single person, and he was that person. We cannot get inside Jesus' mind: but his unambiguous "I am," followed by a reiteration of the prophecy from Daniel, was a statement that although they could kill him, they could not prevent God from raising him from the dead, they could not prevent him from being presented before the Ancient of Days, they could not prevent him from being given authority to rule in the Kingdom of God that would then be established, and they could not prevent the temple from being destroyed. But perhaps things are not quite so simple. Jesus has reordered the prophecy from the Book of Daniel. In the original prophecy, the "one like a son of man" comes "with the clouds of heaven," and *then* he comes to the "Ancient of Days." In Jesus' response to the High Priest, the order is reversed. Either Jesus or the early Christians have reinterpreted the prophecy as saying that Jesus would be given authority to rule, and would then come as both savior and judge to establish the Kingdom of God on earth.[706] What the priests would "see" would be Jesus receiving the authority to rule in the Kingdom of God: so perhaps what they would see would be a Spirit-inspired church that would be a foretaste of the Kingdom of God that would come on Earth at Jesus' return, and then finally the return itself.[707]

Whether Jesus' words during his interrogation were in fact "blasphemy" is open to debate. Jesus was not claiming to be God, which was a claim that it would probably have been impossible for a first century Jew to have made: but presumably what he did say appeared to the high priest to be blasphemy because Jesus was claiming to fulfil a number of significant prophecies in ways in which no-one of that time would have believed possible, with perhaps his claim to be destined for the right hand of God being the deciding factor.[708] How could this Galilean carpenter be Son of God, Messiah, and Daniel's "one like a son of man"? God would never have done that, so it was blasphemy.

But perhaps God has done that. Perhaps this Jesus really was and is Son of God, the servant of God in Isaiah, the Messiah, Daniel's "one like a son of man," and, in the end, a divine being: or rather, action in divine patterns. And perhaps this Jesus was what he would not have been able to conceive—perhaps he was God, living this particular human life. Maybe this is why Jesus had come to believe himself to be Son of God, Daniel's Son of Man, Isaiah's servant of God, and the Messiah: it was the nearest his first century human mind could get to what it really was: the mind of God; and it was the nearest that he could get to the "Son of God" of later Christian belief. Within his human life he would never have been able to grasp that the changing patterns of action that constituted who he was were changing patterns of action that constituted God, so emerging from his subconscious mind would have been a slow recognition that he might in different ways be the fulfilment of prophecies scattered across the scriptures; and he might finally have recognized that all of them referred to the person that he was: hence that "I am," which perhaps he and the High Priest would have recognized as a name of God.[709] But those scattered and then coalescing recognitions were the result of something that could not have come together either in his conscious mind, and probably not in his subconscious mind either: an understanding that can now be ours—that here was God, living our human life, and about to suffer human death, because only in that way could reconciliation occur between God and ourselves.

And might this process have been repeated in other ways during Jesus' life? Jesus would not have been able to understand himself as God going to Jerusalem to suffer a human death in order to achieve reconciliation—reconciliation because then God would eternally experience human life and death: but what was available to Jesus was an understanding stretching across the Jewish law that reconciliation with God could be achieved by a ransom being paid for sin. That is a way in which Jesus could have understood himself as achieving reconciliation between God and humanity, so that is what he said, that is what was written, and that is how Christians the world over still understand reconciliation between God and humanity. When Luke used Mark's Gospel as the backbone for his own, he left out Jesus' "For the Son of Man came not to be served but to serve, and to give his life a ransom for many,"[710] presumably because he thought that his Gentile readers, not being steeped in the Jewish law, would not have understood the reference.[711] This left Luke with something of a theological gap, because no longer could he construct a narrative as to how reconciliation between God and humanity had been achieved by Jesus' death. Luke's Gospel, and his Acts of the Apostles, regard Jesus' death as the necessary prelude to the resurrection, which is what his gospel and its sequel are all about. Jesus' death has no meaning of its own, and in this Luke differed profoundly from Paul. The task for us today is to construct a narrative that is true to the centrality of Jesus' death to reconciliation between God and humanity, without relying on the conceptual structures of the Jewish law: conceptual structures that have too often driven Christian theology into understanding God as demanding the suffering and death of his son: a narrative which for multiple reasons the Christian church should have banished from its theology centuries ago.

Mark has cleared the ground, but he has not constructed the new narrative required. He has gestured towards it by repeating, or himself phrasing, Jesus' response to the High Priest as "I am": both an affirmation that Jesus is "the Son of the Blessed," and the name that God gave to himself when he spoke to Moses from the burning bush.[712] We can now make the new narrative explicit. We can understand the changing patterns of action that constituted Jesus as changing patterns of action that constitute God, and Jesus' suffering and death as the suffering and death of God living a human life and dying a human death: and it is that that constitutes the reconciliation between God and humanity. It is not insignificant that Jesus' "I am" comes at just the point in time at which he is completely alone and facing his death.[713] It is here that reconciliation between God and humanity happens.

We can still, if we wish, continue to employ the notion of ransom: of God demanding a death to make reconciliation possible—but now it is God demanding a human death of God, which means, perhaps, Jesus demanding a human death of himself: although whether Jesus came to understand his death in that way we shall never know. What we can and must abandon is any notion of a parent demanding the death of their child. Whether or not we retain "ransom" language, Jesus' human experience of life, sin, suffering, betrayal, death, and so much else about human life, is now eternally among the changing patterns of action that constitute God. That is what reconciliation means. God is reconciled to us, so we can now be reconciled to God.

## MARK 15:1–20

> 15 As soon as it was morning, the chief priests held a consultation with the elders and scribes and the whole council. They bound Jesus, led him away, and

handed him over to Pilate. ² Pilate asked him, 'Are you the King of the Jews?' He answered him, 'You say so.' ³ Then the chief priests accused him of many things. ⁴ Pilate asked him again, 'Have you no answer? See how many charges they bring against you.' ⁵ But Jesus made no further reply, so that Pilate was amazed.

6 Now at the festival he used to release a prisoner for them, anyone for whom they asked. ⁷ Now a man called Barabbas was in prison with the rebels who had committed murder during the insurrection. ⁸ So the crowd came and began to ask Pilate to do for them according to his custom. ⁹ Then he answered them, 'Do you want me to release for you the King of the Jews?' ¹⁰ For he realized that it was out of jealousy that the chief priests had handed him over. ¹¹ But the chief priests stirred up the crowd to have him release Barabbas for them instead. ¹² Pilate spoke to them again, 'Then what do you wish me to do[e] with the man you call[f] the King of the Jews?' ¹³ They shouted back, 'Crucify him!' ¹⁴ Pilate asked them, 'Why, what evil has he done?' But they shouted all the more, 'Crucify him!' ¹⁵ So Pilate, wishing to satisfy the crowd, released Barabbas for them; and after flogging Jesus, he handed him over to be crucified.

16 Then the soldiers led him into the courtyard of the palace (that is, the governor's headquarters[g]); and they called together the whole cohort. ¹⁷ And they clothed him in a purple cloak; and after twisting some thorns into a crown, they put it on him. ¹⁸ And they began saluting him, 'Hail, King of the Jews!' ¹⁹ They struck his head with a reed, spat upon him, and knelt down in homage to him. ²⁰ After mocking him, they stripped him of the purple cloak and put his own clothes on him. Then they led him out to crucify him.[714]

The high priest had asked Jesus whether he was "the Messiah, the Son of the Blessed One?," and Jesus had given a straight answer: "I am." This had given to the Sanhedrin the basis of the kind of political charge that they would need to present to Pilate if they were to have any hope of Jesus being executed.[715] The trial before Pilate in many ways matches the structure of the one before the Sanhedrin,[716] but the question that he asked was a different one: "Are you the King of the Jews?" Maybe he asked it because the High Priest had suggested it; and perhaps he had already heard about Jesus' entry into Jerusalem on a donkey, and someone had explained to him the meaning of the symbolism. And perhaps the question was asked with a wry smile: for Jesus certainly did not look like a king; and he clearly had no means of taking power if he did think that he was one. Jesus now gave a very different answer from the one that he gave to the high priest: "You say so." He had understood that he was the Messiah and the Son of God. However, he was not sure whether "King of the Jews" was the right title. He was to be the king in the Kingdom of God, but that was to be a kingdom for all

e. Other ancient authorities read *what should I do*
f. Other ancient authorities lack *the many you call*
g. Gk *the praetorium*

nations, and not just for the Jews: so although he would be the servant king of the Jews, that was not all that he would be, which meant that to say that he would be king of the Jews would have been misleading. It would have been doubly misleading because Pilate would have had in his mind a king such as Herod: a puppet king who ruled with limited authority by permission of the Romans. Pilate presumably thought that Jesus wanted to be a king like Herod, but rather less pliable. Hence the question: and hence Jesus' evasive and ambiguous response. Pilate had asked the wrong question. Jesus had no intention of being king just of the Jews, and certainly no intention of being a king in anything like the way that Herod was.[717] As Jesus is recorded as saying to Pilate in John's Gospel: "My kingdom is not of this world." It would encompass this world, but it was not of this world.

And then before Pilate Jesus was silent: again reflecting the passage from Isaiah quoted below, and also one of the psalms:

> [12] Those who seek my life lay their snares;
>
> those who seek to hurt me speak of ruin,
>
> and meditate treachery all day long.
>
> [13] But I am like the deaf, I do not hear;
>
> like the mute, who cannot speak.
>
> [14] Truly, I am like one who does not hear,
>
> and in whose mouth is no retort.[718]

Is silence a pattern of action, or is it an absence of action? It is a pattern of action, because it is two people standing in close proximity to each other, either geographically or virtually, with one listening and one choosing not to speak, both of which result from changing patterns of action in the brain.

Pilate would have been no friend of the priests, and maybe he had warmed to Jesus: perhaps partly on the basis that my enemy's enemy is my friend. So he tried to find a way to release him. There is no independent evidence of a tradition of granting amnesties during festivals,[719] but it is possible that Pilate might have made an occasional habit of doing so; and if he did decide that on this occasion he would release a prisoner requested by the Jewish leaders, then he would no doubt have preferred to release Jesus and to crucify Barabbas, who had taken part in an armed rebellion against Roman rule. But the crowd was restless, and in the end Pilate could see no reason for not giving them what they wanted. So he released Barabbas—a probably unrepentant sinner in a unique manner set free by Jesus' crucifixion—and indulged the crowd by having Jesus flogged, presumably publicly.

And then the soldiers mocked Jesus, dressing him up as a king.[720] Normally it would have been a risky business dressing a prisoner in something royal-looking, putting a crown of thorns on his head, spitting on him, and pretending to do him homage: a senior officer watching them might have thought that the scene looked rather too like his soldiers mocking Caesar. But on this one occasion they all had an excuse: this man had been called the King of Jews, and they were going to show him that he really was not.

There is nothing surprising about any of this behavior by the priests, the crowd, Pilate, or the soldiers. The world is full of acts of cruelty. And now Jesus was feeling the full force of the cruelty listed in Isaiah's description of the suffering of the servant of God:

> ² For he grew up before him like a young plant,
>    and like a root out of dry ground;
> he had no form or majesty that we should look at him,
>    nothing in his appearance that we should desire him.
> ³ He was despised and rejected by others;
>    a man of suffering[u] and acquainted with infirmity;
> and as one from whom others hide their faces[v]
>    he was despised, and we held him of no account. . . .
> ⁷ He was oppressed, and he was afflicted,
>    yet he did not open his mouth;
> like a lamb that is led to the slaughter,
>    and like a sheep that before its shearers is silent,
>    so he did not open his mouth.[721]

But what was the causal link? Did the details of the suffering described in the Isaiah prophecy lead early Christians to assume that these things must have happened to Jesus,[722] or did Christians know that these things happened, and finding them prophesied enabled them to believe that the suffering of the Messiah was within God's will and was not simply an accident of history? Probably both.

The changing patterns of action that constituted Jesus were meeting the changing patterns of action that constituted the cruelty of the priests, the crowd, Pilate, and the soldiers, profoundly changing Jesus' changing patterns of action and therefore the changing patterns of action that constitute God. Here again is reconciliation: God suffering human cruelty—an experience that God now shares eternally with millions of people cruelly treated. Betrayal, injustice, cruelty: all of this is now changing patterns of action that constitute God.

Some in the crowd, and some of the priests, had no doubt gone home: but those who were still there would have witnessed Jesus being taken to be crucified at the rubbish tip outside the city walls. The Romans were practiced at providing cruel

---

u. Or *a man of sorrows*

v. Or *as one who hides his face from us*

spectacles for people's enjoyment, particularly in the Roman Coliseum, with its gladiator fights, and prisoners being dismembered by hungry big cats. And here was just another spectacle: a beaten Jesus being led out to be crucified. He would have been absolutely terrified, because he would have known what awaited him.

Is God a stranger to human emotion? God is Action, the source of all action, and changing patterns of action: changing patterns of action that ever since the universe's creation have engaged with the changing patterns of action that constitute the created order that emerged from the original chaos. The Hebrew scriptures record events and convictions that reveal God not only to be intimately involved with individuals, communities, nations, the planet, and the life of the planet, in all of their diversity, but to be emotionally engaged with all of it. In the Hebrew scriptures, God experiences joy, sorrow, anger, jealousy, and much more. But this was all emotion that God experienced in a relationship with humankind. It was not human emotion, and so was always analogous to human emotion rather than being human emotion. But now in Jesus something new and different has occurred. By living a human life, God has now experienced human emotion: human joy, human sorrow, human anger, human jealousy, human confusion, and much more: and now human terror as well. It was not only pain that Jesus was experiencing, but betrayal, confusion, abandonment, and fear at extreme levels. And so God, constituted by changing patterns of action that constituted Jesus as he was led away to be crucified, is eternally constituted by those changing patterns of action. That is never all that God is: God is Action, the source of all action, the one in whom changing patterns of action are transformed for the Kingdom of God, and the creative source of particular changing patterns of action that constitute who God is: but God is still the changing patterns of action that constituted Jesus on that day in Jerusalem. The betrayal, the confusion, the abandonment, and the abject terror. And perhaps that is why God has eternally been an emotional God: these changing patterns of action that constituted Jesus are eternally the changing patterns of action that constitute God: so the God borne witness to by the Hebrew scriptures is those changing patterns of action that constituted Jesus—it is in Jesus' deeply emotional life, and particularly in the emotional crisis of that Passover festival, that God's eternal emotions are rooted.

## MARK 15:21–41

> 21 They compelled a passer-by, who was coming in from the country, to carry his cross; it was Simon of Cyrene, the father of Alexander and Rufus. 22 Then they brought Jesus[h] to the place called Golgotha (which means the place of a skull). 23 And they offered him wine mixed with myrrh; but he did not take

---

h. Gk *him*

it. ²⁴ And they crucified him, and divided his clothes among them, casting lots to decide what each should take.

25 It was nine o'clock in the morning when they crucified him. ²⁶ The inscription of the charge against him read, 'The King of the Jews.' ²⁷ And with him they crucified two bandits, one on his right and one on his left.ⁱ ²⁹ Those who passed by deridedʲ him, shaking their heads and saying, 'Aha! You who would destroy the temple and build it in three days, ³⁰ save yourself, and come down from the cross!' ³¹ In the same way the chief priests, along with the scribes, were also mocking him among themselves and saying, 'He saved others; he cannot save himself. ³² Let the Messiah,ᵏ the King of Israel, come down from the cross now, so that we may see and believe.' Those who were crucified with him also taunted him.

33 When it was noon, darkness came over the whole landˡ until three in the afternoon. ³⁴ At three o'clock Jesus cried out with a loud voice, 'Eloi, Eloi, lema sabachthani?' which means, 'My God, my God, why have you forsaken me?'ᵐ ³⁵ When some of the bystanders heard it, they said, 'Listen, he is calling for Elijah.' ³⁶ And someone ran, filled a sponge with sour wine, put it on a stick, and gave it to him to drink, saying, 'Wait, let us see whether Elijah will come to take him down.' ³⁷ Then Jesus gave a loud cry and breathed his last. ³⁸ And the curtain of the temple was torn in two, from top to bottom. ³⁹ Now when the centurion, who stood facing him, saw that in this way heⁿ breathed his last, he said, 'Truly this man was God's Son!'ᵒ

40 There were also women looking on from a distance; among them were Mary Magdalene, and Mary the mother of James the younger and of Joses, and Salome. ⁴¹ These used to follow him and provided for him when he was in Galilee; and there were many other women who had come up with him to Jerusalem.[723]

There was nothing extraordinary about Jesus' crucifixion, and nothing surprising about the preliminaries; and for early Christians there would have been nothing surprising about Jesus the Messiah suffering like this, as it was prophesied in the Isaiah passage quoted above.[724] Jesus would have been hung on a cross, his weight suspended on his arms so that he would slowly asphyxiate, and he would have been naked to increase the ignominy of his death.[725] It was a common occurrence, and it is recorded as such, along with some significant details.

    i. Other ancient authorities add verse 28, *And the scripture was fulfilled that says, 'And he was counted among the lawless.'*
    j. Or *blasphemed*
    k. Or *the Christ*
    l. Or *earth*
    m. Other ancient authorities read *made me a reproach*
    n. Other ancient authorities add *cried out and*
    o. Or *a son of god*

Presumably Alexander and Rufus were members of the church for which Mark was writing, or were known to it. Was Simon of Cyrene's carrying of Jesus' cross the beginning of his own discipleship, or was he in the crowd because he was already a follower of Jesus? Is this Simon who carried Jesus' cross a recognition that the apostle Simon had not done so? And is the fact that his sons had gentile names a significant recognition that a gentile had followed Jesus on his way to crucifixion, carrying his cross?[726] We shall never know. What we do know is that this Simon carried Jesus' cross, and was no doubt honored in the church for having done so: and no doubt, by association, Alexander and Rufus would have been honored for being Simon's sons.[727]

It was a compassionate act to offer Jesus wine to drink. Why did Jesus not want to accept the gift of a minor dulling of the pain that he was about to suffer? Because the night before, he had vowed not to drink wine until he drank it in the Kingdom of God? Because he had chosen to experience as much pain as possible?[728] If so, might that have been because in the Garden of Gethsemane he had committed himself to drink the cup of suffering to the dregs? And perhaps he refused the wine because he believed that by doing that the requirement that there should be intense suffering before the birth of the Kingdom of God could be satisfied in full by his death, and the Kingdom could be brought to birth? We don't know. All we know is that Jesus did not drink the wine.

Once Jesus was hung on the cross and it was already difficult for him to breathe, the soldiers were sitting not far away throwing dice for his clothes—a fulfilment of Psalm 22 understood as prophecy:

> they divide my clothes among themselves,
>     and for my clothing they cast lots.[729]

Further echoes of the same psalm can be found throughout the account of Jesus' crucifixion, and particularly in Jesus' words from the cross: so what was the causal connection? Did early Christians and Mark know Psalm 22, know that Jesus had quoted it, and therefore decided that the soldiers must have divided his clothes among them?[730] Or was this a common practice among Roman soldiers after they had hung their victims naked on their crosses? Probably both. What mattered to the early Christians is that what happened to Jesus "fulfilled" the scriptures, as Jesus had predicted that it would.[731]

The "bandits" crucified with Jesus might not have been simply thieves: they might have been insurrectionists, and so might have known Barabbas, and might also have known that he had been released because Jesus had not been.[732] If this was the case, then their attitude to Jesus would have been complicated. We do not hear their words, as we do in Luke's Gospel: all we hear is that they taunted Jesus. We do hear about the mocking words of the inscription fixed to the cross to tell passers-by what crime had been committed:[733] words that were more true than they would have realized, but representing for Jesus a pattern of action very different from the one that the onlookers might have had in their minds. And we hear the words of the mockery of the priests and the passers-by, which Jesus might or might not have been able to hear. Again the words about the temple are repeated: so perhaps Jesus really did say them.

The words that Jesus spoke in what was probably Aramaic,[734] "Eloi, Eloi, lema sabachthani?" are from the beginning of Psalm 22:

> 1 My God, my God, why have you forsaken me?
> 
> > Why are you so far from helping me, from the words of my groaning?[735]

God is still Jesus' God, but it is as "God" that God is addressed, and not as a Father whose will Jesus is determined to do. The sense of abandonment is obvious.[736] Did Jesus mean to quote only the first line? Or perhaps the first verse? Or did he mean to continue to quote the psalm, but was unable to do so? Or did the first verse imply the rest of the psalm, and so represent a whole complex pattern of action from suffering to vindication?[737]

> 2 O my God, I cry by day, but you do not answer;
> 
> > and by night, but find no rest.
> 
> 3 Yet you are holy,
> 
> > enthroned on the praises of Israel.
> 
> 4 In you our ancestors trusted;
> 
> > they trusted, and you delivered them.
> 
> 5 To you they cried, and were saved;
> 
> > in you they trusted, and were not put to shame. . . .
> 
> 21 . . . From the horns of the wild oxen you have rescued[z] me.
> 
> 22 I will tell of your name to my brothers and sisters;[a]
> 
> > in the midst of the congregation I will praise you:
> 
> 23 You who fear the LORD, praise him!
> 
> > All you offspring of Jacob, glorify him;
> > 
> > stand in awe of him, all you offspring of Israel!
> 
> 24 For he did not despise or abhor
> 
> > the affliction of the afflicted;
> > 
> > he did not hide his face from me,[b]
> > 
> > but heard when I[c] cried to him.[738]

z. Heb *answered*
a. Or *kindred*
b. Heb *him*
c. Heb *he*

If Jesus quoted only the first line, or the first verse, then he was feeling utterly abandoned by God: yet another human emotion to add to the list that was now the experience of God. Was he looking into the abyss, and recognizing that maybe death was the end—for himself, for humanity, for any hope of the Kingdom of God's coming? That if there was a God, then either God was powerless, or God did not want to rescue him: both options beyond appalling. And did this first line of the psalm mean that God had indeed abandoned Jesus: that the relationship was at an end—that within God there was experience of the human death of God? But if Jesus intended to continue to quote from the psalm, or the first verse was intended to stand for the whole psalm, then the meaning was very different: the cry from the cross was one of trust in God:[739] that God would rescue him from death, somehow, and that the Kingdom of God would be established.

Either way, the fact that what was happening mirrored a pattern of action to be found in the scriptures revealed it to be within God's will,[740] and so Jesus really was abandoned by God. He had already been abandoned by his disciples, denied by Peter, condemned by both Jewish and Roman authorities, and rejected by the crowd: and now God too had abandoned him.[741] Was this Jesus' humanity, now completely identified with all of sinful humanity, being abandoned by a righteous God?[742] There is no reason to think so. It was God's love for humanity that had given birth to the human life of God. Far from abandoning humanity, God was here utterly identified with us: as identified with us as God could possibly be, by dying a human death. Jesus was abandoned to death by God: God was abandoned to death by God. God was about to die, and God would experience that. Here was a suffering beyond what the universe had ever known, and beyond what had ever been known in any realm of reality.

The bystanders might have been right. Perhaps Jesus was calling for Elijah. Jesus had already recognized that John the Baptist was Elijah, because the changing patterns of action that constituted John were those that constituted Elijah, the prophet who had been taken directly into heaven to await the time at which he would announce the coming of the Messiah who would establish God's reign. Perhaps Jesus was calling him now. Or perhaps he wasn't. Perhaps they were just mishearing the "Eloi, Eloi," "my God, my God," as "Elijah, Elijah." And what was the darkness? Passover is at full moon, so the darkness could not have been an eclipse:[743] so what was it?

Then Jesus died. A death like any other, but far more painful than most.

We do not know which of two temple curtains was torn from top to bottom: the direction of the tear implying that only God could have done it. If it was the outer curtain then the tearing would have been a public event and would have referenced the destruction of the temple that would follow forty or so years later. If it was the inner curtain, then the tearing would not have been visible to the general public, but it would have made accessible the Holy of Holies to which only the High Priest would normally have had access just once a year. The theological meanings of the two tearings would have been different—the one implying a new age without the temple, and the other a new and unmediated relationship between God and humanity—but both would have presaged the beginning of a new age and of a new covenant.[744]

Whether a curtain was torn, or the words are a figurative statement, is not at issue. The restrictive and oppressive temple cult was at an end.[745] No longer was God hidden from the depths of human experience. Reconciliation had been achieved. The changing patterns of action that constitute human life and death were now eternally changing patterns of action that constitute God. And there was a deeper meaning still: God had been rent in two by Jesus' death: God had experienced the death of God. The torn curtain represented both a rending and the uniting that that achieved.

And then for the first time in Mark's Gospel, a human being declares Jesus to be "Son of God."[746] The centurion has seen "this man" both dying and dead, and knows that he is "God's Son." What the centurion might have meant by this would probably not have been what a Christian might have meant or might mean today—the pattern of action in the centurion's mind that gave birth to those words would no doubt have been very different from any pattern of action that might emerge in the minds of anyone who might encounter the pure pattern of those written words today:[747] and what no-one at that time might have felt able to say was that "this man" was God.

Maybe the centurion did recognize who Jesus was. If he had declared Jesus to be a god, which as a Roman would have been a possibility, then this is not what early Jewish Christians would have been able to repeat, and it is not what Mark would have been able to write. The closest they could get was "Son of God": a designation of the kings of Israel. Whether the centurion called Jesus a god or Son of God, he had grasped something of cosmic significance that we can now put like this: Jesus was God dying on a cross; and he was the King whose kingdom was not of this world but would be. And crucially, as far as Mark's Gospel is concerned, the patterns of action represented by "Son of God" and by abandonment by God are entirely compatible,[748] which from the moment of Jesus' crucifixion they are.

At least Jesus did not die entirely alone. His chosen apostles had fled, but the women who had accompanied him during his ministry were still there, watching the gruesome execution: and it is clear from Mark's statement about them that although they had received no attention from him throughout his gospel, they had been as much disciples of Jesus as the men who had been so central to his narrative.[749] It is these women who were the followers—the disciples—at Jesus' crucifixion.[750] Jesus might or might not have been aware of their presence.

Jesus was now dead: The life of God living a human life among us had come to an end: the same end that faces every one of us. Perhaps the poet who has got closest to expressing that is the First World War chaplain and poet Geoffrey Studdert Kennedy, whose experience of the horror of the trenches had led him to the conviction that only a God who had suffered all of that with us could be God for us: and that therefore the Jesus who was dead on a cross was God dead on a cross: our "comrade God." In the poem there is no mention of "Jesus" or "Christ": only of God.

> Only in Him can I find home to hide me,
> 
> Who on the cross was slain to rise again;
> 
> Only with Him, my Comrade God, beside me,
> 
> Can I go forth to war with sin and pain.[751]

It was God who was crucified and who therefore eternally suffers and dies with us. This is how reconciliation constantly occurs. First century Christians would not have been able to put it like that: but Studdert Kennedy could, and so can we.

As the last line of the poem suggests, that was not the end for the God who had experienced human death. Jesus' hope had not been wrong.

## MARK 15:42–16:8

> 42 When evening had come, and since it was the day of Preparation, that is, the day before the sabbath, 43 Joseph of Arimathea, a respected member of the council, who was also himself waiting expectantly for the kingdom of God, went boldly to Pilate and asked for the body of Jesus. 44 Then Pilate wondered if he were already dead; and summoning the centurion, he asked him whether he had been dead for some time. 45 When he learned from the centurion that he was dead, he granted the body to Joseph. 46 Then Joseph[p] bought a linen cloth, and taking down the body[q] wrapped it in the linen cloth, and laid it in a tomb that had been hewn out of the rock. He then rolled a stone against the door of the tomb. 47 Mary Magdalene and Mary the mother of Joses saw where the body was laid.
> 
> 16 When the sabbath was over, Mary Magdalene, and Mary the mother of James, and Salome bought spices, so that they might go and anoint him. 2 And very early on the first day of the week, when the sun had risen, they went to the tomb. 3 They had been saying to one another, 'Who will roll away the stone for us from the entrance to the tomb?' 4 When they looked up, they saw that the stone, which was very large, had already been rolled back. 5 As they entered the tomb, they saw a young man, dressed in a white robe, sitting on the right

p. Gk *he*
q. Gk *it*

side; and they were alarmed. ⁶ But he said to them, 'Do not be alarmed; you are looking for Jesus of Nazareth, who was crucified. He has been raised; he is not here. Look, there is the place they laid him. ⁷ But go, tell his disciples and Peter that he is going ahead of you to Galilee; there you will see him, just as he told you.' ⁸ So they went out and fled from the tomb, for terror and amazement had seized them; and they said nothing to anyone, for they were afraid.ʳ ⁷⁵²

Perhaps there were many like Joseph of Arimathea: conscious that there was something special about Jesus, and hoping that he really would bring in the Kingdom of God that his teaching and healings so vividly promised. And perhaps he was wondering whether Jesus' promise of his resurrection after three days might be true: so a rock tomb was required, and not a burial in the ground.

As we discovered in chapter 6, it was John the Baptist's disciples who buried his body when he was murdered by Herod. This is what disciples do.⁷⁵³ This is not what Jesus' disciples did: it was left to someone on the fringe of the community around Jesus—someone who if a disciple at all was a secret one—to fulfil what the Jews would have regarded as a pious act.⁷⁵⁴ Even though the apostles had disappeared themselves, the women were watching where Jesus was buried, and as soon as the sabbath was over they went to fulfil their culture's normal burial customs for which there had not been time before the burial.

Who was the young man? Might it have been Mark? Or a heavenly messenger?⁷⁵⁵ But rather more importantly: Is this a story that Christians told to express their conviction that Jesus was risen from the dead, just as Jesus told stories to express his conviction that the Kingdom of God would soon be established; or is it an account of events that took place? The first thing to say is that Jesus' resurrection requires neither an empty tomb nor resurrection appearances. Neither appear in the Letter to the Hebrews, where Jesus is described as "a great high priest who has passed through the heavens,"⁷⁵⁶ nor in the early Christian hymn that Paul quotes in his letter to the church in Philippi:

> ⁵ Let the same mind be in you that wasⁱ in Christ Jesus,
>
> ⁶ who, though he was in the form of God,
>> did not regard equality with God
>> as something to be exploited,
>
> ⁷ but emptied himself,
>> taking the form of a slave,
>> being born in human likeness.

r. Some of the most ancient authorities bring the book to a close at the end of verse 8. One authority concludes the book with the shorter ending; others include the shorter ending and then continue with verses 9–20. In most authorities verses 9–20 follow immediately after verse 8, though in some of these authorities the passage is marked as being doubtful.

i. Or *that you have*

> ⁸ And being found in human form,
>> he humbled himself
>> and became obedient to the point of death—
>> even death on a cross.
> ⁹ Therefore God also highly exalted him
>> and gave him the name
>> that is above every name,
> ¹⁰ so that at the name of Jesus
>> every knee should bend,
>> in heaven and on earth and under the earth,
> ¹¹ and every tongue should confess
>> that Jesus Christ is Lord,
>> to the glory of God the Father.⁷⁵⁷

This is exaltation to be with God, with strong echoes of the prophecy in Daniel of

> one like a human being[b]
>> coming with the clouds of heaven.
> And he came to the Ancient One[c]
>> and was presented before him.⁷⁵⁸

The crucifixion is here followed by the exaltation. There is no empty tomb, and there are no resurrection appearances. And perhaps the stories about Jesus' ascension in Matthew's and Luke's Gospels, and at the beginning of the Acts of the Apostles, carry the same message: Jesus had died, and is now with God, and his reign as king in the Kingdom of God has already begun.

But there is a good reason for thinking that Mark is here recording a remembered event: There would have been members of his church who had known those who were eyewitnesses to the events that he was recording. Would he have written his account of the empty tomb if it had not been a remembered event communicated from person to person in the churches?

As has often occurred as we have read Mark's Gospel, we are left with a question: Is the changing pattern of action represented by the pure pattern of the text the changing pattern of action that constitutes narratives told within the church to express Jesus' exaltation to be with God, or does it represent the changing pattern of action that constituted events that happened outside Jerusalem approximately two thousand years ago? Either way, Jesus is risen from the dead; and either way, the Kingdom of God has been established, and Jesus is its servant king.

---

b. Aram *one like a son of man*
c. Aram *the Ancient of Days*

There is one final question to ponder: Why does Mark's Gospel end so abruptly? All of the other gospels end with resurrection appearances: Jesus appears to his disciples in what can only be described as the "spiritual body" that Paul talked about in his letter to the church in Corinth.[759] Mark's Gospel ends with "for they were afraid": *ephobounto gar*, and so with a preposition. There are two main possibilities: Either Mark did write about resurrection appearances, and the end of the original manuscript was lost; or Mark intended to end his gospel in this way.

To take the first possibility: The history of variant manuscripts tells us that accounts of resurrection appearances were added at a later stage, and appear to rely partly on the later gospels. This suggests that all of the extant earlier manuscripts of Mark's Gospel were without accounts of resurrection appearances. It is fairly likely that copies would have been made of Mark's text soon after it was written so that it could be read by other churches, and it is difficult to believe that even if a portion of the original manuscript had become detached, such significant events as resurrection appearances would not have been written into copies of the text: but it is possible that the final page of one of the early complete copies was lost, and also that copies of the original were also lost, so that what was copied thereafter was an incomplete manuscript. As to what an original ending might have contained, the best guess might be a resurrection appearance to the women that encouraged them to speak to the male disciples about their experience rather than remain silent, followed by a meeting between the disciples and Jesus in Galilee, as promised by the young man at the tomb.[760]

Now let us assume that Mark had meant to finish his gospel in this way. Why would he have done that? Perhaps with the purpose of leaving his readers asking what happened next, so that they might realize that they themselves were the continuation of the story: that it was now in them that the Kingdom of God was to come near. Throughout the gospel Jesus has told people to keep secret the activity that was the Kingdom of God coming near, both to preserve his ability to teach and to heal, and to prevent premature misunderstanding. Now the women are told to go to tell the other disciples what they had experienced, and they did not, at least initially.[761] They were terrified. Something out of this world had taken place, something indescribable. There would be ways of telling it, but not yet. Whole new changing patterns of action had taken place. The women had been terrified into silence, but now Mark's readers, having read the whole of the gospel, were in a position to tell the world that the promised Kingdom of God had come in the risen Christ. The way in which Mark completed his gospel could have been a purposeful strategy designed to inspire Christians to fulfil that task. He began his gospel with "The beginning of the good news[a] of Jesus Christ . . . ."[762] What he had written was merely the beginning. The rest was still to come, both in the life of the church, and in Jesus' return and the final establishment of the Kingdom of God in which he would reign as the servant king.

a. Or *gospel*

## Mark's Gospel: An Actological Reading

There is a third possible explanation for the abrupt ending of Mark's Gospel. There was an empty tomb, with a young man sitting in it and giving the message recorded in the text. The women did eventually tell the disciples what they had found at the tomb, the disciples did go to Galilee, and they did see Jesus: because, as we have already noted, there would have been people in the church that Mark was writing for who would have known eyewitnesses of these events. So why didn't Mark write about that meeting? Again, we must raise the possibility that he did, and that that part of his manuscript was lost; but we are also left with the possibility that Mark did not write about the meeting between Jesus and his disciples because it was indescribable. The confused accounts that he had heard did not fit together into a coherent narrative, and every time he tried to create a coherent account, he found that he could not, so he gave up trying. The Kingdom of God had broken into human history, so perhaps it is not surprising that words failed Mark as he tried again and again to put the indescribable into words. If Mark had originally written a longer ending for his gospel, then perhaps it was Mark himself who tore it off. The result is that he has left us knowing that Jesus is going ahead of his disciples to Galilee: Jesus is on the way, still journeying, and inviting us to follow him. This is the pattern of action to which we are invited: a following of Jesus. Mark began his gospel with "The beginning of the good news[a] . . . ."[763] The good news has not ended with the end of the gospel: it continues as the patterns of action represented in it continue to be patterns of action today that call us to conform the patterns of action that constitute who we are to those that constitute the Kingdom of God of which Jesus is now King.

As we have read Mark's Gospel, we have developed two intertwined narratives: that Jesus is the servant of God who suffers death, is revealed to be the "one like a son of man," and who receives authority to rule in the Kingdom of God; and that Jesus is changing patterns of action that constitute God. While we have intertwined the narratives, they have still been separate accounts. We must now bring them together, as we began to do when discussing the account of the woman who anointed Jesus in the house of Simon the leper.[764]

Jesus, the human being who suffers, dies, and is vindicated as the one who will rule in the Kingdom of God, is the one who is constituted by changing patterns of action that constitute God in a way in which no other human being is constituted by such changing patterns of action. And so it is this human being who is God who is "presented to the Ancient One," and who is forever God and ruling in God's Kingdom.

This is my reading of Mark's Gospel. I don't expect it to be yours: but I hope that it will at least encourage you to read Mark's Gospel, and to ask yourself what your own reading of it is.

a. Or *gospel*

# Endnotes

1. NRSV-ANG.
2. France, *The Gospel of Mark*, 24, 27.
3. Cranfield, *The Gospel according to Mark*, 38; France, *The Gospel of Mark*, 49.
4. Matt 1:21, NRSV-ANG.
5. Myers, *Binding the Strong Man*, 64.
6. Myers, *Binding the Strong Man*, 135; Malbon, *Hearing Mark*, 12.
7. Cranfield, *The Gospel according to Mark*, 35–36.
8. Williams, *Meeting God in Mark*, 6–7.
9. NRSV-ANG.
10. Mal 3:1, NRSV-ANG.
11. Myers, *Binding the Strong Man*, 91–136.
12. Myers, *Binding the Strong Man*, 75.
13. Isa 40:3, NRSV-ANG; Cranfield, *The Gospel according to Mark*, 39.
14. NRSV-ANG.
15. Cranfield, *The Gospel according to Mark*, 34–37.
16. France, *The Gospel of Mark*, 10, 88.
17. Wright, *Meeting God in Mark*, 2.
18. John 3:22.
19. Mark 2:15–17.
20. Acts 2:38, NRSV-ANG.
21. France, *The Gospel of Mark*, 55–56.
22. Mark 1:10.
23. Joel 2:28, NRSV-ANG; Cranfield, *The Gospel according to Mark*, 50.
24. Isa 11:1–2, NRSV-ANG.
25. Isa 42:1, NRSV-ANG.
26. Acts 16:7; Phil 1:19.
27. Gal 5:22.
28. Gen 1:2, NRSV-ANG.
29. John 3:8, NRSV-ANG.
30. Acts 2:2–3, NRSV-ANG.
31. Acts 8:12–16, 36–38; 9:18; 10:47–48; 16:15, 33; 18:8, 25; 19:3.
32. NRSV-ANG.
33. Cranfield, *The Gospel according to Mark*, 52.
34. Heb 4:15, NRSV-ANG.
35. Heb 5:1–10.
36. Heb 5:9, NRSV-ANG.
37. Heb 5:9.
38. For instance, Mark 7:24–30.
39. Heb 4:15; 5:8–9, NRSV-ANG.
40. NRSV-ANG
41. Cranfield, *The Gospel according to Mark*, 52.

# Endnotes

42. Matt 3:16.
43. Luke 3:21–22, NRSV-ANG.
44. John 1:32, NRSV-ANG.
45. France, *The Gospel of Mark*, 74.
46. Wright, *Meeting God in Mark*, 5.
47. Mark 15:38–9; France, *The Gospel of Mark*, 74.
48. Mark 14:36, NRSV-ANG.
49. NRSV-ANG.
50. Ps 2:7; Isa 42:1, NRSV-ANG.
51. Mark 14:36, NRSV-ANG.
52. Myers, *Binding the Strong Man*, 120.
53. NRSV-ANG.
54. Cranfield, *The Gospel according to Mark*, 56–57.
55. Myers, *Binding the Strong Man*, 135; Nineham, *The Gospel of St. Mark*, 63.
56. NRSV-ANG.
57. Cranfield, *The Gospel according to Mark*, 58.
58. France, *The Gospel of Mark*, 83.
59. Cranfield, *The Gospel according to Mark*, 58; France, *The Gospel of Mark*, 84.
60. Cranfield, *The Gospel according to Mark*, 59.
61. Cranfield, *The Gospel according to Mark*, 60.
62. Nineham, *The Gospel of St. Mark*, 63.
63. NRSV-ANG.
64. Mark 1:7, NRSV-ANG.
65. Myers, *Binding the Strong Man*, 91.
66. Nineham, *The Gospel of St. Mark*, 67.
67. France, *The Gospel of Mark*, 11–12.
68. Malbon, *Hearing Mark*, 16–17.
69. Nineham, *The Gospel of St. Mark*, 68.
70. France, *The Gospel of Mark*, 30.
71. Cranfield, *The Gospel according to Mark*, 64.
72. Cranfield, *The Gospel according to Mark*, 66; France, *The Gospel of Mark*, 30.
73. Williams, *Meeting God in Mark*, 7.
74. Williams, *Meeting God in Mark*, 8.
75. France, *The Gospel of Mark*, 93.
76. NRSV-ANG.
77. Nineham, *The Gospel of St. Mark*, 70–71.
78. Myers, *Binding the Strong Man*, 120.
79. NRSV-ANG.
80. France, *The Gospel of Mark*, 99.
81. Nineham, *The Gospel of St. Mark*, 67.
82. Wright, *Meeting God in Mark*, 11–12.
83. Cranfield, *The Gospel according to Mark*, 77.
84. Nineham, *The Gospel of St. Mark*, 75.
85. France, *The Gospel of Mark*, 100–101.
86. Nineham, *The Gospel of St. Mark*, 80.
87. France, *The Gospel of Mark*, 43–44.
88. NRSV-ANG.
89. NRSV-ANG.
90. Cranfield, *The Gospel according to Mark*, 84–86.
91. NRSV-ANG.
92. Cranfield, *The Gospel according to Mark*, 88–89.
93. Matt 6:10, NRSV-ANG.
94. Cranfield, *The Gospel according to Mark*, 89–90.

# Endnotes

95. Malbon, *Hearing Mark*, 20.
96. NRSV-ANG.
97. Cranfield, *The Gospel according to Mark*, 92; Williams, *Meeting God in Mark*, 34.
98. Cranfield, *The Gospel according to Mark*, 91.
99. Cranfield, *The Gospel according to Mark*, 94.
100. Wright, *Meeting God in Mark*, 13–15.
101. Cranfield, *The Gospel according to Mark*, 95.
102. NRSV-ANG.
103. France, *The Gospel of Mark*, 114–15.
104. Heb 11:1, NRSV-ANG.
105. Williams, *Meeting God in Mark*, 36.
106. Nineham, *The Gospel of St. Mark*, 91–92.
107. Mark 8:11.
108. John 9:2.
109. France, *The Gospel of Mark*, 125.
110. Cranfield, *The Gospel according to Mark*, 100.
111. Cranfield, *The Gospel according to Mark*, 276.
112. Dan 7:9–14, NRSV-ANG. In Daniel 7:13, the original means "Son of man." It might have been better to leave the translation like that rather than interpret it as "human being."
113. France, *The Gospel of Mark*, 127–28.
114. Cranfield, *The Gospel according to Mark*, 274.
115. Wright, *Meeting God in Mark*, 17.
116. NRSV-ANG.
117. Cranfield, *The Gospel according to Mark*, 102; France, *The Gospel of Mark*, 132; Wright, *Meeting God in Mark*, 20.
118. Cranfield, *The Gospel according to Mark*, 104–105.
119. Mark 12:18–27.
120. Nineham, *The Gospel of St. Mark*, 96–97.
121. Matt 21:31, NRSV-ANG.
122. France, *The Gospel of Mark*, 131.
123. Nineham, *The Gospel of St. Mark*, 98.
124. For instance, Acts 11:3 and Gal 2:12.
125. Cranfield, *The Gospel according to Mark*, 101.
126. NRSV-ANG.
127. Cranfield, *The Gospel according to Mark*, 108; France, *The Gospel of Mark*, 137–38.
128. Mark 4:29.
129. Luke 14:13–23.
130. Nineham, *The Gospel of St. Mark*, 102.
131. Isa 53:8, NRSV-ANG; Cranfield, *The Gospel according to Mark*, 110.
132. NRSV-ANG.
133. NRSV-ANG.
134. Cranfield, *The Gospel according to Mark*, 115.
135. Wright, *Meeting God in Mark*, 27,
136. France, *The Gospel of Mark*, 145.
137. Cranfield, *The Gospel according to Mark*, 118.
138. Nineham, *The Gospel of St. Mark*, 105–106.
139. Deut, 23:25; Cranfield, *The Gospel according to Mark*, 114.
140. Exodus 20:10, NRSV-ANG.
141. NRSV-ANG.
142. Myers, *Binding the Strong Man*, 140.
143. Nineham, *The Gospel of St. Mark*, 110.
144. Cranfield, *The Gospel according to Mark*, 121; Williams, *Meeting God in Mark*, 34.
145. For instance: Josh 8; Deut 1:34–45.

# Endnotes

146. Wright, *Meeting God in Mark*, 29–31.
147. NRSV-ANG.
148. NRSV-ANG.
149. Nineham, *The Gospel of St. Mark*, 114; France, *The Gospel of Mark*, 159.
150. France, *The Gospel of Mark*, 159–60.
151. France, *The Gospel of Mark*, 163.
152. Wright, *Meeting God in Mark*, 34.
153. Nineham, *The Gospel of St. Mark*, 115.
154. Cranfield, *The Gospel according to Mark*, 128.
155. Malbon, *Hearing Mark*, 26.
156. 1 Cor 12; Eph 4:1–16.
157. NRSV-ANG.
158. Gen 1:2.
159. Wright, *Meeting God in Mark*, 36.
160. France, *The Gospel of Mark*, 171.
161. Nineham, *The Gospel of St. Mark*, 44–45.
162. Myers, *Binding the Strong Man*, 137.
163. France, *The Gospel of Mark*, 171, 173.
164. Malbon, *Hearing Mark*, 27.
165. Nineham, *The Gospel of St. Mark*, 118.
166. France, *The Gospel of Mark*, 177.
167. Cranfield, *The Gospel according to Mark*, 142.
168. NRSV-ANG.
169. France, *The Gospel of Mark*, 156–57, 186.
170. Nineham, *The Gospel of St. Mark*, 122–23.
171. Mark 10:24, NRSV-ANG.
172. John 13:1–20; 19:26
173. Mark 6:3, NRSV-ANG.
174. Mark 1:14–15; France, *The Gospel of Mark*, 180.
175. France, *The Gospel of Mark*, 178.
176. NRSV-ANG.
177. Malbon, *Hearing Mark*, 29.
178. France, *The Gospel of Mark*, 183.
179. France, *The Gospel of Mark*, 184.
180. Cranfield, *The Gospel according to Mark*, 150.
181. France, *The Gospel of Mark*, 189.
182. Isa 55:10–13, NRSV-ANG.
183. Wright, *Meeting God in Mark*, 43.
184. Nineham, *The Gospel of St. Mark*, 132.
185. Nineham, *The Gospel of St. Mark*, 130.
186. NRSV-ANG.
187. Nineham, *The Gospel of St. Mark*, 131.
188. France, *The Gospel of Mark*, 194–95.
189. France, *The Gospel of Mark*, 199.
190. Isa 6:10.
191. Nineham, *The Gospel of St. Mark*, 137; Malbon, *Hearing Mark*, 31.
192. Cranfield, *The Gospel according to Mark*, 153.
193. France, *The Gospel of Mark*, 199.
194. Cranfield, *The Gospel according to Mark*, 157.
195. France, *The Gospel of Mark*, 200–201.
196. Williams, *Meeting God in Mark*, 42.
197. Mark 4:22; France, *The Gospel of Mark*, 201.
198. Nineham, *The Gospel of St. Mark*, 133, 140.

# Endnotes

199. France, *The Gospel of Mark*, 202–203.
200. Cranfield, *The Gospel according to Mark*, 160.
201. Nineham, *The Gospel of St. Mark*, 131.
202. Cranfield, *The Gospel according to Mark*, 158–61.
203. NRSV-ANG.
204. Cranfield, *The Gospel according to Mark*, 164–65.
205. France, *The Gospel of Mark*, 209–210.
206. Cranfield, *The Gospel according to Mark*, 165.
207. Nineham, *The Gospel of St. Mark*, 32.
208. Matt 6:14–15; 18:23–32.
209. Matt 25:14–30
210. Nineham, *The Gospel of St. Mark*, 142.
211. NRSV-ANG.
212. France, *The Gospel of Mark*, 212.
213. Mark 4:1–9.
214. France, *The Gospel of Mark*, 214–15.
215. Joel 3:12–13, NRSV-ANG; Wright, *Meeting God in Mark*, 48.
216. NRSV-ANG.
217. France, *The Gospel of Mark*, 217.
218. Ezek 17:22–23, NRSV-ANG; Wright, *Meeting God in Mark*, 50.
219. Malbon, *Hearing Mark*, 33.
220. Matt 21:31.
221. NRSV-ANG.
222. France, *The Gospel of Mark*, 219–20.
223. France, *The Gospel of Mark*, 222, 224–25.
224. Gen 1:1–2.
225. Pss 89:8–9; 93:3–4; 106: 8–9; Isa 51:9b–10; Nineham, *The Gospel of St. Mark*, 146–47.
226. Dan 7:13, NRSV-ANG.
227. Ps 44:23–24; 104:6–7.
228. Nineham, *The Gospel of St. Mark*, 147.
229. Wright, *Meeting God in Mark*, 52–53.
230. Heb 11:1, NRSV-ANG.
231. Malbon, *Hearing Mark*, 37.
232. NRSV-ANG.
233. Nineham, *The Gospel of St. Mark*, 153.
234. Nineham, *The Gospel of St. Mark*, 153.
235. Cranfield, *The Gospel according to Mark*, 180.
236. Wright, *Meeting God in Mark*, 57.
237. Nineham, *The Gospel of St. Mark*, 151.
238. Mark 6:11.
239. Mark 5:16; France, *The Gospel of Mark*, 231.
240. Cranfield, *The Gospel according to Mark*, 182.
241. France, *The Gospel of Mark*, 233.
242. NRSV-ANG.
243. Cranfield, *The Gospel according to Mark*, 185.
244. Nineham, *The Gospel of St. Mark*, 158.
245. Williams, *Meeting God in Mark*, 36.
246. France, *The Gospel of Mark*, 235.
247. Nineham, *The Gospel of St. Mark*, 160.
248. John 11:1–44.
249. Cranfield, *The Gospel according to Mark*, 189.
250. Myers, *Binding the Strong Man*, 197–98.
251. NRSV-ANG.

## Endnotes

252. John 19:27; Acts 1:14.
253. Isa 8:14; 28:16; Nineham, *The Gospel of St. Mark*, 163, 165.
254. France, *The Gospel of Mark*, 241–42.
255. Luke 1:46–55.
256. Mark 4:24; Matt 25:14–30.
257. Cranfield, *The Gospel according to Mark*, 197.
258. NRSV-ANG.
259. France, *The Gospel of Mark*, 245.
260. France, *The Gospel of Mark*, 246–47.
261. Cranfield, *The Gospel according to Mark*, 200.
262. France, *The Gospel of Mark*, 247.
263. Nineham, *The Gospel of St. Mark*, 169.
264. Cranfield, *The Gospel according to Mark*, 203.
265. Luke 10:29–37.
266. Jas 5:14.
267. Malbon, *Hearing Mark*, 42.
268. NRSV-ANG.
269. Mal 4:5.
270. Nineham, *The Gospel of St. Mark*, 173.
271. France, *The Gospel of Mark*, 252–53
272. NRSV-ANG.
273. Cranfield, *The Gospel according to Mark*, 214–15.
274. Myers, *Binding the Strong Man*, 205–207.
275. Cranfield, *The Gospel according to Mark*, 216, 221.
276. Wright, *Meeting God in Mark*, 79.
277. France, *The Gospel of Mark*, 267.
278. Cranfield, *The Gospel according to Mark*, 222.
279. Nineham, *The Gospel of St. Mark*, 179.
280. Isa 25:6–8; 55; 65:13–14; Nineham, *The Gospel of St. Mark*, 179.
281. Nineham, *The Gospel of St. Mark*, 178.
282. John 6; Nineham, *The Gospel of St. Mark*, 179.
283. Luke 8:1–3.
284. NRSV-ANG.
285. France, *The Gospel of Mark*, 261–62.
286. Mark 14:36, NRSV-ANG.
287. Nineham, *The Gospel of St. Mark*, 181, 184.
288. Job 9:8; Ps 77:19; Isa 43:16; Nineham, *The Gospel of St. Mark*, 181.
289. Cranfield, *The Gospel according to Mark*, 228.
290. Wright, *Meeting God in Mark*, 83.
291. 1 Cor 16:22, NRSV-ANG.
292. Job 9:8, NRSV-ANG; Isa 43:16, NRSV-ANG; cf. Ps 77:19.
293. France, *The Gospel of Mark*, 270.
294. Exodus 3:14.
295. France, *The Gospel of Mark*, 274.
296. Malbon, *Hearing Mark*, 45.
297. NRSV-ANG.
298. Luke 24:13–35.
299. NRSV-ANG
300. Cranfield, *The Gospel according to Mark*, 236.
301. Wright, *Meeting God in Mark*, 86.
302. Acts 10:1–11:26.
303. France, *The Gospel of Mark*, 278.
304. Jer 31:33, NRSV-ANG; Cranfield, *The Gospel according to Mark*, 245.

## Endnotes

305. France, *The Gospel of Mark*, 292–94.
306. Nineham, *The Gospel of St. Mark*, 192.
307. NRSV-ANG.
308. France, *The Gospel of Mark*, 296.
309. Cranfield, *The Gospel according to Mark*, 248.
310. Cranfield, *The Gospel according to Mark*, 249.
311. Myers, *Binding the Strong Man*, 204.
312. France, *The Gospel of Mark*, 294.
313. France, *The Gospel of Mark*, 16.
314. Acts 13:46; 18:6.
315. Nineham, *The Gospel of St. Mark*, 200–201.
316. Heb 5:8.
317. NRSV-ANG.
318. Cranfield, *The Gospel according to Mark*, 252.
319. France, *The Gospel of Mark*, 303.
320. Isa 35:5–6, NRSV-ANG; Nineham, *The Gospel of St. Mark*, 202.
321. NRSV-ANG.
322. France, *The Gospel of Mark*, 307.
323. Nineham, *The Gospel of St. Mark*, 208; France, *The Gospel of Mark*, 305.
324. Nineham, *The Gospel of St. Mark*, 207.
325. Acts 15:1–35.
326. Acts 8:1–11:30; Gal 2:11–14; 1 Cor 11:17–12:31.
327. Malbon, *Hearing Mark*, 49.
328. NRSV-ANG.
329. Num 14:11, 22; Nineham, *The Gospel of St. Mark*, 210.
330. Deut 18:15.
331. France, *The Gospel of Mark*, 310.
332. John 14:6, NRSV-ANG.
333. NRSV-ANG.
334. France, *The Gospel of Mark*, 314.
335. Myers, *Binding the Strong Man*, 231.
336. NRSV-ANG.
337. France, *The Gospel of Mark*, 320–21.
338. Mark 7:31–37; Nineham, *The Gospel of St. Mark*, 217.
339. Nineham, *The Gospel of St. Mark*, 218.
340. France, *The Gospel of Mark*, 7.
341. Malbon, *Hearing Mark*, 52; Wright, *Meeting God in Mark*, 107.
342. Cranfield, *The Gospel according to Mark*, 268; France, *The Gospel of Mark*, 322–23.
343. Cranfield, *The Gospel according to Mark*, 270.
344. Wright, *Meeting God in Mark*, 108; France, *The Gospel of Mark*, 331.
345. France, *The Gospel of Mark*, 327.
346. Nineham, *The Gospel of St. Mark*, 224–25.
347. Myers, *Binding the Strong Man*, 235; Malbon, *Hearing Mark*, 58.
348. NRSV-ANG.
349. France, *The Gospel of Mark*, 333.
350. Cranfield, *The Gospel according to Mark*, 272–73, 275.
351. Isa 53:3–8, NRSV-ANG; Cranfield, *The Gospel according to Mark*, 277.
352. France, *The Gospel of Mark*, 334–35.
353. Nineham, *The Gospel of St. Mark*, 228.
354. Studdert Kennedy, *The Hardest Part*, 71, 95.
355. Studdert Kennedy, *The Hardest Part*, 131–32.
356. Nineham, *The Gospel of St. Mark*, 226; France, *The Gospel of Mark*, 339.
357. Myers, *Binding the Strong Man*, 11.

# Endnotes

358. Cranfield, *The Gospel according to Mark*, 282; France, *The Gospel of Mark*, 339-40.
359. Cranfield, *The Gospel according to Mark*, 282; France, *The Gospel of Mark*, 341.
360. France, *The Gospel of Mark*, 341.
361. Nineham, *The Gospel of St. Mark*, 33, 37-38.
362. Cranfield, *The Gospel according to Mark*, 285.
363. Nineham, *The Gospel of St. Mark*, 231-32.
364. Cranfield, *The Gospel according to Mark*, 286; France, *The Gospel of Mark*, 333.
365. Wright, *Meeting God in Mark*, 112.
366. France, *The Gospel of Mark*, 342-43.
367. France, *The Gospel of Mark*, 245.
368. France, *The Gospel of Mark*, 345.
369. NRSV-ANG.
370. Mal 4:5-6; Nineham, *The Gospel of St. Mark*, 235.
371. Deut 18:15-18.
372. Wright, *Meeting God in Mark*, 114; Cranfield, *The Gospel according to Mark*, 293.
373. France, *The Gospel of Mark*, 348.
374. Mal 4:5-6; Nineham, *The Gospel of St. Mark*, 235.
375. Deut 18:15-18.
376. Exodus 16:10; 24:18.
377. Exodus 34:29-35; France, *The Gospel of Mark*, 348.
378. Zech 14:16-19; Rev 21:1-4; Nineham, *The Gospel of St. Mark*, 237.
379. Cranfield, *The Gospel according to Mark*, 293.
380. Mark 9:1, NRSV-ANG; Nineham, *The Gospel of St. Mark*, 237.
381. NRSV-ANG.
382. Malbon, *Hearing Mark*, 61.
383. Mark 12:18-27; Acts 23:6-10.
384. France, *The Gospel of Mark*, 357.
385. France, *The Gospel of Mark*, 358.
386. Cranfield, *The Gospel according to Mark*, 298; Nineham, *The Gospel of St. Mark*, 239.
387. France, *The Gospel of Mark*, 358-59.
388. NRSV-ANG.
389. France, *The Gospel of Mark*, 361.
390. France, *The Gospel of Mark*, 362-65.
391. Exodus 32 and 33; Nineham, *The Gospel of St. Mark*, 245.
392. France, *The Gospel of Mark*, 365-66.
393. Cranfield, *The Gospel according to Mark*, 301, 305.
394. France, *The Gospel of Mark*, 368-69.
395. Malbon, *Hearing Mark*, 63.
396. Josh 8; 1 Kgs 18:40.
397. NRSV-ANG.
398. France, *The Gospel of Mark*, 371.
399. Nineham, *The Gospel of St. Mark*, 248; France, *The Gospel of Mark*, 370-71.
400. Myers, *Binding the Strong Man*, 257.
401. France, *The Gospel of Mark*, 373.
402. France, *The Gospel of Mark*, 374.
403. Matt 18:1-5, NRSV-ANG.
404. Cranfield, *The Gospel according to Mark*, 308.
405. France, *The Gospel of Mark*, 375.
406. NRSV-ANG.
407. France, *The Gospel of Mark*, 376.
408. Nineham, *The Gospel of St. Mark*, 254.
409. France, *The Gospel of Mark*, 376-77.
410. Nineham, *The Gospel of St. Mark*, 252.

# Endnotes

411. Luke 23:43.
412. France, *The Gospel of Mark*, 382–83.
413. France, *The Gospel of Mark*, 381.
414. Nineham, *The Gospel of St. Mark*, 255–57; France, *The Gospel of Mark*, 385.
415. NRSV-ANG.
416. France, *The Gospel of Mark*, 386.
417. Gen 2:24, NRSV-ANG; Wright, *Meeting God in Mark*, 132.
418. Cranfield, *The Gospel according to Mark*, 319; France, *The Gospel of Mark*, 387.
419. Deut 24:1–4; Nineham, *The Gospel of St. Mark*, 262.
420. Deut 22:22; Nineham, *The Gospel of St. Mark*, 261.
421. Cranfield, *The Gospel according to Mark*, 321; Malbon, *Hearing Mark*, 66.
422. Some of the commentaries consulted suggest that Mark's Gospel was written before or after 70 CE in a Gentile context, and possibly in Rome. Myers disagrees, locating Mark and the writing of his gospel in Galilee before 70 CE: Myers, *Binding the Strong Man*, 40–41.
423. Nineham, *The Gospel of St. Mark*, 266; France, *The Gospel of Mark*, 393.
424. 1 Cor 7:10–15.
425. Cranfield, *The Gospel according to Mark*, 321.
426. NRSV-ANG.
427. Cranfield, *The Gospel according to Mark*, 324; France, *The Gospel of Mark*, 395.
428. Nineham, *The Gospel of St. Mark*, 268.
429. France, *The Gospel of Mark*, 43–44.
430. Acts 16:33.
431. Myers, *Binding the Strong Man*, 288.
432. NRSV-ANG.
433. France, *The Gospel of Mark*, 400.
434. France, *The Gospel of Mark*, 407–408.
435. Nineham, *The Gospel of St. Mark*, 273.
436. France, *The Gospel of Mark*, 409.
437. Cranfield, *The Gospel according to Mark*, 329.
438. Nineham, *The Gospel of St. Mark*, 271–72.
439. Cranfield, *The Gospel according to Mark*, 331.
440. Nineham, *The Gospel of St. Mark*, 272.
441. NRSV-ANG.
442. France, *The Gospel of Mark*, 413.
443. France, *The Gospel of Mark*, 414–15.
444. Nineham, *The Gospel of St. Mark*, 278, 284.
445. Acts 12:2.
446. Hos 6:1–2.
447. France, *The Gospel of Mark*, 417.
448. France, *The Gospel of Mark*, 416.
449. John 13:1–17.
450. France, *The Gospel of Mark*, 409, 419.
451. Nineham, *The Gospel of St. Mark*, 280.
452. Nineham, *The Gospel of St. Mark*, 31; France, *The Gospel of Mark*, 420.
453. Isa 53:3–8, NRSV-ANG; Cranfield, *The Gospel according to Mark*, 277.
454. Cranfield, *The Gospel according to Mark*, 338,
455. Gen 22:1–14.
456. Mark 2:1–12.
457. Williams, *Meeting God in Mark*, 64.
458. 1 Pet 2:24, NRSV-ANG.
459. France, *The Gospel of Mark*, 421.
460. NRSV-ANG.
461. Nineham, *The Gospel of St. Mark*, 282; France, *The Gospel of Mark*, 421.

462. France, *The Gospel of Mark*, 423.
463. Matt 15:14; 23:16, 24, NRSV-ANG.
464. France, *The Gospel of Mark*, 423.
465. Malbon, *Hearing Mark*, 72.
466. John 14:6, NRSV-ANG.
467. Nineham, *The Gospel of St. Mark*, 283; France, *The Gospel of Mark*, 425.
468. Cranfield, *The Gospel according to Mark*, 346.
469. Mark 8:24-25.
470. Nineham, *The Gospel of St. Mark*, 19-23.
471. Malbon, *Hearing Mark*, 70-72.
472. Nineham, *The Gospel of St. Mark*, 51.
473. NRSV-ANG.
474. France, *The Gospel of Mark*, 427.
475. France, *The Gospel of Mark*, 431.
476. Nineham, *The Gospel of St. Mark*, 293-94; France, *The Gospel of Mark*, 428-29.
477. Zech 9:9, NRSV-ANG.
478. France, *The Gospel of Mark*, 430.
479. France, *The Gospel of Mark*, 429, 434.
480. Mark 10:45, NRSV-ANG.
481. Zech 9:10, NRSV-ANG.
482. Cranfield, *The Gospel according to Mark*, 353-54.
483. NRSV-ANG.
484. Nineham, *The Gospel of St. Mark*, 294; France, *The Gospel of Mark*, 435-36.
485. Wright, *Meeting God in Mark*, 151-52.
486. Myers, *Binding the Strong Man*, 322-23.
487. Nineham, *The Gospel of St. Mark*, 299.
488. France, *The Gospel of Mark*, 447.
489. France, *The Gospel of Mark*, 440-41.
490. Cranfield, *The Gospel according to Mark*, 356.
491. Heb 11:1, NRSV-ANG.
492. Mark 9:24, NRSV-ANG.
493. Mark 10:27, NRSV-ANG.
494. John 20:11-18, NRSV-ANG.
495. Mark 9:24, NRSV-ANG.
496. Mark 10:27, NRSV-ANG.
497. Matt 6:12; 18:23-35; Luke 11:4.
498. France, *The Gospel of Mark*, 448.
499. NRSV-ANG.
500. Isa 56:3-8, NRSV-ANG.
501. Deut 23:1, NRSV-ANG.
502. Mal 3:1, NRSV-ANG.
503. Jer 7:11, NRSV-ANG.
504. Jer 7:12-15; Mark 13:2; France, *The Gospel of Mark*, 446.
505. Hos 9:15, NRSV-ANG.
506. Zech 14:21, NRSV-ANG.
507. Nineham, *The Gospel of St. Mark*, 301.
508. Ezek 40-48; France, *The Gospel of Mark*, 438.
509. Nineham, *The Gospel of St. Mark*, 302.
510. Cranfield, *The Gospel according to Mark*, 359.
511. Mark 15:29-30, 38; France, *The Gospel of Mark*, 437.
512. Mark 14:47.
513. Luke 22:38, NRSV-ANG.
514. Matt 5:17, NRSV-ANG.

# Endnotes

515. Myers, *Binding the Strong Man*, 352–3; Malbon, *Hearing Mark*, 79.
516. NRSV-ANG.
517. Cranfield, *The Gospel according to Mark*, 362.
518. France, *The Gospel of Mark*, 453.
519. Luke 11:20, NRSV-ANG.
520. NRSV-ANG.
521. Nineham, *The Gospel of St. Mark*, 310–12.
522. Isa 5:1–7.
523. Isa 5:1–7, NRSV-ANG.
524. Cranfield, *The Gospel according to Mark*, 368; France, *The Gospel of Mark*, 460.
525. France, *The Gospel of Mark*, 460–61.
526. Acts 6:8–8:3.
527. Ps 118:22–23.
528. France, *The Gospel of Mark*, 462–3.
529. NRSV-ANG.
530. Nineham, *The Gospel of St. Mark*, 316.
531. Cranfield, *The Gospel according to Mark*, 371–72; France, *The Gospel of Mark*, 465–66, 468; Wright, *Meeting God in Mark*, 162–63.
532. John 8:2–11.
533. John 8:2–11.
534. Rom 13:1–7; Titus 3:1; 1 Pet 2:13–17; France, *The Gospel of Mark*, 466, 469.
535. NRSV-ANG.
536. Nineham, *The Gospel of St. Mark*, 319; France, *The Gospel of Mark*, 470–71.
537. Nineham, *The Gospel of St. Mark*, 321.
538. 1 Cor 15:44, NRSV-ANG.
539. Exodus 3:6.
540. France, *The Gospel of Mark*, 471–72.
541. NRSV-ANG.
542. France, *The Gospel of Mark*, 477–78.
543. Exodus 20:1, NRSV-ANG.
544. Nineham, *The Gospel of St. Mark*, 324–25.
545. Deut 6:4–5, NRSV-ANG.
546. Lev 19:18, NRSV-ANG.
547. France, *The Gospel of Mark*, 477.
548. France, *The Gospel of Mark*, 478, 481.
549. Cranfield, *The Gospel according to Mark*, 380.
550. John 3:2, NRSV-ANG.
551. John 7:50.
552. John 19:39.
553. Mark 15:43, NRSV-ANG.
554. John 19: 38, NRSV-ANG.
555. Acts 9:1–18.
556. 1 Cor 13:4–6, NRSV-ANG.
557. Nineham, *The Gospel of St. Mark*, 325.
558. Cranfield, *The Gospel according to Mark*, 376.
559. NRSV-ANG.
560. Cranfield, *The Gospel according to Mark*, 381–83.
561. Nineham, *The Gospel of St. Mark*, 329, 331.
562. France, *The Gospel of Mark*, 487.
563. Psalm 110:1–2, NRSV-ANG.
564. Matt 1:1–17.
565. Luke 3:23–38.
566. Rom 1:3–4.

# Endnotes

567. France, *The Gospel of Mark*, 484–85.
568. Ps 2:7, NRSV-ANG.
569. Dan 7:13–14, NRSV-ANG.
570. NRSV-ANG.
571. Nineham, *The Gospel of St. Mark*, 335.
572. France, *The Gospel of Mark*, 492–93.
573. Malbon, *Hearing Mark*, 84.
574. Matt 25:14–30.
575. Matt 6:12, NRSV-ANG.
576. Matt 6:10, NRSV-ANG.
577. Luke 19:9, NRSV-ANG.
578. Matt 20:15–16, NRSV-ANG.
579. NRSV-ANG.
580. France, *The Gospel of Mark*, 32.
581. France, *The Gospel of Mark*, 496.
582. Malbon, *Hearing Mark*, 85.
583. France, *The Gospel of Mark*, 495.
584. Cranfield, *The Gospel according to Mark*, 392; France, *The Gospel of Mark*, 498.
585. Nineham, *The Gospel of St. Mark*, 341.
586. Nineham, *The Gospel of St. Mark*, 340.
587. France, *The Gospel of Mark*, 502–503, 508–509.
588. Cranfield, *The Gospel according to Mark*, 388.
589. France, *The Gospel of Mark*, 410–11.
590. France, *The Gospel of Mark*, 412.
591. Nineham, *The Gospel of St. Mark*, 345.
592. Col 1:24, NRSV-ANG.
593. Nineham, *The Gospel of St. Mark*, 351.
594. Myers, *Binding the Strong Man*, 328–9.
595. NRSV-ANG.
596. Malbon, *Hearing Mark*, 76.
597. Cranfield, *The Gospel according to Mark*, 388.
598. Nineham, *The Gospel of St. Mark*, 350.
599. Nineham, *The Gospel of St. Mark*, 347.
600. France, *The Gospel of Mark*, 517.
601. Nineham, *The Gospel of St. Mark*, 348.
602. France, *The Gospel of Mark*, 517.
603. France, *The Gospel of Mark*, 519.
604. Acts 2:5–11; 1 Cor 12:10; 14:1–19.
605. France, *The Gospel of Mark*, 513.
606. NRSV-ANG.
607. France, *The Gospel of Mark*, 523.
608. France, *The Gospel of Mark*, 525.
609. Myers, *Binding the Strong Man*, 335–8; Wright, *Meeting God in Mark*, 181–82.
610. Cranfield, *The Gospel according to Mark*, 402, 404.
611. Isa 6:13.
612. Matt 3:10, NRSV-ANG.
613. Col 1:24, NRSV-ANG.
614. NRSV-ANG.
615. Cranfield, *The Gospel according to Mark*, 406.
616. Nineham, *The Gospel of St. Mark*, 356.
617. Dan 7:13–14, NRSV-ANG.
618. Ezek 37:1–14.
619. Hos 6:2, NRSV-ANG.

# Endnotes

620. Phil 2:5–11, NRSV-ANG.
621. Dan 7:13–14, NRSV-ANG.
622. Heb 4:14, NRSV-ANG.
623. France, *The Gospel of Mark*, 535.
624. France, *The Gospel of Mark*, 537.
625. France, *The Gospel of Mark*, 501, 533.
626. NRSV-ANG.
627. France, *The Gospel of Mark*, 539.
628. Cranfield, *The Gospel according to Mark*, 408.
629. Cranfield, *The Gospel according to Mark*, 409.
630. France, *The Gospel of Mark*, 538–39.
631. Rev 21:1–4.
632. Mark 12:25, NRSV-ANG.
633. 1 Cor 15:44, NRSV-ANG.
634. France, *The Gospel of Mark*, 541.
635. France, *The Gospel of Mark*, 543–44.
636. Nineham, *The Gospel of St. Mark*, 361.
637. Nineham, *The Gospel of St. Mark*, 33.
638. Cranfield, *The Gospel according to Mark*, 390–91.
639. Nineham, *The Gospel of St. Mark*, 358, 361.
640. NRSV-ANG.
641. Zech 9:9, NRSV-ANG.
642. France, *The Gospel of Mark*, 557.
643. Jeffrey Archer, *The Gospel according to Judas*, London: Macmillan, 2007
644. Cranfield, *The Gospel according to Mark*, 415; Malbon, *Hearing Mark*, 89.
645. Nineham, *The Gospel of St. Mark*, 372.
646. Malbon, *Hearing Mark*, 90.
647. Cranfield, *The Gospel according to Mark*, 415–16; Myers, *Binding the Strong Man*, 359.
648. France, *The Gospel of Mark*, 555.
649. NRSV-ANG.
650. Nineham, *The Gospel of St. Mark*, 381; France, *The Gospel of Mark*, 559.
651. Myers, *Binding the Strong Man*, 363.
652. Myers, *Binding the Strong Man*, 354–55.
653. Mark 14:18b, 20; Ps 41:9, NRSV-ANG.
654. Dan 7:13, original Aramaic, NRSV-ANG; Nineham, *The Gospel of St. Mark*, 378.
655. Isa 53:1–9, NRSV-ANG.
656. Mark 10:45.
657. Nineham, *The Gospel of St. Mark*, 380.
658. Malbon, *Hearing Mark*, 90; France, *The Gospel of Mark*, 567.
659. 1 Cor 11:24, NRSV-ANG.
660. Myers, *Binding the Strong Man*, 362.
661. Luke 24:13–35.
662. Cranfield, *The Gospel according to Mark*, 426.
663. France, *The Gospel of Mark*, 569.
664. Cranfield, *The Gospel according to Mark*, 427; France, *The Gospel of Mark*, 568–70.
665. John 19:34.
666. Wright, *Meeting God in Mark*, 194.
667. Nineham, *The Gospel of St. Mark*, 383.
668. France, *The Gospel of Mark*, 569.
669. Gen 31:43–55; Exodus 24:6–11.
670. Malbon, *Hearing Mark*, 91.
671. NRSV-ANG.
672. Zech 13:7, NRSV-ANG; France, *The Gospel of Mark*, 575.

# Endnotes

673. France, *The Gospel of Mark*, 573–76.
674. Matt 14:30.
675. France, *The Gospel of Mark*, 622.
676. Gal 2:11–14.
677. 1 Cor 13.
678. John 21:15–19.
679. Rom 12:3–8; 1 Cor 12:12–31; Eph 4:1–16.
680. 1 Cor 13.
681. France, *The Gospel of Mark*, 576–77.
682. Matt 28:16–20.
683. Wright, *Meeting God in Mark*, 199.
684. Mark 16:7; France, *The Gospel of Mark*, 619.
685. Myers, *Binding the Strong Man*, 346–47.
686. NRSV-ANG.
687. France, *The Gospel of Mark*, 587.
688. Matt 6:13, NRSV-ANG.
689. Ps 22:20, NRSV-ANG.
690. Ps 31:9–10, NRSV-ANG.
691. Nineham, *The Gospel of St. Mark*, 390.
692. France, *The Gospel of Mark*, 580, 584.
693. Cranfield, *The Gospel according to Mark*, 433.
694. Williams, *Meeting God in Mark*, 56.
695. Isa 53:7, NRSV-ANG.
696. France, *The Gospel of Mark*, 595.
697. Myers, *Binding the Strong Man*, 356, 368–69; Malbon, *Hearing Mark*, 92–93.
698. France, *The Gospel of Mark*, 596–97.
699. NRSV-ANG.
700. Isa 53:7, NRSV-ANG.
701. John 2:19, NRSV-ANG.
702. Cranfield, *The Gospel according to Mark*, 440–41; France, *The Gospel of Mark*, 601–603.
703. Cranfield, *The Gospel according to Mark*, 442.
704. France, *The Gospel of Mark*, 605.
705. Malbon, *Hearing Mark*, 94; France, *The Gospel of Mark*, 609, 611.
706. Cranfield, *The Gospel according to Mark*, 444–45.
707. France, *The Gospel of Mark*, 612–13.
708. France, *The Gospel of Mark*, 615–16.
709. Exodus 3:13–14, NRSV-ANG.
710. Mark 10:45, NRSV-ANG.
711. Mark 10:41–45; Luke 22:24–27.
712. Exodus 3:13–14.
713. Williams, *Meeting God in Mark*, 59.
714. NRSV-ANG.
715. Mark 14:61–62; France, *The Gospel of Mark*, 617, 624–25.
716. Myers, *Binding the Strong Man*, 372–73.
717. France, *The Gospel of Mark*, 628.
718. Ps 38:12–14, NRSV-ANG; Nineham, *The Gospel of St. Mark*, 412.
719. France, *The Gospel of Mark*, 629.
720. France, *The Gospel of Mark*, 637–38.
721. Isa 53:2–3, 7, NRSV-ANG.
722. Nineham, *The Gospel of St. Mark*, 21.
723. NRSV-ANG.
724. Nineham, *The Gospel of St. Mark*, 421.
725. Wright, *Meeting God in Mark*, 212.

726. Myers, *Binding the Strong Man*, 385.
727. France, *The Gospel of Mark*, 641.
728. Cranfield, *The Gospel according to Mark*, 455, 457; France, *The Gospel of Mark*, 643.
729. Ps 22:18, NRSV-ANG.
730. Nineham, *The Gospel of St. Mark*, 21.
731. Mark 12:10; 14:49, NRSV-ANG; France, *The Gospel of Mark*, 640.
732. France, *The Gospel of Mark*, 646.
733. France, *The Gospel of Mark*, 646.
734. France, *The Gospel of Mark*, 652.
735. Ps 22:1, NRSV-ANG.
736. France, *The Gospel of Mark*, 652.
737. Nineham, *The Gospel of St. Mark*, 428.
738. Ps 22:2–5, 21b–24, NRSV-ANG.
739. Malbon, *Hearing Mark*, 96.
740. Nineham, *The Gospel of St. Mark*, 428.
741. Williams, *Meeting God in Mark*, 56.
742. Cranfield, *The Gospel according to Mark*, 458.
743. France, *The Gospel of Mark*, 651; Wright, *Meeting God in Mark*, 215.
744. France, *The Gospel of Mark*, 657.
745. Myers, *Binding the Strong Man*, 390.
746. Malbon, *Hearing Mark*, 97.
747. France, *The Gospel of Mark*, 661.
748. France, *The Gospel of Mark*, 653.
749. France, *The Gospel of Mark*, 661–65.
750. Myers, *Binding the Strong Man*, 396.
751. Studdert Kennedy, *The Unutterable Beauty*, 31.
752. NRSV-ANG.
753. Malbon, *Hearing Mark*, 43.
754. France, *The Gospel of Mark*, 666–67.
755. Cranfield, *The Gospel according to Mark*, 465.
756. Heb 4:14, NRSV-ANG.
757. Phil 2:5–11, NRSV-ANG.
758. Dan 7:13, NRSV-ANG.
759. 1 Cor 15:44, NRSV-ANG.
760. Wright, *Meeting God in Mark*, 221–24; France, *The Gospel of Mark*, 673–76, 684.
761. Williams, *Meeting God in Mark*, 47–48.
762. Mark 1:1, NRSV-ANG.
763. Myers, *Binding the Strong Man*, 397–99; Malbon, *Hearing Mark*, 99–100.
764. Mark 14:3–9.

# Bibliography

Church of England. *Common Worship: Services and Prayers for the Church of England.* London: Church House Publishing, 2000.

Cranfield, C.E.B.. *The Gospel According to Mark*. Revised edition. Cambridge: Cambridge University Press, 1977.

France, R.T.. *The Gospel of Mark: A Commentary on the Greek Text.* Grand Rapids, MI: William B. Eerdmans, 2002.

Malbon, Elizabeth Struthers. *Hearing Mark: A Listener's Guide*. Harrisburg, Pennsylvania: Trinity Press International, 2002.

Myers, Ched. *Binding the Strong Man: A Political Reading of Mark's Story of Jesus.* Maryknoll, NY: Orbis Books, 2003.

Nineham, D.E.. *The Gospel of St. Mark*. London: Adam and Charles Black, 1963.

Studdert Kennedy, Geoffrey. *The Hardest Part*. London: Hodder and Stoughton, 1919.

———. *The Unutterable Beauty*. London: Hodder and Stoughton, 1941.

Temple, William. *Readings in St John's Gospel: First and Second Series*. London: Macmillan, 1968.

Torry, Malcolm. *Actology: Action, Change and Diversity in the Western Philosophical Tradition*. Eugene, OR: Resource Publications/Wipf and Stock, 2020.

———. "Action, Patterns and Religious Pluralism." *Theology* CVI (830) (2003) 107–18.

———. "'Logic' and 'Action': Two New Readings of the New Testament." *Theology* CXI (860) (2008) 93–101.

———. "A Neglected Theologian: John Sandwith Boys Smith." *Theology* CVII (836) (2004) 89–104.

———. "On Completing the Apologetic Spectrum." *Theology* CIII (812) (2000) 108–15.

———. "Testing Torry's model." *Theology* CIX (851) (2006) 343–52.

———. "Two Kinds of Ambiguity." *King's Theological Review* III (1) (1980) 24–28.

Williams, Rowan. *Meeting God in Mark*. London: SPCK, 2014.

Wright, Tom. *Mark for Everyone*. Second edition. London: SPCK, 2004.

# Subject Index

action in (changing) patterns, *passim*
Ancient One, 38–39, 89, 146, 203, 217, 222–23, 228, 232–34, 245, 272, 274
   *see also* God
Andrew (apostle), 19–20, 25, 41, 57, 221
apostles, xvii, 41, 57–60, 85, 102–5, 109–12, 122, 126, 131–32, 137, 175, 226, 229, 266, 269, 271
arrest (of Jesus), 20, 194, 200, 239–40, 252–53, 255
authority, 2, 22–24, 34–40, 48–49, 57–58, 60, 64, 87, 92, 98, 102, 110, 123, 127, 142–43, 146, 150, 154, 157, 159, 196–99, 232, 235, 237, 245, 248, 255, 258–59, 262, 271, 274

baptism, 5–7, 9–10, 66, 125, 140, 167, 174, 196, 256
   of Jesus, 5–7, 10–14, 17, 36, 148, 254
   *see also* John the Baptist
Bartimaeus, 153, 179–81, 184, 196, 217
Beelzebul, *see* Satan
Bethany, 182, 187, 191, 239–40
betrayal, 57, 149, 156, 184, 207, 225, 239, 242–45, 249, 252, 260, 263–64
blindness, xvi, 96, 129, 138–41, 153, 179–81, 257
burial (of Jesus), 212, 239–40, 271

children, 2, 50, 64–67, 79, 84, 95, 108–9, 112–13, 124–26, 130, 153, 156–58, 160–61, 165–70, 174, 176, 178, 180, 207–8, 219–21, 223, 225, 230, 241, 243, 255, 260
command, commandment, 18–19, 21–24, 32–33, 42, 51, 69, 77–78, 98, 120, 122, 153, 161, 163, 166, 170, 178, 185, 189, 191, 197, 201, 210–11, 214, 226, 235, 250
crucifixion, 12, 26, 46, 119, 141, 145, 147–48, 161, 178–79, 184–86, 194, 202, 213, 223, 226, 248, 252, 261–66, 269–72

deafness, 127, 129, 138, 140, 262
death, 17, 67, 92, 65, 95–96, 101, 107, 142, 150, 164, 173, 208–9, 225–26, 243
   of God, *see* God, death of
   of Jesus, *see* Jesus, death of
demon possession, *see* evil spirits
denial, 142, 145, 151, 248–53
devil, *see* Satan
divorce, *see* marriage

Emmaus, road to, 119, 246
eschatology, 196, 221, 241
Eucharist, 10, 43, 66, 112, 131–32, 168, 245, 247–48, 251
   *see also* Last Supper
evil, 15, 17, 22, 28–29, 31–32, 58–63, 89, 92–95, 102–4, 106, 108, 120, 124, 126–27, 146, 155–56, 159, 168, 184, 188, 190–91, 196, 220, 226, 230, 238, 261
   powers of, 15, 17, 70–71
   spirits, 15, 17, 22–28, 30–32, 51, 57, 60, 62, 91–94, 102–4, 111, 114, 119, 124–25, 128, 134, 140, 143, 146, 153–54, 157, 159, 172, 197, 202, 218, 226, 232
   *see also* Satan

fasting, 44–45, 153
feeding of the four/five thousand, 44, 109–13, 116–17, 124, 130–33, 137–38, 245
fig tree, 187–91, 235

Galilee, 4, 9, 15, 17, 21, 28, 30–32, 56, 63, 83, 86, 90, 105, 112, 115, 156, 220, 224, 248, 251, 254, 265, 271, 273–74
   Lake/Sea of, 19, 54, 76, 92, 127, 130, 172
Gennesaret, 117–19
Gethsemane, 12, 20, 28, 194–95, 250, 252–56, 266

## Subject Index

God, *passim*
    death of, 146, 178–79, 241, 247, 254, 259–60, 268–70
    suffering of, 152, 263
    *see also* Ancient One
growing seed, parable of, *see* seed, parable of

healing (miracles), xiv, 1, 4, 20, 23–28, 31–40, 46–47, 49, 51–56, 67, 70–71, 73, 75, 85–86, 92–103, 106, 112, 118–19, 121, 123–30, 134, 138–41, 146, 152–56, 159, 172, 179–82, 184, 195–96, 220, 226, 230, 232, 240, 254, 271
    *see also* miracles
Hebrew scriptures, ix, 2, 4, 45, 53, 93, 117, 119, 121, 155, 194, 198–99, 210–11, 223, 226, 231–32, 264
Herod, Herodians, 40, 51, 105–9, 135–37, 183–84, 203–5, 262, 271
Holy Communion, *see* Eucharist
Holy Spirit, 5, 7–9, 13, 16–17, 60, 63–64, 66, 85, 114, 128, 138, 146, 182, 198–99, 204, 215, 225, 227–28

Jairus, 95
James (apostle), 19, 21, 25, 41, 57, 95, 146–50, 174–76, 221, 252
James (Jesus' brother), 58, 65, 67, 98, 250
Jerusalem, 4–5, 15, 17, 20, 54, 58, 60, 63, 90, 119, 122, 131–32 138, 141, 153, 156, 174–75, 177, 179–89, 191, 194–96, 201, 217, 220–22, 228–29, 239–41, 246, 254–55, 259, 261, 264–65, 272
    triumphal entry into, 182–87
Jesus, *passim*
    death of, 1, 5, 18, 24, 40, 45–46, 52, 62, 73, 103, 107, 119, 137, 143–46, 150, 152, 156, 164, 174–80, 183–85, 194–95, 200, 202, 204, 221–24, 227, 231, 233, 235, 240–41, 243–54, 256–60, 265–66, 268–70, 272, 274
    *see also* suffering
John (apostle), 19, 21, 25, 41, 57, 67, 95, 146–50, 159, 174–76, 221, 252
John the Baptist, 5–17, 44–45, 105–9, 125, 138, 140, 152, 161, 194–98, 200, 202, 222, 230, 268, 271
Judas Iscariot (apostle), 57, 110, 168, 239–40, 243, 245, 249, 252, 258

Kingdom of God, *passim*

Last Supper, 67, 112, 132, 168, 245–48, 255–56
    *see also* Eucharist

lawyers, 96
Lazarus, 98, 196
Levi (apostle), 41–44, 52
Lord's Supper, *see* Eucharist; Last Supper

marriage, 163–66, 182, 207–9, 212, 237, 241, 246
Martha, 196
Mary (Jesus' mother), 65–67, 98–100
Mary (sister of Martha), 196
Mary Magdalene, 190, 265, 270
Messiah, 2, 5–7, 15–17, 78, 112–13, 123, 138, 140–46, 150, 153, 169, 175, 179, 184–85, 188, 194–96, 203–4, 215–18, 222–23, 228, 232, 240–41, 250, 256, 258–59, 261, 263, 265, 268
miracles, 87–91, 113–17
    *see also* feeding of the four/five thousand; healing miracles
mustard seed, parable of, 83–87
    *see also* seed, parable of; sower, parable of

nard, 239
Nazareth, 3, 9–10, 21, 99–101, 112, 119, 142–43, 179, 241, 249, 271
New Testament, ix, xiii, xv, xix, 55, 189, 198–99, 214, 223, 226, 257

Old Testament, *see* Hebrew Scriptures

parables, 18, 23, 43–44, 60, 64, 67–87, 92, 99–100, 103, 112, 119–20, 125, 134, 149, 162, 169, 188–90, 194, 200–204, 219–20
paralysis, 35–40, 51, 140
Passover, 167, 183, 189, 239, 242–43, 255, 264, 268
persecution, 62, 72, 75, 89–90, 115, 132, 146, 162, 170, 172, 198, 201–2, 204, 208, 213, 222, 224–26, 229, 235, 238
Peter (apostle) (Simon Peter), 7, 19–20, 25–26, 28, 32, 41, 57–58, 93, 95, 98, 122, 132, 138, 140–50, 153, 162, 172, 175, 181, 184–85, 187, 191, 195, 216–18, 221, 248–54, 256, 258, 268, 271
Pharisees, 4, 40–42, 44, 48–49, 51–53, 96, 119–21, 133–35, 137, 151, 163, 181, 204–5, 208, 212
Pilate, 133, 257, 261–63, 270
prayer, 13, 28–31, 44, 59, 96, 103–4, 108, 113–14, 117, 125, 128–9, 153–57, 187, 190–93, 195, 197–99, 207, 218, 220, 226–28, 235, 240, 250, 252–54

# Subject Index

rabbi, 41, 146, 148, 164, 176, 187, 191, 196–97, 210–11, 217, 253–54

repentance, 5–7, 9–10, 12–13, 17–18, 20, 22, 24, 30, 41–44, 46, 53, 93, 101–102, 107, 126, 140, 148, 168, 222, 230
see also sinner (unrepentant)

resurrection, xv–xvi, 1, 5, 7, 18, 24, 40, 42, 49–53, 56–58, 85, 97–99, 103, 105, 109–10, 122, 137–38, 142–44, 146–52, 156, 174–76, 180, 183–85, 188, 190, 195, 203–4, 207–9, 221–22, 227–28, 232–37, 241, 246, 248, 251–52, 257, 260, 270–73

sabbath, 4, 21, 46, 48–54, 93, 98, 121–23, 142, 192–93, 195, 270–71

Sadducees, 42, 151, 207–8, 210

Sanhedrin, 261

Satan, 10, 15–16, 20, 23, 33, 36, 60–64, 72, 75, 125, 142, 254

seed, parable of, 80–83
see also mustard seed, parable of; sower, parable of

Simon Peter, see Peter (apostle)

Simon the Zealot (apostle) (Simon the Cananaean), 41, 57

sin, 6–7, 10–12, 16, 36–37, 44, 60, 64, 93, 125–26, 178, 190, 207, 222, 225, 236, 259–60, 270

sinner (unrepentant), 40–46, 72, 87, 107, 113, 125–26, 160–61, 167, 176, 220–21, 229–30, 252, 262
see also repentance

soldiers, 106, 246, 261–63, 266

Son of David, 39, 179–80, 184, 196, 215–18

Son of God, 1–3, 15, 39, 54–56, 199, 202–3, 217–18, 234, 258–59, 261, 265, 269

Son of Man, 35–36, 38–39, 48–49, 89, 92, 122, 141–44, 146, 150, 152, 156, 174, 176, 182, 194, 197, 202–3, 217–18, 222, 231–37, 241–45, 252, 255–56, 258–60, 272, 274, 277n112,

sower, parable of, 68–76
see also mustard seed, parable of; seed, parable of

storm, 89–91, 114–17, 188

suffering, 11–12, 22, 25, 29, 33, 45, 62, 78, 89–90, 92, 95, 107, 126, 142–46, 150, 152, 156, 158, 161–62, 174–79, 181–85, 194, 204, 222–26, 228–31, 234, 236, 238, 243–45, 247–49, 253–55, 258–60, 263, 265–68, 270, 274

Syrophoenician woman, 124, 127, 131, 197, 199, 230

tax (collector), 40–44, 87, 110, 176, 194, 204–7, 220–21, 230

temple, 3–4, 13, 41, 46, 141, 182–83, 187–89, 191–96, 215, 219–23, 226–30, 235–36, 238, 243, 253, 255–58, 265, 267–69

temptation, 10–12, 16–17, 101, 125, 252–53

tradition, 17, 24, 27, 37, 44, 46, 49, 61–62, 79, 96, 101–2, 107, 114–15, 120–21, 123, 132, 140, 162, 169–70, 176, 185–86, 188, 206, 210–11, 219, 222, 226, 240, 243, 247, 249, 262

transfiguration, the, 146–50, 224

trial, 48, 141, 156, 197, 217, 225–27, 233, 249–50, 252–53, 257, 261

vineyard, 200–204, 220

wealth, 50, 72, 75, 84, 121, 132, 170, 173, 213, 219–20

widow, 207–8, 218–21

Word of God, xv, 120, 129, 199

# Scripture Index

Superscript numbers indicate endnote numbers. The endnotes for pages i to xx are on page xxi, and the endnotes for pages 1 to 274 are on pages 275 to 290.

### Genesis
1:1–2 — 89 [224]
1:2 — 9 [28], 60 [158]
2:24 — 163 [417]
22:1–14 — 178 [455]
31:43–55 — 247 [669]

### Exodus
3:6 — 210 [539]
3:13–14 — 259 [709], 260 [712]
3:14 — 117 [294]
16:10 — 148 [376]
20:1 — 211 [543]
20:10 — 49 [140]
24:6–11 — 247 [669]
24:18 — 148 [376]
34:29–35 — 148 [377]

### Leviticus
19:18 — 211 [546]

### Numbers
14:11 — 134 [329]
14:22 — 134 [329]

### Deuteronomy
1:34–45 — 53 [145]
6:4–5 — 211 [545]
18:15–18 — 148 [371], 148 [375]
18:15 — 134 [330]
22:22 — 164 [420]
23:1 — 193 [501]
23:25 — 49 [139]
24:1–4 — 164 [419]

### Joshua
8 — 53 [145], 155 [396]

### 1 Kings
18:40 — 155 [396]

### Job
9:8 — 115 [288], 117 [292]

### Psalms
2:7 — 14 [50], 217 [568]
22:1 — 267 [735]
22:2–5 — 267 [738]
22:18 — 266 [729]
22:20 — 253 [689]
22:21b–24 — 267 [738]
31:9–10 — 254 [690]
38:12–14 — 262 [718]
41:9 — 244 [653]
44:23–24 — 89 [227]
77:19 — 115 [288], 117 [292]
89:8–9 — 89 [225]
93:3–4 — 89 [225]
104:6–7 — 89 [227]
106: 8–9 — 89 [225]
110:1–2 — 216 [563]
118:22–23 — 203 [527]

## Scripture Index

### Isaiah
| | |
|---|---|
| 5:1–7 | 200[522], 201[523] |
| 6:10 | 73[190] |
| 6:13 | 229[611] |
| 8:14 | 99[253] |
| 11:1–2 | 8[24] |
| 25:6–8 | 112[280] |
| 28:16 | 99[253] |
| 35:5–6 | 129[320] |
| 40:3 | 4[13] |
| 42:1 | 8[25], 14[50] |
| 43:16 | 115[288], 117[292] |
| 51:9b–10 | 89[225] |
| 53:1–9 | 244–45[655] |
| 53:2–3 | 263[721] |
| 53:3–8 | 144[351], 177[453] |
| 53:7 | 255[695], 257[700], 263[721] |
| 53:8 | 45[131] |
| 55 | 112[280] |
| 55:10–13 | 69[182] |
| 56:3–8 | 193[500] |
| 61:1–2 | xvi[31] |
| 65:13–14 | 112[280] |

### Jeremiah
| | |
|---|---|
| 7:11 | 193[503] |
| 7:12–15 | 194[504] |
| 31:33 | 122[304] |

### Ezekiel
| | |
|---|---|
| 17:22–23 | 83[218] |
| 37:1–14 | 233[618] |

### Daniel
| | |
|---|---|
| 7:9–14 | 38–39[112] |
| 7:13–14 | 217[569], 232[617], 234[621] |
| 7:13 | 38–39[112], 89[226], 244[654], 272[758] |

### Hosea
| | |
|---|---|
| 6:1–2 | 175[446] |
| 6:2 | 233[619] |
| 9:15 | 194[505] |

### Joel
| | |
|---|---|
| 2:28 | 7[23] |
| 3:12–13 | 81[215] |

### Zechariah
| | |
|---|---|
| 9: 9 | 183[477], 239[641] |

| | |
|---|---|
| 9:10 | 185[481] |
| 13:7 | 249[672] |
| 14:16–19 | 148[378] |
| 14:21 | 194[506] |

### Malachi
| | |
|---|---|
| 3:1 | 3[10], 193[502] |
| 4:5–6 | 148[370], 148[374] |
| 4:5 | 106[269] |

### Matthew
| | |
|---|---|
| 1:1–17 | 216[564] |
| 1:21 | 1[4] |
| 3:10 | 230[612] |
| 3:16 | 13[42] |
| 5:17 | 195[514] |
| 6:10 | 29[93], 220[576] |
| 6:12 | 190[497], 220[575] |
| 6:13 | 253[688] |
| 6:14–15 | 79[208] |
| 14:30 | 249[674] |
| 15:14 | 180[463] |
| 18:1–5 | 158[403] |
| 18:23–35 | 190[497] |
| 18:23–32 | 79[208] |
| 20:15–16 | 221[578] |
| 21:31 | 42[121], 87[220] |
| 23:16 | 180[463] |
| 23:24 | 180[463] |
| 25:14–30 | 79[209], 100[256], 219[574] |
| 28:16–20 | 251[682] |

### Mark
| | |
|---|---|
| 1:1 | 1–3, 273[762] |
| 1:2–3 | 3–4 |
| 1:4–8 | 5–9 |
| 1:7 | 17[64] |
| 1:9–13 | 9–17 |
| 1:10 | 7[22], 12 |
| 1:11 | 14 |
| 1:12 | 15 |
| 1:13 | 16 |
| 1:14–15 | 17–19, 67[174] |
| 1:16–20 | 19–21 |
| 1:21–28 | 21–25 |
| 1:29–34 | 25–28 |
| 1:32–34 | 27 |
| 1:35–39 | 28–31 |
| 1:40–45 | 31–35 |
| 2:1–12 | 35–40, 178[456] |
| 2:13–17 | 40–44 |
| 2:15–17 | 7[19] |

## Scripture Index

| Reference | Pages |
|---|---|
| 2:18–20 | 44–45 |
| 2:21–22 | 45–48 |
| 2:23–28 | 48–51 |
| 3:1–6 | 51–54 |
| 3:7–12 | 54–57 |
| 3:13–19a | 57–60 |
| 3:19b–30 | 60–64 |
| 3:31–35 | 64–67 |
| 4:1–9 | 67–71, 81[213] |
| 4:10–20 | 71–76 |
| 4:21–25 | 76–80 |
| 4:22 | 74[197] |
| 4:24 | 100[256] |
| 4:26–29 | 80–83 |
| 4:29 | 44[128] |
| 4:30–34 | 83–87 |
| 4:35–41 | 87–91 |
| 5:1–20 | 91–95 |
| 5:16 | 94[239] |
| 5:21–43 | 95–98 |
| 6:1–6a | 98–101 |
| 6:3 | 67[173] |
| 6:6b–13 | 102–5 |
| 6:11 | 93[238] |
| 6:14–29 | 105–9 |
| 6:30–44 | 109–13 |
| 6:45–52 | 113–17 |
| 6:53–56 | 117–19 |
| 7:1–23 | 119–23 |
| 7:24–30 | 12[38], 123–27 |
| 7:31–37 | 127–30, 138[338] |
| 8:1–10 | 130–33 |
| 8:11–13 | 133–35 |
| 8:11 | 37[107] |
| 8:14–21 | 135–38 |
| 8:22–30 | 138–41 |
| 8:24–25 | 180[469] |
| 8:31–9:1 | 142–46 |
| 9:1 | 150[380] |
| 9:2–8 | 146–50 |
| 9:9–13 | 150–52 |
| 9:14–29 | 152–56 |
| 9:24 | 189[492], 190[495] |
| 9:30–37 | 156–58 |
| 9:38–50 | 159–62 |
| 10:1–12 | 163–66 |
| 10:13–16 | 167–69 |
| 10:17–31 | 170–74 |
| 10:24 | 66[171] |
| 10:27 | 189[493], 190[496] |
| 10:32–45 | 174–79 |
| 10:41–45 | 260[711] |
| 10:45 | 184[480], 245[656], 260[710] |
| 10:46–52 | 179–82 |
| 11:1–11 | 182–87 |
| 11:12–26 | 187–91 |
| 11:12–24 | 191–96 |
| 11:27–33 | 196–99 |
| 12:1–12 | 200–204 |
| 12:10 | 266[731] |
| 12:13–17 | 204–7 |
| 12:18–27 | 42[119], 151[383], 207–10 |
| 12:25 | 237[632] |
| 12:28–34 | 210–14 |
| 12:35–37 | 215–18 |
| 12:38–44 | 218–21 |
| 13:1–8 | 221–25 |
| 13:2 | 194[504] |
| 13:9–13 | 225–28 |
| 13:14–23 | 228–31 |
| 13:24–27 | 231–35 |
| 13:28–37 | 235–38 |
| 14:1–11 | 239–42 |
| 14:3–9 | 274[764] |
| 14:12–25 | 242–48 |
| 14:18b | 244[653] |
| 14:20 | 244[653] |
| 14:26–31 | 248–52 |
| 14:32–52 | 252–56 |
| 14:36 | 14[48], 15[51], 114[286] |
| 14:47 | 194[512] |
| 14:49 | 266[731] |
| 14:53–65 | 256–60 |
| 14:61–62 | 261[715] |
| 14:66–72 | 248–52 |
| 15:1–20 | 260–64 |
| 15:21–41 | 264–70 |
| 15:29–30 | 194[511] |
| 15:38–39 | 13[47] |
| 15:38 | 194[511] |
| 15:42–16:8 | 270–74 |
| 15:43 | 212[553] |
| 16:7 | 252[684] |

## Luke

| Reference | Pages |
|---|---|
| 1:46–55 | 100[255] |
| 3:21–22 | 13[43] |
| 3:23–38 | 216[565] |
| 4:18–19 | xvi[31] |
| 8:1–3 | 112[283] |
| 10:29–37 | 103[265] |
| 11:4 | 190[497] |
| 11:20 | 197[519] |
| 14:13–23 | 44[129] |
| 19:9 | 220[577] |
| 22:24–27 | 260[711] |
| 22:38 | 194[513] |

## Scripture Index

| | |
|---|---|
| 23:43 | 161 [411] |
| 24:13–35 | 119 [298], 246 [661] |

### John

| | |
|---|---|
| 1:1–3 | xv [11] |
| 1:14 | xv [11] |
| 1:32 | 13 [44] |
| 2:19 | 257 [701] |
| 3:2 | 212 [550] |
| 3:8 | 9 [29] |
| 3:22 | 7 [18] |
| 6 | 112 [282] |
| 7:50. | 212 [551] |
| 8:2–11 | 207 [532], 207 [533] |
| 9:2 | 37 [108] |
| 10:30 | xiii [7] |
| 11:1–44 | 98 [248] |
| 13:1–20 | 67 [172] |
| 13:1–17 | 176 [449] |
| 14:6 | 135 [332], 180 [466] |
| 16:32 | xiii [8] |
| 17:21 | xiii [9] |
| 19:26 | 67 [172] |
| 19:27 | 99 [252] |
| 19:34. | 246 [665] |
| 19:38 | 213 [554] |
| 19:39 | 212 [552] |
| 20:11–18 | 190 [494] |
| 20:28 | xv [12] |
| 21:15–19 | 250 [678] |

### Acts

| | |
|---|---|
| 1:14 | 99 [252] |
| 2:2–3 | 9 [30] |
| 2:5–11 | 227 [604] |
| 2:38 | 7 [20] |
| 6:8–8:3 | 203 [526] |
| 8:1–11:30 | 132 [326] |
| 8:12–16 | 9 [31] |
| 8:36–38 | 9 [31] |
| 9:1–18 | 213 [555] |
| 9:18 | 9 [31] |
| 10:1–11:26 | 122 [302] |
| 10:47–48 | 9 [31] |
| 11:3 | 43 [124] |
| 12:2 | 175 [445] |
| 13:46 | 125 [314] |
| 15:1–35 | 131 [325] |
| 16:7 | 8 [26] |
| 16:33 | 9 [31], 169 [430] |
| 18:6 | 125 [314] |
| 18:8 | 9 [31] |
| 18:25 | 9 [31] |
| 19:3 | 9 [31] |
| 23:6–10 | 151 [383] |

### Romans

| | |
|---|---|
| 1:3–4 | 216 [566] |
| 3:30 | xvi [29] |
| 8:33 | xvi [17] |
| 9:16 | xvi [18] |
| 12:3–8 | 251 [679] |
| 13:1–7 | 207 [534] |

### 1 Corinthians

| | |
|---|---|
| 1:19 | xvi [30] |
| 3:7 | xvi [19] |
| 7:10–15 | 165 [424] |
| 10:13 | xvi [30] |
| 11:17–12:31 | 132 [326] |
| 11:24 | 245 [659] |
| 12 | 59 [156] |
| 12:6 | xvi [20] |
| 12:10 | 227 [604] |
| 12:12–31 | 251 [679] |
| 13 | 250 [677], 251 [680] |
| 13:4–6 | 214 [556] |
| 14:1–19 | 227 [604] |
| 15:44 | 209 [538], 237 [633], 273 [759] |
| 16:22 | 117 [291] |

### 2 Corinthians

| | |
|---|---|
| 1:9 | xvi [21] |
| 1:18 | xvi [30] |
| 1:21 | xvi [22] |
| 4:6 | xvi [23] |
| 8:16 | xvi [24] |

### Galatians

| | |
|---|---|
| 2:11–14 | 132 [326], 250 [676] |
| 2:12 | 43 [124] |
| 3:20 | xvi [29] |
| 5:22 | 8 [27] |

### Ephesians

| | |
|---|---|
| 3:9 | xvi [25] |
| 4:1–16 | 59 [156], 251 [679] |

### Philippians

| | |
|---|---|
| 1:19 | 8 [26] |
| 2:5–11 | 233–34 [620], 271–72 [757] |
| 2:13 | xvi [26] |

## Scripture Index

**Colossians**
1:24     224[592], 231[613]

**1 Thessalonians**
2:4     xvi[27]

**1 Timothy**
6:17     xvi[28]

**Titus**
2:13     xv[14]
3:1     207[534]

**Hebrews**
4:14     234[622], 271[756]
4:15     11[34], 12[39]
5:1–10     11[35]
5:8–9     12[39]
5:8     126[316]
5:9     11[36], 12[37]
11:1     36[104], 89[230], 189[491]

**James**
5:14     103[266]

**1 Peter**
2:13–17     207[534]
2:24     178[458]

**2 Peter**
1:1     xv[15]

**Revelation**
21:1–4     148[378], 236[631]

www.ingramcontent.com/pod-product-compliance
Lightning Source LLC
Chambersburg PA
CBHW081144230426
43664CB00018B/2800